THE ADAMS FEDERALISTS

The ADAMS FEDERALISTS

BY

MANNING J. DAUER

1953

Baltimore: The Johns Hopkins Press

Copyright 1953, The Johns Hopkins Press
Distributed in Great Britain by Geoffrey
Cumberlege: Oxford University Press, London
Printed in the U. S. A. by J. H. Furst Co.

Library of Congress Catalog Card Number: 53–11171

Preface

THE " why " in history and in the other social sciences is one of those perennial questions. Students of anthropology give a picture of primitive man which is fairly uniform in certain respects. Regardless of place or time primitive man is sure that virtually all causation is outside his control—events are inspired by spirits, devils, or some other unknown. All of this is some distance removed from an essay on the formative period of American political parties, which is the subject matter of this book. But it is not without point. The question of theories of causation is related to the matter of research methodology. Whatever methodology is pursued means the acceptance of some theory of causation. Some students of the social sciences attempt to ignore the problem of method. Others examine it.[1] Without attempting a review of historiography, it is of some importance to review some recent writings and establish their points of view.

Thirty years ago historians still living today began to study the origin of the party divisions in American history. Without considering here those studies relating to the colonial period, I should mention several writers who have treated the revolutionary period and the constitutional period. Arthur Meier Schlesinger in his *Colonial Merchants and the American Revolution*[2] finds the origin of the pre-Revolutionary American Whigs in the American mercantile groups. Somewhat earlier, Charles A. Beard had presented a rather extreme statement of the economic basis of politics in his *Economic Interpretation of the Constitution of*

---

[1] A survey of some theories is found in Rice, Stuart A., *Methods in Social Sciences* (Chicago, 1931); also see Rice, Stuart A., *Quantitative Methods in Politics* (New York, 1928); Strayer, J. R. (ed.), *The Interpretation of History* (Princeton, 1943); Beard, Charles A., and Beale, Howard K., *Essays in Theory and Practice in Historical Study: A Report of the Committee on Historiography, Social Science Research Council* (New York, 1946). In political science the most valuable work is Easton, David, *The Political System* (New York, 1953).

[2] (New York, 1918).

v

the United States.[3] Discussing the dividing line between parties, he then wrote a more balanced work in his *Economic Origins of Jeffersonian Democracy.*[4] These writings have influenced the interpretation of American history ever since. Also Frederick Jackson Turner, in his later writings, and especially *The United States, 1830-1850,*[5] arrived at something of a synthesis of social, economic, and political history.

The method adopted herein is not so conclusive, although definitely influenced by these earlier works. All that has been definitely attempted is to follow a formula stated recently by Professor R. M. MacIver as: " causal analysis centers its attack on the investigation of differences between comparable situations." [6] At the same time the reader of this work should have two other explanations. First, there are several threads throughout this work, since I have found it necessary to undertake a treatment which seeks to present multiple causation. Second, I shall attempt, in line with Max Weber's dicta on the need of an explanation as to values, to state the frame of reference of the work.

In the United States from 1789-1803 there existed a developing national state, sparsely settled. What were the factors that promoted the successful development of this experiment in self-government? What role did political theory, economic theory, social, sectional, economic and class divisions play? How did the background of experience as British colonies affect the new state? How did the great continental struggle between France and England play its role in the American picture? How far were political parties the means of reconciling group conflicts in the central government? How far was geographic isolation from Europe a factor in permitting the United States opportunity to develop apart from the conflicts elsewhere? Other states were emerging at this period. Still later, as in the nineteenth century,

---

[3] (New York, 1913).

[4] (New York, 1915).

[5] (New York, 1935).

[6] " History and Social Causation," in *The Tasks of Economic History* (New York, 1943), 143-44.

Germany and Italy became unified. But during this time the United States continued the successful development of self-government along the pattern already set by England. Numerous crises occurred but were surmounted. What factors distinguished American development from that of these European continental nations and states? If some answer (even tentatively) can be given to the problems raised, then perhaps some light may be shed on the difficulties attendant upon the development of self-government in a new area.

The point of view of this book is that the first duty of the student of the social sciences is to depict the actual social structure of a period. If this period is one in the past, this is primarily the work of the social, economic, and cultural historian. The next point of view is that theories and governmental policies must be examined in relation to their effect upon various groups of the population, comprising sections of different economic, religious, and cultural background. Finally, in a political society with free elections, and with some experience in politics, the elections should be examined to ascertain whether or not there are patterns of political behavior. In this book the voting pattern of members of the United States House of Representatives in the period 1794-1802 is examined to see if it reflects the point of view of their constituents. For this purpose some 105 votes have been charted and analyzed, and the information given in the appendices. The narrative considers the point of view of the political leaders, their economic and political ideas and policies against this background.

The period that has been chosen is a good one because it covers both the rise and breakup of the first American political party alignments. Specifically, the analysis of the Hamiltonian Federalists versus the Jeffersonian Republicans has mainly confirmed earlier interpretations, especially those of Beard. There does emerge, however, a better understanding of other political leaders including John Adams and John Taylor. As a by-product, articles interpreting them have been published by me earlier.[7] I am

[7] Cf. Dauer, Manning J., " The Political Economy of John Adams," *Political Science Quarterly*, LVI, 545-72; and Dauer, Manning J. and Hammond,

grateful to the editors of the *Political Science Quarterly* for permission to reprint much of my article on "The Political Economy of John Adams" as Chapter 4 of this book.

This book has been in progress since 1931. One of the chief difficulties was the task of constructing the vote charts. This necessitated much work in establishing the boundaries of election districts for members of the United States House of Representatives. To do this it was necessary to trace the laws in the early session acts of State legislatures, then to find contemporary maps showing the county lines. Finally, there was the problem of using contemporary newspapers, biographies, and correspondence to determine the location of the congressmen in their districts. A preliminary version of part of this work constituted my doctoral dissertation at the University of Illinois in 1933 (unpublished).

Under the Historical Records Project of the W. P. A., Clifford Lee Lord, now Director of the State Historical Society of Wisconsin, directed a research project to map all the votes of congress in the manner I have indicated. This was not known to me until the publication of his *Atlas of Congressional Roll Calls for the Continental Congress*.[8] After World War II the unfinished materials of the larger project for the congresses after 1789 were housed at Columbia University. Dr. Lord kindly permitted me to examine these materials. The only parts I examined were those concerning the working maps and the lists of congressmen by districts. The project is, however, incomplete for the years of the Federalist period, and much of the material had not been checked. Consequently, it was necessary to return to the checking of maps, charts, and congressmen from source materials. If completed, the herculean work on the votes of all the congresses would be of inestimable importance for American historians and other students of the social sciences. It would provide a means of checking social and economic data against political trends and voting behavior. An equally important need is for a searching study which would provide election returns. Such a compilation

Hans, "John Taylor, Democrat or Aristocrat?" *Journal of Politics*, VI, 381-403.   [8] (New York, 1943).

of election returns could be used in countless studies. Where greater detail is necessary, voting behavior in comparable studies of state legislatures could provide information on the alignment of political groups. It is regrettable that data such as this, including election returns, is not readily provided by state and local historical societies. It is also regretable that more dissertations and monographs do not treat such topics, which could be useful in broader interpretations.

The objection may be made that all of this is a multiplication of detail. But is this true? As matters are, much that is written is merely descriptive or narrative. How can we integrate political history with social and economic data before we know the skeleton of the story, before we have the basic facts? Again, how can we evaluate theorists—political, economic, or religious—before we can determine the effects of their theories on broad sections of the population? How can we evaluate political leadership unless we have objective data as to the effects of policies on divergent sections and groups?

Today there is an appreciation of such material in the field of public opinion sampling. We also have much data to determine the effect of advertising, especially in measurement techniques, to determine the effect of radio advertising. But often data to analyze more important social phenomena are lacking, or are not used. In the absence of data, writers may deny its utility. Recently Allan Nevins has written an essay in the *New York Times* denying that basic differences are apparent among American political parties.[9] As to one interpretation of history, Bernard DeVoto has denounced, " the naive mythology called economic determinism." [10] Perhaps the extreme type of interpretation attacked is an oversimplification, but Mr. DeVoto has offered nothing more convincing than one writer controverting another. Or again, in times of stress, we have heroic attempts to determine cause by writers attempting to treat a long period, or even all

---

[9] *New York Times Magazine*, July 18, 1948, 5 ff.
[10] *The Year of Decision, 1846* (New York, 1943) 11, quoted by MacIver, *op. cit.*

world history, in accord with some philosophy of history. Frequently these take the form of mechanistic or cyclical theories developed in periods of sharp disillusionment. But are the social sciences at the stage to permit such mechanistic theories to be proven? Do such mechanistic theories actually provide an explanation of the social process? Or, in a more sophisticated age than that of primitive man, do they merely provide an explanation freeing man of his own responsibility for his actions? Such a cyclical theory was attempted by Oswald Spengler after World War I in his *Decline of the West*.[11] During the depression of the 1930's Arnold J. Toynbee's *A Study of History* [12] appeared. This work in the one volume abridgment has received wide popular acclaim since World War II. Finally, Charles A. Lindbergh has added an even more mystical statement in his recent book, *Of Flight and Life*.[13]

The objection to these cyclical attempts, it seems to me, is that they attempt to formulate laws and rules for the social sciences. But these laws and rules are by analogy to mathematical patterns already predetermined, or in some cases the pattern is determined intuitively by the writer. Then the data from the social sciences is selected to fit the pattern.[14]

Certainly the student of the social sciences should try to formulate laws when possible. But the most fruitful results have come from those studies which analyzed the data first, and then attempted to formulate conclusions and laws. To illustrate the procedure discussed, certain studies in various fields of the social sciences may be considered.

In sociology some of the studies which carefully analyze segments of the population produce results so indisputable as to

[11] Originally *Der Untergang des Abendlandes* (München, 1919-22) translated, New York, 1926-28.

[12] (Oxford, 1934-1939). One volume abridgment by Somervell, D. C., same title (New York, 1946).

[13] (New York, 1948).

[14] Analysis of social phenomena which proceeds by analogy to the laws of either physical or biological sciences, which have been evolved from data in those fields, is also likely to produce strange results in the social sciences.

limit the scope of debate. For example, the Lynds' studies of American culture in *Middletown* and in *Middletown in Transition* [15] provide accurate data on life and culture in a small American urban center. The case and survey methods employed by Gunnar Myrdal and associates in *An American Dilemma* [16] provide material on the Negro in America that is most useful. Regional studies such as Rupert B. Vance's *Human Geography of the South* and Howard W. Odum's *Southern Regions* [17] are also comprehensive. The study by William I. Thomas and Florian Znaniecki, *The Polish Peasant*,[18] and by E. A. Stauffer and others on *The American Soldier* [19] employ significant empirical methods. *The American Soldier* also verges into the area of social psychology.

Some writings in economics also fall in the categories being considered. Many of the studies of the United States Census Bureau have long been indispensable for basic data. Government reports such as those of Sir William Beveridge [20] in England, or the reports on income of the Federal Reserve Board,[21] the reports on living costs of the United States Bureau of Labor Statistics,[22] various studies on distribution of wealth, and the data provided by the Council of Economic Advisors [23] to the President, the monographs of the Senate Committee on the *Investigation of*

[15] Lynd, Robert S. and Helen M. (New York, 1930); and Lynd, Robert S. and Helen M. (New York, 1937).

[16] 2 vols. (New York, 1944).

[17] (Chapel Hill, 1935) and (Chapel Hill, 1936). *The Report of Economic Conditions of the South* (Washington, 1938) should also be noted.

[18] 2nd ed., 2 vols. (New York, 1927).

[19] (2 vols., Princeton, 1949). Merton, Robert K. and Lazarsfeld, Paul F., have edited an appraisal of this work under the title *Studies in the Scope and Method of " The American Soldier."* (Glencoe, Ill., 1950).

[20] *Social Insurance and Allied Services* (London, 1942); also see his *Full Employment in a Free Society* (London, 1944).

[21] U. S. Federal Reserve Bulletin (Washington, 1915-   ).

[22] *Monthly Labor Review* (Washington, 1915-   ) also *Wages and Hours of Labor series* (Washington, 1913-1934).

[23] U. S. Council of Economic Advisors. *Economic Indicators* (Washington, 1949-   ); *The Economic Reports of the President* as transmitted to the Congress, Jan. 1949, from Government Printing Office, Washington, various dates.

Concentration of Economic Power,[24] are all examples of analyses presenting pertinent data.

In the field of political science, certain works which use the quantitative approach may be mentioned. These include *A Study of War*, by Quincy Wright and his University of Chicago associates.[25] While some of the materials in the appendices to this work are of interest, others are probably too ambitious in the light of the data available. But there are in this work many interesting and suggestive ideas. Professor William Anderson's *The Units of Government in the United States*[26] is another type of work which prepares the way for analysis and appraisal. Writings on political parties and groups will be considered presently.

While giving a general endorsement to the quantitative method in the social sciences, it should be recognized that statistics do not interpret themselves. Nor is the mere accumulation of unrelated facts an end in itself. To indulge in that would be as escapist as romanticism itself. The student in the social sciences, when he turns to the present, is faced with the pressure of tremendous decisions which must be made every day. But at the same time there is the necessity for trying to develop techniques whereby competent students of the same question may independently come closer to comparable results when studying the same questions. This is one of the difficulties in any governmental system. Perhaps in countries with a background of democratic experience, the public may develop a degree of sophistication which stands it in good stead. But if the democratic process is to operate in countries without such background, any criteria which might be evolved to aid in the appraisal of problems in the social sciences would be of great value. For that matter such would also be the case in any state. Not the least of the problems to be studied is the operation of the democratic process itself.

---

[24] 76th Congress, 3rd Session, Temporary National Economic Committee, *Monographs* 1-43 (Washington, 1940-41); and *Final Report and Recommendations of the T N E C* (77th Congress, 1st Session, Washington, 1941).

[25] 2 vols. (Chicago, 1942).

[26] (Chicago, 1942).

Questions as to the stability of the democratic process to varying cultures, to countries at varying levels of political and economic development, with varying types of resources—all these might better be answered if there could be better analysis of the operation of the democratic process itself.

The scope of this present work is merely suggestive. I have had to omit certain detailed analyses which would have required more time and additional data to complete. Furthermore, complete accuracy on all the maps and district lines is not claimed. Local study in various areas may readily provide corrections. Nor is the claim made that the social and economic data are treated or evaluated in terms of their full influence; only here and there have inter-relationships which are apparent been examined. That is the most that can be stated. Statistical techniques might also be used if some of the data were secured in greater detail for certain localities.[27]

Some may raise the question, why is the work of analyzing the composition of the House of Representatives' Districts, and of charting the votes necessary? Why not simply write the political narrative from published and unpublished correspondence, the newspapers and pamphlets, the debates in congress, and other sources? I believe the best answer has been given by Prof. William F. Ogburn of the University of Chicago in the following parable: [28]

I once heard of a man who was wonderfully skilled as a wool-tester. He could feel a piece of wool with his fingers and tell how durable it would be, how much warmth it would hold, how much shoddy was in it, and could describe many other qualities of the wool and of the sheep that produced it. He could not, though, transmit his art to others, for he scarcely knew how he did it, though his results were

---

[27] Cf. Gosnell, Harold F., *Machine Politics: Chicago Model* (Chicago, 1937), especially pp. 91-125 and App. B., pp. 205-209. Rice, *Quantitative Methods in Politics*; and in part in V. O. Key, *Southern Politics* (New York, 1949).

[28] In the Foreword to Gosnell, *Machine Politics: Chicago Model*, xi. Also cf. the earlier work of Ogburn, W. F. and Talbot, N. S., " A Measurement of the Factors in the Presidential Election of 1928," *Social Forces*, **VIII**, 175-83 (1929).

good. About the same time I read an account of a method, developed
in a laboratory, of measuring the properties of wool with the aid of a
microscope, by counting the fibers, by measuring thickness, and by
dimensioning air pockets and enumerating them per unit of area.
By this means the weight of blankets necessary on a night with a
temperature of, say, 30 degrees to keep the air surrounding the body
at 98.6 degrees could be determined by anyone who could count and
measure.

Thus the hope is that by establishing certain facts basic to the
narrative, it may be possible to demonstrate certain points which
will find general acceptance. There may be less room for argument,
greater chance that other investigators will find the materials
presented lead to the same conclusions.

On the other hand, others may feel that with the statistical
methods of multiple correlation and factor analysis which are
available, the use of quantitative methods is far too scanty in this
study. I am aware of this. The only defense is that for later
periods the availability of economic data, and the availability
of election returns, makes the use of such techniques possible.
But a great deal more spade work would need to be done to
assemble election returns before anything like such a method
could be used in the period prior to 1800. Likewise more careful
examination as to the availability of tax rolls, church preferences,
etc., would have to be made on a local basis.

Another limitation on this work is that it does not attempt a
history of the period or its events. The chief events of the period
are mentioned, but most attention is given to the Adams wing of
the Federalist party, and the program which Adams stood for.
This is the explanation for the rather long chapters on the
political and economic ideas of John Adams. At the same time
the chapters use Adams as the vehicle, because of two factors.
First, the beliefs of Hamilton and Jefferson have previously been
fully treated by other writers already named. Second, because
of his mid-way position between the two, the main schools of
political and economic ideas can be brought in fairly accurate
perspective. From this examination, the attempt is made to show

the interplay of these political and economic ideas with the actually developing economic and political life of the country, and to suggest certain conclusions as to their influence.

The conclusions of this study, expressed in Chapter 17, emphasize the importance of the function of political parties in the democratic process. A number of studies on later periods of American politics have reached much the same conclusion. Under this interpretation one of the primary results is the reconciliation of a majority of group interests, economic, sectional, religious, and social, into the common policy of a political party. Part of this idea was expressed by A. F. Bentley in his *Process of Government*,[29] which was generally influenced by G. Ratzenhofer[30] and the works of sociologists contemporary with him. Other writers who have been concerned with the problem of groups in politics include, in broader scope, A. N. Holcomb,[31] Charles E. Merriam,[32] Peter H. Odegard,[33] E. P. Herring,[34] Merle Fainsod,[35] and Wilfred E. Binckley.[36] Charles A. Beard, Harold F. Gosnell and V. O.

---

[29] (Chicago, 1908); also, D. P. Truman, *The Governmental Process* (New, York, 1951).

[30] *Wesen und Zweck der Politik.* 3 vols. (Leipzig, 1893). Possibly the corporative idea of some of the theorists of the Middle Ages and early modern period may also be mentioned. But to carry this idea too far can result in emphasis on particularism, which is beside the point. The essence of the contemporary idea is that a common policy emerges and results in action. Whether this is a resultant, a compromise, or a major modification of separate group desires into something approaching a national policy, this common policy does develop. That the two-party rather than the multi-party system is more likely to produce a positive program instead of a compromise of stalemate, is the conclusion of most present-day students, especially those who have studied the problem comparatively with European parties. My own study touches but lightly on this question of the two-party versus the multi-party system.

[31] *The New Party Politics* (New York, 1933), and *The Middle Class in American Politics* (Cambridge, Mass., 1940).

[32] *The American Party System* (New York, 1949).

[33] *American Politics* with E. A. Helms (New York, 1947).

[34] *Group Representation before Congress* (Baltimore, 1929).

[35] With Lincoln Gordon, *Government and the American Economy* (New York, 1948).

[36] *American Political Parties: Their Natural History* (New York, 1943).

Key, Jr.,[37] have already been mentioned. More specialized studies by E. E. Schattschneider,[38] H. L. Childs,[39] Belle Zeller [40] and Paul Lazarsfeld [41] also shed light on the problem. Finally, David Easton's *The Political System* is an excellent systematic analysis and criticism of the study of the group process.

I wish to express my indebtedness to officials of the Library of Congress, the National Archives, the Boston Public Library, the Massachusetts Historical Society Library, Widener and Langdell Libraries of Harvard University, the Library of the Pennsylvania Historical Society, the Maryland Historical Society, the University of Illinois Library and the University of Florida Library. For help at various stages of this work I also wish to thank the late Professors Marcus Lee Hansen, L. M. Larson, T. C. Pease, and J. G. Randall, of the University of Illinois, and Professors S. E. Morison and Frederick Merk of Harvard, Professor Howard K. Beale of the University of Wisconsin, Drs. Thomas P. Martin and A. O. Sarkissian of the Library of Congress, Professor Hans Hammond of Rutgers University, and my colleagues at the University of Florida, including Professors James Miller Leake, R. S. Johnson, and John G. Eldridge. Several past and present graduate assistants, including Messrs. George Wolff, Dwynal Pettengill, Hugh D. Price, Robert J. Frye, and Richard Letaw have assisted in the making of the maps, checking data, and indexing.

Special acknowledgment is due to two of my colleagues, Professor William G. Carleton and Professor Arthur W. Thompson, to Professor C. Vann Woodward of the Johns Hopkins University, and to Professor Dumas Malone of Columbia University, all of whom have read the entire manuscript and offered many helpful suggestions and criticisms. However, I alone am responsible for any errors in the completed work.

[37] Also see his *Politics, Parties, and Pressure Groups* (New York, 1947).

[38] *Party Government* (New York, 1942) and *Politics, Pressures and the Tariff* (New York, 1935).

[39] *Labor and Capital in National Politics* (Columbus, 1929).

[40] *Pressure Politics in New York* (New York, 1937).

[41] *The People's Choice*, 2nd ed. (New York, 1948).

Table of Contents

List of Tables

List of Maps

HOUSE OF REPRESENTATIVES VOTING RECORD

Congress and Session

List of Vote Charts

THE ADAMS FEDERALISTS

Chapter 1

The Basis of
Early Political Divisions

I. COMMERCIAL GROUPS

How and why did American political parties begin? During the period before the Revolution, divisions appeared. The colonial period was full of political conflicts within each colony. On the eve of the Revolution, the division of Whig versus Tory developed in every colony, and Whigs and Tories alike united among the colonies. During the Revolution, this division passed beyond the political level to the level of civil war. But by the end of the Revolution, in 1783, the Tories had either migrated or been suppressed. Soon, however, a new division appeared—Federalist versus Anti-Federalist. Should the thirteen states unite in a stronger form of government, or retain the weak union of a confederation?

Although political parties fought over the issue of adopting the new constitution which established a federal form of government, their continuation on a national basis and their role in the government were not fully foreseen by the makers of the Constitution. Nor do writers on parties of this period more than partially understand their role. The ideas held by Hamilton, Madison, and Jay as expressed in *The Federalist* [1] are not so discerning on this subject as on others. There was discussion of " Factions " and the influence these would have. But the assumption was that any factions, or political parties, would be local or regional. It was foreseen that there would be continuing differences among social, economic, and geographic groups; but how these would be expressed was a speculative matter.

[1] Hamilton, Alexander; Madison, James; and Jay, John; *The Federalist*, H. C. Lodge, ed. (New York, 1895).

3

To understand how parties were so quickly established, it is necessary first to survey the new United States of the 1790's. The census of 1790 shows the total population of the thirteen states as 4,009,000 in round numbers. By 1800 this had increased to just over 5,300,000, most of which was agrarian population. In 1790, Philadelphia, the largest city, had a population (including suburbs) of 42,444; New York, 33,133; Boston, 18,038; and in the South, Charleston, the largest city, 16,359. In 1790 only four per cent of the country's population, or 131,396 people lived in cities of over 8,000, only 201,655 in cities and towns over 2,500. Even by 1800 the number of people in urban communities of over 2,500 had reached but 322,371.[2]

The early American economist, Samuel Blodget, presents the following table as an estimate of the employment of the population of the United States in 1805. Actually, the proportions of various classes in this study appear to be well calculated.

TABLE 1 [3]

ECONOMIC CLASSES IN THE UNITED STATES, 1805

Classes	Employment Category	Total Persons, United States
Slaves to planters	300,000	800,000
Slaves variously employed	100,000	200,000
Free planters and Agriculturists	1,200,000	4,800,000
Mechanical Artisans	100,000	500,000
Fishermen	6,000	30,000
Seamen, &c.	110,000	400,000
Professional and all others not enumerated	50,000	250,000
	1,866,000	6,180,000 *

* Blodget or his printer missed this one. The actual total is 6,980,000.

The striking point about this estimate is that, eliminating the slaves, 80 per cent of the economic groups, as well as 80 per cent of the population appear as agricultural. If anything, the propor-

---

[2] Bureau of the Census, *A Century of Population Growth* (Washington, 1909), 11, 15; Bureau of the Census, *Historical Statistics of the United States, 1789-1945* (Washington, 1949), 29, Series B 145.

[3] Blodget, Samuel, *Economica* (Washington, 1810), 89.

tion of the population in agriculture is smaller in 1805 than at the earlier period from 1790-1800. The overwhelming numerical superiority of the agricultural groups is apparent.

This estimate is also confirmed by another set of figures. Because of the self-sufficient nature of much of the farming, and the smallness of the domestic market, figures on exports are of considerable importance in estimating the proportion of the population in various phases of economic life. In 1804 Albert Gallatin, Secretary of the Treasury, reported United States' exports of domestic products as follows: [4]

Products of the Sea	3,420,000
Products of the Forest	4,630,000
Products of Agriculture	30,890,000
Products of Manufactures	2,100,000
Uncertain	430,000
	$41,470,000

Another estimate, which gives private national income for 1799 by classes of economic enterprise helps to fill out the picture of the national economy. This estimate is:

TABLE 2 [5]

PRIVATE NATIONAL INCOME BY INDUSTRIES, 1799

(*In millions of dollars*)

Industry	Income	Percent of total income
Agriculture	264	39.6
Mining	1	.1
Manufacturing	32	4.8
Construction	53	7.9
Transportation and Communication	160	23.9
Trade	35	5.3
Services	64	9.6
Finance and others	59	8.8
TOTAL	668	100.0

[4] Blodget, *Economica*, 119.
[5] Bureau of Census, *Historical Statistics of the United States*, 14 (Series A 151-64).

This table also is important in showing the greater proportionate income of such industries as finance, shipping, and trade, despite the smaller proportion of individuals in these enterprises.

While in New England the decentralization of the shipbuilding industries makes the calculation of the extent of agricultural *versus* commercial sections difficult, it is doubtful if even in this section the direct mercantile interests had sufficient votes to carry a single state. Even in New England in 1800 it is estimated that, of a total population of 1,078,546, the population of commercial towns came only to about 145,000.[6] John A. Krout and Dixon Ryan Fox state that during the period around 1800 " at least nine Americans out of ten, even in commercial New England, dug their living from the land."[7] This statement is indisputable for the country as a whole; but because of the importance of shipping, shipbuilding, and the fisheries, it is probably an over-statement for much of New England and especially for eastern New England. But it serves to point up the political problem generally. Any political party which wished to maintain a majority had to secure considerable agrarian support.

On the other hand, Alexander Hamilton's policy was the basis of the Federalist party program. Initially, in 1790, his program of a strong central government commanded fairly broad support. Washington, as president, became the symbol of this policy. But opposition to a strong central government already had arisen over the adoption of the Constitution.[8] While this opposition somewhat disintegrated as the new government started, it soon reappeared. As Beard has shown in his *Economic Origins of Jeffersonian Democracy*, the basis of the Jeffersonian Republican

[6] Cf. Bidwell, Percy W., " Rural Economy in New England at the Beginning of the Nineteenth Century," *Transactions of the Connecticut Academy of Arts and Sciences* (New Haven, 1916), XX, 296 and Appendix II to this book, pp. 275-87.

[7] *The Completion of Independence, 1789-1830* (Vol. V of *A History of American Life,* A. M. Schlesinger, ed., New York, 1944), 92.

[8] Beard, Charles A., *Economic Interpretation of the Constitution of the United States* (New York, 1913), and the numerous studies by various authors on the struggle for adoption of the Constitution in state conventions.

party's strength was agrarian.[9] With the United States so strongly agrarian, why, then, did the Jeffersonian party not become successful upon the retirement of Washington in the presidential contest of 1796?

There are a variety of reasons for this. But one of the central ones is the support of the Federalist party by agricultural sections throughout the country. This is also the explanation of John Adams' strength in the Federalist party. By centering attention on the Adams supporters, instead of on the Hamilton supporters, it becomes apparent that the history of the decline of the Federalist party is largely the history of the step-by-step loss of the agrarian elements from the party. It also becomes apparent that religious and cultural factors influenced the extent to which agrarian elements tied in with Federalism or Jeffersonian Republicanism. As the series of eleven maps and eight vote charts show,[10] in most states the general pattern is that the more self-sufficient farming sections and the " mechanic interests " of the cities are the centers of Jeffersonian strength. The extreme Federalists are found among the commercial and shipping sections, and the exporting agricultural sections are somewhat less intensely Federalist. A more detailed survey of the various Republican and Federalist centers in 1796, together with the influences which predominated in determining the political character of these sections, is found in Appendix II.

. The soundness of the position taken by Charles A. Beard, that the Federalist policy favored the commercial groups, while the Republicans represented the agrarians, is accepted as fundamental.[11] However, although this is true of the Federalist *policy;* yet Federalist *support* was derived from a broader basis. In general, the Half-Federalists, as those who deviated from Hamiltonian orthodoxy are called, are to be found in farming sections.

This analysis differs from the position taken by A. M. Simons in his statement: " Three divisions of the ruling class united to

[9] (New York, 1915).
[10] Maps 1-11, Vote Charts 1-8 (Appendix III).
[11] Beard, *Economic Origins of Jeffersonian Democracy, passim.*

form the constitution and establish the new government. These were the merchants, the manufacturers, and the planters. The first two at once formed an alliance against the latter to secure control of the government. In this alliance the first dominated, since the carrying trade was by far the most highly developed. Its units of capital were larger, its owners more clearly conscious of their class interests, and better equipped to further those interests than the owners of the essentials of any other industry." [12] The disagreement is not with the idea that shipping and commercial interests dominated Federalist policy — this is perfectly correct. But the disagreement is with the idea that virtually all of the agrarians left the Hamiltonian leadership immediately after the new government began. Moreover the commercial and manufacturing groups were not sufficiently numerous to carry elections — even with a limited franchise.

The wealthy commercial groups that constituted the strongest of the Hamiltonian Federalists were principally in shipping and shipbuilding, handicraft manufactures, the export and re-export trade, retail merchandising and banking. The most important of these groups were the shipowners and shipbuilders. Table 3 (p. 9) shows the ratio of foreign trade tonnage per inhabitant by states in 1801. Table 4 (p. 10) shows the concentration of the export and re-export trade in these same states. These last figures are significant to show in which state the mercantile business is concentrated. It should be understood that Table 3 is on the basis of port clearances, and the fact that the figures are by states does not mean that the goods were produced in that state, only that they were shipped abroad through ports so located. The figures for 1801 are also not divided between export of domestic production and re-exports, state totals not being available until the later years, 1803-1805. However, it should be stated that in 1801 the total exports and re-exports are almost equal, over $46 million in value for each category.

As is well known, the heaviest concentration of shipping was in New England. In 1801, Massachusetts, New Hampshire, Rhode

---

[12] Simons, A. M., *Social Forces in American History* (New York, 1911), 108.

TABLE 3 [13]

RATIO OF FOREIGN TRADE TONNAGE TO INHABITANTS BY STATES, 1801

State	Inhabitants	Total Tons	Tons per Inhabitant
Vt.	154,465	0	0
N. H.	183,858	18,379	0.099
Mass.	574,564	241,319	0.57
R. I.	69,122	23,747	0.34
Conn.	251,002	34,465	0.14
N. Y.	589,051	106,023	0.18
N. J.	211,145	1,046	0.0049
Penn.	602,365	109,036	0.18
Del.	64,273	2,752	0.04
Md.	341,648	55,986	0.16
Va.	880,200	44,850	0.05
N. C.	478,103	21,812	0.046
S. C.	345,591	51,192	0.15
Ga.	162,686	7,758	0.048

Island and Connecticut contained 1,078,546 persons (based on the census of 1800) and had 417,910 tons of shipping. The remaining states and territories, with a population of 4,229,931 had only 400,483 tons of shipping. This total of over 818,000 tons in foreign trade in 1801 is probably somewhat padded. Hutchins, the best recent authority, accepts the statement of Albert Gallatin that this figure is over 200,000 tons too high. Their estimate for 1800 shows tonnage in foreign trade to be between 500,000 and 525,000; in coastal trade, about 240,000; with the grand total, including fishing and whaling vessels, about 770,000 in 1800.[14] In the four New England States enumerated, there were .38 tons of shipping per inhabitant; in the rest of the country there were but .095 tons per inhabitant — 400 per cent more in New England than in the rest of the country.

[13] Seybert, Adam, *Statistical Annals* (Philadelphia, 1818), 308; 321. Pitkin, Timothy, *A Statistical View of the Commerce of the United States of America* (Hartford, 1817), 435-36.

[14] Hutchins, John G. B., *The American Maritime Industries and Public Policy, 1789-1914* (Cambridge, Mass., 1941), 225-26. No state figures are given on the basis of which a corrected table for the lower figures might be presented.

Outside New England, of the Middle Atlantic States, New York and Pennsylvania have the greatest amount of shipping; while of the Southern States, Maryland and South Carolina register considerable tonnage. The comparison of this factor with the areas showing Federalist strength shows a direct correlation.

TABLE 4 [15]

VALUE OF EXPORTS BY STATES, 1801

State	Total Exports in 1801 Domestic and Foreign	Percentage that foreign goods re-exported is of total exports, 3 yr. average, 1803-1805
N. H.	$ 555,055	20-30%
Vt.	57,267	20-30
Mass.	14,870,556	30-70
R. I.	1,832,773	40-60
Conn.	1,446,216	2-5
N. Y.	19,851,136	30-50
N. J.	25,406	0
Penn.	17,438,193	40-50
Del.	662,042	40-80
Md.	12,767,530	30-60
D. of C.	894,467	2-10
Va.	5,655,574	3-10
N. C.	874,884	1-2
S. C.	14,304,045	10-40
Ga.	1,755,939	2-3
Miss.	1,095,412	0
Tenn.	29,430	0
TOTAL	94,115,925	

The importance of this shipping can best be understood if comparison be made with England. This also brings out the fact that the American shipbuilding trade was well established from colonial times. On the eve of the American Revolution, in 1774, there were a total of only 600,000 tons of British shipping engaged in foreign trade according to one estimate,[16] while another places

---

[15] Pitkin, Timothy, *A Statistical View of the Commerce of the United States*, 52.

[16] Hutchins, *American Maritime Industries*, 155.

the total British merchant marine at 979,000 tons.[17] The same
sources estimate the American built ships in the English foreign
trade in 1774 at 200,000 tons. By 1800, British shipping had
increased considerably, having reached approximately 1,905,438
tons — double the total of 1774.[18] But even this was insufficient
to carry the increased volume of trade. England was forced to
admit much neutral tonnage to her waters, including tonnage of
the United States.[19] Against this total for British shipping, U. S.
shipping in foreign trade was between 500,000 and 525,000 tons
by 1800. One estimate places the freight profits per ton on
shipping during this period at $50 to $70 annually. Net annual
income of the United States merchant marine is put at $32,000,000
annually after 1794.[20] But in addition to this income the American
economy was further affected favorably by the income from shipbuilding. Virtually all of the American tonnage was American
built. Therefore, added to those drawing income from the shipping industry are the large numbers working in shipbuilding.
Shipbuilding, moreover, extended far up the New England rivers,
and in the bays of the deeply indented coast. Many of those
who are classified as living on farms were also working in shipbuilding, cutting timber for ships, and otherwise dependent on
the industry.[21] There is even the case of two shipbuilders who
built a West Indian schooner on the side of Mount Ossipee in
the White Mountains and hauled it twenty-five miles over winter

[17] Hunter, Henry C., *How England Got its Merchant Marine* (New York,
1935), 307.

[18] McArthur, John, *Financial and Political Facts of the Eighteenth Century*
(London, 1801), 242; Marshall, John, *A digest of All the Accounts . . . Relating to Great Britain* (London, 1834), 225-26; Chalmers, George, *An Estimate
of the Comparative Strength of Great Britain* (new edition, London, 1810),
308. This last source places ships cleared outward from England in 1800 at
1,269,329 tons of British shipping and 654,713 tons of foreign.

[19] Marshall, *Digest of All the Accounts*, places U. S. ships cleared from
English ports at 112,696 tons in 1800.

[20] Clark, Victor S., *History of Manufactures in the United States* (New
York, 1929 edition), I, 237.

[21] Morison, Samuel E., *Maritime History of Massachusetts* (Boston, 1921),
96-118.

snows to water.[22] This particular incident occurred later than
1800, but it illustrates the geographic decentralization of the
industry. Further, the tonnage built was great during the period
from 1789-1800. In the earlier year total American tonnage in
foreign trade was only 124,000 tons. In 1795 and 1796 the output
was 100,000 *additional* gross tons per year.[23] Even accepting the
low figure of about 500,000 tons for American shipping in 1800,
the increase of tonnage in foreign trade from 1789 to 1800 was
over 400 per cent. Consequently the general interest in shipping
in New England and the other shipping states was widespread.
Members of many families shipped as sailors, many built ships,
and others were engaged in the fisheries. All in all, it is difficult
to separate the population in New England between those dependent on agriculture and those dependent on shipping and the
maritime industries. Of course not all those connected with the
maritime industries followed the lead of the great merchants and
shippers into the Federalist party. But it would be equally wrong
to classify all of the rural population as agrarian. Turning to
the commercial leaders, it is fairly easy to see how the rapid
expansion of their industry would lead them to feel that national
policy should support them — even to the extent of dreaming of
an American Empire as a counterpart to the British.

Because of the French Revolution, and the resulting warfare
between England and France, French shipping was almost driven
from the seas.[24] But England was not able to build shipping with
sufficient rapidity to replace that of the enemy powers. Even
before the Revolution the decline of her own timber resources had
caused her to depend increasingly on the colonies.[25] At the same
time her own increasing manufactures provided many items of
export. This gap in available shipping was filled by American
and other foreign shipping, creating a noncompetitive situation
wherein the British navy controlled the seas, and the British and
American merchant marines were the chief beneficiaries. Incidents

[22] Hutchins, *American Maritime Industries*, 191.
[23] *Ibid.*, 224; 185.
[24] Hutchins, *American Maritime Industries*, 184, 223.
[25] *Ibid.*, 130, 175.

over impressment of seamen by the British angered Americans concerned with individual rights and were played up in the Jeffersonian press. But to the Federalists, and especially the shipping interests, these were minor irritations. There was actually a community of interest between American and British shipping throughout the period of the French Revolution and the Napoleonic Wars — interrupted eventually by Jefferson's Embargo Act and then by the War of 1812.[26]

By 1800 shipping from Salem and Boston, as well as that from New York and Philadelphia, was of great importance in the Far East, including China and the East Indies.[27] Much of this trade was carried on with English manufactures. In some cases American ships carried these goods direct; other ships stopped to trade some of the English cargo for furs supplied by the Indians of the Northwest Pacific Coast of North America. These furs had special value in Canton.[28] Then the goods of the Far East were brought back to world markets which grew up in American ports. So important was this trade that shortly after 1800 Salem, Massachusetts, had become " the world emporium for pepper," [29] and was thought to be so important in the East Indies as to rank as one of the great countries of the world! [30] The interest of the great merchants in this world-wide trade was one of the primary reasons for the difference in outlook of the commercial leaders of Boston, Salem, New York and Philadelphia from the rest of the Federalists. This outlook naturally left them even more widely separated from the self-sufficient agrarians who predominated in the Jeffersonian party. In addition to the foreign market, merchants could also sell in the urban domestic market. But this type of trade was probably small in volume. Villagers grew their own food, and one estimate places the total population of those in Northern urban centers which were not

---

[26] *Ibid.*, 188; 288.
[27] Morison, *Maritime History of Massachusetts*, 27-40; 64-78.
[28] *Ibid.*, 52-63.
[29] *Ibid.*, 79-95.
[30] *Ibid.*, 84.

largely self-sufficient at no more than 200,000 in 1800.[31] Probably not over half this number should be added for the South.

Another important influence among the commercial Federalists was banking. In the first place, the increase in banks after 1784 was rapid. In the second place, banks were concentrated in the states with shipping and export business. The distribution of state banks by states in 1801 was as follows:

TABLE 5

DISTRIBUTION OF STATE BANKS BY STATES, 1801 [32]

State	No. of Banks	Bank Capital
Maine	1	$ 300,000
New Hampshire	1	400,000
Vermont	0	
Massachusetts	6	3,850,000
Connecticut	5	2,000,000
Rhode Island	5	1,070,000
New York	5	4,720,000
Pennsylvania	2	5,000,000
New Jersey	0	
Maryland	2	1,600,000
Delaware	1	110,000
Virginia	0	
North Carolina	0	
South Carolina	2	3,000,000
Georgia	0	
Kentucky	0	
Tennessee	0	
District of Columbia	2	1,500,000
TOTAL	32	$23,550,000

Including the Bank of the United States after 1790, the increase of bank capital and the circulation of bank notes is shown for various periods in the following table:

[31] Bidwell, Percy W. and Falconer, John I., *History of Agriculture in the United States, 1620-1860* (New York, 1941), 132.

[32] *Monthly Summary of Commerce and Finance of the United States for . . . 1899*, New Series, Vol. 6 (House Document No. 573, Pt. I, 55th Congress, 2nd Session, Washington, 1899), 208-209.

TABLE 6

STATISTICAL RESUME OF BANK CAPITAL AND CIRCULATION IN THE
UNITED STATES FROM 1780 TO 1811 [33]

(*Figures in millions except first and last columns*)

Banks (including Bank of the U. S. after 1790)

Year	Number	Capital	Circulation	Specie	Total	Population	per Capita
1784	3	2.1	2.0	10.0	12.0	3.0	$4.00
1790	4	2.5	2.5	9.0	11.5	3.8	3.00
1795	24	21.0	16.0	19.0	35.0	4.5	7.77
1800	29	31.3	15.5	17.5	33.0	5.3	6.22
1805	76	50.5	26.0	17.5	43.5	6.2	7.00
1811	89	52.7	28.1	30.0	58.1	7.3	8.00

Here again, the concentration appears in the seven states of Massachusetts, Rhode Island, Connecticut, New York, Pennsylvania, Maryland, and South Carolina. In addition to those directly connected with shipping, banking, and the general mercantile interests, the professional groups, including the lawyers, usually supported the Federalists. It was always a good point for Republican propaganda to advertise a candidate as not being a lawyer.

The Federalists also derived support from manufacturing although the extent of this was limited because of the relative unimportance of commercial manufacturing. Agricultural sections carried on household manufactures; but the products were absorbed by the family making them.[34] One writer on the period has aptly called it " The Age of Homespun." [35] Hence the

[33] Hepburn, A. Barton, *History of Currency in the United States* (New York, 1924), 87. Other authorities differ as to the number of banks. For 1795 Walter Buckingham Smith and Arthur Harrison Cole give 21; and for 1812, 119. *Fluctuations in American Business, 1790-1860* (Cambridge, Mass., 1935), 5. Wettereau gives the number of state banks in 1791 as 5, 23 in May of 1796, and 84 in January, 1811. Wettereau, J. O., " New Light on the First Bank of the United States," *Pennsylvania Magazine of History*, LXI, 279.

[34] Tryon, Rolla M., *Household Manufactures in the United States, 1640-1860* (Chicago, 1917), 130-42; Clark, *History of Manufactures in the United States*, I, 234.

[35] Bidwell, " Rural Economy in New England," *loc. cit.*, 366-68; Schaper,

domestic market for manufactures was relatively small, and in it there was competition between American and British goods.[36] It is true that there was manufacture of such goods as gunpowder, paper, furniture, agricultural implements, some metals and glass; and Pennsylvania was the chief manufacturing state.[37] But despite Hamilton's Report on Manufactures, issued on December 5, 1791,[38] little development in this field took place until the embargo acts and the War of 1812 interrupted trade with England. Until then commercial capital had been attracted mainly to shipping and the mercantile trade. It should also be noted that export of American manufactures was small, coming to but $2,100,000 as late as 1803.[39]

Before leaving the commercial sections of the population, it should be clearly understood that not all of the town and city vote was Federalist. Charles A. Beard, in his *Economic Origins of Jeffersonian Democracy* has carefully considered the basic division of the urban vote between the Federalists and the Republicans.[40] By mapping the wards in the elections of 1800 in New York City, he has pointed out that the wards with high property valuation were Federalist, while those with low property valuation were Republican. No comparable detail is available for the earlier elections, but the same general trend is consistently noted in the press — the Republican appeal in the cities is chiefly directed to the " mechanic " or laboring groups. Detail of this is supplied when the newspaper comments are considered throughout this study. Beard also observes that in 1800 the same division as to Federalists and Republican areas of strength appeared in Philadelphia and Charleston.[41] Once again, the type of appeal to the voters points to this same division in the earlier

W. A., " Sectionalism in South Carolina," *American Historical Association Report, 1900*, I, 278-79.

[36] Clark, *History of Manufactures*, 233-62.

[37] *Ibid.*, 231.

[38] Hamilton, Alexander, *The Works of Alexander Hamilton*, John C. Hamilton, ed. (New York, 1851), III, 192-284.

[39] Blodget, *Economica*, 119.

[40] 383-87.   [41] *Ibid.*, 388.

elections and also in the City of Boston. This strength of the Republicans in the cities had existed in some cases before 1794. But by the time of the congressional elections of that year, the democratic societies were well organized and played a vital role in all the coastal towns and cities.[42] Clearly the democratic clubs modeled on those of France were especially effective in urban areas, although not confined to them by any means.[43] If, as Beard has justly observed, the basis of the city divisions between Republican and Federalist is economic, yet the potential Republican strength in most cities was not effective until organized through the democratic clubs. And in no case was this more evident than in the temporary capital city, Philadelphia.[44]

With the stronger organization of political parties, Republican strength clearly began to encroach on that of the Federalists in the cities and towns. This makes it the more necessary to observe other factors which account for Federalist strength among the agrarian elements. Even though the commercial strength extends into the rural areas of New England because of the importance of shipping, an analysis of the agrarian sections to disclose the basis of Federalist strength in farm areas is clearly necessary.

[42] Link, Eugene P., *Democratic-Republican Societies, 1790-1800* (New York, 1942); Miller, William, " First Fruits of Republican Organization: Political Aspects of the Congressional Election of 1794," *Pennsylvania Magazine of History*, LXIII, 118-43; Luetscher, George D., *Early Political Machinery in the United States* (Philadelphia, 1903); Fee, Walter R., *The Transition from Aristocracy to Democracy in New Jersey* (Somerville, N. J., 1933); Robinson, William A., *Jeffersonian Democracy in New England* (New Haven, 1916).

[43] Miller, William, " The Democratic Societies and the Whiskey Insurrection," *Pennsylvania Magazine of History*, LXII, 324-49; McLaughlin, J. F., *Mathew Lyon* (New York, 1900).

[44] Miller, William, " First Fruits of Republican Organization," *Pennsylvania Magazine of History*, LXIII, 142; and Tinkcom, Harry M., *Republicans and Federalists in Pennsylvania, 1790-1801*.

Chapter 2

The Basis of
Early Political Divisions

II. AGRICULTURAL GROUPS, SOCIAL, RELIGIOUS, AND OTHER FACTORS

FEDERALIST strength in agricultural areas was chiefly centered in those farming sections which were least self-sufficient economically, but in which much of the crop was produced for the market. With the exception of the small domestic market, this meant the foreign export market. In 1804 the products of agriculture sent abroad came to $30,890,000.[1] This was 75 per cent of the value of all domestic exports. The chief exports were cotton, sugar, tobacco, cattle, butter, cheese, flaxseed, and grains. In the South especially the period was one of transfer in many areas from tobacco to wheat.[2]

The Federalist agricultural sections can be found by considering four factors: (1) soil, (2) exporting agricultural areas, (3) ratio of slaves to white population in the South, and (4) per capita wealth. The relative size of farms would also be important, but data on this point are not available. Soil areas of the United States are best treated by three general maps. Two of the maps in Paullin's *Historical Atlas* covering Physical Divisions, when compared with Maps 1-11 giving the political complexion of the districts, show a concentration of Federalist strength in the coastal

[1] Blodget, *Economica*, 119.
[2] Gray, Lewis C., *History of Agriculture in the Southern United States, to 1860* (Washington, 1863), I, 679, 681, 740; Bidwell and Falconer, *History of Agriculture in the Northern United States*, 136; Craven, A. O., *Soil Exhaustion as a Factor in the Agricultural History of Virginia and Maryland, University of Illinois Studies in the Social Sciences* (Urbana, Ill., 1926), XIII, No. 1, 76-77.

plain area of the Southern and Middle Atlantic States.[3] If we compare the same maps of political areas with the map of soil districts, the Federalist strength appears in the coastal plain of yellowish sandy loams, and in the alluvial soils of the river basins.[4] And if we make a comparison with the map entitled " Natural Land Use Areas " presented by Lewis C. Gray,[5] the areas are generally those below the Piedmont sections in the Southern and Middle Atlantic States, which is the same region with somewhat different nomenclature. In the Southern States these were also the areas of larger plantations and of concentration of slave holding. Paullin's maps of 1790 and 1800 [6] giving slave-white ratios by counties show in Maryland, Virginia, North Carolina, South Carolina, and Georgia certain areas of high slave concentration: over 50 per cent, and 30-50 per cent. Comparing these areas of high slave concentration with Federalist voting strength in the South, (Maps 1-11, Appendix III), it is apparent that generally the greatest Federalist strength is in these same counties. Some exceptions are apparent. The Seventh North Carolina District departs from this pattern throughout the entire period; the influences operating in this district and the " Ninety-Six " District of South Carolina, as well as those in western North Carolina in the election for the Sixth Congress will be considered later. Geographic and economic factors did not prove to be dominant in these last named instances.

One other matter of considerable importance must be considered. Soil alone was not the decisive item. The coastal plain sandy loam soils are not notably rich. The alluvial soils are, but those outside the river bottoms were early subject to soil exhaustion. However, the plantation economy was concentrated in these areas during the decade under consideration, since they were easily cleared and more readily accessible to river trans-

[3] Paullin, Charles O., *Atlas of the Historical Geography of the United States* (Washington, 1932), Plate 2B.

[4] Paullin, Plate 2C.

[5] *History of Agriculture in the Southern United States to 1860*, I, frontispiece.

[6] Plates 67B and 67C.

portation. This leads to another primary factor, that of adequate transportation to market. In areas otherwise comparable, the factor of river transportation is frequently decisive. This was important throughout all agricultural areas, north and south. The chief river systems are shown on Plate I of B. H. Meyer's *History of Transportation in the United States Before 1860.*[7] These river systems in 1900 are listed in Table 7 by Atlantic Seaboard States. For the sake of brevity, tributaries of these rivers are not listed.

TABLE 7

NAVIGABLE RIVERS BY STATES, ATLANTIC SEABOARD, 1900

Maine	Virginia
Penobscot	*Rappahannock*
Kennebec	*York*
	James
Connecticut	North Carolina
Connecticut	*Roanoke*
New York	*Neuse*
Hudson	*Cape Fear*
	South Carolina
Pennsylvania–New Jersey	*Peedee*
Delaware	*Santee*
	Edisto
Maryland–Delaware	South Carolina–Georgia
Nanticoke	*Savannah*
Maryland–Virginia	Georgia
Potomac	*Altamaha*

Also river systems flowing into the Mississippi are not given. The intent is simply to show, by concentrating on the main eastern systems, the importance to agriculture of river transportation. In the period of 1800, certain problems are apparent in using a map of 1900. But by checking against other data, the problem is not insuperable.

The main difficulty in using a later listing of these rivers is that while all of them were of importance in the period 1790-1800, navigation was at this earlier period of a different character from that at the date of Meyer's map. Water transportation was

[7] (Washington, D. C., 1917).

more freely used than was the case a hundred years later. In the first place, the extensive systems of small rivers in a coastal area like that of the Chesapeake Bay were generally used. In the second place, in the period of the 1790's the height of navigation on the various rivers was higher than is shown by Meyer's map. Above and between rapids rafts were used, and goods were then transshipped to small craft after smoother waters were reached. This is apparent from information given by contemporary geographers such as Jedediah Morse,[8] other information from earlier chapters of Meyer's *History of Transportation* and statements in such works as Dwight's *Travels.*[9]

To consider one river system in the light of this information in contemporary newspapers, the Shenandoah River of Virginia, even before the building of the Potomac Canal, was used to carry goods to the Potomac and thence to the Ocean. Advertisements of markets and agents along the river show the trade to have been extensive. This had political impact on the entire Shenandoah Valley and was one of the reasons why Federalism was strong in the valley. For another example, the Connecticut River was actually used not only throughout its course through central Massachusetts, but also for shipments from eastern Vermont. This and other factors resulted in eastern Vermont being consistently Federalist in the period under study, while western Vermont, across the Green Mountains, was Republican (cf. Maps 1-11). "So long as 20-ton sailboats were deep-water craft, the coast-line extended to the head of river navigation in a sense no longer true since goods are carried by steam. Middletown, 200 miles nearer Cuba than Boston, and 100 miles nearer the farming section of central New England than New York, was an active port for West Indian commerce. Hudson maintained several whaling ships; Albany traded directly with Calcutta; and even Troy supported a river fleet. Georgetown and Richmond loaded

[8] Morse, Jedediah, *American Gazeteer* (second edition, Boston, 1804) was checked for each major and most minor rivers. Also cf. Meyer, *op. cit.*, 65-93; Morse, J., *The American Geography* (Elizabethtown, 1789).

[9] Dwight, Timothy, *Travels in New England and New York* (4 vols., New Haven, 1821-1822).

flour, and the latter city coal, on vessels that carried their cargoes without transshipment to northern ports." [10]

In the 1790's the first effects of canal building also began to be felt. By 1797 the sections of the Middlesex Canal between the Concord and the Merrimack Rivers in Massachusetts were in use.[11] The Santee and Cooper Rivers in South Carolina were connected by 1800, permitting craft from Columbia, South Carolina, to reach Charleston.[12] In New York, a canal at Little Falls permitted navigation of the Mohawk River from Schenectady to Fort Schuyler (Utica) by 1795.[13] Canal projects were launched for the Potomac in Virginia. Many other canal companies were also being started before 1800.

One other factor is the extent to which road transportation was developed to enable farmers to get their goods to market. In most of the country, road development was poor and therefore did not offer an alternative mode of transport or supplement water transportation. People might migrate over such poor roads, but goods could not be transported in quantity. In two areas this was not the case. By 1790 an extensive system of roads had developed into Philadelphia, supplementing the Delaware River. This was one of the factors which made Philadelphia the chief city in the country. It enabled the farmers of Lancaster, Chester, Montgomery, Berks, and Bucks Counties to get their goods to market. Those of eastern Lancaster and York Counties used the Susquehanna River to market goods in Baltimore.[14] The other state in which there was considerable development of road transportation was Connecticut. This system of roads, supplementing the Connecticut River, was attested to by Dwight and Morse.[15]

[10] Clark, *History of Manufactures*, 335.

[11] Roberts, Christopher, *The Middlesex Canal* (Cambridge, Mass., 1938), 103.

[12] Harlow, A. F., *Old Towpaths* (New York, 1926); Meyer, *History of Transportation*, 278.

[13] Meyer, *History of Transportation*, 173.

[14] Bidwell, Percy W. and Falconer, John I., *History of Agriculture in the Northern United States*, 138-39.

[15] Also cf. Meyer, *op. cit.*, 64.

It enabled the farmers to haul the products of the small Connecticut farms to markets.

Data on per capita wealth in land, by counties, have only been found available for Massachusetts. This material is considered in Appendix II as it covers but one state. In general, the trend is for the counties to show Federalist trends if there be a high per capita property valuation; while the poorer counties in per capita wealth show a Republican trend. Inquiry at the National Archives treasury section has shown no extant copies of the 1799 house and land tax valuation figures by counties. Published figures do show the house and land tax figures by states, and these have been mapped by Paullin.[16] Figures given show a fairly high uniform per capita valuation for most of the New England and Middle Atlantic States, with a fairly low uniform valuation for the South. New Hampshire and Vermont occupy an intermediate position. But there is no apparent guarantee that the treasury supervisors, who were named by states, followed a uniform plan of valuation. In the absence of proof that they did, skepticism is in order as to the meaning of the figures given. There is a curiously uniform tendency in most of the states (although this does not apply to New York and Pennsylvania) for the land valuation per acre to reflect the density of population per acre. This relationship becomes more apparent in extending the examination to the direct tax levied during the War of 1812, to see whether or not this factor is of importance. In the light of this trend it seems best to ignore the data. In general, the figures on ratio of slaves to whites, already considered, are believed to be most significant for the Southern States as an index to per capita farm wealth by counties.

From this survey of the agrarian exporting sections it becomes plain that politically they have much in common with the commercial elements. It was the coalition of these two elements which had effected the adoption of the Federal Constitution.[17] In order

---

[16] Plate 152B.

[17] Libby, Orin G., *Geographical Distribution of the Vote of the Thirteen States on the Federal Constitution* (Madison, Wisconsin, 1894). Map at frontispiece and preface by Frederick J. Turner.

to distinguish the agrarian sections, the term " radical agrarians "
will be applied to the more self-sufficient farmers, regardless of
section or location. For the wealthier farmers, those who produced
an appreciable quantity of goods for market, " conservative
agrarian " will be used.

In general it was a characteristic of the radical agrarians to
disregard the importance of commerce, and not to care whether
the small amount of goods they produced for market was carried
by European or American vessels. There was a great distrust of
lawyers. In regard to money, this group was prone to favor
unregulated paper currency. Banks were generally distrusted as
concentrating power and weath in the hands of the rich. All
of this then raises the question: how far did all agrarians, both
wealthy and poor, stay together; how far did wealthy agrarians
unite instead with the commercial interests? Usually this de-
pended upon both sectional factors and the issues in a particular
election; how this varied from election to election will presently be
considered throughout this study. Sectionally an important item
was the proportion of commercial interests in the section or state.
A nucleus of commercial leaders usually organized the Federalists.
Then the more wealthy agrarians lined up with them. On the other
hand, with little commercial business there was not a strong Federalist nucleus. Then the wealthy agrarians tended toward the
straight agrarian or Republican party. In other words, in Virginia,
the Republicans included a greater proportion of moderately
wealthy farmers than was the case in South Carolina [18] or New
England.

With the general introduction of banks, some change began to
appear in the ideas of this middle group (the wealthy agrarians).
If banks were to be introduced, many of this type felt that the
proper way to meet the issue was by the establishment of agrarian
banks. Jefferson, for example, suggested to Madison that this
would be the best method of offsetting the influence of the

[18] Phillips, Ulrich B., " The South Carolina Federalists," *American Historical
Review*, XIV, 530.

Richmond branch of the Bank of the United States.[19] This point is of considerable importance, for on this policy many of the wealthier agrarians throughout the union were to be won over to Republicanism. This group did not, however, share the enthusiasm of the radicals for paper money, in this respect sharing the views of their more conservative colleagues who were Federalists.

The richer agrarians, concentrated in the South along the tidewater, were generally Federalists. Motivated by the same distrust of democracy as was current among the commercial interests, they joined with this group in warding off such doctrines. After 1792 the growing radicalism of the French Revolution strengthened this feeling.[20]

In addition to, or in combination with, purely economic factors, social and cultural factors played a determining role in a few states. Religious affiliation, similar cultural and historical background, and recency of immigration, together with country of origin, are secondary factors which likewise proved to be of some importance. In general, the Congregationalist Church was the most important of all the religious denominations in political influence. No other denomination is credited by contemporary observers with the same proportionate influence. A number of sources, including the maps showing religious affiliation, present a high concentration of members of this denomination in areas of New England, western New York, and the Wyoming Valley of Pennsylvania. This most important of all church influences benefitted the Federalists. In the New England States this is a commentary on the influence of the established church. The Congregationalist Church remained the established church in Massachusetts until 1833, in New Hampshire until 1817, and in Connecticut until 1818.[21]

---

[19] Jefferson to Madison, Philadelphia, July 3, 1792, *Works of Thomas Jefferson*, Ford, ed. (New York, 1904), VII, 98.

[20] A more detailed consideration of the economic party divisions is found in App. II.

[21] Sweet, W. W., *The Story of Religion in America* (New York, 1930), 275.

The strongest organization of the Congregationalist clergy held sway in Connecticut. Timothy Dwight, President of Yale University, was the head of the hierarchy. He was called " Pope Dwight " in the Republican press.[22] This clerical influence in Connecticut supplemented economic factors, which alone were hardly sufficient to account for the political homegeneity of Connecticut. It is true that the state was prosperous. By the system of roads and by shipment down the Connecticut River farmers could readily get their crops to market. But there was no great port. In other New England States, shipping, a primary influence toward Federalism, was more important than in Connecticut. How, then, explain the difference in political allegiance to Federalism between Connecticut and Rhode Island? The outstanding difference is that which existed between the Congregationalist Church in Connecticut in contrast with the heritage of the Baptist Church in Rhode Island from the days of Roger Williams. Probably in Connecticut the influence of religion was stronger in politics than in any other single state.[23] To a lesser degree, this same influence was also felt in Massachusetts and New Hampshire, and as Congregationalism spread into western New York and the Wyoming Valley of Pennsylvania, Federalist strength appeared in these areas, although not for so long a period.[24]

Maps on the location of the religious denominations are difficult to secure for the exact period under study. There are, however, a series of maps in Paullin's *Atlas* for the eve of the American Revolution, 1775-1776. Using these maps together with denominational histories, a fair degree of certainty as to the areas of concentration of the religious strength of the denominations emerges. The general pattern shows that the Episcopalian Church membership in the South was concentrated in the coastal plain

[22] Beard, *Economic Origins of Jeffersonian Democracy*, 365.

[23] Purcell, R. J., *Connecticut in Transition, 1775-1818* (Washington, 1918); Beard, *Economic Origins of Jeffersonian Democracy*, 365.

[24] Sweet, W. W., *Religion on the American Frontier, 1783-1850*, Vol. 3, *The Congregationalists* (Chicago, 1939); Atkins, G. G., and Fagley, F. L., *History of American Congregationalism* (Boston, 1942).

area from which Federalists drew their strength. In the Middle Atlantic States the Episcopalians were most numerous in the first settled areas of New York, Pennsylvania, Maryland and New Jersey.[25] It might be argued that the Episcopalians could have moved inland by 1790 or 1800, but the religion of the Piedmont and frontier sections was that of the Protestant evangelical denominations. The evidence for this is clear when data concerning the Presbyterians, Methodists and other denominations are considered, and state histories confirm this as well.[26] In Connecticut until after 1800 the Episcopalians, being among the wealthier of the community, allied with the Congregationalists. In turn the Congregationalists recognized the alliance by such devices as a Yale honorary degree.[27] As the Republicans gained strength, some Episcopalians joined with the other dissenters — the Methodists, Baptists, and Presbyterians — after 1800. But the early Connecticut and New England Republicans included few Episcopalians.

The Catholic Church was divided as to political alliance. The older Catholic congregations, established in the original colony of Maryland, had long since become a minority denomination in their state. But among their members were the more influential of the planters. Concentrated in the tidewater and along the Eastern Shore of Maryland,[28] they were led by Archbishop John Carroll of the famous Carroll family of Maryland. In 1784, prior to his consecration as Archbishop, Carroll reported the number of Catholics in Maryland as approximately 16,000, with 7,000 in Pennsylvania, 1,500 in New York, and 200 in Virginia.[29] This group was predominantly Federalist, and Charles Carroll of Carrollton was the leader of the Maryland Federalists. On the

[25] Paullin, C. O., *Historical Atlas*, Plate 82C.

[26] Manross, W. W., *A History of the American Episcopal Church* (New York, 1935), 183-84.

[27] Greene, M. L., *The Development of Religious Liberty in Connecticut* (Boston, 1905), 393 ff.

[28] Paullin, *op. cit.*, Plate 82K.

[29] Sweet, *Story of Religion in America*, 295; Maynard, Theodore, *The Story of American Catholicism* (New York, 1941), 163 ff.; Shea, John G., *Life and Times of Archbishop Carroll* (New York, 1888).

other hand, after the Revolution a new wave of Irish Catholic
migration came to the cities of New York, Philadelphia, and
Boston. These belonged to the laboring classes and were predominantly Jeffersonian. They were denounced in all the Federalist papers, and in a famous speech by Federalist Representative
Harrison Gray Otis of Boston, as the " Wild Irish." [30]

The other religions whose members originally supported the
Federalists were the German Reformed, Dutch Reformed, and
Lutheran denominations, concentrated chiefly in lower New York,
eastern Pennsylvania, and New Jersey.[31] But in Pennsylvania, at
least, following the levy of the direct tax of 1799, this allegiance
shifted to the Republicans in the agricultural counties.[32] Consequently it would appear that the denominational control was not
so important as economic and political factors.

In the areas of Republican superiority the chief denominations
were the Baptists who were concentrated in Rhode Island and in
the Piedmont sections,[33] the Methodists and Presbyterians, also
concentrated in the back country geographically; and these same
denominations plus the Irish Catholics in the towns.[34] The
evangelical denominations coincided in their outlook with the
smaller farmers and the more individualistic feelings of the
frontier. With some strength in upstate New York, they became

---

[30] Morison, S. E., *Life and Letters of Harrison Gray Otis* (New York, 1912),
I, 108; Cobbett, William, *Detection of a Conspiracy formed by the United
Irishmen, with the Evident Intention of Aiding the Tyrants of France in
Subverting the Government of the United States of America* (Philadelphia,
1798).

[31] Morse in his *American Gazetteer* accounts for the chief denominations in
Pennsylvania by sections of the state and at times by counties. For other
states he is not so specific. Paullin's maps of 1775-1776 are: German Reformed, 82F; Dutch Reformed, 82H; Lutheran, 82G.

[32] Maps 8-11, Appendix III; Chapter 12 and 13, *Infra*.

[33] Paullin, *op. cit.*, Plate 82D; Sweet, W. W., *Religion on the American
Frontier: The Baptists, 1783-1830* (New York, 1931), Ch. II.

[34] *Ibid.*, Plate 82B (Presbyterian); Sweet, W. W., *Religion on the American
Frontier*, Vol. II, *The Presbyterians, 1783-1840* (New York, 1936); Buckley,
J. M., *A History of Methodists in the United States* (New York, 1907);
Stevens, Abel, *History of the Methodist Episcopal Church in the United States
of America* (New York, 1864?), III.

increasingly numerous in central and western Pennsylvania, in the upland, small farm, poorer counties of north and central New Jersey, which tended toward Republicanism, in the central sections of Maryland, and in the general Piedmont and western regions of the rest of the South. An exception to this trend is the heavily Presbyterian Seventh North Carolina District, which was Federalist. Deists were generally supposed to have supported Jefferson, but to account for this group geographically is difficult.[35] The Quakers, strongest in Pennsylvania, were generally Federalists, except when war threatened.[36] Other minor denominations were too small in number of members to require detailed consideration.

A few districts, influenced by cultural and historical factors throughout the period of this study, continually returned Federalist representatives although the districts were in the Piedmont area of small farms. One of these, with a population heavily Presbyterian, was the Seventh North Carolina District, in the area around Fayetteville (cf. Maps 1-11). It was settled just before the Revolution by Highland Scotch Presbyterians. During the Revolution sentiment was Loyalist, and the Tories from this area supplied the troops on the British side at the Battle of Moore's Creek Bridge. After 1789 the district refused to support the former Whigs who dominated the Republican Party in the state, and William Barry Grove, a Federalist, was constantly returned as the district's representative.[37]

Factors of language and historical background were apparent

[35] Koch, G. Adolf, *Republican Religion: The American Revolution and the Cult of Reason* (New York, 1933), pp. 83, 251 ff.; Morais, Herbert M., *Deism in Eighteenth Century America* (New York, 1934), especially Ch. V. Some Federalists, including John Adams, were considered as deists, but the bulk of deist influence was certainly towards Jefferson. The orthodox clergy, especially in New England, violently attacked Jefferson for his deism.

[36] Sharpless, Isaac, *Two Centuries of Pennsylvania History* (Philadelphia, 1900), 233; Jones, Rufus M., *The Quakers in the American Colonies* (London, 1911), 565; Sharpless, Isaac, *A Quaker Experiment in Government* (Philadelphia, 1902).

[37] Wagstaff, H. M., ed., " Letters of William Barry Grove," *Sprunt Historical Monographs*, IX, No. 2 (Chapel Hill, 1910).

in other districts to be considered in the analysis by states which follows. Among these were the German counties of eastern Pennsylvania, which were Federalist. These have already been considered in connection with the religious affiliations of the sections of that state. In some cases factors of culture and historical background aided the Republicans. The bitter opposition of the Irish to England had influence in driving the Irish Catholics of the cities toward Republicanism. This appeal was stressed by the Jeffersonian press. French immigration was slight, but what French there were were inclined toward Jefferson.

Political leadership was reflected in the choice of some districts. On the Jeffersonian side John Langdon appeared in the Senate from New Hampshire. Samuel Adams continued to win the governorship of Massachusetts while the state was overwhelmingly Federalist. Robert Goodloe Harper, noted as one of the most eloquent speakers of the time, was elected originally as a Republican from the upstate, Piedmont, Ninety-Six District of South Carolina. Then he shifted parties and became a staunch Federalist. Despite this fact he continued to carry his district. But as soon as he retired from the house, he was succeeded by a Republican. The same type of control was exercised by Theodore Sedgwick, Speaker of the House, over the First Western District of Massachusetts in the Berkshires. Whenever he ran, the district elected him, a staunch Federalist. When he did not run it elected a Republican. Other districts of course show variation from election to election, but none show the same consistent departure from the general economic and social pattern except those from which Harper and Sedgwick were chosen (cf. Maps 1-11).

In addition to the general trend of political events of the period, which is treated later, there were certain political events which affected sentiment in areas that economically might have been expected to be Republican. One of these was the Federalist policy of providing for a standing army. This attracted certain support in the far western districts of the Southern States and in Georgia, where Indian problems were acute. The specific elections are treated in detail at the proper place. Another Republican measure that caused an adverse reaction in the western districts of the

Southern States and throughout Georgia during 1798-1799 was the threat of disunion offered by the Virginia and Kentucky Resolutions. This was apparent in the elections for the Sixth Congress (cf. Maps 8-10, Appendix III). Even though it was the Kentucky legislature which had adopted the resolutions, the sentiments expressed were too extreme for Georgia, western North Carolina and South Carolina. Along with sentiment against France that was aroused by the XYZ dispatches, these measures helped to carry the day temporarily for the Federalists. On the other hand, this development is not noticeable in the frontier areas in Pennsylvania in elections for Congress but it did affect state elections (cf. Maps 8-10, Appendix III).

Another political policy with effects on elections in 1798 was the Federalist tax program. As already noted, this proved decisive in alienating certain of the agricultural sections of the states of Pennsylvania and New York which had elected Federalists until the enactment of the direct tax. Fries's Rebellion and its aftermath are considered in the narrative at the proper point. Also already noted is the reaction of moderates in the far South against the Virginia and Kentucky Resolutions. This reaction took place in the region where there was strongest Republican support. But in the same elections for the Sixth Congress, political moderates in New England distrusted the war aims of the extreme Federalists, with the result that in the elections of 1798 Republicans made gains in that section. This again is treated in the concluding chapters.

The following summary is of the relative weight of different factors in the various elections for the federal House of Representatives which are considered on the vote charts and maps (bye-elections having been excluded from the count). This summary is compiled by using the voting maps as the base maps and superimposing overlays made up from the other maps which have been cited. One hundred and six representatives appear on the voting record during four congresses. This gives a total of 424 to be accounted for. The choice of 360 of the representatives fits into the pattern of the geographic and economic composition of

the districts and states considered. Thirty-three of the representatives chosen can be attributed primarily to the influence of
religious and cultural factors considered in combination. Four of
the elections turned primarily on the historical and cultural
factors operating in the district. Five of the representatives can
best be accounted for on the basis of their political leadership
transcending all other factors. Seventeen of the representatives
were chosen because of certain special political factors operating
in their districts more heavily in a particular election than in the
country at large. These include districts on the frontier which
returned Federalists because of demand for support against the
Indians, although the general composition of the district as to
other factors would argue for the choice of Republican representatives. In the case of five of the districts, as represented in
particular congresses, not enough is known to explain what factors
operated.[38]

If the ultimate effect of these group divisions were a coalition
into two parties, yet party issues were not so clearly defined in
the first three Congresses. Most of those elected to the House
were party men. But even as late as the elections for the Fourth
Congress, 1794, a few could ignore the growing party divisions.
There was still a tendency for many of the leaders of the Revolution to cling together despite other issues. By the time the
Fourth Congress closed in 1797, party lines were more tightly
drawn.

The voting behavior of the members of the House of Representatives during the Fourth Congress is analyzed in Appendix II,
and is also the basis of the Vote Charts and Maps in Appendix
III. Maps 1, 2, and 3 record the voting record of the Fourth
Congress. Three major groups appear on these maps: the Federalists, the Republicans and the moderates. The moderates were
those usually associated with Adams. How strong was this group?
How is it connected with his political and economic ideas? These
are questions to explore carefully.

Twenty-nine moderates appear on the voting chart for the

[38] This paragraph is considered further in Appendix V.

Fourth Congress.[39] How do these fall as to the party classification under which they were elected? At the start of the Congress, Fisher Ames wrote that forty-nine Federalists and fifty-six Anti-Federalists had been elected.[40] Evidently he was not counting Tennessee, whose representative, Andrew Jackson, appeared only for the second session. Our classification as to party affiliation at the start of the Congress shows one member as doubtful, 48 Federalists, and 57 Republicans (Vote Chart II and Table 15). On the basis of their voting, fifteen of these Federalists are classified as moderates, while three additional actually vote with the Republicans (Map 3). The Republicans produce fourteen moderate Republicans and one renegade who votes with the Federalists.

At the close of the Fourth Congress it is evident that party lines are still somewhat flexible. The Federalist leaders in their correspondence complain more than do the Republican leaders about their inability to hold their followers in line on votes. The writings of Hamilton, Wolcott, Ames, Cabot, and others voice more complaints than do those of Jefferson, Madison, Monroe, and Macon. With the advent of the Fifth Congress, the party lines become more sharply drawn. The bitterness attending the debates over the Alien and Sedition Laws and the tension over relations with France were felt sharply in the next Congress.

By 1796, moreover, the disposition to continue electing Revolutionary leaders, even though of the opposition, had practically ceased. First John Hancock and then Samuel Adams had held the governorship in Massachusetts. Both were in sympathy with Jefferson. But Samuel Adams had already been opposed by Federalists, who ran Caleb Cushing in 1794. After his defeat for elector from Boston in 1796, Samuel Adams did not again make the race for governor. In 1798, referring to the political situation at this earlier date, Pickering wrote to Henry Dearborn: " I recollect that when you first came to Congress you mentioned

[39] Also cf. summary in Table 15, p. 297.
[40] Ames to Thomas Dwight, Dedham, December 30, 1795; Ames, Seth, ed., *Works of Fisher Ames* (Boston, 1854), I, 180.

to me a conversation you had had with Mr. Ames at Boston when he told you that it was necessary to take a side and stick to it; and that in answer you reprobated the principle; and added that an honest and independent member would vote sometimes on one side and sometimes on the other, as truth and the public good should require.—— But you on important measures voted uniformly with the opposition." [41]

This reversal of sentiment toward old Revolutionary leaders is typified in an incident involving John Langdon of New Hampshire. In Philadelphia a toast was given at a Republican dinner:

" John Langdon, an old whig."

Whereupon Porcupine wrote: " Do you know what an old Whig is reader? It is a very ill looking, nasty, despised and neglected thing, fit for nothing but to be trodden under foot, or thrown in the dunghill." [42] The growth of party feeling had reached the point that the demand was for party men. This was increasingly evident in the congresses following 1796.

[41] Pickering to Henry Dearborn, Philadelphia, August 1, 1798. Pickering *Mss.* 9/127.

[42] Cobbett, William, *Political Censor*, VIII, January, 1797; in *Porcupine's Works* (London, 1800), IV, 366.

Chapter 3

The Political Theories of
John Adams

THE political writings of John Adams naturally are important in establishing his position in the Federalist party. The number of these works and the strong influence of the views expressed concerning his administration and general political career make them of especial interest. There have been a number of surveys of the political ideas of John Adams.[1] However, the purpose of this and the succeeding chapter is somewhat different from the studies of those who have previously treated the subject.

---

[1] In addition to the longer general histories which give more or less attention to this topic, the following specialized works are of interest: Walsh, Correa M., *The Political Science of John Adams* (New York, 1915), the most detailed and scientific treatment; Morse, Anson D., "The Politics of John Adams," *American Historical Review*, IV, 292-312; Thorpe, Francis N., "The Political Ideas of John Adams," *Pennsylvania Magazine*, XLIV, 1-46; and Beard, Charles A., Chapter XI in his *Economic Origins of Jeffersonian Democracy*; Warren, Charles, "John Adams and American Constitutions," *Kentucky State Bar Association Proceedings*, 27th annual meeting. Moreover, the various biographers of Adams touch upon the subject; Adams, John Quincy and Adams, Charles Francis, *Life of John Adams* (Vol. I of the *Life and Works of John Adams*), (Boston, 1856); Chinard, Gilbert, *Honest John Adams* (Boston, 1933); Morse, John T., Jr., *John Adams* (Boston, 1884); Irelan, John Robert, *History of the Life, Administration, and Times of John Adams* (Vol. II of *The Republic*), (Chicago, 1886); Chamberlain, Mellen, *John Adams, the Statesman of the American Revolution* (Boston, 1898); Adams, James Truslow, *The Adams Family* (New York, 1932); Ford, Worthington C., "John Adams," in *Dictionary of American Biography*, I, 72-82. Other writings include Parrington, Vernon L., *Main Currents in American Thought* (New York, 1927) I, 292-306; Koch, Adrienne, and Peden, William, *Selected Writings of John and John Quincy Adams* (New York, 1946); Bowen, Catherine D., *John Adams and the American Revolution* (Boston, 1950).

Zoltan Haraszti has published an excellent analysis of the thought of John Adams in his *John Adams & the Prophets of Progress* (Cambridge, Massachusetts, 1952); a work which appeared too late for detailed use in my own book. Alfred Iacuzzi's, *John Adams, Scholar* (New York, 1952) is also too recent to have been extensively used.

The purpose here is not to study the views of John Adams as an end in itself, but rather to lay the foundation for the analysis of the Federalist party. The writings of Adams on government [2] fall into three periods. The first period lasted until about 1786, marking a time in which his views were in virtual conformity with those of Jefferson, Madison, and similar leaders.[3] The second period begins with his residence in England in 1786. By this time the unsettled conditions under the Articles of Confederation together with his study of the British Constitution caused him to conceive a deep admiration for the British system. Further Adams had never liked the unicameral legislature of certain American states. The operation of these unicameral legislative systems — that sponsored by Franklin in Pennsylvania, and imitated by the State of Georgia — was abhorrent to Adams. Such disturbances as Shays's Rebellion in Massachusetts, accompanied by agitation for the abolition of the Senate, interference with the courts, and threats to the rights of property, had an even deeper

[2] The chief of these are: *Dissertation on the Canon and Feudal Law* (1765); (*Works*), III, 447; *Novanglus* (1774); (*Ibid.*), IV, 3; *Thoughts on Government* (1776); (*Ibid.*), 189; *Defense of the Constitutions of Government of the United States of America*, 3 vols. (1787, 1788); (*Ibid.*), IV, 271, V, VI, 3; *Discourses on Davila* (1790); (*Ibid.*), VI, 223; *Four Letters—between John Adams and Samuel Adams on Government* (1790); (*Ibid.*), VI, 405; *Three Letters to Roger Sherman on the Constitution of the United States* (1789); (*Ibid.*), VI, 427; *Letters to John Taylor . . .* (1814); (*Ibid.*), 443; *Review of the Propositions for Amending the Constitution, Submitted by Mr. Hillhouse to the Senate of the United States, in 1808*; (*Ibid.*), VI, 523.

[3] The system he advocated in his *Thoughts on Government* is perhaps the best criterion. (*Works*), IV, 189 ff. This provided for a bicameral legislature, the lower house of which was to be elected by the people. This house was to choose the members of the upper chamber. The executive should be chosen by joint vote of the two houses. He should have a negative vote on all laws (one feature certainly, which was not very popular at this period). Elections should be annual, " there not being in the whole circle of the sciences, a maxim more infallible than this, ' where annual elections end, there slavery begins.'" The central government should consist of a Congress with adequate representation, whose " authority should sacredly be confined to . . . : war, trade, disputes between colony and colony, and the post office, and the unappropriated lands of the crown . . ." This was written in January, 1776. Adams, Charles Francis, *Letters of John Adams, Addressed to His Wife* (Boston, 1841), I, 273.

influence.[4] Another factor which was probably not without weight, arose from the status of Adams himself. No longer was he a rebel. He had made a name for himself and held a position in society. This was not without its effect.

At any rate, despite frequent denials to old friends,[5] it is perfectly clear that during these years in England his point of view underwent a great transition. The system which he outlined at this time may be regarded as dominating his outlook during the rest of the time that he remained active in politics. Consequently it is important to examine it in some detail.

The third period of Adams' political thought came after his retirement from active politics in 1801. In it he returns to his earlier, more liberal position on many points. But even then he retained many of the ideas of his second period.

Naturally the ideas of Adams in his second period, 1786-1801, are most important for the Federalist era. Therefore attention is centered on them here. His ideas are systematically presented, chiefly in the *Defense*, the first part of which was written before the Philadelphia Convention. Starting with a view of human nature, which Adams, with Hobbes, believed was dominated by a seeking for self-interest, he never ceased to emphasize that self-interest exceeds all other human motivating forces. This, he believed, must be recognized in formulating any successful system of government.[6] Perhaps the best generalization which he felt could be drawn from the importance of self-interest is that the passion for distinction is the dominating motive in man.[7] With some this is expressed by the pursuit of riches.[8] With scholars it is expressed in a seeking for acclaim. Men do not learn dead

---

[4] *Defense*, III (*Works*), VI, 11. Further he refers to the " Lawless, tyranni-cal rabble . . . . . of Berkshire . . . Massachusetts." *Ibid.*, 116.

[5] Adams to Benjamin Rush, New York, April 4, 1790. Biddle, Alexander, *Old Family Letters* (Philadelphia, 1892), Series A, 57.

[6] *Defense*, III (*Works*), VI, 57. The extent to which the *Defense*, Adams' longest work is a " paste and scissors " compilation of quotations from earlier works, is interestingly brought out by Haraszti in his *John Adams & the Prophets of Progress*, 155-64.

[7] *Discourses on Davila* (*Works*), VI, 232.

[8] *Ibid.*, 237.

languages and toil through research for pleasure.[9] Because individuals have conflicting aims, human existence is a struggle among the various classes.[10] " It is very easy to flatter the democratical portion of society, by making such distinctions (based on their supposed superior virtue) between them and the monarchical and aristocratical; but flattery is as base an artifice, and as pernicious a vice, when offered to the people, as when given to others. There is no reason to believe the one much honester or wiser than the other; they are all of the same clay; their minds and bodies are alike. The two latter have more knowledge and sagacity, derived from education, and more advantages for acquiring wisdom and virtue. As to usurping others' rights, they are all three equally guilty when unlimited in power. . . ." [11]

It will be noted that Adams emphasizes a difference in classes, which, he held, arise naturally from society due to differences in ability.[12] Such a thing as complete equality is absurd. " The people in all nations are naturally divided into two sorts, the gentlemen and simplemen, a word which is here chosen to signify the common people." Who are gentlemen? " By gentlemen are not meant the rich or the poor, the high-born or the low-born, the industrious or the idle; but all those who have received a liberal education, an ordinary degree of erudition in liberal arts and sciences. . . ." On the other hand, " By the common people we mean laborers, husbandmen, mechanics, and merchants, in general, who pursue their occupations and industry without any knowledge in liberal arts and sciences. . . ." But would there be, from generation to generation, a considerable transition from one class to the other? Not at all, for, " We must nevertheless, remember, that *generally* those who are rich, and descended from families in public life, will have the best education in arts and sciences, and therefore the gentlemen will ordinarily, notwithstanding some exceptions to the rule, be the richer, and born of more noted families." [13]

---

[9] *Ibid.*, 239-40.   [10] *Defense*, III (*Works*), VI, 10.

[11] *Ibid.*   [12] *Ibid.*, I (*Works*), IV, 392.

[13] *Defense*, III (*Works*), VI, 185; the same idea is stated in *Davila* (*Works*), VI, 280; " Leisure for study must ever be the path of a few."

Adams believed the differences among classes are based on nature, and that among these classes a constant struggle takes place in society, the aristocracy against the democracy. This has always been the case, and always will be.[14] Where the system of government is not designed to place a check upon this conflict, the aristocracy usually gain control.[15] Even in America, where property is widely diffused, this is the case.[16] Whenever it has happened that the people temporarily secure all power, they have fallen under the sway of demagogues who have set up a new aristocracy,[17] or have fallen into a state of anarchy, from which the result has been the same.[18] The outcome is that the only way of securing liberty and preventing oppression is to arrange a system of government in which there will be a balance of the rich against the poor; while an independent arbitrator, holding equal power with these two groups, is a *sine qua non* for a successful system.[19]

For Adams the legislature, the body which made the laws, was the crucial point of the system. The inspiration for his most detailed work, the *Defense*, arose from a desire to refute a letter of M. Turgot,[20] which Adams looked upon as advocating the concentration of all legislative power in one assembly. Consequently, it is to the balancing of power in this branch of the government that he gives most attention.

The power of government, sovereignty, resides in the people.[21]

---

[14] Adams to Alexander Jardine, New York, June 1, 1790; *Works*, IX, 569.

[15] *Defense*, I (*Works*), IV, 381.

[16] *Ibid.*, 444.

[17] *Defense*, III (*Works*), VI, 11.

[18] *Defense*, I (*Works*), IV, 298; more exactly, handwritten note by John Adams in his copy of William Godwin's *Enquiry Concerning Political Justice* (Philadelphia, 1796), I, 133. Godwin had written, ". . . Anarchy is a *short lived* [underlined by Adams to show the point to which his note has reference] mischief, while despotism is all but immortal." Note in the handwriting of Adams: "Why? because it soon convinces Men that Despotism is the least evil of the Two." The bulk of the John Adams library is now in the Boston Public Library, where it was examined.

[19] *Defense*, I (*Works*), IV, 285.

[20] The letter is printed in Adams, *Works*, IV, 278-81.

[21] *Defense*, I (*Works*), IV, 404-405.

But, the people do not form a coherent body. Hence it is necessary that they be represented in chambers conforming to their divisions; one for the rich and one for the poor.[22] It is an absolute necessity that the legislature shall thus mirror the composition of the country at large.[23] Each of the branches, the senate and house, must agree upon a measure before it can become a law.[24]

Yet, these two equal elements could not alone be expected to form the correctly balanced system. The third element, which is raised to the level of an equivalent order, is the executive.[25] The executive must have an absolute veto over the acts of the senate and house. Thus he becomes a part of the legislative system.[26] His function is to hold the balance between the two contending orders. It is to his self interest not to permit either to gain the supremacy.

. . . It is the true policy of the common people to place the whole executive power in one man, to make him a distinct order in the state, from whence rises an inevitable jealousy between him and the gentlemen; this forces him to become a father and protector of the common people, and to endeavor always to humble every proud, aspiring senator, or other officer in the state, who is in danger of acquiring an influence too great for the law or the spirit of the constitution. This influences him to look for merit among the common people, and to promote from among them such as are capable of public employments; so that the road to preferment is open to the common people much more generally and equitably in such a government than in an aristocracy, or one in which the gentlemen have any share in appointments to office.

From this deduction, it follows, that the precept of our author, [Marchamont Nedham] ' to educate children (of the common people) in principles of dislike and enmity against kingly government, and enter into an oath of abjuration to abjure a toleration of kings and kingly powers,' is a most iniquitous and infamous aristocratical arti-

---

[22] *Ibid.*, 284.
[23] *Ibid.*, 228.
[24] *Defense*, III (*Works*), VI, 65.
[25] *Davila* (*Works*), VI, 340-41.
[26] *Defense*, I (*Works*), IV, 579, 358.

fice, a most formal conspiracy against the rights of mankind, and against that equality between the gentlemen and the common people which nations have established as a moral right, and law should ordain as a political right, for the preservation of liberty.

By kings and kingly power, is meant both by our author and me, the executive power in a single person. . . . [27]

Thus the people should support the executive who would assure justice for them against the aristocracy. In similar manner he functions as a prop for the rights of the aristocracy. " If it is asked, when will this negative be used? it may be answered, perhaps never. The known existence of it will prevent all occasion to exercise it; but if it has not a being, the want of it will be felt every day." [28]

This executive should have the absolute power of appointment to office, making treaties, and declaring war, in addition to the veto.[29] This will enable him to maintain his independent position and will assure his freedom of action in maintaining the balance. His position is, in many respects, the keystone of the system.

As contrasted with this system, Adams strongly believed no other could be permitted. Some have contended, he argued, that a benevolent absolute monarchy is the best of all possible systems, but this is denied.[30] In Europe, even monarchical courts are realizing the advantages to be derived from the balanced system, and are introducing some of its features.[31] The two worst possible types of government, where there is least regard for life, liberty, and property, are an oligarchy, in which an unchecked aristocracy controls, and a democracy, in which the common people hold unchecked sway. The former type has many examples in Greek and Roman history,[32] in Italian history,[33] and at present, in

---

[27] *Defense*, III (*Works*), VI, 186.

[28] *Ibid.*, 65.

[29] Adams to Samuel Adams, Richmond Hill (N. Y.), July 18, 1789, *Works* VI, 43-51. Reference is to the American Constitution.

[30] *Defense*, I (*Works*), IV, 289.

[31] *Ibid.*

[32] *Ibid.*, 271 ff.

[33] *Defense*, II and III (*Works*), V, *passim*.

Poland. In the last instance the powerful nobility have had all control, their estates being hereditary, while that of the monarch is elective, and the people are unrepresented.[34]

In regard to democracy, the results are equally destructive.

Suppose a nation, rich and poor, high and low, ten millions in number, all assembled together; not more than one or two millions will have lands, houses, or personal property; if we take into the account the women and children, or even if we leave them out of the question, a great majority of every nation is destitute of property, except a small quantity of clothes, and a few trifles of other movables. Would Mr. Nedham be responsible that, if all were to be decided by a vote of the majority, the eight or nine millions who have no property, would not think of usurping over the rights of the one or two millions who have? Property is surely a right of mankind as really as liberty. Perhaps, at first, prejudice, habit, shame or fear, principle or religion, would restrain the poor from attacking the rich, and the idle from usurping on the industrious; but the time would not be long before courage and enterprise would come, and pretexts be invented by degrees, to countenance the majority in dividing all the property among them, or at least, in sharing it equally with the present possessors. Debts would be abolished first; taxes laid heavy on the rich, and not at all on the others; and at last a downright equal division of every thing be demanded and voted. What would be the consequence of this? The idle, the vicious, the intemperate, would rush into the utmost extravagance of debauchery, sell and spend all their share, and then demand a new division of those who purchased from them. The moment the idea is admitted into society, that property is not as sacred as the laws of God, and that there is not a force of law and public justice to protect it, anarchy and tyranny commence. If 'THOU SHALT NOT COVET,' and 'THOU SHALL NOT STEAL,' were not commandments of Heaven, they must be made inviolable precepts in every society, before it can be organized or made free.[35]

Under neither of these forms, oligarchy or democracy, is liberty to be expected. For liberty is only the enjoyment of the operation of equal laws; it does not presuppose equality in any other respect.

[34] *Defense*, I (*Works*), IV, 361; *Ibid.*, 366.
[35] *Defense*, III (*Works*), VI, 8-9.

Although, among men, all are subject by nature to *equal laws* of morality, and in society have a right to equal laws for their government, yet no two men are perfectly equal in person, property, understanding, activity and virtue, or ever can be made so by any power less than that which created them. . . .[36]

These equal laws enable the rich and poor to " have equal powers to defend themselves. . . ." [37] But this cannot be without a balanced system, which must include a moderator, " Always ready, always able, and always interested to assist the weakest." [38] Without this balance, judiciary, bar and the press will represent only the tyrannical majority.[39]

It may be noted here, that while Adams regards the three separate departments of government, legislative, executive, and judicial, as constituting one form of balance,[40] this is not that form of balance with which he is chiefly concerned. The function of the judiciary, for example, is of vital importance in administering equal laws, but this branch is dependent upon the perfection of the legislative balance. Moreover, the inclusion of the executive, with his absolute veto, in the legislative department is another illustration of the violation of the departmental balance in his system. In fact, it is logical to draw the conclusion that the system of division of departmental functions into legislative, executive, and judicial branches is, with Adams, merely a matter of administrative convenience. In his mind it is the legislative balance which is of vital importance, and the legislature is regarded as the predominating part of the governmental system. The chief reason for delegating such strong executive powers to the head of the government is to enable him to be independent in his relations with the two houses.[41]

[36] *Davila* (*Works*), VI, 285-86.
[37] Adams to Thomas Brand-Hollis, of London; Quincy, June 11, 1790, *Works*, IX, 570.
[38] *Ibid*.   [39] *Defense*, III (*Works*), VI, 58.
[40] Adams to Benjamin Rush, Braintree, December 2, 1788, *Works*, IX, 556.
[41] *Defense*, I (*Works*), IV, 290. " . . . If the executive power, or any considerable part of it, is left in the hands either of an aristocratical or a democratical assembly, it will corrupt the legislature as necessarily as rust corrupts iron. . . ."

Clearly, this projected system is based upon the idea of the English Constitution in vogue at the time. In particular Adams follows, quotes at great length, and has the highest praise for De Lolme.[42] There is a similar use of such authorities as Bolingbroke, Harrington, and Locke.[43] For the English Constitution Adams has the highest praise: " I only contend that the English Constitution is, in history, both for the adjustment of the balance and the prevention of its vibrations [i. e., the prevention of violent changes of control between complete aristocratic domination, and complete democratic control], the most stupendous fabric of human invention; and that the Americans ought to be applauded instead of censured, for imitating it as far as they have done." [44] In regard to this constitution, the only reform which would be of value is the reform of the representation in the commons.[45] Not only the people of England,[46] but also the people of Europe,[47] are warned that they will defeat themselves by seeking to overthrow the King and the nobles. The only justifiable reform is the introduction of a representative democratic branch in order to perfect a balanced system.[48] Next to the British system, highest praise is bestowed upon the Macedonian republic of ancient Greece: " The Macedonian republic may then, with propriety, be called monarchical, and had the three essential parts of the best of all possible government; it was a mixture of monarchy, aristocracy, and democracy." [49]

[42] De Lolme, J. L., *The Constitution of England*, published in Holland in 1770; in England in 1775. Of all works on the English Constitution Adams followed this most closely.

[43] Lord Bolingbroke (Henry St. John), *Dissertation on Parties* (1734); *Idea of a Patriot King* (1738). The influence of these works on Adams' concept of the function of the executive is strong. Locke, John, *Essay Concerning Human Understanding* (1690); *Letter Concerning Toleration* (1690); Harrington, James, *Oceana* (1656) were others who strongly influenced Adams. In addition he had read the leading Roman and Greek philosophers and historians and was thoroughly familiar with the French writers. Of these he especially admired Montesquieu.

[44] *Defense*, I (*Works*), IV, 358.

[45] *Ibid.*

[46] *Ibid.*, 468.

[47] *Ibid.*, 297.

[48] *Ibid.*

[49] *Ibid.*, 553.

Adams next considers whether or not it is possible to have such a balanced system without two hereditary branches to the government. In regard to America, the answer is that at present it is well not to follow England in the matter of an hereditary first magistrate and senate; but if property becomes concentrated in a few hands, it may be necessary to hold a new convention to change nearer to the British Constitution.[50] Should elections become turbulent, of which there is no appearance at present, this change would need to be instituted.[51]

Past history has never revealed a long continued success for the experiment of a government entirely elective.

It should always be remembered, that this is not the first experiment that ever was made in the world of elections to great offices of state; how they have hitherto operated in every great nation, and what has been their end is very well known. Mankind have universally discovered that chance was preferable to corrupt choice, and have trusted Providence rather than themselves. First magistrates and senators had better be made hereditary at once, than that the people should be universally debauched and bribed, go to loggerheads, and fly to arms regularly every year. Thank Heaven! Americans understand calling conventions; and if the time should come, as it is very possible it may, when hereditary descent shall become a less evil than fraud and violence, such a convention may still prevent the first magistrate from becoming absolute as well as hereditary.[52]

The private correspondence of Adams is equally explicit. To Rush he wrote:

---

[50] *Ibid.*, 339.

[51] *Ibid.*

[52] *Defense*, III (*Works*), VI, 56-57. For the same idea, see also *Ibid.*, 25; 67: Where turbulence has resulted from a completely elective system, " The evils may be lessened and postponed, by elections for longer periods of years, till they become for life; and if this is not found an adequate remedy, there will remain no other but to make them hereditary. The delicacy or the dread of unpopularity that should induce any man to conceal this important truth from the full view and contemplation of the people, would be a weakness, if not a vice." In *Davila*, written in 1790, and appearing in installments in the *Gazette of the United States* of that year, he is particularly concerned over the dangers of an elective first magistrate. *Works*, VI, 254.

I do not 'consider hereditary Monarchy or Aristocracy as Rebellion against Nature.' On the contrary I esteem them both as Institutions of admirable wisdom and exemplary Virtue in a certain stage of Society in a great nation. The only Institutions that can possibly preserve the laws and Liberties of the People, and I am clear that America must resort to them as an Asylum against discord, Seditions and Civil War, and that at no very distant period of time. I shall not live to see it—but you may. I think it therefore impolitick to cherish prejudices against Institutions which must be kept in view as the hope of our Posterity. I am by no means for attempting any such thing at present. Our Country is not ripe for it in many respects [one, he later stated, being the lack of basis for an hereditary nobility, which must accompany the establishment of an hereditary executive], and it is not yet necessary, but our ship must ultimately land on that shore or be cast away.[53]

Likewise, in private conversation, Adams at times voiced a preference for an hereditary aristocracy and executive.[54] In view of

[53] Adams to Rush, New York, June 9, 1789, *Old Family Letters*, 38. Adams' *Works*, IX, 566, contain a later letter to Rush, written from New York, April 18, 1790, which was prompted by a memorandum on Adams which Rush drew up and submitted to him. Not liking the statements there made, he wrote a denial, totally incompatible with sentiments expressed in earlier letters, from which series the above quotation comes. None of these earlier letters are given in the *Works*, and the denial alone is printed. For the statement by Rush, cf. f. [92] to this chapter, *post*.

[54] John Langdon (Senator from New Hampshire), Portsmouth, New Hampshire, to Samuel Ringgold of Hagerstown, Md.; October 10, 1800; Boston, Massachusetts, *Independent Chronicle*, November 24, 1800; " In the conversation held between Mr. Adams, Mr. Taylor [Senator John Taylor of Virginia] and myself, Mr. Adams certainly expressed himself (as far as my memory serves me) in the very words mentioned in your letter, viz., that he hoped or expected to see the day when Mr. Taylor or his friend Mr. Giles [William Branch Giles, Representative from Virginia] would be convinced that the people of America would not be happy without an hereditary Chief Magistrate and Senate——or at least during life . . ." From Taylor's account of the same incident, John Taylor to Daniel Carrol Brent; Caroline (Va.), October 9, 1796. Dodd, William E., " Letters of John Taylor," *Branch Historical Papers* (Richmond, 1903); II, 267, it appears that this conversation took place in 1794. Adams later wrote an explanation to Langdon, Quincy, February 27, 1812; *Letters By Washington, Adams, Jefferson and Others . . . to John Langdon* (Philadelphia, 1880), 18-19.

this, his preference for such a system was known to his contemporaries, and has been recognized by modern writers.[55]

It will be noticed that the English system, as Adams conceived it, was not that which actually existed at the time he was writing. In the actual system there was little power in the hands of the monarch. The ministry, responsible to Parliament, exercised the executive powers. Adams' concept of the government was that of De Lolme and other contemporary commentators who had advanced but little beyond the concept first definitely, and erroneously, formulated by Montesquieu.

In regard to other features of Adams' system, a few deserve to be noticed here. The people are regarded as " the original and fountain of all power and government." [56] For maladministration hereditary officials may always be subject to deposition, for after having been set up by the people, they may be changed by the same power.[57] Apparently, however, while elective or administrative officials may be impeached, only revolution could accomplish this in the case of hereditary officers. Tyrannicide is upheld, in case of necessity, to be as justifiable as, " To hang a robber or kill a flea." [58] From this it is apparent that he subscribed to the theory of the social contract, and believed in the right of revolution. He also clearly held that no man could be above the law.[59]

Adams believed that there should be a permanent navy, but not a standing army.[60] He strongly upheld the ideal of universal education.[61] He did not subscribe to the idea of rotation in office.[62] Finally, he held that public service should be sufficiently remunerative to attract good men.[63] Judges, he held, should be appointed for life.[64]

[55] Walsh, Chapter XVIII.
[56] *Defense*, III (*Works*), VI, 117.
[57] *Ibid.*
[58] *Defense*, III (*Works*), VI, 130.
[59] *Ibid.*, 187.
[60] *Ibid.*, 168.
[61] *Ibid.*
[62] *Ibid.*, 52.
[63] *Ibid.*, 14.
[64] *Defense*, II (*Works*), V, 180.

Having discussed the most perfect system, that having hereditary offices in certain branches, Adams next considered the effect of introducing the elective executive and elective senate. The balance in this latter elective system would not have the perfection to be derived from a completely independent executive. Obviously there does not exist a third group in the state to elect him, a group separate from that choosing the senate and house.

Yet, Adams emphasized, there must be a separate basis of representation for the three branches.[65] The best Adams could propose was that the executive not be chosen by the legislature, but by the people. But this choice should be independent of party; from this idea, Adams never deviated throughout his entire career.[66] The rich should be represented in the Senate — in fact segregated in that chamber, in order that they would not acquire too great influence.[67] The lower chamber was to be representative of the common people. With these changes, there would be no other departure from the system already outlined.

But even if all officers be elective, titles would be absolutely necessary to uphold the dignity of the government, secure respect for it in foreign eyes, and reward those who have merit.[68] It was

[65] *Defense*, III (*Works*), VI, 118.

[66] For example, his review of a proposed amendment in 1808, *Works*, VI, 539.   [67] *Defense*, I (*Works*), IV, 290-91.

[68] Adams to Rush, New York, June 9, 1789; *Old Family Letters*, 38. " I do not abhor Titles, nor the Pageantry of Government. If I did I should abhor Government itself, for there never was, and never will be, because there never can be, any government without Titles and Pageantry. There is not a Quaker Family in Pennsylvania, governed without Titles and Pageantry; not a school, not a college, not a club can be governed without them.

" ' I love the people.' with you — too well to cheat them, lie to them or deceive them."

Similarly, in *Davila*, (*Works*), VI, 243-44, he states that titles and distinctions are necessary in a republic to provide adequate reward for the desire for distinction, " To such means as these, or to force and a standing army, recourse must be had for the guardianship of laws and the protection of the people...."

In another letter to Rush, *Old Family Letters*, 41-43; Richmond Hill, July 5, 1789, " It is to make offices and laws respected: and not so much by the virtuous part of the Community, as by the Profligate, the criminal and abandoned, who have little reverence for Reason, Right or Law, divine or human. These are overawed by Titles frequently, when Laws and Punishments cannot restrain them...."

this belief which caused him to make such strenuous efforts for the adoption of a suitable system of titles at the first meeting of the Senate.[69]

As to parties, Adams has no illusions but that political parties would exist. The advantage in a free government is that they operate in the open,[70] while the balance secures the rights of the minority.[71] Yet there is danger from this source in a system where all officers are elective. This is particularly the case in regard to the executive. An hereditary monarch is recognized as being above parties, and as being disinterested. He is the subject of universal respect and adulation. When there is an elective monarch, how would he be regarded?

In elective governments, something very like this always takes place towards the first character. His person, countenance, character, and actions, are made the daily contemplation and conversation of the whole people. Hence arises the danger of a division of this attention. Where there are rivals for the first place, the national attention and passions are divided, and thwart each other, the collision enkindles fires; the conflicting passions interest all ranks; they produce slanders and libels first, mobs and seditions next, and civil war, with all her hissing snakes, burning torches, and haggard horrors at last.

This is the true reason, why all civilized free nations have found, by experience, the necessity of separating from the body of the people, and even from the legislature, the distribution of honors, and conferring it on the executive authority of government. When the emulation of all the citizens looks up to one point, like the rays of a circle from all parts of the circumference, meeting and uniting in the center, you may hope for uniformity, consistency, and subordination; but when they look up to different individuals, or assemblies, or councils, you may expect all the deformities, eccentricities, and confusion of the Ptolemaic system.[72]

From this it is apparent that Adams expected all parties in the state to accept the disinterestedness of the executive. The impli-

[69] Maclay, William, *Journal* (Beard edition, New York, 1927), 1 ff.
[70] *Defense*, I (*Works*), IV, 587-88.
[71] *Defense*, III (*Works*), IV, 109.
[72] *Davila* (*Works*), VI, 255-56.

cation is that there are certain questions upon which all are supposed to be united. To carry party strife too far would be to approach disloyalty. Naturally, where the line of demarcation between party opposition and disloyalty was to be drawn would always be a question difficult to decide.

In the use of the words " democracy " and " republic " by Adams there is considerable significance. To him democracy was always a system in which the people choose representatives to an all-powerful unicameral legislature. This he never ceased to condemn.[73] On the other hand Adams' conception of a republic comprised all possible variations of a system which he might approve. Perhaps the most inclusive definition is the following: ". . . Whenever I use the word republic with approbation, I mean a government in which the people have collectively, or by representation, an essential share in the sovereignty."[75] Consequently, under the head of a republic a limited monarchy is included. To his friend Benjamin Rush he wrote: "You seem determined not to allow a limited monarchy to be a republican system, which it certainly is, and the best that has even been tryed. . . ."[75] Both the English and the American governments are classified as limited monarchies, the American because its branches perform the same functions as the English.[76] On one occasion the definition of a Republic is simply " a government whose sovereignty is vested in more than one person."[77]

Adams was critical of those features of the American Constitution that departed from his own ideas. The first volume of his *Defense of American Constitutions* reached Philadelphia just as the Convention assembled. "A numerous edition of it was soon abroad in Philadelphia, another in New York and a third in Boston," wrote Adams, " and the public voice was so decidedly

---

[73] *Defense*, I (*Works*), IV, 301-302. Here he states that this system has never worked and never will.

[74] Adams to Samuel Adams, New York, Oct. 18, 1790. *Works*, VI, 415.

[75] Adams to Rush, New York, June 19, 1789, *Old Family Letters*, 39.

[76] Adams to Roger Sherman, New York, July 17, 1789, *Works*, VI, 428. Same to same, New York, July 18, 1789, *Ibid.*, 429; *Defense*, I (*Ibid.*), IV, 296.

[77] Adams to Roger Sherman, New York, July 17, 1789, *Ibid.*, 428.

in favor of it, that it revived the hopes and strengthened the hands of the convention. It soon dissipated the vapours of Franklin's foggy system, demolished Hamilton's airy castles, and united the Convention in the plan they finally adopted, and Franklin himself thought fit at last to yield in his assent. It contributed also to unite the assemblies of the several states in the acceptance and adoption of it." Franklin, however, believing in a straight democratic system with a unicameral legislature, could only sign with a tear.[78] Thus, Adams credited his own writings with great influence over the constitutional convention and approved, in general, the final draft as submitted for ratification to the states.

It so happened that the Constitution reached him as he was completing the third volume of the *Defense*. Consequently, he appended to this volume a note of praise for the Constitution: " It is now in our power to bring this work to a conclusion with unexpected dignity . . . ," he declared. The former Confederation had a council which was only a diplomatic body. Now, however, a new Constitution, on the principles advocated in his work, had been written. It was a result of " accommodation." But provision was made for its amendment. " The conception of such an idea, and the deliberate union of so great and various a people in such a plan, is, without all partiality or prejudice, if not the greatest exertion of human understanding, the greatest single effort of national deliberation that the world has ever seen. . . ." [79] In his official capacity, he wrote to Jay, voicing the same sentiments.[80]

In private letters, however, he was more critical. Jefferson wrote to him expressing the fear that the executive was too strong. In reply, Adams asserted that he feared this officer would not be sufficiently independent. The necessity of Senate approval for appointments strongly limited the independence of

[78] *Boston Patriot*, April 15, 1812; Quincy, February 9, 1812. This is one of a series written by Adams from 1809 to 1813 in the *Patriot*.
[79] *Defense*, III (*Works*), VI, 219.
[80] Adams to Jay, London, December 16, 1787; *Works*, VIII, 466.

the executive. He feared the influence of the aristocracy.[81] Even more explicit was the statement in one of his letters to Samuel Adams, in which he asserted that there was great danger because of the powers given to the senate. Not only might this aristocratic body encroach upon the executive, but there was even the possibility that this branch would swallow up the house as well as the executive.[82] Likewise, he believed the qualified veto to be too weak; it should be absolute,[83] and the president should also have the unrestrained power of making treaties and declaring war.[84] Changes such as these should be made as soon as possible.[85] It is clear that he would have welcomed such modifications had the time been ripe for them.

In Adams' concept of the new American government the idea of a judicial negative never crossed his mind. In fact, he believed the important check would be that exercised by the executive over the legislative. Primarily the executive needed the absolute veto for this purpose. Without such a check he feared the legislature would be free to enact whatever laws it desired.

A divided sovereignty in one, a few or many has no balance, and therefore no laws. A divided sovereignty without a balance, in other words, where the division is unequal, is always at war, and consequently has no laws. In our constitution the sovereignty,—that is, the legislative power,—is divided into three branches. The house and senate are equal, but the third branch, though essential, is not equal. The president must pass judgment upon every law; but in some cases his judgment may be overruled. These cases will be such as attack

---

[81] Adams to Jefferson, London, December 6, 1787; *Ibid.*, 464.

[82] Adams to Samuel Adams, Richmond Hill (N. Y.), July 18, 1789; *Works*, VI, 431.

[83] *Ibid.* and Adams to R. Sherman, New York, July, 1789, *Works*, VI, 432-38.

[84] *Ibid.*

[85] Adams to Richard Price, New York, May 20, 1789; *Works*, IX, 559. " Our new Constitution is found in part upon its [my book's] principles, and the enlightened part of our communities are generally convinced of the necessity of adopting it, by degrees, more completely." Also see Adams to Richard Price, New York, April 19, 1790; *Ibid.*, 564.

his constitutional power; it is, therefore, certain he has not equal power to defend himself, or the constitution, or the judicial power, as the senate and house have.[86]

During the first years under the constitution, Adams was as concerned as the strongest of Federalists about checking the popular tide. " In this country the pendulum has vibrated too far to the popular side, driven by men without experience or judgment, and horrid ravages have been made upon property by arbitrary multitudes or majorities of multitudes. France has severe trials to endure from the same cause. Both have found, or will find, that to place property at the mercy of a majority who have no property is ' *committere agnum lupo*.' My fundamental maxim of government is, never to trust the lamb to the custody of the wolf. If you are not perfectly of my mind at present, I hereby promise and assure you that, you will live to see that I am precisely right. Thus arrogantly concludes your assured friend." [87]

However, with the development of Hamilton's financial plans, the establishment of the Bank of the United States, and the growing speculation which went on in the country, Adams began to change his mind. He early took steps to deny imputations of monarchism which were certainly deserved.[88] After his election to the presidency, he publicly denied, both in his farewell address to the senate [89] and in his inaugural,[90] that he had ever entertained the idea or had hoped for either an hereditary senate or executive, or that both should be hereditary; or further, that they should be for life. After leaving official life, these denials, which needed to be constantly repeated, were often given to his correspondents.[91]

The point naturally arises as to how Adams could, with sincerity, give such a sweeping denial on all of these points. Even

[86] Adams to Roger Sherman, Richmond Hill, N. Y., July 17, 1789; *Works*, VI, 431.
[87] Adams to Richard Brand-Hollis, June 11, 1790; *Works*, IX, 571.
[88] Adams to Jefferson, July 29, 1791; *Works*, VIII, 506-509; also cf. IX, 566.
[89] *Annals of Congress* (Washington, 1849), VI, 1550, Feb. 15, 1797.
[90] *Ibid.*, 1583; March 4, 1797.
[91] See final chapter.

John Adams' closest friend, Benjamin Rush, accepted the argument that Adams had once turned to a favorable view of monarchism. In 1790 he wrote to Adams:

" In my notebook I have recorded a conversation that passed between Mr. Jefferson and myself on the 17th of March, of which *you* were the principal subject. We both deplored your attachment to monarchy and both agreed that you had changed your principles since the year 1776." [92] Yet, in my mind there is no question but that Adams was sincere in his later denials. He was never one to check back on his earlier pronouncements or correspondence. He was probably able to believe that he had always merely considered monarchy proper as a way out in case of certain eventualities.[93]

In his later career, particularly after 1809, when John Quincy Adams left the Federalists, Adams' condemnation of the American aristocracy became severe and bitter.[94] Yet, in this change, there is no serious inconsistency with his system. If the aristocracy proved able to uphold their position without being hereditary, well and good. The position which Adams himself held was always that of his independent executive, looking over the field and placing his weight with that group whose rights appeared to be threatened.

Thus it should be apparent that there was a sharp line of demarcation between the thought of Adams on the one hand and that of Hamilton and the New England " Tie-Wig " (commercial Federalist) group on the other. The one thought that either the rich or the poor would be equally tyrannical when in power; the other believed that only the rich had the right to rule, and that it was necessary that the government should be conducted by them.

[92] Rush to Adams, Philadelphia, April 13, 1790. *Letters of Benjamin Rush,* ed. L. H. Butterfield (Princeton, 1951), I, 546. Also see same to same, June 15, 1789, I, 516; and July 21, 1789, I, 522. For Adams' immediate denial of Rush's statement, cf. Adams, *Works,* IX, 566.

[93] Haraszti, in *John Adams & the Prophets of Progress* has a good summary of the problem of Adams' monarchism, 40-42. Haraszti's view that Adams was merely endorsing monarchy to stir up thought, is not a sufficient explanation in my opinion. [94] See final chapter of this book.

Chapter 4

The Economic Ideas of
John Adams [1]

THE review of the political principles of John Adams should have established the fact that Adams' primary difference from the other Federalist leaders arose from his distrusting the aristocracy as well as distrusting the people. Consequently, he would be expected to oppose measures benefiting the aristocracy as opposed to the interests of the people as a whole. On this point there is an interesting conversation between Jefferson, Hamilton, and Adams, which aptly sums up the situation:

The . . . conversation . . . by some circumstance, was led to the British Constitution, on which Mr. Adams observed, ' purge that constitution of its corruption and give to its popular branch equality of representation, and it would be the most perfect constitution ever devised by the wit of man.' Hamilton paused and said, ' purge it of its corruption, and give to its popular branch equality, and it would become impracticable government: as it stands at present, with all its supposed defects, it is the most perfect government which ever existed.' And this was assuredly the exact line which separated the political creeds of these two gentlemen. The one was for two hereditary branches and an honest elective one; and the other, for an hereditary King, with a House of Lords and Commons corrupt to his will, and standing between him and the people.[2]

---

[1] This chapter closely follows my " Political Economy of John Adams," *Political Science Quarterly*, LVI (1941), 545-72; Also on the economic ideas of Adams cf. Spengler, J. J., " Political Economy of Jefferson, Madison and Adams " in Jackson, David K., ed., *American Studies in Honor of William K. Boyd* (Durham, N. C., 1940) and " Regal Republic of John Adams " by Joseph Dorfman in his *The Economic Mind in American Civilization* (New York, 1946) I, 417-33.

[2] *The Complete Anas of Thomas Jefferson* (Franklin B. Sawvel, ed., New York, 1903), 36-37. Conversation recorded in April, 1791; explanation written on February 4, 1818.

Unlike Hamilton, then, Adams did not favor the wealthy class over the others. This was what was so confusing to the Hamiltonian Federalists. They thought it was an accepted convention that all Federalists talked of protecting the poor. So much had to be stated for public consumption. But in practice, the government naturally should be run by and for the " wise, rich, and good." [3] Could it be possible that Adams was so naive as to mean what he wrote and said? If so, precisely how did he differ from the orthodox Federalists? What effect did this difference have? These are questions that need a more complete answer.

To begin with, the background and the whole outlook of Adams differed materially from that of such spokesmen of the commercial group as Hamilton, Gouverneur Morris and Robert Morris.[4] It is true that Hamilton and Adams had a common background in training for the law. Before the Revolution, moreover, Adams maintained a general practice in the commercial city of Boston. But at the start of the Revolution he abandoned this practice, never thereafter to return to it, nor to be connected with the affairs of commerce. He devoted his time exclusively to farming and to public affairs. In contrast, Hamilton developed a large legal practice and became the spokesman for the trade and commerce of New York.

As a product of New England, Adams was naturally acquainted with the importance of commerce and the fisheries. It was one of his proudest boasts that he had been responsible for the clauses in the Treaty of 1783 protecting the rights of New England in the fisheries.[5] Fundamentally, however, he never moved far from the position of the Physiocrats. In 1778 he wrote to Ralph Izard:

Your sentiments of the fisheries as a source of wealth, of commerce, and naval power are perfectly just. Nevertheless, agriculture is the most essential interest of America, and even of the Massachusetts

---

[3] Adams, James T., *New England in the Republic, 1776-1850* (Boston 1926), 212.

[4] Beard, *op. cit.*, 318-19; Parrington, *op. cit.*, I, 326.

[5] See especially the *Diary* for November, 1782, *Works*, III, 300-39.

Bay: and it is very possible to injure both by diverting too much of the thoughts and labor of the people from the cultivation of the earth to adventures upon the sea.[6]

Not all of his pronouncements expressed such a partiality for agriculture. When he was president, Adams, like Jefferson, spoke of the importance of commerce and specifically recommended its protection to the Congress.[7]

Another factor which caused a difference in viewpoint between Adams and the commercial group was Puritanism.[8] Although in sectarian outlook Adams, being virtually a Unitarian, had no particular bias from his New England background, on moral questions he was strongly influenced. His strict moral code caused him to condemn anything which smacked of speculation. This reinforced his Physiocratic prejudice against many of the practices of the commercial interests.[9]

The first phase of Adams' economic opinions to be considered here is his position in relation to various schools of economic thought. He was one of the most widely read men in the America of his time. Though best informed in the fields of history, politics and theology, he was also well read in the field of economics. First of all, he was fully familiar with the colonial controversies and pamphlets on the question of paper money. Furthermore, the works of many leading economists are in his library, and an examination of his books shows that in many of them he made marginal comments.[10] In addition, there are references to other economists in his correspondence.

In general Adams followed the older theorists rather than his

---

[6] Sept. 25, 1778, Wharton, Francis, *Revolutionary Diplomatic Correspondence of the United States* (Washington, 1889), II, 743.

[7] *Annals of Congress*, VII, 631-32, Fifth Cong., 2d sess., Nov. 23, 1797.

[8] Biographies already cited and Gilbert Chinard, *Jefferson et les idéologues* (Paris and Baltimore, 1925), 226-87.

[9] Beard, *op. cit.*, 318-19; Parrington, *op. cit.*, I, 320.

[10] The library of John Adams in the Boston Public Library was examined. A number of books once in it are now missing. Fortunately a catalogue of the library was published when the books were given to the city of Quincy. See *Deeds and other documents relating to the several pieces of land, and to*

contemporaries.[11] This was especially true in the case of money, since he was an admirer of the works of Sir Isaac Newton [12] and John Locke. Many views expressed in the latter's *Some Considerations of the Consequence of the lowering of interest and raising the value of Money* (1691) are echoed by Adams.

When more general writers are considered, Adams is disappointing. Differences among schools of thought seem to escape him. In a letter to Jefferson he called François Quesnay, author of the *Tableau économique* (1758), " the grand master " [13] and expressed admiration of the *Encyclopédie*, the third edition of which (Genève, 1778-1779) was in his library. In general these two works are in agreement, for Quesnay was a contributor to the *Encyclopédie*. On the other hand, in the same letter Adams commented favorably on the writings of two mercantilists, Sir James Steuart [14] and Isaac de Pinto.[15] He also approved of Adam Smith,

the Library presented to the town of Quincy by President Adams, together with a catalogue of the books (Cambridge, 1823).

Haraszti, in *John Adams & the Prophets of Progress*, has reproduced these marginal comments to show the opinions of Adams in relation to the authors Adams has read.

[11] Adams to John Taylor, March 18, 1819, *Works*, X, 375-76.

[12] He would probably have known the two most widely printed of Newton's reports as Master and Worker of the Mint, *Report to the Lord High Treasurer on the value of foreign gold and silver coins . . .* , 7th July 1702, and *On the state of gold and silver coins of the kingdom, and on the relative value of gold and silver*, 21st September 1717. Adams at times shows understanding of some features of the quantity theory and did know Gresham's law. Other refinements and differences of theory escaped him. For the best review of the subject of early monetary theory see Arthur E. Monroe, *Monetary Theory before Adam Smith* (Cambridge, Mass., 1923).

[13] March 2, 1819, Chinard, *Jefferson et les idéologues*, 270. While no copy of the *Tableau économique* is in the list presented to the town of Quincy, there are Quesnay's *Essai physique sur L'oeconomie animale* (Paris, 1747, 3 vols.); *Philosophie rurale* (Amsterdam, 1763, 3 vols.); and *L'ami des hommes; ou Traité de la population* (1759, 3 vols. in 5). The last two works are the products of collaboration with others.

[14] He was the author of *An Inquiry into the Principles of Political Economy* (London, 1767, 2 vols.). His work was soon overshadowed in England by that of Smith, but had considerable influence on the later German historical school. A copy of the 1770 edition is in the Adams library.

[15] Author of *Essai sur la luxe* (Amsterdam, 1762) and *Traité de la circulation et du crédit* (Amsterdam, 1771).

the founder of classical economics. Two copies of *The Wealth of Nations* are in his library, one of the second English edition (1788) and one of the French translation (1781). Apparently the theoretical differences among these schools of thought are dismissed with the statement that they contain " mysteries, paradoxes, and enigmas." Despite the approbation Adams expressed several times for Adam Smith, specific references to his works are rare, and certainly on most questions, Adams accepted other writers. He reserved his highest praise for the Physiocrats, and undoubtedly rejected Smith's more advanced theories on banking.

Toward the close of his life, after the friendship with Jefferson had been renewed, Adams received from the Virginia statesman a copy of Comte Antoine Louis Claude Destutt de Tracy's *A Treatise on Political Economy*, which had been translated by Jefferson from the French and printed in the United States.[16] In an unpublished letter to Jefferson, Adams had given permission to publish his letter endorsing the work.[17] Apparently, however, Jefferson never released it to the press. Destutt de Tracy was a follower of Adam Smith, though certainly not one of his clearest expositors. Finally, at the close of his career, Adams ran the gamut of economic theory by endorsing Daniel Raymond.[18] Raymond is distinguished as an early American nationalist, and a strong proponent of protection. He violently attacked the free trade ideas of Adam Smith.[19] He also opposed Adam Smith on the question of banking.[20] By this time Adams was convinced that the growing industry of the United States needed a protective tariff. On that score the strongly nationalist ideas of Raymond probably appealed to him. Consequently he wrote a

---

[16] (Georgetown, 1817). A preface was written by Jefferson.

[17] April 2, 1819, in Jefferson *Papers* (Manuscript Division, Library of Congress).

[18] *The Elements of Political Economy* (Baltimore, 1820). The similarity between the ideas of Raymond and Friedrich List's *National System of Political Economy* (1841) is noted in Charles P. Neill's *Daniel Raymond* (Baltimore, 1897), 46 *et seq.*

[19] Raymond, *op. cit.* (2d ed., Baltimore, 1823), I, 125-257, 328-29; II, 125-57.

[20] *Ibid.*, II, 198-253.

letter of endorsement, which appeared as a preface to later editions of the work.[21] It is probable that the reason Adams was more friendly to manufacturing than to commerce and banking was that to him, as to others with a Physiocratic background, it appeared more productive, thus being comparable to agriculture. At the same time, it was something which could be developed in the United States, and Adams was ever a strong nationalist.

The chief common conception of virtually all these writers, with which Adams agreed, was the natural law theory of his time. In this way he was prone to justify his beliefs. On specific questions of economic theory many of the treatises which he found praiseworthy lack internal consistency. This probably contributed to Adams' confusion, but he showed little ability to discriminate among the various schools. It must be remembered, however, that many of Adams' pronouncements were put down in the midst of controversy, and that he drew on his own experience rather than on the theorists for his economic ideas. His inconsistent endorsements of theoretical economists probably arose from the fact that he read them for specific points of policy rather than for their general philosophies.

Before proceeding with an analysis of how Adams put his economic ideas into practice, and thus developed many specific points of disagreement with the Federalists, one other phase of his general system of ideas should be noted. His political opinions first coincided with those of the orthodox Federalists during the period of constitution making, just prior to the ratification of the Federal Constitution. But among the Federalist conservatives there was always a lingering suspicion of Adams because of his radical tendencies during the Revolution. As is well known, he was prominent in the early debates in the Continental Congress. He was foremost in pressing for the adoption of drastic measures against England. His political ideas at this time were correspondingly radical.[22] It was only with the close of the Revolution that he became more conservative, and it was after 1787 that he

[21] Daniel Raymond, *Political Economy* (Baltimore, 1840).
[22] Walsh, *op. cit.*, ch. II.

produced such political writings as his *Defense of the Constitutions of Government of the United States* (1787-1788),[23] *Three Letters to Roger Sherman, on the Constitution of the United States* (1789),[24] and *Discourses on Davila* (1790).[25] These aroused enthusiasm among the conservatives and were largely responsible for alienating him from the Republicans. Among the stanch Federalists, however, the memory of the earlier period must have lingered.[26]

Adams' position on those economic issues which fell within the realm of practical politics was at no time acceptable to the commercial group. Instead he was surprisingly in agreement with the agrarians, even when he opposed them on particular points of political theory and outlook. This can best be demonstrated by examining the position which he took on the chief economic issues of his day.

The commercial groups' distrust of Adams was not lulled by the policy which he followed in making peace with England. In 1779 he had urged that the United States prepare to supplant British trade by enlarging that with France and other continental countries, even terming England a natural commercial rival.[27] Despite his recommendations, Adams was empowered by Congress in 1779 to negotiate a treaty of commerce with England when peace negotiations were begun. Subsequently this power was revoked by Act of Congress of July 12, 1781.[28] Adams thereupon

[23] *The Works of John Adams*, IV, V, VI.

[24] *Works*, VI, 427-36.

[25] *Works*, VI, 227-403.

[26] It should be remembered that the commercial interests had moved rather slowly to the support of the Revolution, and many in fact had become Tories or remained neutral. After 1783 they were again united. As Arthur M. Schlesinger states: " . . . Once more united, the mercantile interests became a potent factor that led to the establishment of the United States Constitution." *The Colonial Merchants and the American Revolution, 1763-1776* (New York, 1918), 606. Also see Charles A. Beard, *An Economic Interpretation of the Constitution of the United States.*

[27] Adams to President of Congress, Aug. 4, 1779, Wharton, *op. cit.*, III, 281; and Adams to Genêt, May 1, 1780, *Ibid.*, 687.

[28] *Works of John Adams*, VII, 453; *Journals of the Continental Congress* (Washington, 1909), Aug. 14, 1779, XIV, 956; and XX, 744.

urged the necessity of continuing such authorization with the result that, upon a motion drawn up and introduced by Hamilton, the authority to negotiate such a treaty was vested in Adams, Franklin, and Jay in instructions adopted May 1, 1783.[29]

After the treaty of peace with England and his subsequent appointment as the first United States minister to England, Adams devoted considerable attention to the matter of a commercial treaty, but these efforts were not at all fruitful. Disappointed, he began to urge retaliation by Massachusetts and the other states of the Confederation, writing to this effect to the governor of Massachusetts. At the same time Adams urged fulfillment of the obligations assumed by the United States under the Treaty of 1783 in the matter of paying the debts owed to British merchants. This was as far as he was willing to go to conciliate England. Meanwhile, to assure independence from England, he thought that the policy of the United States should be directed to building up American manufacturing.[30]

In view of the difficulties attendant upon our early relations with England, probably no negotiator could have succeeded; but Adams' policy displeased those who were advocates of placating England. After he returned to the United States and had been chosen Vice-President, the question once more arose as to the choice of a representative to negotiate such a treaty.

Between 1787 and 1790, Beckwith, the unofficial agent of Britain to the United States, reported in a long series of communications the attitude of the Federalists on the question of a British treaty. He found such representatives of the commercial interests as Hamilton, Jay, and Fisher Ames anxious for a close connection with England.[31] He likewise found these leaders critical

---

[29] *Works of John Adams*, I, 400, and VIII, 146; *Journals of the Continental Congress*, XXIV, 320.

[30] Adams to Samuel Adams, 1785, *New York Public Library Bulletin*, VIII, 240; Also Jan. 26, 1786, and June 2, 1786, *Ibid.*, X, 241-43.

[31] One estimate of the volume of trade to England and her dependencies puts the total as high as 50 per cent of all U. S. exports in 1790-1791. Johnson, Emory R., and others, *History of Domestic and Foreign Commerce of the United States* (Washington, 1915), 20-23.

of Adams and determined that the latter should not again be sent to England. On this question their attitudes toward Adams and Jefferson were surprisingly similar. They felt that neither would be willing to yield enough to make the American terms acceptable to England. This information was duly transmitted to Lord Grenville,[32] Secretary of State for the Home Department, who, in 1791, became Secretary of State for Foreign Affairs.[33]

Although unsatisfactory as a possible negotiator, Adams won some support from the Federalists because of other aspects of his commercial policy. During the Napoleonic wars an extensive list of restrictions upon American commerce was introduced by England.[34] In response, the measures proposed by the Republicans in Congress were those of retaliation rather than negotiation. Adams expressed strong disapprobation of one such proposal: that the British debts be sequestered.[35] Two additional retaliatory measures, one suspending all commercial intercourse with England and another laying an embargo on British goods, were killed in the Senate by the deciding vote of Adams.[36] Finally, Adams strongly favored both the opening of negotiations for Jay's Treaty and its ratification.[37]

The essential differences between Adams and the Hamiltonian

[32] Lord Dorchester to Lord Grenville, Oct. 25, 1789 and May 27, 1790, Brymner, Douglas, ed., *Report on the Canadian Archives for 1890* (Ottawa, 1890), 121 *et seq.* and 133 *et seq.* Also Bemis, Samuel Flagg, *Jay's Treaty* (New York, 1923), 64-66.

[33] Fitzpatrick, Walter, ed., *The Manuscripts of J. B. Fortesque, Esq.* (Historical Manuscripts Commission, London, 1892-1927), I, xv-xvi.

[34] Mahan, Alfred T., *The Influence of Sea Power upon the French Revolution and Empire* (Boston, 1892), I, 241-42. For a list of British restrictions, see Clauder, Anna Cornelia, *American Commerce as Affected by the Wars of the French Revolution and Napoleon* (Philadelphia, 1932), 30.

[35] To Abigail Adams, April 1, 1794, *Letters . . . to His Wife*, II, 148.

[36] Adams to Abigail Adams, April 15, 1794, *Ibid.*, 155; *Annals of Congress*, IV, 87; *Porcupine's Gazette*, November 1799, as quoted in William Cobbett's *Porcupine's Works* (London, 1801), VI, 111. On other occasions, such as the neutrality act concerning France, the vote of the Vice-President was employed for Federalist proposals. *Annals of Congress*, IV, 66-67; and Adams to Abigail Adams, March 12, 1794, *Letters to Wife*, II, 146.

[37] Adams to Abigail Adams, Jan. 7, March 13, 25, April 16, 19, 1796, *Letters to Wife*, II, 198-223.

Federalists, however, were on fiscal and banking questions. The funding system and the assumption of state debts had met with the hearty approval of Adams. His endorsement of the plans was noted with disapproval by the more extreme Republicans.[38] With Adams the sole objective was the re-establishment of public credit.[39] While never approving the speculation in these securities (especially where it was carried on by members of the government),[40] and refusing, of course, to participate in it himself,[41] he rejoiced in the rise of the price of the securities to par.[42] On the other hand he did not accord Hamilton great personal credit for this or other fiscal proposals, nor did he have a high opinion of Hamilton's knowledge of matters of finance.[43] The Secretary's policies, he thought, achieved success because the new government had strength and adequate sources of revenue. They were formulated, moreover, on the advice of men who had served in the financial department of the government from the outbreak of the Revolution.[44]

[38] *The Journal of William Maclay*, 318 *et seq.*

[39] Adams to Benjamin Rush, Jan. 25, 1806, *Old Family Letters*, 98.

[40] Adams to Benjamin Waterhouse, May 9, 1813, Ford, Worthington C., ed., *Statesman and Friend* (Boston, 1927), 99.

[41] Adams to Rush, Aug. 25, 1811, *Old Family Letters*, 351. It is amusing to note that, in a particularly misanthropic moment, Adams wrote that a dominating factor in determining the location of the capitol was Washington's desire to dispose of lands at a profit. Same to same, Aug. 14, 1811, *Ibid.*, 345.

[42] Same to same, Jan. 25, 1806, *Ibid.*, 98.

[43] Same to same, Aug. 23, 1805, *Ibid.*, 75.

[44] *Ibid.* " His knowledge of the great subjects of Coin and commerce and their intimate Connection with all Departments of every Government . . . was very superficial and imperfect." Adams declared that Hamilton got his knowledge from Duer, the brother-in-law of Rose, Departmental Secretary under Pitt. Further, " Duer had been long Secretary to the Board of Treasury." Other men in the department, " Lee, Osgood, and Livingston were all men of abilities. . . . " Moreover Oliver Wolcott had seven years of experience with Connecticut finance. The only change from the old Congress was to make a secretary, " so that I see no extraordinary reason for so much exclusive Glory to Hamilton. . . . " This is, of course, too extreme a statement; but for further discussion of the origins of Hamilton's ideas on central banking, the funding system, and sinking fund, see Wettereau, James O., " Letters from Two Business Men to Alexander Hamilton on Federal Fiscal Policy, November, 1789," *Journal of Economic and Business History*, III, 667. For origins of his ideas

More to the point than Adams' efforts to show that Hamilton was not responsible for the detail of the Treasury's fiscal operations, is the general parallel between Hamilton's program and that introduced in England a century earlier. My colleague, William G. Carleton, has noted that the program of Hamilton followed closely the plans for a national debt and the Bank of England as introduced by Charles Montague in England between 1692 and 1694.[45] These plans led to Montague's appointment as Chancellor of the Exchequer in 1694 and at the same time established the connection between the Whig party and the commercial classes of England. Subsequently this plan of operations extended to the sinking fund, and the policy of Montague was expanded by Walpole. All of this was a pattern which Hamilton followed closely, both as to economics and as to the political effect of such measures in solidifying the support of commercial groups to the party which followed such a program.

While Adams approved the establishment of a system of taxation to provide the necessary revenue, he expressed alarm at the resulting burden. In this respect he showed far more concern than did Hamilton. Moreover, he was disturbed at the size of the public debt, whereas Hamilton regarded it at this time as a means of increasing the interest of the financial and commercial groups in the government.[46] Adams' views on these matters were expressed to his wife: " While I confess the necessity of it, and see its importance in giving strength to our government at home

on manufacturing, see Rezneck, Samuel, " The Rise and Early Development of Industrial Consciousness in the United States, 1760-1830," in *Ibid.*, IV, 790 *et seq.*, with special reference to Benjamin Rush and Tench Coxe. For the view that the claims of Coxe concerning Hamilton's " Report on Manufactures " are not justified in the form advanced by Coxe, see Hutcheson, Harold, *Tench Coxe* (Baltimore, 1938), 100; and Arthur H. Cole, *Industrial and Commercial Correspondence of Alexander Hamilton* (New York, 1928). Also on the ideas of the time, see Konkle, B. A., *Thomas Willing* (Philadelphia 1937); and East, Robert A., *Business Enterprise in the American Revolutionary Era* (New York, 1938), especially ch. xiii. Jensen, Merrill, in his *The New Nation* (New York, 1950), has a good survey of American finances during the Confederation, 382-98.

[45] " Macauley and the Trimmers," *American Scholar*, XIX, 73-82.

[46] Beard, *Economic Origins of Jeffersonian Democracy, passim.*

and consideration abroad, I lament the introduction of taxes and expenses which will accumulate a perpetual debt and lead to future revolutions." [47] Again he wrote: "We have very disagreeable business to do in finding ways and means for the expenses we have already incurred. It grieves me to the heart to see an increase of our debt and taxes. . . ." [48] At the same time he was not in sympathy with the Republicans, who were advocating costly measures against England. Even during his own administration in 1798 Adams voiced opposition to many expenditures forced upon him by Congress and expressed the view that the Federalists would create among the taxpayers an overwhelming reaction against the government. [49] To Congress, in his annual message in 1797, he expressed concern over the size of the United States debt, and at the same time pointed to abuses in the British funding system. [50]

During the formative period of fiscal policy, 1790-1792, Adams did, however, support Hamilton on a sufficient number of questions to be viewed as generally favorable to him. At the time of the investigation of the Treasury Department by the House of Representatives in 1793, Adams strongly supported Hamilton and termed him " a faithful servant . . . [whose] character will shine all the brighter." [51] Likewise, although condemning Adams in other respects for his fiscal views, Hamilton acknowledged in his public pamphlet in 1800: "It is, in particular, a tribute due from me, to acknowledge that Mr. Adams being in quality of Vice-President, ex-officio, one of the Trustees of the Sinking-Fund, I experienced from him the most complete support." [52]

Banking was the most important economic subject on which

[47] May 5, 1794, *Letters to Wife*, II, 158.
[48] April 3, 1794, *Ibid.*, II, 150.
[49] Adams to McHenry, Oct. 22, 1798, *Works*, VIII, 612; Sedgwick to Hamilton, Feb. 7, 1799, Hamilton's *Works* (Hamilton, ed.), VI, 393.
[50] *Annals of Congress*, VII, 633-34, Nov. 23, 1797.
[51] Adams to Abigail Adams, Jan. 24 and Feb. 27, 1793, *Letters to Wife*, II, 121, 127.
[52] Hamilton, Alexander, *Letter Concerning the Public Conduct and Character of John Adams* (New York, 1800), 9-10, in *Works of Alexander Hamilton* (Hamilton, ed.); VII, 693.

fundamental differences appeared between Adams and the Hamiltonian group. To understand this fully it is necessary to consider both the political situation of the period and Adams' theories of banking. There were three main currents of thought concerning banking at this time. The Federalists, best represented by the Hamiltonian group, demanded banks to supply credit for their commercial needs. At the same time they insisted that whatever banks were established should be operated on a sound basis, so that a stable system of credit and paper money might result. Finally, realizing that profits would accrue from banking, they desired a political monopoly of banking for their own purposes.

The Republicans, on the other hand, were not unified in their point of view. The most orthodox group, for which John Taylor was spokesman, opposed all banks which might perform the function of discount or issue paper money. This group was composed of " hard money " proponents. The majority of the party, however, were usually favorable toward banks when any practical question of policy was under discussion. Debtors in the cities sympathized with this attitude. Most of the city merchants were Federalists, but some were Republicans. This latter group desired the Republicans to support banks which they (the Republican merchants) might control.[53] Finally as the tide of sentiment for banks rose, certain of the anti-bank Republicans were willing to yield on grounds of political expediency. At one time, when the Bank of the United States threatened to establish a branch at Richmond, Jefferson suggested that the Republicans should charter a state bank.[54]

[53] For example, there is the case of the Manhattan Company of New York for which Aaron Burr and other Republicans secured a charter as a water company. A clause in the charter permitted this to become a bank of discount. It was incorporated on April 2, 1799, and began operations in September of that same year. Webster, Noah, *Miscellaneous Papers* (New York, 1802), 19. Pomerantz, Sidney, in his *New York: An American City* (New York, 1938), has shown that the Federalists had knowledge of the purposes of Burr at the time the vote was taken on the bill (187-90).

[54] Jefferson to Madison, July 3, 1792, *Jefferson's Works* (Ford, ed.), VII, 98. Also see Wettereau, J. O., " New Light on the First Bank of the United States," *Pennsylvania Magazine of History*, LXI, 281, where Jefferson is shown

These, then, were the three main political factors in the situation. The Federalists generally supported sound, conservative, commercial banking. Some of the Republicans desired banks of greater or less degree of soundness. Finally the more consistent agrarians (a minority of the Republicans) opposed all banks of discount and all paper money, whether issued by banks or by the government.

In connection with the views of Adams concerning banks, the status of banking theory at this time must be briefly examined. All banks which were chartered issued paper money. Consequently, few writers of the period wrote about banks apart from the question of paper money and inflation. Adams therefore approached the question through a discussion of paper money. During the Revolution the issue of almost unlimited amounts by the Continental Congress had resulted in the virtual repudiation of the Continental currency. It was with banks, after their establishment, that the problem of note issue was more intimately associated.[55] At the same time the banks created commercial credit simply through discounting paper. This last function, discount, and the creation of deposit credit were but little understood at this time.[56] Adams believed the effects of both note issue and discount were inflationary, and hence that both were wrong. His failure to distinguish between the two functions, however, makes his presentation confusing.

Approaching this subject, then, through a consideration of Adams' views on paper money, we find that in 1789, in response to a query on the subject, he replied that at that time there was no sound basis for credit. " No man of common sense will trust us. As long as unlimited democracy tyrannized over the

---

to have been a borrower from the Bank of the United States. The same article established the nature of the business of the bank, which made loans chiefly to manufacturers, master mechanics, wholesalers and wealthy landowners.

[55] Miller, Harry E., *Banking Theories in the United States before 1860* (Cambridge, Mass., 1927), chaps. IV, V, VI. This work briefly mentions the opposition of Adams to banks. *Ibid.*, 20. The opinion is expressed that only the Republicans opposed the national bank, a view with which the present writer disagrees. *Ibid.*, 24.

[56] Hamilton, for example, regarded bank credit as capital. *Ibid.*, 82.

rich, no man of property was safe." [57] Shays's Rebellion was still fresh in Adams' mind. Apparently, it was the demand for cheap money, sponsored chiefly by the inflationist wing of the Republican Party, which Adams most feared at this juncture. In opposing such a demand, he was in accord with Federalist orthodoxy. In the same letter he stated that he hoped there would be no necessity at all for paper money. Instead, "the cash paid in imposts will immediately be paid to creditors, and by them circulated in society." [58] It is noteworthy that Adams' correspondent here, James Sullivan of Boston, was the author of a sharp attack on Hamilton's banking policies in the *Path to Riches* (1792). In this he also follows the argument of Dr. Richard Price, another close friend of Adams.[59]

When the question of the establishment of a national bank arose, these views concerning banks of issue and discount were reflected in Adams' outline of the type of national bank which should be established. As to its constitutionality, he had no doubts. Furthermore, following the same plan as did Sullivan, he agreed that such a bank should be established. To that extent, he was in accord with orthodox Federalist theory. Adams always was a strong nationalist, never an adherent to the idea of States' rights. Thus, he was in disagreement with the Republicans. When it came to the purpose for which these national powers should be used, however, he disagreed with the Federalists. In 1794 he wrote, "One Bank of the United States with its branches strictly limited in its operations, would be useful . . ."; [60] and again he wrote:

A national bank of deposit I believe to be wise, just, prudent, economical, and necessary. But every bank of discount, every bank by which interest is to be paid or profit of any kind made by the deponent, is downright corruption. It is taxing the public for the benefit

---

[57] Adams to James Sullivan, Sept. 17, 1789, *Works*, IX, 562.

[58] *Ibid.*

[59] Cf. *On the Nature of Civil Liberty* (London, 1776).

[60] Jan. 12, 1794, *Letters to Wife*, II, 138.

and profit of individuals; it is worse than old tenor, continental currency, or any other paper money. . . .[61]

More information is given in a very important passage of an
unpublished letter from Adams to Jefferson:

> The Medici rose to the despotism of Europe, ecclesiastical, & politi-
> cal, by the machinery of banks, hundreds of mushrooms or Jonah's
> gourds have sprung up in one night in America by the strength of
> the same rotten manure. How has it happened that the bank of
> Amsterdam has for so many years conducted all most all the com-
> merce of Europe without making any profit to the proprietors, and
> how has it happened that religious liberty, fiscal science, coin & com-
> merce, & every branch of political economy should have been better
> understood and more honestly practiced in that Frog land, than any
> other country in the World.[62]

Examination of the plan of the Bank of Amsterdam, or Amsterdam Wisselbank, will likewise clarify Adams' stand on discounting.
This bank was founded in 1609. It was designed to be primarily
a money-changing institution. So varied were the coins then in
circulation that it was a great convenience to be able to deposit
specie and receive a standard-value bank money in return. A
fee was paid by *depositors* for keeping money on deposit. The
bank had no right to loan deposits. All specie paid in was supposed
to be available at any time. The bank was given a monopoly of
all money-changing and deposit business, although this was not
enforced. It was controlled by a board of depositors and city
officials. All profits went to the City of Amsterdam, which from
1609 to 1796 is estimated to have received 12,256,000 guilders.[63]

---

[61] Adams to Benjamin Rush, Aug. 28, 1811, *Works*, IX, 638. Elsewhere
Adams wrote that this bank should be " inexorably limited to ten or fifteen
millions of dollars." Same to same, Aug. 23, 1805, *Old Family Letters*, 76.

[62] Jan. 29, 1819, in Jefferson Papers (Manuscript Division, Library of Con-
gress). There is rather close agreement between this account and that by
Adam Smith in *The Wealth of Nations*. *Cf.* Cannan edition (London, 1904),
I, 442-50.

[63] Richard Van der Borght, " History of Banking in the Netherlands," in
Sumner, William Graham, ed., *History of Banking in All Nations* (New York,
1896), IV, 188-371. A fact, of which Adams apparently was not aware, is that

In contrast to this system the Bank of the United States was formed with a capital of $10,000,000. It had the power to issue paper money equal to this capital, to create deposit credit, and to make loans upon adequate security.[64] The issue of paper money by the bank was $1,225,000 on January 22, 1792; $3,700,000 a year later; and $6,539,428 on November 26, 1801. Specie held varied from a low of $500,000 in 1795 to over $5,000,000 in 1801 and over $8,000,000 in 1802.[65] Loans in 1809 were $15,000,000. It did act as a check upon the depreciated currency of some state banks by refusing to accept notes not redeemable in specie. The bank paid dividends of about eight per cent per annum.[66]

In 1793 Adams wrote, " I consider myself already as taxed one-half of my salary and one-half of all the interest of my money to support bankers and bankrupts." [67] Now this argument is apparently virtually an echo of contemporary Republican arguments. Regarding a contemporary pamphlet which he sent Abigail Adams he wrote: ". . . This production is said to have been written by a Senator from Virginia, Mr. Taylor; I know not how truly. It is like his style, spirit, opinions and sentiments. There is too much foundation for some of his observations. . . ." [68]

The pamphlet in question is probably that one entitled: *An Enquiry into the Principles and Tendency of Certain Public Measures*.[69] Taylor represented the ideas of the group which in

the bank had secretly been granting loans to the Dutch East India Company since 1657. This was generally suspected by 1789, and resulted in depreciation of the bank money. In 1796, public recognition of the fact was made, and the bank reorganized. It struggled on until 1819, when it was finally liquidated. This, of course, does not affect the theory of the bank so far as Adams' ideas are concerned.

[64] Hepburn, A. Barton, *History of Currency in the United States*, 84.

[65] Wettereau, in *Pennsylvania Magazine of History*, LXI, 283.

[66] Hepburn, *op. cit.*, 84; also see Holdsworth, John T., *The First Bank of the United States* (Washington, 1910). The bank charter is given in Holdsworth, 126-32.

[67] Jan. 9, 1793, *Letters to Wife*, II, 117.

[68] Jan. 12, 1794, *Ibid.*, II, 138.

[69] (Philadelphia, 1794). This pamphlet was published anonymously. Another anonymous pamphlet by Taylor is *An Examination of the Late Proceedings*

this chapter have been called orthodox agrarian. Naturally his first argument is that the bank is unconstitutional. As has been shown above, Adams held directly opposite views on this point. Taylor advocated the eradication of banks through legislation in the larger states prohibiting the circulation of any bank paper. These measures were to be directed against the Bank of the United States.[70] On the other hand, Adams' plan was for a federal bank to drive out all state banks and all paper money. A further method advocated by Taylor was for two-thirds of the state legislatures, or as many as possible, to protest the action of Congress. Thus, although agreeing in the economic reasons for opposing banks, the two differ in their political means of solving the problem; Taylor voiced the States' rights and Adams the nationalist point of view.

Adams' contention that banks through certain functions robbed the community followed the argument which in Taylor's writings proceeded as follows: All income is derived from labor, something cannot be created from nothing. Consequently someone has to work to pay the interest on bank credit. How has this credit been created? It is not derived from specie, which would offer some real basis for loans. Instead, three-fourths of the capital is required to be in government bonds. These were probably acquired by persons profiting from speculations in the funding system. Now, on the basis of these bonds paper money is issued, creating additional false capital to be loaned out at interest. Thus, it is contended, an engine is set up, controlled by the rich

in Congress, respecting the Official Conduct of the Secretary of the Treasury (Richmond, 1793). A third is *A Definition of Parties; or The Political Effects of the Paper System Considered* (Philadelphia, 1794). There is a possibility that the pamphlet sent by Adams, and to which the letter refers, was the 1793 pamphlet. However, the part of these with which Adams was chiefly concerned, as the context of his letter shows, is the discussion of the banking and paper systems, on which Taylor touched in all three of the pamphlets.

While the later correspondence between Taylor and Adams has attracted comment in Simms, Henry H., *The Life of John Taylor* (Richmond, 1932), chapter vii, this early endorsement has not been emphasized. Also see Mudge, E. T., *The Social Philosophy of John Taylor of Caroline* (New York, 1939).

[70] Taylor, *An Enquiry into the Principles and Tendency of Certain Public Measures*, 80.

and operating to draw into their hands additional funds. This income is a tax on labor, which is alone capable of production.[71] Taylor does not, however, deny to all capital the right to receive interest; for in the matter of private loans, where specie is the basis of the transaction, there is no speculative value set up, and the transaction is based on a reasonable limit.[72] But in regard to the bank, he insists that the bill should have been called, "An act for taxing the community by the establishment of a bank, and dividing the money so raised among sundry members of Congress and certain other individuals therein named. . . ." [73]

While the ideas of both Taylor and Adams are marked by a failure to comprehend the principle of credit, they are founded on a real grievance; namely, that the great increase in the volume of money in circulation between the years 1790 and 1795 had a definite inflationary effect. During these years the per capita circulation rose from $3.00 to $7.77, over two and a half times, while the number of banks increased from four to twenty-four, with a corresponding increase in credit facilities (cf. Table 6).[74] Bank loans and discounts were probably in excess of $20,000,000 by 1800.[75]

---

[71] *Ibid.*, 12-19. This conception of a labor theory of value follows Locke and other English mercantilists. In a later period apologies to Marx would be in order.

[72] *Ibid.*, 16.   [73] *Ibid.*, 33.

[74] Hepburn, *op. cit.*, 87. A general description of early state banks is found in Dewey, Davis R., *State Banking before the Civil War* (Washington, 1910).

An interesting list of the banks chartered through 1801 is given by Webster, Noah, *Miscellaneous Papers*, 31-33. He estimates the total number of banks, counting the Bank of the United States as one bank, at 30; and total capitalization of all at $23,612,000. This is in general agreement with Table 6.

Also Adams to F. A. Vandercamp, Feb. 16, 1809, *Works*, IX, 610. "Our medium is depreciated by the multitude of swindling banks, which have emitted bank bills to an immense amount beyond the deposits of gold and silver in their vaults, by which means the price of labor and land and merchandise and produce is doubled, tripled, and quadrupled in many instances. Every dollar of a bank bill that is issued beyond the quantity of gold and silver in the vaults, represents nothing, and is therefore a cheat upon somebody."

[75] Shultz, William J., and Caine, M. R., *The Financial Development of the United States* (New York, 1937), 127-28.

Of course, not all of the changes in prices could be attributed solely to banks. But banks of this period did not follow sound practices. Absence of experience led to many mistakes. The range of business fluctuations was therefore made greater by the practices followed by banks.[76]

The rise in prices was affected by the following items, among others: (1) high prices abroad for American products and heavy export of these products, (2) the inflow of specie, and (3) the expanding issue of bank notes and expansion of bank credit. Therefore, it is wrong to attribute changes in prices solely to the banks, as did Adams.[77]

It was the belief of Adams that in a correct monetary system, gold and silver are but commodities; and that these would be attracted in sufficient quantities to provide an adequate circulating medium, just as a supply of any goods would be attracted by the demand for it. No suitable replacement which would maintain a constant value could be found.[78]

His statements contain at least two fallacies. In the first place, it is not correct to say that when gold or silver is coined there is no change in the value as a result. Adams confuses the price of specie with its value, a common error. In the second place, the idea that through some natural law a sufficient volume of gold and silver would flow into the country has no substantial basis. While sale of products abroad would, of course, bring specie into the country when exports exceed imports, there would be no

---

[76] Smith and Cole, *op. cit.*, 32-33.

[77] For detail on price fluctuations see Chapter III of Smith and Cole, and especially Chart 4. In general there were three periods of prosperity in 1790-1801. The first was accompanied by the speculation in bank securities, and closed in 1792. At that time Weighted Index A (Wholesale Domestic Commodity Prices in Boston) reached a low of 82. A rise then occurred to a high point of 138 in 1796. The next low point was 106 in 1798. A new high of 141 was reached in 1801. *Ibid.*, 146. For Index B (Wholesale Imported Commodity Prices in Boston) see *Ibid.*, 147. Schultz and Caine estimate specie in circulation increased from $10,000,000 in 1790 to as much as $20,000,000 in 1800, *op. cit.*, 128.

[78] Adams to John Taylor, March 18, 1818, *Works*, X, 375-77. Again he wrote, " . . . A circulating medium of gold and silver only ought to be established . . . ," to Benjamin Rush, Aug. 28, 1811, *Ibid.*, IX, 638.

guarantee that the amount would suffice for business purposes, assuming a price level as expressed in contracts and other term obligations. Adams seems almost to imply that gold and silver have an intrinsic value. If this be true he does not show an understanding of money as a medium of exchange, nor does he show a consistent adoption of the quantity theory of money. If some aspects of the quantity theory appear at times, on other occasions Adams seems to hold to a commodity theory, a supply theory, or even more primitive ideas. Neither he nor Taylor shows, moreover, any understanding of credit. Throughout, they have a valid point as to the unfair advantage over other citizens which a charter for a bank of discount gives to the stockholders of the bank in enabling them to profit for themselves. But this is an argument for governmental ownership of credit facilities or for the mutualization of credit, not that such transactions should be abolished as serving no useful purpose.

To return to the pamphlet by Taylor, he concludes that the result of the banking and funding systems would be to corrupt the members of Congress. Instead of senators and representatives speaking the voice of their constituents, they would speak the voice of the bank. Further he holds that this would tend to make them representatives of an aristocracy which may be expected to result finally in the establishment of a monarchy. He then proceeds to launch an attack upon the philosophy of Adams in regard to a natural aristocracy.[79] At that point, of course, Taylor and Adams would part company.

Illustrative of Adams' attitude toward the state banking systems, is an instructive incident of 1792. At that time there was already one bank in Boston, the Massachusetts Bank which served the commercial interests. In the move to establish another bank, the Union Bank, it was considered desirable to draw upon the support of Governor Hancock and his party, many of whom were agrarian Republicans. Accordingly the charter of the bank specified that one-fifth of the bank funds should be appropriated to loans outside of Boston for the benefit of agriculture

[79] *An Enquiry into the Principles and Tendency of Certain Public Measures,* 24-25, 28-29, 36-37.

in sums not less than $100 nor more than $1,000 secured by mortgages on real estate, and having not less than one year to run.[80]

This happened in the year that Quincy was separated from Braintree, Adams wrote. As its representative Quincy chose Peter Boylston Adams, brother of John Adams.

He also was a Man of Sense, Spirit and Honour. Upon the Question of the Union Bank he saw its corrupt Tendency and gave his Nay against it. The Gallery was full of Speculators, and upon his Nay being pronounced the Cry in the Gallery, loud enough to be heard by many, was " God damn the Nays, who would have expected a Nay from that Quarter? " [81]

Quite evidently, the speculators, in the light of orthodox Federalist finance, had not expected such a development. On the same vote a Dr. Tufts of Weymouth voted with P. B. Adams. Both

lost their Elections in 1793 by a single vote of each against our Union Bank. Two honnester Men, or more disinterested, or independent, can no where be found; no, nor more popular Men. Yet both fell sacrifices to a single vote against a Bank. These two cases were so remarkable, such decisive demonstrations of Banking Corruption that they ought to be detailed and held up as Beacons. But they would have no effect.[82]

In this matter, however, the " Democrats cannot complain of superior virtue, [John] Hancock and [Moses] Gill, [Charles] Jarvis, [Benjamin] Austin and all the Democrats were engaged [in] the Union Bank." [83] While this bank had Republican support, most state banks were established by Federalists. To his wife, Adams wrote: " I have the same aversion to the multiplication of banks, and the same apprehension of their pernicious tendency, as you express." [84]

---

[80] Winsor, Justin, *Memorial History of Boston* (Boston, 1881), **IV**, 153.
[81] Adams to Rush, Jan. 17, 1811, *Old Family Letters*, 276.
[82] Same to same, Dec. 27, 1810, *Ibid.*, 273.
[83] *Ibid.* All of those named are prominent Massachusetts Republicans. Gill became a Federalist after 1793.
[84] Jan. 9, 1793, *Letters to Wife*, **II**, 117.

These views upon finance, as Adams wrote to Jefferson, were not kept to himself, but were expressed.[85] The result was that, although in 1792 he had the united support of the Federalist party, a reconciliation having taken place after the attempt to undermine him in 1789, in 1796 there was considerable opposition to him within the Federalist party.

Bearing all these factors in mind, it is well to attempt some conclusion as to where Adams stood in relation to these economic questions, and to summarize the political implications which may be drawn therefrom. There are certain peculiarities in his position. In general, he stood midway between the Hamiltonians and the Jeffersonians. From the standpoint of political theory, this was probably the reason that in his political writings he called attention to the necessity for a " balance " [86] between the conflicting groups, which should be supplied by the independent executive. He wrote of this in his formal works as the attempt to maintain a balance between aristocracy and the general mass of the people. In reality, however, this was but a part of the conflict. There was also taking place a conflict between agrarians and the commercial interests. Spokesmen for the first group were Jefferson and Taylor; for the second, Hamilton and his cohorts. The first group broadened the basis of its support by identifying its cause with that of popular government, and thus won the political conflict.[87]

[85] March 2, 1819, Chinard, *Jefferson et les idéologues*, 270.

[86] *Defense of the Constitutions of Government of the United States*, III, in *Works*, VI, 65; *Davila* in *Works*, VI, 340-41.

[87] The general understanding between Adams and Jefferson is well brought out in the second volume of Dumas Malone's excellent and definitive biography of Jefferson, *Jefferson and the Rights of Man* (Boston, 1951).

Chapter 5

John Adams and the
Federalist Party, 1788-1796

DURING John Adams' ministry to England under the Confederation he formed certain opinions and attitudes toward
England which are important. First, the foreign policy which he
urged on the Congress of the Confederation differed from that
of the Hamiltonians both then and later, so that they found it
unsatisfactory. Second, the opinions are the basis for Adams' own
ideas as to policy toward England, when later he was Vice-
President and then President. His ideas are best set forth in two
letters to Samuel Adams written in 1786. In England he found
great jealousy toward America. The basis of this was the natural
resentment against the independence of the colonies and the fear
of a potential rival in the field of shipping.[1] Furthermore, many
in England regarded America as already inclining so strongly
toward France as to be completely alienated from England on
matters of foreign policy. Neutrality was not believed to be within
the competence of America. "Indeed they really do not think
us of much consequence. We have no Navy; and are akward in
Uniting in anything."[2] Adams felt that a policy of neutrality
should be pursued so long as possible by America. War would be
deeply regretted. However, "It is much to be desired that our
Commerce with all other nations may be increased, especially
France, and Holland, and lessed with England as much as possible,
until she shall put it on a more liberal Footing. The Political
Friendship too of France, Spain and Holland should be cultivated
as much as possible without involving us too far."[3]

[1] John Adams to Samuel Adams, London, Jan. 26, 1786; *New York Public
Library Bulletin*, X, 241. Same to same, London, June 2, 1786, *Ibid.*, 242-43.
[2] Same to same, London, Jan. 26, 1786, *Ibid.*, 241.
[3] John Adams to Samuel Adams, London, Jan. 26, 1786; *New York Public
Library Bulletin*, X, 241.

However, Adams was entirely of the opinion that the treaty of 1783 should be rigidly observed by the United States. Then, and only then it would be possible to demand justice from England. Yet he was not for taking the discriminations of England without retaliation. " [We] must oppose Navigation Acts to Navigation Acts or [we shall] . . . never have a free Commerce with any Part of the British Empire." [4] These views, and his lack of success in negotiating a commercial treaty with England did not endear him to the hearts of the pro-British Federalists. Rather they served to create an impression that he was too anti-British.

With the return of Adams to the United States he at once came into prominence as a candidate for the vice-presidency. At one time he considered taking a seat in the final session of the old Congress, there being a demand that he take the presidency of that body. However he decided not to do this. A suggestion that he take a senatorial seat from Massachusetts in the new federal Congress was declined on the ground that the office would be beneath him. [5] Thus he definitely indicated what position he would consider.

Meanwhile, with Washington as the leading candidate, it was obvious that someone from the North would be needed to balance the ticket. George Clinton became the candidate of the Anti-Federalists. John Hancock, like Adams, from Massachusetts, was apparently in a receptive mood for the presidency or vice-presidency. At this juncture, according to a letter by Adams in 1807, Hamilton sent General Henry Knox to Massachusetts to look over the ground. "Hamilton had insinuated into him that I should not harmonize with Washington, and (would you believe it?) that John Adams was a man of too much influence to be so near Washington! In this dark and insidious manner did this intriguer lay schemes in secret against me, and like the worm at the root of the peach, did he labor for twelve years, under-

[4] Adams to Samuel Adams, London, June 2, 1786. *Ibid.*, 242-43.
[5] Adams to Theophilous Parsons, Braintree, Nov. 2, 1788, *Works*, VIII, 484.

ground and in darkness. . . ." [6] However, his own popularity was too great to permit such plans to succeed in 1788.

Credence is lent to this statement by the fact that Adams and Knox became quite close later on account of the intrigue over who should be second in command of the army to Washington in 1798. As a result of being displaced in the command by Hamilton, Knox discussed matters with Adams. Further, the letters of Hamilton during 1788 and 1789 show clearly that Hamilton was only brought to grant partial support to Adams after exhausting other possibilities. To Madison, then one of the Federalists, Hamilton wrote that he was supporting Adams, though " Not without apprehensions on the score we talked about." This decision in favor of Adams was dictated by two considerations which Hamilton stated: first, Adams desired to defer to a later date any important amendments to the constitution, a course which Hamilton generally approved; second, Adams was important in the Eastern States. Should he not be granted the vice-presidency he might become disgruntled and strengthen the opposition; or he would have to be nominated to some office for which he was less suited. Knox, who was evidently being considered, would decline to run on account of the need of making money.[7]

In similar tenor Hamilton wrote to Theodore Sedgwick: " On the question between Mr. H[ancock] and Mr. A[dams], Mr. King will probably have informed you that I have, upon the whole, concluded that the latter ought to be supported. My measures will be taken accordingly. I had but one scruple, but after mature consideration, I have relinquished it. Mr. A., to a sound understanding, has always appeared to me to add an ardent love for the public good, and, as his further knowledge of the world seems to have corrected those jealousies, which he is represented to have once been influenced by, I trust nothing of the kind

---

[6] Adams to Mercy Warren, Quincy, July 20, 1807. *Massachusetts Historical Society Collections*, Ser. 5, IV, 334.

[7] Hamilton to Madison, New York, November 23, 1788. Hamilton's *Works* (Lodge, ed.), VIII, 203.

suggested in my former letter will disturb the harmony of the administration." [8]

At the same time Hamilton was taking pains to see that there should be no danger of Adams securing the first place. That this proceeded as much from a desire to lessen the number of votes for Adams in order to cause a reflection upon his popularity, as from a desire to protect Washington, is revealed by the tactics which he pursued. In Connecticut an express arrived the day before the electors voted stating that Hamilton had calculated the question exactly and found that by throwing away three votes from Adams in New Jersey and two in Connecticut there there would be a correct outcome.[9] At the same time he wrote to James Wilson of Pennsylvania that he had written to Connecticut to drop two votes and would have the same number discarded in New Jersey. He calculated that through the scattering of votes in the South it would be best to allow for dropping at least eight from Adams. Pennsylvania should throw away three or four. Hamilton was even ready to risk the defeat of Adams, " for God's sake let not our zeal for a secondary object defeat or endanger a first. I admit that in several important views and particularly to avoid disgust to a man who would be a formidable head to Anti-Federalists —— it is much to be desired that Adams may have the plurality of suffrages for Vice-President; but if risk is to be run on one side or on the other can we hesitate where it ought to be preferred? " The letter closes with the recommendation that, " if there appears to you to be any danger, will it not be well for you to write to Maryland to qualify matters there? " [10]

There is also an interesting letter to Wilson from the Rev. William Smith, D. D., who wrote from Maryland on January 19

[8] Hamilton to Theodore Sedgwick, New York, November 9, 1788. *Ibid.*, 211.

[9] Col. Jeremiah Wadsworth wrote Hamilton from Hartford that Hamilton's instructions had been followed and two votes dropped from Adams. Feb., 1789, *Hamilton Papers*, (Library of Congress) 7/942; Trumbull to Adams, Adams' *Works*, VIII, 484. Date not given but from the context the letter must have been written immediately after the electors met.

[10] Hamilton to James Wilson, New York, Jan. 25, 1789. *Pennsylvania Magazine*, XXIX, 210-11.

to the same effect, suggesting that all of the middle states throw away a number of votes and that Connecticut be communicated with.[11] This may show either that Hamilton had spread his ideas even further, which is not improbable, or that a number of people were apprehensive of the same outcome as Hamilton feared. Be this as it may, it was not expected that Adams would appreciate these efforts; and in view of Hamilton's opinion of Adams, it is likely that he was anxious to place Adams in a position which would reflect upon the support he commanded.

When the returns were in, there were sixty-nine electoral votes for Washington and thirty-four for Adams, distributed as follows: [12]

TABLE 8

PRESIDENTIAL ELECTION OF 1788–1789

State	Wash.	Adams	Jay	Hancock	Scattering
New Hampshire	5	5			
Massachusetts	10	10			
Connecticut	7	5			2
New Jersey	6	1	5		
Pennsylvania	10	8		2	
Delaware	3		3		
Maryland	6				6
Virginia	10	5	1	1	3
South Carolina	7			1	6
Georgia	5				5
	69	34	9	4	22

At a result of this nature, Adams was greatly angered. To his friend, Benjamin Rush, he wrote: " Is not my election to this office, in the scurvey manner in which it was done, a curse rather than a blessing? Is this Justice? Is there common sense or

[11] Smith to Wilson, Chester, Kent Co., Md., Jan. 19, 1789, *Ibid.*, XVII, 204.
[12] Stanwood, Edward, *History of the Presidency*, I, 27.

decency in this business? Is it not an indelible stain on our Country, Countrymen and Constitution? I assure you I think it so, and nothing but an apprehension of great Mischief, and final failure of the Government from my Refusal and assigning my reasons for it, prevented me from Spurning it." [13]

Having saved the country by not resigning, Adams entered upon his duties of presiding over the Senate. His efforts in behalf of titles, and his motive for desiring them have been recounted in Chapter 3. Needless to say this did not endear Adams to the more democratic elements of the country.

General Schuyler, Senator from New York, reported that in the Senate Adams spoke against levying retaliatory duties against Great Britain on account of England's failure to abandon the Western posts.[14] Hamilton, though, was at this time uncomplimentary in his remarks about the recently concluded ministry of Adams to England. For this reason he opposed using Adams again as a negotiator, stating: "Undoubtedly, we have not in some former instances been exempt from this sort of inconvenience [that the representative was not sufficiently friendly to England], to which the manner of naming to public appointments under our old government not a little contributed. The case is now altered, these nominations originate with General Washington, who is a good judge of men, and the gentleman to be employed in this business, is perfectly master of the subject, and if he leans in his bias towards any foreign country, it is decidedly to you." [15]

At this same time another incident shows that Federalists were lukewarm towards Adams. There was a report that Washington was soon to retire. Senator Johnson declared that Adams' un-

---

[13] Adams to Rush, New York, May 17, 1789; Biddle, Alexander, *Old Family Letters*, 36.

[14] Lord Dorchester to Lord Grenville, Quebec, Oct. 25, 1789. Enclosure, "Conversations with Different Persons." *Canadian Archives, 1890,* 121 ff. Schuyler also stated the Senate had not appropriated for a minister as it was thought he would not be sufficiently favorable.

[15] Dorchester to Grenville, Quebec, May 27, 1790. Enclosure, *Canadian Archives, 1890,* 127.

popularity to the South (it was at this time that the *Discourses on Davila* were appearing in the *Gazette of the United States*) would prevent his election. He thought that Jay would be a proper person.[16]

During his first term as Vice-President, Adams and Jefferson continued on good terms. There was considerable correspondence between them. Jefferson congratulated Adams on his election to the vice-presidency.[17] Adams had written to Jefferson in 1787 declaring that he looked with terror on the idea of election to high office. Such experiments had failed before.[18] Similar doubts were expressed publicly in Adams' *Discourses on Davila*. Consequently, when in 1791 Jefferson's letter endorsing the principles of Paine's *Rights of Man* was published without his consent as a preface to the pamphlet, he considered he should write a letter to Adams explaining the preface.[19] The preface included a statement that this pamphlet was an excellent antidote to heresies now being propagated. Adams accepted the apology, and took the opportunity to deny that he ever had any " design or desire " to introduce either an hereditary senate or executive.[20]

During his first term as Vice-President, Adams, by his casting vote, upheld the power of the President to remove appointees without the consent of the Senate.[21] He was in favor of Philadelphia as the location of the capitol, not the Potomac.[22]

An incident of Hamilton's lack of sympathy for Adams at this time is given by Jefferson in his *Anas*. At the time *Davila* was appearing, Jefferson discussed this essay of Adams' with Hamilton. The latter expressed general condemnation of Adams' writings, and particularly *Davila*, as tending to keep public apprehension aroused and preventing a fair trial for the new government.[23]

---

[16] Same to same Sept. 25, 1790. Enclosure, *Canadian Archives, 1890*, 152.

[17] Jefferson to Adams, Paris, May 10, 1789; Adams' *Works*, VIII, 488.

[18] Adams to Jefferson, London, Dec. 6, 1787; *Ibid.*, 465.

[19] Jefferson to Adams, July 17, 1791, and same to same, Aug. 30, 1791, *Ibid.*, 504, 509.

[20] Adams to Jefferson, Braintree, July 29, 1791. *Ibid.*, 507.

[21] Adams, C. F., *Life of John Adams, Works*, I, 449.

[22] Adams to Rush, Quincy, Dec. 28, 1807. *Old Family Letters*, 175.

[23] *Complete Anas of Thomas Jefferson*, 44. Conversation with Hamilton on Aug. 13, 1791.

With the approach of the election of 1792 it was obvious that Adams should receive Federalist support. His election was a test of strength, as everyone rallied to the support of Washington. The Republican paper, the *National Gazette,* strongly supported George Clinton of New York. Privately Jefferson wrote, " The occasion of electing a Vice-President has been seized as a proper one for expressing the public sense on the doctrines of the mono-crats. There will be a strong vote against Mr. Adams, but the strength of his personal worth and his services will, I think prevail over the demerits of his political creed." [24]   Thomas Jefferson himself continued his friendship with Adams and even recommended Adams to the Virginia electors.[25]

Hamilton urged Adams to return early to Philadelphia from Quincy. He feared that a late arrival would supply ammunition for attacks. To his followers he wrote that Adams should be supported.[26] After the election he expressed gratification over the success which Adams had (cf. Table 9), declaring that it was " as great a source of satisfaction as [the election] of Mr. Clinton would have been of mortification and pain to me." [27]   The best evidence of all is that Adams stated he had Hamilton's support in 1792.[28]

For once unanimity in favor of Adams existed among the rest of the extreme Federalists. Charles Carroll of Carrollton, the leader of the Hamilton faction in Maryland, gave support and rejoiced in the victory.[29] Likewise the Wolcotts in Connecticut [30]

---

[24] Jefferson to Thomas Pinckney, Dec. 3, 1792.   Jefferson's *Works,* VI, 144.

[25] Malone, Dumas, *Jefferson and the Rights of Man* (Boston, 1951), 482.

[26] Hamilton to Adams, Philadelphia, Sept. 9, 1792. Adams' *Works,* VIII, 514; Hamilton to John Steele, Philadelphia, Oct. 15, 1792. Hamilton's *Works* (Lodge, ed.), VIII, 288.

[27] Hamilton to Jay, Philadelphia, Dec. 18, 1792. *Ibid.,* 291.

[28] Adams' *Works,* VI, 543.

[29] Carroll to John Henry, Annapolis, Dec. 3, 1792, and same to same, Dec. 16, 1792.   Rowland, Kate M., *Life and Correspondence of Charles Carroll of Carrollton* (New York, 1898), II, 190; 193.

[30] Oliver Wolcott to Oliver Wolcott, Sr., Philadelphia, Oct. 8, 1792. Also same to same, Oct. 16, 1792 and again same to same Nov. 21. Also Oliver Wolcott, Sr., to Frederick Wolcott, Middleton, Conn., Dec. 15; likewise Oliver Wolcott, Sr., to Oliver Wolcott, Middleton, Conn., Dec. 5.   Gibbs, George,

and Rufus King in New York [31] favored Adams.

In the press the chief battle concerned the alleged monarchism of Adams. *Davila* had been discontinued on account of the furor it aroused, and the storm was yet raging. In the *Gazette of the United States,* there were strenuous efforts to combat this sentiment, and to set forth Adams' merits.[32]

With the resumption of his duties as Vice-President, Adams continued to support the Federalist program, but with no better success in securing the confidence of the Hamiltonian group. His sympathies were with Hamilton for whom he had high praise as an upright and honorable official when the House investigation of the Treasury was in progress early in 1793.[33] Of some of the Republicans at this time he wrote, " We have our Robespierres and Marats, whose wills are good to do mischief, but the flesh is weak." [34] When the question of American neutrality arose in connection with the Treaty of Alliance with France, he, as one of the earliest American advocates of neutrality, and also as an early opponent of the French Revolution, naturally favored the administration policy.[35] He felt that the French Revolution was leading to dangerous experiments, and the excesses indicated too sharp a departure from a balanced government.

During 1794 on several occasions when close votes occurred in the Senate, the vote of Adams was of vital importance. On three votes in connection with the bill to enforce American neutrality, the casting vote of Adams saved this from defeat.[36]

Memoirs of the Administration of Washington and Adams, edited from the Papers on Oliver Wolcott (to be cited hereafter as Gibbs, *Wolcott*) (New York, 1846), I, 80-83.

[31] King to R. Southgate, Sept. 30, 1792. King, Charles R., *Life and Correspondence of Rufus King* (New York, 1896), I, 430.

[32] *Gazette of the United States,* 1792.

[33] Adams to Abigail Adams, Philadelphia, Jan. 24, 1793. *Letters to Wife,* II, 121.

[34] Same to same, Philadelphia, Jan. 14, 1794, *Ibid.,* 120.

[35] Same to same, Philadelphia, Dec. 19, 1793, *Ibid.,* 133.

[36] *Annals of Congress,* IV, 66-67. March 12, 1794. Also Adams to Abigail Adams, Philadelphia, March 12, 1794. *Letters to Wife,* II, 146.

TABLE 9

PRESIDENTIAL ELECTION OF 1792 [37]

(Electoral vote by states)

State	Washington	Adams	Clinton	Jefferson	Burr
New Hampshire	6	6			
Vermont	3	3			
Massachusetts	16	16			
Rhode Island	4	4			
Connecticut	9	9			
New York	12		12		
New Jersey	7	7			
Pennsylvania	15	14	1		
Delaware	3	3			
Maryland	8	8			
Virginia	21		21		
North Carolina	12		12		
South Carolina	8	7			1
Georgia	4		4		
Kentucky	4			4	
	132	77	50	4	1

In like manner his vote was necessary to kill two of the three important measures proposing discriminatory commercial legislation against England that passed the House. The three measures were: first, an act providing for the sequestration of British debts; second, an act suspending commercial intercourse with England; and third, an act levying an embargo on British goods. All of these he strongly disapproved.[38] The sequestration of British debts was defeated without his vote, but that suspending commercial intercourse required it.[39] Likewise, on April 28, he killed the bill levying an embargo.[40] In connection with this last measure there is an interesting incident. Senator James Ross of

[37] Stanwood, *History of the Presidency*, 39.

[38] Adams to Abigail Adams, Philadelphia, April 7, 1794. *Letters to Wife*, II, 153.

[39] Adams to Abigail Adams, Philadelphia, April 15, 1794. *Letters to Wife*, II, 155.

[40] *Ibid.*

Pennsylvania was of the extreme Hamiltonian Federalists. On earlier votes during that day he was present. On this important measure, he did not vote. These circumstances make credible an incident which is described by Porcupine: He declares that on the third day of Mr. Ross's senatorship,[41] on a question to suspend the commercial intercourse with England,[42] Ross at first voted against it, but left as two more senators for the bill came into the Senate. " By this act of Mr. Ross the question was supported by 13 against 13, and the Vice-President, Mr. Adams, was forced to commit himself by giving his casting negative to the third reading of the bill. It has been suspected and alleged, that the party among the Federalists who are enemies of Mr. Adams meant to sacrifice him in the gap, and it is well to know that Mr. Ross's particular friends tried to get Mr. Pinckney elected President, instead of Mr. Adams, in 1796." [43]

The appointment of Jay to negotiate with England Adams highly approved.[44] He also approved the Federalist policy of denying to Gallatin his seat in the Senate,[45] although Gallatin received the impression that Adams was in favor of him.[46] The services of Adams as a commissioner of the sinking fund, in which capacity he acted in agreement with Hamilton, have been mentioned in Chapter 4.

In other respects, however, he continued to show independence of the extreme Federalists. When the Federalists opposed Samuel Adams in the Massachusetts gubernatorial contest John Adams

[41] Ross had taken his seat on April 24, hence the 28th was the third day he attended. *Annals of Congress*, IV, 87, April 24, 1794.

[42] He is mistaken, having confused the non-intercourse and embargo acts.

[43] *Porcupine's Gazette*, November, 1799; *Porcupine's Works*, XI, 111. The account of Ross's actions is in accordance with the *Annals*. With Ross present the Federalists had fourteen votes on an early test of strength over the measure. With Ross absent and two more Republicans present, the vote was thirteen to thirteen.

[44] Adams to Abigail Adams, Philadelphia, April 19, 1794. *Letters to Wife*, II, 156.

[45] Same to same, Philadelphia, March 2, 1794. *Ibid.*, 144.

[46] Albert Gallatin to Mrs. Gallatin, Philadelphia, March 5, 1794. Adams, Henry, *Life of Albert Gallatin* (Philadelphia, 1879), 121.

disapproved strongly, holding that the great services Samuel
Adams had rendered during the Revolution were such that he
deserved to be continued in office.[47] After the election he rejoiced
that Adams had won, stating: " I should have thought human
nature dead in the Massachusetts if it had been otherwise." [48]
This is indicative of a tendency which was always strong in
Adams, a partiality to Revolutionary Whigs and a distrust of
old Tories. In this he followed in the tradition of the Republicans.
In this same election he wished that his good friend Elbridge
Gerry, rather than Moses Gill, had been chosen Lieutenant-
Governor. Gerry was a Middlesex County follower of Adams who
had opposed the adoption of the Constitution. Although distrusted by the ruling Massachusetts Federalists of the Essex
Junto, he was not yet active in opposition to the Federalists. This
predilection for Gerry led Adams and Cabot into quite a dispute
before several other Federalists. Dining one night at Wolcott's,
King, George Cabot, and Oliver Ellsworth started a conversation
derogatory to Gerry. Adams at once defended him strongly,
asserting that his merits were inferior to none except the present
Governor, Samuel Adams.[49] Gerry is one of the best examples of
the type of moderate whom the Essex Junto in Massachusetts
distrusted, but who had the complete confidence of Adams.

Another story illustrative of the extent to which the Federalists
felt uncertain of Adams was told by George Cabot long after the
event took place. Cabot was sent to sound out Adams on the
question of the dismissal of Genêt, French Minister to the United
States who was meddling in American politics, trying to create
opposition to the policy of neutrality. Cabot was sent because
the policy of demanding Genêt's recall was so controversial it
was thought necessary to assure all possible support from doubt-

[47] Adams to Abigail Adams, Philadelphia, April 7, 1794, *Letters to Wife*,
II, 154.
[48] Same to same, April 19, 1794. *Ibid.*, 157. The conduct of the Federalists
in the election he termed " an egregious blunder." Same to same, May 17, 1794.
Ibid., 160.
[49] Adams to Abigail Adams, May 21, 1795. Adams' *Works*, I, 479.

ful persons.[50] Of course Adams was strongly in favor of the measure. It was a general characteristic of the Hamiltonian wing to view Adams as further removed from them than he was.

Adams and the other Federalists also differed over the founding of the democratic clubs in the United States. He wrote that he had, in his youth, always found pleasure in such organizations, and that he felt they had a perfect right to exist. Naturally he did not approve disorders on the part of the clubs.[51]

Just as Adams and Jefferson had maintained a fairly close relationship during Adams' first term as Vice-President, they continued on this basis during the second term. They continued to exchange several friendly letters. The main point of interest was the proposal made to both of them to aid in the transfer of the Academy of Geneva to the United States. Other topics were discussed as well.[52]

With the publication of Jay's Treaty, the most heated political discussion of this period took place. Adams strongly favored ratification. He thought that Washington should not have hesitated an instant in signing it.[53] The right of the House to ask for papers he believed in, but trusted that it would not be abused.[54] If the House withheld the appropriation he believed that the Senate and Executive would be reduced to virtual nullity. In this respect he shared with the rest of the Federalists distrust over the pretentions of the more popular branch of the legislature.[55] Those of the Massachusetts Federalists who voted with the opposition he scored strongly, and thought the people should not return them. These included J. B. Varnum, W. Lyman, and Henry Dearborn.[56] The opposition of Samuel Adams to the treaty he regretted, but looked upon the Federalists as partly responsible,

[50] Lodge, Henry Cabot, *Life and Letters of George Cabot* (Boston, 1877), 64.
[51] Adams to Abigail Adams, December 14, 1794. *Letters to Wife*, II, 172.
[52] Jefferson to Adams, Monticello, Dec. 6, 1795 and same to same, Monticello, Feb. 28, 1796. Adams' *Works*, VIII, 516-17.
[53] Adams to Abigail Adams, Jan. 7, 1796. *Letters to Wife*, II, 198.
[54] Same to same, April 19, 1796. *Ibid.*, 223.
[55] Same to same, March 13, 1796. *Ibid.*, 210.
[56] Same to same, March 25, 1796. *Ibid.*, 221.

as they had stirred him up. He asserted that he did not believe in opposing Samuel Adams.[57]

Attending the debates in the House over the appropriation for the Treaty, Adams and Supreme Court Justice James Iredell, who went together, were moved to tears by the famous oration of Fisher Ames on the Federalists' side.[58] Thus it was that the last important measure of Washington's administration was brought to a successful issue. From this time everything in politics looked towards the coming election of Washington's successor to the presidency.

[57] Adams to Abigail Adams, Philadelphia, April 16, 1796. *Ibid.*, 221.
[58] Adams to Abigail Adams, Philadelphia, April 30, 1796. *Letters to Wife,* II, 226.

Chapter 6

The Election of 1796

B^Y 1796 it was generally known that Washington would retire. He evidently looked upon Adams as his successor. In March he had a conference with Adams and stated that his decision in favor of retirement had definitely been made. The two then went over general policies. Adams was surprised to find that they were in such close agreement. Upon the attitude to be pursued toward France and England, quite evidently that of neutrality, they were in accord. They also held the same views upon the American parties.[1]

At this juncture an interesting maneuver is recorded by Adams, which likewise demonstrates the general recognition of the gap between him and Hamilton. Apparently it involved a hint at running him on the ticket with Jefferson, the latter to be President. He unfolded it to his wife: " The Southern gentry are playing, at present, a very artful game, which I may develope to you in confidence hereafter, under the seal of secrecy. Both in conversation and in letters they are representing the Vice-President as a man of moderation. Although rather inclined to limited monarchy, and somewhat attached to the English, he is much less so than Jay or Hamilton. For their part, for the sake of conciliation, they should be very willing he should be continued as Vice-President, provided the Northern gentlemen would consent that Jefferson should be President. I must humbly thank you for your kind condescension, Messieurs Transchesapeakes." [2]

Despite this recognition by Washington, Adams was not at all sure that he could secure the support of the Federalists. The great propaganda campaign in favor of the ratification of Jay's

---

[1] Adams to Abigail Adams, Philadelphia, March 25, 1796. *Letters to Wife,* II, 214.

[2] Adams to Abigail Adams, Philadelphia, Jan. 23, 1796. *Letters to Wife,* II, 192.

Treaty he thought might culminate in the substitution of Jay for himself. At this time Robert Goodloe Harper, the prominent representative from South Carolina, wrote one of his pamphlets in defense of Jay's Treaty.[3] In it he defended Jay and asserted that Jay was no enemy of France. On January 19, 1796, Jay wrote to Harper thanking him for this remark and declaring that he would take the opportunity to clarify his position. He is a partisan of no country, desiring that America should not meddle in foreign politics. Pointing out that he is not of British descent, he could have no prejudice for England on that account. He admires the English institutions and the character of the nation. America has modeled on these.

As one despising arbitrary governments, Jay declared that he rejoiced at first in the French Revolution. But the more radical tendencies of the French Revolution, as expressed in the second constitution and the execution of Louis XVI, he deplored. He still expressed hope that France would achieve a free government and independence from foreign danger, but that no European power would achieve supremacy. In conclusion, Jay summarized his program in a letter written from London to the Secretary of State. He asserts that he daily becomes more convinced of English friendship for America. " Let us cherish it. . . . Let us cultivate friendship with all nations." [4] In subsequent editions of the pamphlet this letter was uniformly included.

To his wife, in regard to this, Adams wrote: " The letter from Jay in the enclosed pamphlet is called by the southern gentlemen, an electioneering letter. The toasts in the enclosed paper are no doubt electioneering toasts. If Washington continues, [This is before their conference], I suppose Jefferson and Jay may both be set up for President and Vice President both, and let the lot come out as it will, the chief contest will be between these two, according to present appearances." [5]

[3] Harper, Robert Goodloe, *Address to His Constituents Containing His Reasons for Approving of the Treaty . . . with Great Britain . . .* (Philadelphia, 1796).

[4] Harper, Robert Goodloe, *Select Works* (Baltimore, 1814), 43-46.

[5] Adams to Abigail Adams, Philadelphia, Feb. 20, 1796. *Letters to Wife,* II, 203.

The toasts lend credence to the fears thus expressed. That aristocratic organization, the First Troop of Philadelphia Cavalry, held a banquet at this time. Toasts were drunk to Jay, Hamilton and Adams, with ten, eleven and nine cheers respectively being given as each was proposed.[6] In New York the " Sons of Herman " toasted Jay in the regular order, and then the chair gave the volunteer toast, " The true and virtuous patriot John Jay," which was greeted with nine cheers.[7] In Boston and Newburyport, Massachusetts, Adams and Jay were toasted together.[8]

The general uncertainty which Adams felt as to his own position was frequently stated in his letters to his wife. He was able to view with equanimity the idea that either Jay or Jefferson should succeed. " The government will go on as well as ever. Jefferson could not stir a step in any other system than that which is begun. Jay would not wish it." [9] Later he was more apprehensive should the choice fall to Jefferson. " The great affair is as it was. I hear frequent reflections which indicate that Jefferson, although in good hands, he might do very well; yet, in such hands as will hold him, he would endanger too much." [10]

By the close of February and the first of March, many had spoken to him, and he was assured that " the succession would not be passed over." [11] However, he still conjectured that Patrick Henry, Jefferson, Jay, and Hamilton would all be voted for.[12] He was determined not to serve if the election should go into the house. Only if he had a clear mandate by a majority of all the electoral votes would he serve.[13]

As a matter of fact support for Adams was strong. As Mr.

---

[6] *Gazette of the United States*, Feb. 25, 1796.

[7] *Ibid.*, Feb. 27, 1796. Some allowance might be made for the fact that after from twelve to twenty regular toasts, the assemblage would usually be in a condition to cheer with great enthusiasm, thus the greater number accompanying volunteers.

[8] *Gazette of the United States*, Feb. 22, 1796.

[9] Adams to Abigail Adams, Feb. 15, 1796. *Letters to Wife*, II, 201.

[10] Same to same, Feb. 27, 1796, *Ibid.*, 204.

[11] Same to same, Feb. 27 and March 1, 1796, *Ibid.*, 204; 206.

[12] *Ibid.*

[13] Adams to Mrs. Adams, April 9, 1796. *Letters to Wife*, II, 217.

Gibbs has put it, he was the " inevitable candidate." [14] There is
no evidence, however, that Adams had a part in choosing his
running mate. This was the work of the leader of the party.

In selecting the ostensible candidate for Vice-President, the
goal of Hamilton was not to choose someone like Jay, who would
split the party openly, but to select a Southern candidate. Votes
would be then sought for him in the North on the ground that he
should receive equal support with Adams. But there would be
hope of Southern votes detached from Adams to bring him in
ahead. Such a candidate should be able to pass in the South
as a moderate.

The first idea which occurred was that Patrick Henry should
be run with Adams. Hamilton had Rufus King write to John
Marshall about the matter. The latter then had General Henry
Lee approach Henry. It must have appeared, even if not
specifically stated, that should Henry run, he would have a good
chance in the manner outlined above. At any rate, Henry,
apparently because he was apprehensive of the difficulties of high
office, declined.[15]

Because of doubt as to Patrick Henry's availability, even before
the refusal, King suggested that as Thomas Pinckney of South
Carolina was just returning with a good treaty with Spain, which
would make him popular in the South and West, why not run
him.[16] The idea met with Hamilton's favor. In fact, he liked
it better than the other.[17] Accordingly Thomas Pinckney's
candidacy was launched by the Hamilton group.

[14] Gibbs, *Wolcott*, I, 378.

[15] Marshall to King, Richmond, April 19, 1796, Hamilton Papers (Library
of Congress), 28/3880, and May 24, 1796, King's *King*, II, 48. The explanation of Henry's transition from opposition to the constitution to Federalism is
given in a passage from a letter written by Edward Carrington to George
Washington, Oct. 13, 1796: " We know too that he is improving his fortune
fast, which must additionally attach him to the existing Government & order,
the only Guarantees of property." Beveridge, Albert, *Life of John Marshall*
(Boston, 1916), II, 125, note 3.

[16] King to Hamilton, May 2, 1796. King's *King*, II, 46; Hamilton's *Works*,
VI, 113.

[17] Hamilton to King, May 4, 1796. King's *King*, II, 47; Hamilton's *Works*,
VI, 114.

The idea that the choice was to be between Henry and Pinckney for the vice-presidency received general circulation. In 1796 it would have been difficult to make an arrangement which would assure the election of a preferred candidate without handling the matter as Hamilton had in 1789, i. e. deliberately scatter some of the votes among various candidates for the vice-presidency. The criticism advanced of the system then pursued was that it was obviously pressed beyond possible necessity. The fact that electors would all vote on the same day precluded any general agreement to wait and let the last of those voting withhold votes from Pinckney if necessary.

The policy which Hamilton pursued, however, was that of insisting upon an equal vote for Adams and Pinckney in the states above the Potomac, while the South Carolina situation was obviously in favor of Pinckney. The only way there could have been a good chance for the election of the two candidates would have been for the party to have a large majority. By 1800 parties were sufficiently stable that the electors could be better relied on. In 1796, this was not the case.

There are several points of view from which the Federalists approached the election. To a certain extent these have been presented by Chauncy Goodrich. First there were those who felt that the election of Adams was the chief aim of the Federalists, and all efforts should be directed towards this goal. Second, a considerable number felt that the election would be so close that it would not be possible to do otherwise than to vote equally for both — that to throw away votes from Pinckney would be to run the risk of complete defeat. Third, there were those who preferred Pinckney as President and Adams as Vice-President to the possibility of Jefferson as Vice-President. As a subdivision of this third group, or more exactly what would be a fourth group, Goodrich admits that there were probably some in Pennsylvania who preferred Pinckney to Adams.[18]

Goodrich's analysis gives a correct view of the situation. That the group which preferred Pinckney was not confined to Penn-

---

[18] Goodrich to Oliver Wolcott, Sr., Philadelphia, Dec. 17, 1796. Gibbs, *Wolcott*, I, 411.

sylvania is quite evident. The letter did not state that such was
the case. It now becomes of interest to trace the campaign
between the Republicans on the one hand, and the divided
Federalists on the other.

Apparently there was either something like a caucus in the
spring of 1796 to ratify Hamilton's choice, or the news was passed
around. In July, William Loughton Smith wrote from Charleston
that before leaving Philadelphia it was understood that the
candidates would be Adams and Pinckney.[19] In September there
were apparently still loose ends to be caught up, as Jay was being
discussed in Delaware.[20]

Various methods were pursued to persuade New England to
vote unanimously for Adams and Pinckney. Oliver Wolcott, of
Connecticut, who succeeded Hamilton as Secretary of the
Treasury, wrote to his father, Oliver Wolcott, Sr., that New
England and the South should vote unanimously for both candidates. He gave assurances that the middle states would throw
away votes to bring in Adams. It would not do for either the
South or New England to do this, as the two should build up
faith in each other within the party.[21] Whether this advice was
merely being passed on by Wolcott, and he gave it in good faith,
or whether he realized that nothing of the sort would happen in
the middle states, does not appear. At any rate he anticipated
there might be an untoward result, as he stated, " It is possible
that the events may be different from our wishes, but it will
be the fault of the constitution if such be the case." [22] After
Adet's famous message on behalf of Jefferson, threatening a war
on the part of France were Jefferson not elected, Wolcott declared
that this would probably prevent Southern votes for Adams.
The consequence would be the election of Pinckney. This would

---

[19] Smith to King, Charleston, July 23, 1796.   King's *King*, II, 66.

[20] William Vans Murray to James McHenry, Sept. 24, 1796. Steiner, Bernard C., *Life and Correspondence of James McHenry* (Cleveland, 1907), 198.

[21] Wolcott to Wolcott, Sr., Philadelphia, Oct. 16, 1796.   Gibbs, *Wolcott*, I,
387.

[22] Wolcott to Wolcott, Sr., Philadelphia, Oct. 17, 1796.   Gibbs, *Wolcott*, I,
387.

be regretted, as Adams was the better; but to try to bring him in involved too great a risk.[23]

This point of view became generally accepted among those not in favor of risking the chance for Adams alone, or those not in favor of Adams at all. The equal vote for both in the East would bring about the choice of Pinckney. From New York, Judge R. Troup, who was closely in touch with Hamilton's ideas, informed Rufus King, who had just been sent as Minister to England, that the New York electors would all vote for Adams and Pinckney. " I am inclining to think, and such is the inclination of our friends here, that Mr. Adams will not succeed; but we have Mr. Pinckney completely in our power if our Eastern friends do not refuse him some of their votes under an idea that if they vote for him unanimously, they may injure Mr. Adams. Upon this subject, we are writing all our Eastern friends and endeavoring to make them accord with us in voting unanimously both for Mr. Adams and Mr. Pinckney." [24]

In Philadelphia, the same idea was held by the wealthy Senator William Bingham. He declared that Adams' friends might count upon a small majority, but that on so momentous an occasion it was agreed among them not to risk this. " It is therefore deemed expedient to recommend to Federal Electors an uniform vote to give for Mr. Pinckney, which with those he will obtain to the Southward, detached from Mr. Adams, will give him a decided majority over the other Candidates." [25] It is a safe assumption that his fellow senator, James Ross, was anxious that this should be the outcome.

Fisher Ames agreed that the proper thing to do would be to vote equally for Adams and Pinckney.[26] He thought, though, that the entire matter would look very odd. Moreover it would present the procedures of American elections in a curious light to Europe. Unaware of the degree to which the knowledge of

[23] Same to same, Philadelphia, Nov. 19, 1796, and Nov. 27, 1796. *Ibid.*, 396; 402.

[24] Troup to King, New York, Nov. 15, 1796. King's *Works*, II, 110.

[25] Bingham to King, Philadelphia, Nov. 29, 1796. King's *Works*, II, 112.

[26] Ames to Thomas Dwight, Dedham, Oct. 25, 1796. Ames's *Works*, I, 204.

Hamilton's support of Pinckney would spread, he expected
Pinckney to receive Republican votes in the South in preference
to Adams.[27]

In the press the schism in the Federalist ranks was as noticeable
as in the private correspondence. The longest series in opposition
to Adams which the *Gazette of the United States* published was
that by "A Federalist." The attack pursued was dual. In order
to aid Pinckney in the South, the monarchical aspects of Adams'
creed were set forth. One of the first of these pieces states: " The
opinions of Mr. Adams in favor of an hereditary President and of
an hereditary senate, and his desire to see them introduced
among us, *are the great objections* to him, which prevail conclu-
sively with all the friends of the federal Constitution, who are
opposed to his election. Hence we see, that though Mr. Pinckney
is understood to be set up by the same persons, no objections
whatever have been made to him. This gentleman gives rise to
no alarm even among the friends of other candidates, because he
is universally admitted to be *a friend to representative or elective
government.* Nay, even the papers characterized as Anti-federal
and Jacobin, have not sounded any alarum concerning the Republican Pinckney." [28]

On the other hand, for the extreme Federalists, the argument
took the trend that Adams in matters of finance was no better
than Jefferson; that he did not have the confidence of those who
are or were connected with the treasury department. This aspect
of the case has been treated in Chapter 4. The significance of this
series is apparent as the *Gazette* was the Federalist organ. It
carried the legal advertisements, the Senate advertisements, and
those of all the departments. Many of the articles which set forth
policy reflected the opinions of some of the Hamilton wing of
the party, as is true of this series.

" The Federalist " stated that Jefferson was too democratic, but
that Pinckney should be perfectly satisfactory as between the

---

[27] Ames to C. Gore, Philadelphia, Dec. 3, 1796. *Ibid.*, 205.
[28] *Gazette of the United States*, Nov. 9, 1796.

monarchist Adams and the democrat. He proceeded to show that there was no reason for a Federalist to prefer Adams to Jefferson.[29]

In reply to this series " Philo-Adams "[30] charged that "A Federalist " was a noted Tory, one " Janus " who had influence with the present government. He had welcomed the British when they took Philadelphia. Adams aroused the Tories by the publication of his letters to Dr. Calkoen on the American Revolution,[31] wherein he mentioned them by name. " Janus " should recognize that if his efforts resulted in Federalist defeat, by his opposing their candidate, Jefferson was no more favorable to Tories than was Adams.

" Union Among Federalists " defended Adams.[32] " Thousands "[33] and other correspondents[34] demanded the exclusion of "A Federalist " from the Gazette. What did a Federalist paper mean by permitting such attacks? " Eastern Shore," the pseudonym of William Vans Murray, representative from Maryland, pointed to the danger of a Federalist schism throughout the union, and urged all Maryland electors to support Adams.[35]

The longest series of articles setting forth the Federalist position in the campaign was written by William Loughton Smith under the name of " Phocion." Smith was a representative from Charleston, S. C., and a partisan of Hamilton. " Phocion " ran in the Gazette[36] and a number of other papers. It appeared as a pamphlet as well.[37] William Vans Murray wrote articles in the

[29] Ibid., Nov. 9, 11, 15, 16, 24, 29, 30, 1796.
[30] Gazette of the United States, Dec. 1, 1796.
[31] Adams' Works, VII, 265 ff. These were published in 1790.
[32] Gazette of the United States, Dec. 2, 1796. From the Maryland Herald.
[33] Ibid., Nov. 19, 1796. [34] Ibid., Nov. 26, 1796.
[35] Ibid., Dec. 5, and 6, 1796. From the Maryland Journal, dated October 19, 1796.
[36] Started in the Gaeztte on October 14, 1796.
[37] Smith, William Loughton, The Pretensions of Thomas Jefferson to the Presidency Examined; and the Charges against John Adams Refuted. . . . n. p. October, 1796. Part II, November, 1796. So little attention was given to the merits and services of Adams in this pamphlet, that Adams and Gerry suspected it was part of the plot to pay attention chiefly to attacking Jefferson, while giving little attention to the Federalist candidate. Gerry to Adams, Cambridge, Feb. 3, 1797. Adams' Works, VIII, 520-21. Also Ibid., 524 n. 1.

Gazette [38] in addition to those named. These were published along with " Phocion " in pamphlet form.[39]

That there was considerable danger from the charges of monarchism is certain. Particularly in Virginia was this the case. The impression was generally held that Adams was a High-Federalist, even a Monarchist. Leven Powell, the one Virginia Federalist elector who was chosen, in his circular letter to the freeholders of Loudoun and Fauquier Counties, declared that he was for a man who was neither of the British nor the French party. Consequently, as he regarded Adams and Jefferson as the representatives of these two groups, he first declared he would support Patrick Henry. He averred that Fisher Ames, who had travelled through Virginia, declared Henry to be preferable to Adams, who was regarded as too pro-British.[40] " Civis," a writer whose name was synonymous with the Junto, denied this on behalf of Ames.[41] Another of the Virginia electors was for Adams and Henry.[42] The Virginia Republicans declared that Henry was simply being held up as a stalking horse for Adams, who was the real candidate.[43] Powell actually cast his vote for Adams and Pinckney. Upon being elected to Congress he found he had been mistaken about Adams, and in 1800 became a strong supporter of the Adams branch of the Federalist party.

Robert Goodloe Harper of South Carolina fully approved the plan to run Pinckney ahead of Adams. He felt that the plan of presenting Pinckney as more moderate than the monarchist Adams was winning some Republicans. Writing to Hamilton he held out hopes for electoral votes for Pinckney from South Carolina, Georgia, and North Carolina. He declared that the

[38] Starting in the *Gazette* on Nov. 5, 1796.

[39] Murray, William Vans, *A Short Vindication of Mr. Adams' Defense of American Constitutions*, added to Part II of the above. This is designed to remedy part of the deficiencies of Smith's pamphlet, in the manner indicated in note 37.

[40] *Gazette of the United States*, Sept. 15, 1796; Oct. 6, 1796.

[41] *Ibid.*, Oct. 11, 1796.

[42] Richmond *Virginia Gazette* (Nicholson's), Oct. 8, 1796. Charles Simms to the Freeholders of Prince William, Stafford, and Fairfax counties.

[43] Fredericksburg *Virginia Herald*, Oct. 21, 1796.

Pinckneys themselves were working strongly for Adams, but since they had left the state, Adams' South Carolina electoral votes may well have declined from three to two.[44]

Amidst the cross-currents a curious one developed from New Jersey. Jonathan Dayton, member of the House of Representatives, communicated with Theodore Sedgwick, Senator from Massachusetts and a chief lieutenant of Hamilton. Dayton sought to convince Sedgwick that Aaron Burr was independent of the Republicans, and that the only chance of defeating Jefferson was for the Federalists to abandon both Adams and Pinckney, who could not be elected in any event, and make an agreement with Burr. Meanwhile they should support him in New Jersey and elsewhere. Dayton was close to Burr, it should be noted. Sedgwick sent copies of this correspondence to Hamilton, but Hamilton merely endorsed it, " concerning Dayton's intrigue for Burr." Hamilton, quite clearly, had no idea of endorsing Burr.[45]

In Connecticut one aspect of the campaign is interesting as indicating the extreme provincialism of this state. One of the writers in the *Connecticut Courant,* " Pelham," asserted that the time was drawing nigh when a separation of the New England States from the Union should be considered. In order to prevent the corruption of French influence this would be necessary. " I shall . . . endeavor to prove," he states, " the impossibility of an union for any long period in the future, both from the moral and political habits of the citizens of the Southern states; and finally examine carefully to see whether we have not already approached the era when they must be divided." [46] This sectional bias was to be the nemesis of Pinckney in Connecticut.

Reports of the Federalist intrigue against Adams were published in the Republican press. The Boston *Chronicle* declared that the Secretary of State, Timothy Pickering, was intriguing against Adams because he would not follow the exact policy of Hamilton.

[44] Harper to Hamilton, Raleigh, N. C., Nov. 4, 1798, Hamilton *Papers,* 29/3789-3790.

[45] The correspondence is dated from Nov. 12 to Nov. 19, 1796 and the originals are in the Hamilton *Papers,* 29/4002.

[46] Welling, " Connecticut Federalism," *loc. cit.,* 280 ff.

This was commented upon by the Philadelphia *Aurora*.[47] The *Chronicle* as well as the southern Republican papers were constantly attacking Adams and supporting Jefferson. Selections from "A Federalist" appeared in the Republican press.[48]

The Massachusetts situation in regard to Adams and Pinckney was set forth by George Cabot in a letter to Oliver Wolcott. He declared that no decision had yet been reached, nor would one be reached until the actual time for voting. If the electors could make Adams President and Pinckney Vice-President this would be done. But if it were fairly certain that Adams could not be carried, while Pinckney could, the latter would be given equal support. He assured Wolcott that proper attention would be given towards securing an equal vote for Pinckney.[49] After the election he asserted that he was for Adams, but not for risking anything to elect him.[50]

Such an idea as this concerning the outlook in Massachusetts must have been known to Hamilton. Apparently he attempted to supply the stimulus which would cause the electors to support Pinckney. In the Boston *Centinel* of December 7, just as the electors were meeting, the following paragraph appeared, under a New York date line of November 26: " We have good authority to believe the election of electors in Vermont is invalid — being grounded on a *Resolve* of the Legislature, not a law."

Underneath this there appeared a note by the editor declaring that it was certainly to be hoped that this would not be true. If so, it shows the " necessity of union in the electors." Then there follows an article by a " True American," declaring: " The account received in town yesterday of the probable loss of the Vermont votes for President and Vice President, may have an unfortunate effect on the decision of the Electors of this State. Every one feels deeply interested in the event, and the subject was yesterday discussed in the different private circles. Too many opinions have appeared to preponderate in favor of supporting

[47] *Chronicle*, Dec. 10, 1796, and *Aurora*, Dec. 19, 1796.
[48] *Chronicle*, Dec. 1, 1796.
[49] Cabot to Wolcott, Nov. 30, 1796. Lodge's *Cabot*, 112.
[50] Same to same, April 3, 1797, Gibbs, *Wolcott*, I, 448.

Mr. Pinckney, at the risque of sacrificing Mr. Adams; but it will become the electors to consider that the people at large ought to be their guide. . . ." The writer further declares that Adams' own feelings, and the reward which he deserves should be gravely considered. He will probably exceed Jefferson even without Vermont.

". . . Shall a momentary pusillinamity in Mr. Adams's friends put Mr. Pinckney in the presidential chair? Shall we by grasping at a shadow, lose the substance? No, Mr. Russell,[51] Firmness is expected in the electors, and from their characters we may fairly presume they will not disappoint the public." [52]

In the next issue comes the announcement of the vote cast by both Massachusetts and Rhode Island. Three of Massachusetts' sixteen electors had not voted for Pinckney; the same was true of all four in Rhode Island. On the Vermont matter the following note appears: "A gentleman who left Vermont on Tuesday last says he heard nothing in the state of any informality in the choice of the Electors. . . ." [53] Finally, on December 28 comes this intelligence:

Vermont, December 14

We have seen in the Centinel a doubt of the validity of our votes for President and Vice-President, but we can have no idea on what ground that doubt is founded. There is a law in this state which points out the mode of appointing Electors, and they were made agreeably to that law. Our votes were unanimous for Adams and Pinkney [sic]; and our prayer is that they may fill the first and second offices in the general government; and then they will be well filled.[54]

For what seems to be the source of this entire affair there is a letter from Stephen Higginson, prominent Boston merchant, and the member of the Junto closest to Hamilton. On December 9 he wrote that Hamilton's letter containing the intelligence about Vermont had enabled him to secure all but three votes for Pinckney. Prior to this the majority had been for throwing away

---

[51] Major Benjamin Russell, editor of the *Centinel*.
[52] *Centinel*, Dec. 7, 1796.
[53] *Ibid.*, Dec. 10, 1796.   [54] *Ibid.*, Dec. 28, 1796.

their votes. Adams' particular friends have succeeded with three of the electors. He further conjectures that if the rest of the New England states have voted for both equally, the votes detached from Adams which Pinckney will receive in the South and middle states should bring him in. He expects that Adams will fail, and will be greatly angered.[55] As Higginson, in common with a practice which extended to Cabot and Jonathan Jackson, as well as to other members of the Junto, burned his papers,[56] it is a safe assumption that the letter of Hamilton will never be recovered.

There were puzzled comments in the Philadelphia papers, but no confirmation of irregularity in the Vermont vote was forthcoming. Madison wrote to Jefferson on December 25, " Unless the Vermont election, of which little has of late been said, should contain some fatal vice in it, Mr. Adams may be considered as the President elect." On January 8, he wrote again, " If the Vermont votes should be valid, as is now generally supposed, Mr. Adams [is elected]." [57] Nothing arose about this matter in Congress, and Adams as Vice-President was permitted to accept and count the returns without question.

The question naturally arises, what was the source of Hamilton's information; and how seriously did he regard it? There could have been nothing more opportune than such intelligence as this, enabling him to sound the alarm just as the Massachusetts electors were about to cast their votes. The date of his letter as given by Higginson is November 28; the newspaper dispatch appeared in the *Centinel* on December 7, based on news from New York of November 26. It is highly probable that the *Centinel* story is simply based on Hamilton's letter. Moreover, it is not probable that the point raised would have affected the validity of the returns, even if true.[58]

[55] Higginson to Hamilton, Boston, Dec. 9, 1796. Hamilton's *Works*, VI, 185.

[56] Higginson, Thomas Wentworth, *Life and Times of Stephen Higginson* (Boston, 1907), 183-84.

[57] Madison to Jefferson, Philadelphia, Dec. 25, 1796 and same to same, Jan. 8, 1797. Madison's *Works* (Congress ed.), II, 109-10.

[58] In regard to the power of the legislature in choosing electors the Consti-

TABLE 10 [59]

ELECTORAL VOTE FOR PRESIDENCY IN 1796

State	Adams	Jefferson	Pinckney	Burr	S. Adams	Ellsworth	Scat.
New Hampshire	6					6	
Vermont	4		4				
Massachusetts	16		13			1	2
Rhode Island	4					4	
Connecticut	9		4				5
New York	12		12				
New Jersey	7		7				
Pennsylvania	1	14	2	13			
Delaware	3		3				
Maryland	7	4	4	3			2
Virginia	1	20	1	1	15		4
N. Carolina	1	11	1	6			5
S. Carolina		8	8				
Georgia		4					4
Kentucky		4		4			
Tennessee		3		3			
	71	68	59	30	15	11	22

tution (Art. II, Sect. 1) states, " Each State shall appoint, in such manner as the Legislature thereof may direct, a number of electors, equal to the whole number of Senators and Representatives. . . . " At this time the majority of the electors were chosen by the State Legislatures, in such manner as was agreed by law beforehand.

It is of interest to consider the decision of Chief Justice Fuller in the case of *McPherson* v. *Slacker* (1892). After considering the above clause, he declared, " . . . The legislative power is the supreme authority except as limited by the constitution of the state. . . .

.   .   .   .

" . . . The legislature possesses plenary authority to direct the manner of appointment, and might itself exercise the appointing power by joint ballot or concurrence of the two houses, or according to such mode as designated." 146 *United States Supreme Court Reports*, 25.

The microfilm of the *Journal* of the Vermont General Assembly shows that the first law providing for choice of electors was passed on November 1, 1791, concurred in by the Governor and Council on Nov. 3, and duly became a law. *Journal, 1791*, 37, 44, 47. At the next session a bill was enacted providing for a time and place of meeting for the electors. *Journal, 1792*, 88, 98, 102. Electors were chosen under this act in 1792. There is no difference between the procedure for enactment of these acts and any others.

[59] Stanwood, Edward, *History of the Presidency*, 51.

It now remains to consider the results of the election. The point which is most interesting is that involving the motives which brought about a preference for Adams in certain states. Table 10 shows the electoral vote by states.

In regard to Pennsylvania Goodrich indicates that some of the Federalists of that state had endangered the Federalist ticket by reason of opposition to Adams. Apparently he is inclined to place part of the blame for the loss of Pennsylvania on this schism. In view of the attacks on Adams in the *Gazette,* this is not an illogical conclusion. Also he no doubt has reference to one of the two Federalist electors voting for Jefferson and Pinckney. He mentions Hamilton's writing to Connecticut in an effort to secure an equal vote for Pinckney, but attributes all Hamilton's efforts to a desire to prevent the choice of Jefferson as Vice-President.[60] As the situation in Pennsylvania is of particular interest in comparison with 1800, the returns in Table 11 are of value.

These total a majority for Adams of 980. When the returns for the western counties of Fayette, Green, and Westmoreland were added, Jefferson had a majority of 120 out of the entire 20,000 votes cast. Two Federal electors were chosen, being ahead of the lowest Republicans. One of these voted for Adams and Pinckney, the other for Jefferson and Pinckney. A study of the popular vote shows the extent to which the Federalists were dependent upon agrarian support. (Map 1 and Appendix I give the location of the counties.) The subsequent disintegration of this agrarian support under the impact of the direct tax is to be observed by comparing this election with the election of 1800, to be considered hereafter. In 1796 the Federalists came close. In 1800 they were swamped in the popular vote.

In New England two factors produced a preference for Adams. The first of these was local pride and sectional feeling. This is best exemplified in the case of Connecticut. There the electors based their disregard of Hamilton's instructions on reasons which may be described as a concentration of New England provincialism. Oliver Wolcott, Sr., one of the electors, and Governor of

[60] Goodrich to Wolcott, Dec. 17, 1796. Gibbs, *Wolcott*, I, 413.

TABLE 11 [61]

PENNSYLVANIA POPULAR VOTE FOR ELECTORS IN 1796 BY COUNTIES

County	Adams	Jefferson
Philadelphia City	1,091	1,733
Philadelphia County	391	1,833
Lancaster	2,061	619
Bucks	1,001	361
Cumberland	238	857
Berks	576	722
Northumberland and Lycoming	32	802
Dauphin	464	233
York	3,224	141
Delaware	313	129
Chester	530	120
Northampton	370	460
Montgomery	533	333
Luzerne	407	8
Lafayette	406	66
Majorities [62]		
Mifflin		402
Huntingdon	291	
Bedford		171
Somerset	22	
Allegheny		315
Washington		1,258
Franklin		106

the state, wrote his son, the Secretary of the Treasury, that they had preferred Adams. In the first place they looked upon him as the best and most experienced. Second, they felt that the choice of Pinckney might look like a partial victory for Adet. Third, Pinckney was not known in Connecticut. Fourth, Pinckney had been abroad and consequently absent from his country for some time. He might have absorbed corrupting ideas.[63]

[61] Richmond *Virginia Gazette* (Nicholson's), Nov. 26, 1796, for all returns except those for Lafayette Co., which are from Adams, *Gallatin*, 177.
[62] Richmond *Virginia Argus* (Pleasant's), Nov. 26, 1796.
[63] Wolcott, Sr., to Wolcott, Litchfield, Dec. 12, 1796. Gibbs, *Wolcott*, I, 408.

In Massachusetts, on the other hand, the Junto supported the plans for giving an equal vote for Pinckney. The letter of Higginson to Hamilton ascribed the three votes not given to Pinckney as due to the influence of Adams' particular friends. Such a one was Elbridge Gerry, who gave a preference to Adams.[64] His relations with Adams, and his part in trying to achieve a union between Jefferson and Adams, will be considered in the next chapter in more detail. Starting in 1800, though continuing to support Adams, he became the leader of the Republicans and led a considerable secession from the Federalists.

Rhode Island always had a strong leavening of moderate agrarians among the Federalists. These were headed by Governor Fenner. His first preference was generally for the Republican candidate. This was the case in 1792 [65] and probably in 1800.[66] However, he was responsible in this latter election for Rhode Island's giving to Adams the only votes detached from C. C. Pinckney, and was regarded by Adams as one who preferred him among the Federalists.[67]

In New Hampshire there was a situation not unlike that in Massachusetts. There the Federalist electors included Judge Walker, a moderate who in 1800 was to head the Republicans. He, too, was a particular friend of Adams.[68]

In Maryland at this time, Charles Carroll, who commanded the High-Federalists of that state, supported Adams.[69] It is likely that the detached votes for Adams in the state are to be attributed to the influence of supporters such as Murray, who was willing to see a working arrangement made with Jefferson.[70] One of the

[64] Gerry to Jefferson, Cambridge, March 2, 1797. Austin, J. T., *Life of Elbridge Gerry* (Boston, 1828-9), II, 124.

[65] Theodore Sedgwick to [John?] Lowell [Jr.?], Philadelphia, Nov. 28, 1792. Lowell *Mss* (Boston, Mass.).

[66] John Rutledge to Alexander Hamilton, Newport, R. I., July 17, 1800. Steiner, *McHenry*, 463 n.

[67] Adams' *Works*, VI, 544.

[68] Benjamin Russell to Harrison Gray Otis, Boston, March 14, 1800. Otis *Mss*. Also *Centinel*, March 22, 1800.

[69] Carroll to McHenry, Dec. 12, 1796. Steiner, *McHenry*, 208.

[70] Murray to McHenry, The Hague, June 22, 1797. Steiner, *McHenry*, 229.

votes Adams obtained in this state was from a Republican elector, Plater, who voted for both Adams and Jefferson.[71]

The generalization which may be made is that most of these votes which were for Adams alone can be attributed to the influence of moderates — those, who, in most part, were to be driven from the party by the extremist legislation of the next four years, and who represent the agrarian influence. This will become more apparent when the course of Gerry, the Fenners, and Judge Walker is further traced.

Adams had hopes of even more of this support from moderates than he received. Pennsylvania's leading Republican was Thomas McKean, an old Revolutionary leader. Adams was highly pleased with the support of Gerry and hoped that McKean might likewise vote for him. He looked upon this as the test of whether or not Samuel Adams would support him. The answer was that McKean was further detached than was Gerry. The only Pennsylvania vote for Adams was that of the Federalist elector.[72]

It is interesting to find that whereas almost any candidate was preferred to Adams in Virginia in September and October, the course which the campaign had taken made the Republican leaders sympathetic toward him. According to Adams, William B. Giles, one of the narrowest of the Virginia agrarians, stated: " '. . . the point is settled. The V. P. will be President. He is undoubtedly chosen. The old man will make a good President too.' (There's for you) ' But we shall have to *check* him a little now and then. That will be all.' . . .

" The gentlemen with whom I have conversed, have expressed more affection for me than they ever did before, since 1774. They certainly wish Adams elected rather than Pinckney. Perhaps it is because Hamilton and Jay are said to be for Pinckney." [73]

Adams fully and correctly appraised the situation in the same letter. " I am not enough of an Englishman, nor little enough of a Frenchman, for some people. These would be very willing

[71] Carroll to McHenry, Dec. 5, 1796. *Ibid.*, 204.

[72] Adams to Mrs. Adams, Philadelphia, Jan. 11, 1797 and same to same, Dec. 8, 1796, *Letters to Wife*, II, 239; 234.

[73] Adams to Mrs. Adams, Philadelphia, Dec. 12, 1796, *Works*, I, 495.

that Pinckney should come in chief. But they will be disappointed."

He preferred that Jefferson rather than Pinckney should come in as Vice-President. " If Colonel Hamilton's personal dislike of Jefferson does not obtain too much influence with Massachusetts electors, neither Jefferson will be President, nor Pinckney Vice-President." [74] Further, he made this preference known to the Federalists.[75]

In regard to Hamilton, he stated: " There have been manoeuvers and combinations in this election that would surprise you. I may one day or another develop them to you.

" There is an active spirit in the Union who will fill it with his politics wherever he is. He must be attended to, and not suffered to do too much." [76]

[74] *Ibid.*

[75] According to Pickering he made this statement after the election to Benjamin Goodhue, Senator from Massachusetts. Pickering to Timothy Williams, Philadelphia, May 19, 1800. Pickering *Mss.* 13/516. Also, Pickering to John Pickering, Jr., Philadelphia, May 17, 1800. *Ibid.*, 13/539.

[76] Adams to Mrs. Adams, Philadelphia, Dec. 12, 1796, *Works*, I, 495.

Chapter 7

Aftermath of the Election

THE Republicans had waged a vituperative campaign against Adams. Despite this they hoped that the efforts of the Hamiltonians might have sufficiently estranged Adams from the Federalists to make possible a coalition with him on the basis of a moderate program. Jefferson drew up a letter to Adams assuring him that he would be glad to accept the vice-presidency, and that there should be no barrier between them. " The public & the papers have been much occupied lately in placing us in a point of opposition to each other. I trust with confidence that less of it has been felt by ourselves personally." He had never thought that he would win. Always he had served as Adams' junior, and would continue in this position with pleasure. Should the election go into the house, he would withdraw in favor of Adams.[1]

The letter was enclosed in one written to Madison, which sets forth the aim he had in view. " If Mr. Adams can be induced to administer the government on its true principles, & to relinquish his bias to an English constitution, it is to be considered whether it would not be on the whole for the public good to come to a good understanding with him as to his future elections. He is perhaps the only sure barrier against Hamilton's getting in." [2]

Madison, however, felt it would be best not to deliver the letter. He had written to Jefferson urging his acceptance of the vice-presidency, " There is reason to believe that your neighborhood to Adams may have a valuable effect on his councils, particularly in relation to our external system. You know that his feelings will not enslave him to the example of his predecessor. It is certain that his censure of our paper [money] system & the intrigues at New York for setting P. above him, have fixed an

---

[1] Jefferson to Adams, Monticello, Dec. 28, 1796. Jefferson's *Works*, VII, 95.
[2] Jefferson to Madison, Jan. 1, 1797, Jefferson's *Works*, VII, 95.

enmity with the British faction . . . add to the whole that he is said to speak of you now in friendly terms and will no doubt be soothed by your acceptance of a place subordinate to him." [3]

Yet Madison thought it unwise to transmit Jefferson's letter to Adams. He informed Jefferson that Adams had already been judiciously apprised of Jefferson's disposition in regard to him. His ticklish temper being what it was, it would probably be best not to risk such a step as the delivery of the letter. Moreover, he was already fully aware of Hamilton's " treachery," which Jefferson had taken care to deplore in the letter he wrote. Another consideration was that it would be questionable wisdom to impart such material in writing when it might afford the means for future embarrassment if the policy of Adams should later be such as would require virulent denunciation. Another consideration was that many of the Republicans would not approve of deprecating the attacks made during the campaign. There was already friction on that score within Republican ranks. Such a step as this might appear as a repudiation of certain of their own friends.[4]

One of those most anxious to see the new administration divorce itself from many of the old policies was Elbridge Gerry. Soon after the election Gerry wrote to Mrs. Adams warning Adams against his cabinet, and urging cooperation with Jefferson. This letter is of considerable interest.

True it is that an 'assemblage of fortunate circumstances' to favor his administration 'has been the singular lot' of the predecessor in office, & *he* is in my opinion a very great & good character: but it is said nevertheless, & if true, to be lamented that by the wiles of insidious & unprincipled men, he has nominated to offices foreign as well as domestic, some characters which would not bear the public test, & are a reproach to religion morality good government & even to decency, he is likewise charged with manifesting a disposition of extending his power at the expense of the constitution, & notwithstanding the virulence of party [Gerry is inclined to accept much of this]. I must confess however, that wise & politic as it may be to mark the great

---

[3] Madison to Jefferson, Dec. 19, 1796. Madison's *Works*, VI, 300-302.
[4] Madison to Jefferson, Jan. 15, 1797. Madison's *Works*, VI, 302.

hazards which have exposed to danger this skilful pilot, I have the highest respect for him & think there are few (if any) characters who are his equals in history ancient or modern.

I have been long acquainted with Mr. Jefferson & conceiving that he & Mr. Adams have had a mutual respect for each other: conceiving also that he is a gentleman of abilities, integrity, altho not entirely free from a disposition to intrigue, yet in general a person of candor & moderation, I think it is a fortunate circumstance that he is Vice President & that great good is to be expected from the joint election.

The insidious plan to bring a third person into the presidential chair arose from a corrupt design of influencing his administration, as is generally conceived. Whether his want of experience will justify the expectation, I will not pretend to say, but sure I was from good information that the supporters of Mr. Jefferson give Mr. Adams a decided preference as well for his abilities as his independent spirit.[5]

Gerry also warned Adams about Timothy Pickering, Secretary of State. Pickering had prepared an answer to charges by the French Minister, Adet. In this he emphasized the importance of John Jay in the negotiations with England for the Treaty of Peace of 1783. This emphasis minimized the importance of Adams in the negotiation.[6] However he was unable to make any impression upon Adams regarding the loyalty of the cabinet. Adams replied, " Pickering and his colleagues are as much attached to me as I desire. I have no jealousies from that quarter." [7] Indeed the change of any of the cabinet, particularly in view of the strained relations between Federalist factions, would have been the signal for open war. There was then no precedent for a change of officials with a new administration. In fact the cabinet officers were regarded as being in office until they chose to retire.

At one point Adams, who always recognized the danger of giving play to his natural irascibility, was willing to believe that Hamilton's attempt had only been dictated by a desire to insure the election of Pinckney over Jefferson, or at most was due to a

[5] Gerry to Abigail Adams, Cambridge, Jan. 7, 1797. Gerry *Mss.* (Words in parentheses struck out.)

[6] Gerry to Adams, Cambridge, Feb. 3, 1797. Adams' *Works*, VIII, 520.

[7] Adams to Gerry, Philadelphia, Feb. 13, 1797. *Ibid.*, 522. Also Adams to Gerry in *Massachusetts Historical Society Collection*, Vol. 73, 331.

fear that it would not be safe to risk everything on Adams.[8] Several days later, however, he received intelligence from a friend in Albany that was of such a nature as to confirm his worst suspicions about Hamilton's policy of opposing him.[9]

In his effort to effect a union between Jefferson and Adams, Gerry wrote to Jefferson in the same vein as he wrote to Adams, urging cooperation. He informed Jefferson that it was with great pain that he had not voted for Jefferson in his capacity as elector. Only knowledge of the superior claims of Adams, and the realization that he would be cancelling his vote, had prevented him from voting for both.[10] Jefferson replied that the result of the election was in accord with his own desires, and that he hoped there would be no friction between the two executive officers. On his part he desired to cooperate.[11]

Adams indicated that he, too, wished that differences might be buried, and that he might have Republican approval. He trusted that " the party who have embarrassed the President and exerted themselves to divide the election " would not continue this policy. " I have seen," he wrote, " a disposition to acquiesce, and hope it will increase." [12] With Adams as with Jefferson, Gerry continued to urge cooperation between the two as late as July. Benjamin Rush also made every effort to bring about cooperation between Adams and Jefferson.[13]

Much of the material on this proposed reconciliation between Adams and the Republicans became public. The extent to which Madison exhibited the letter of Jefferson, " in confidence," has not been realized. It became known detail by detail to the Federalists.[14] Moreover it was the subject of discussion in the

[8] Adams to Gerry, Philadelphia, Feb. 13, 1797. Adams' *Works*, VIII, 522.
[9] Adams' *Works*, VIII, 524.
[10] Gerry to Jefferson, March 27, 1797. Austin, *Gerry*, II, 134-36.
[11] Jefferson to Gerry, Philadelphia, May 13, 1797. *Ibid.*, 136-42.
[12] John Adams to Caroline Adams Smith, Philadelphia, Feb. 21, 1797. DeWindt, Caroline A., *Correspondence of Miss Adams*, II, 48-49.
[13] Gerry to Jefferson, July 6, 1797. *New England Historical and Genealogical Register*, XLIX, 438; Rush to Jefferson, Philadelphia, Jan. 4, 1796, *Letters of Benjamin Rush*, I, 784.
[14] Theodore Sedgwick to Rufus King, Philadelphia, March 12, 1797, King's *King*, II, 156.

press. One correspondent in the *Centinel*, the organ of New England Federalism, declared that this would mean the acceptance of the office by Jefferson. " The event, we hope, will

> ' *Unite the roses, red and*
> *white together . . .* ' " [15]

Thereupon, in the next issue, a militant Federalist, in high indignation, replied, " The correspondent who so sanguinely expects the union of ' the roses red and white,' by the election of Messrs. Adams and Jefferson, to the Executive chairs, will assuredly be disappointed. Fire and frost are not more opposite in their natures than those characters are; and the prosperity, honor, and dignity of the United States, depend on an administration *perfectly* federal. That those gentlemen differ essentially on the leading principles of government is certain; and that Adams will remain unshaken in his, cannot be questioned." [16]

In this the issue is fairly joined. On the one hand there was a party of moderation, as represented by such as Gerry; on the other the High-Federalists, demanding complete proscription of the opposition and obedience to their own desires.

If there existed a division in the ranks of the Federalists as to how to accept the possibility of Republican cooperation, the Republicans publicly presented a united front in welcoming the change of administration. Benjamin Franklin Bache, editor of the *Aurora*, gave orders not to admit paragraphs unfavorable to Adams. " ' Let us give him a fair trial,' said this editor to one of his correspondents, ' and then, if he actually does wrong, our censures will fall with the greater weight.' " [17] In 1801 Mr. Callender expressed the matter thus with his customary purity of outlook. " Had he [Adams] attempted to steer a middle course between the two parties, and to make a moderate use of his immense official patronage in securing friends, his interest must infallibly have been supported by an overwhelming majority of

---

[15] *Centinel*, Jan. 14, 1797.
[16] *Ibid.*, Jan. 18, 1797.
[17] Callender, James T., *Sketches of the History of America for 1798* (Philadelphia, 1798), 232-33.

citizens. Without competition, or disturbance, he might have enjoyed his beloved salary, to the end of his life." [18]

The announcement of the Republican attitude appeared in the *Aurora* on December 21, 1796. The article states that Washington seems to arrogate great merit to himself for retiring voluntarily. As a matter of fact no credit is due, for the real source of this decision is a " consciousness that he would not be re-elected, [rather] than a want of ambition or lust of power." The Republicans would have united with the supporters of Adams in placing him above Washington. The reason for this preference is that " There can be no doubt that Adams would not be a *puppet* — that having an opinion and judgment of his own, he would act from his impulses rather than the impulses of others — that possessing great integrity, he would not sacrifice his country's interests at the shrine of party — and that being an enemy to the corruptions which have taken place by means of funding systems, he would not lend his aid to the further prostitution of the American character." Moreover, Adams is an aristocrat in theory only, Washington in practice. "Adams has the simplicity of a republican, but . . . Washington has the ostentation of an eastern bashaw. . . ." [19]

In like manner the *Independent Chronicle* declared, " The republicans anxiously wish the President at Mount Vernon, and Mr. Adams in the exercise of the important office, . . . and that he may in every respect shun the pernicious example of his predecessor, is the sincere wish and fond hope of every real American." [20] Advice was freely tendered to Adams that his cabinet should be remade. Theirs was the responsibility of causing the neglect of the Vice-President during the preceding six years. Perhaps Pickering can explain this. [21]

It needs no comment upon this campaign to point out that in it there is no great subtlety. It naturally was perfectly evident

[18] Callender, J. T., *Prospect Before Us*, II, Part 2 (Richmond, 1801), 34-35. This part of the *Prospect* was written from Richmond Jail. *Ibid.*, 16.

[19] *Aurora*, Dec. 21, 1796.

[20] *Chronicle*, March 6, 1797.

[21] *Aurora*, Feb. 13, 1797; *Chronicle*, March 5, 1797.

to Adams that the chance of securing this support at the same time as retaining that of the Federalists was a manifest impossibility. Furthermore, despite the opposition of a portion of the Federalists, it was to the great mass of this party that he owed his election and his sympathies were largely with this group of the Federalists. Adams himself, in general policy, had not yet reached the position of most of the political moderates.

Be this as it may, many of the Federalists were greatly worried. Sedgwick wrote that it had been intended for all from the East of the Delaware to vote equally for Pinckney and Adams. " Had those views, and in them I concurred, prevailed," he stated, " the former would have become president and the latter continued in his former station. What effects that arrangement would have produced can now only be a subject of conjecture. The attempt, however, has afforded abundant matter for Jacobinical intrigue." He gave in detail the content of Jefferson's undelivered letter to Adams, and pointed out the sentiments expressed in Jefferson's speech on assuming the vice-presidency were of the same tenor.[22]

From Boston Higginson wrote to Hamilton that he was being charged by the friends of Adams with a desire to defeat Adams, and that it was likewise stated Hamilton had opposed Adams because he would be unable to rule him. Among the special partisans of Adams there was general rejoicing over the selection of Jefferson rather than Pinckney.[23] Ames had heard of the letter written by Jefferson. He declared, " such hypocrisy may dupe very great fools, but it should alarm all other persons." He feared that this design to deceive Adams might not be without success.[24] Naturally the efforts of the Republican press were commented upon by the members of this group.[25]

Hamilton was less alarmed than many of his followers. He wrote, " Our Jacobins say, they are well pleased, and that the

---

[22] Sedgwick to R. King, Philadelphia, March 12, 1797. King's *King*, II, 156.

[23] Higginson to Hamilton, Boston, Jan. 12, 1797. Hamilton's *Works* (Hamilton, ed.) VI, 191.

[24] Ames to Thomas Dwight, Philadelphia, Jan. 5, 1797. Ames's *Works*, I, 213.

[25] C. Goodrich to Oliver Wolcott, Philadelphia, Jan. 9, 1797. Gibbs, *Wolcott*, I, 417.

lion and lamb are to lie down together. Mr. Adams's Personal friends talk a little in the same way." He, however, was skeptical that there would be any such outcome and placed his trust in Adams' integrity to the Federalist cause.[26]

Troup pointed out that New York and New Jersey gave all their votes to Adams and Pinckney; consequently charges by the Adams' factions were unjust.[27] As, however, it was not the purpose of Hamilton to create an open break, but to arrange matters so that it would appear that Pinckney had won by reason of a natural popularity in the South, this was beside the point.

There is an interesting side light of this period which deserves to be recorded. The *Gazette* ran a brief note, " Evidence of Monarchy," " The Vice President of the United States was seen handing Buckets in one of the lanes the other morning at the Fire." [28] This was probably the fire recorded several days before under " Melancholy and Distressing," in which fire Mr. and Mrs. Andrew Brown and their three children were fatally burned.[29]

As the administration of Washington was brought to a close the cloud appeared upon the horizon which was to overspread the entire administration of his successor. C. C. Pinckney had been sent as minister plenipotentiary to France, to negotiate a treaty which would settle the differences between the two countries. Meanwhile American commerce was receiving very serious losses from the depredations of the French. The demands of the shippers that the government afford protection to them and secure redress from France became more and more insistent. Desiring to permit his successor to have a free hand in the policy which would be formulated, Washington postponed any decision. As a consequence, this question, the decision upon which would largely determine the character of the new administration's policy, awaited the inauguration of Adams.

[26] Hamilton to King, Feb. 15, 1797. Hamilton's *Works* (Hamilton, ed.), VI, 206.

[27] Troup to R. King, Jan. 28, 1797. King's *King*, II, 135.

[28] *Gazette of the United States*, Jan. 30, 1797.

[29] *Ibid.*, Jan. 27, 1797. It is barely possible that the fire in question was that in the malt room of Thomas Morris's Brew House. *Ibid.*, Jan. 20, 1797.

Chapter 8

Starting the Administration

THE inaugural address of Adams was very well received by all but the most extreme Federalists.[1] In it he took occasion to reassert the sentiments he had delivered before the Senate, denying an attachment to hereditary government, and denying any design or desire to see any more permanent tenure of office established in the United States. In addition to these statements he set forth his creed of government in a single sentence which fills two printed pages. One of the most important declarations he made was for absolute impartiality among all nations. Going further than this he declared he felt " a personal esteem for the French nation, formed in a residence of seven years, chiefly among them, and a sincere desire to preserve the friendship which has been so much for the honor and interest of both nations." On domestic policies, he pledged himself to an administration which would consider the interest of all, " without preference or regard to a northern or southern, eastern or western position." [2]

Adams had evidently deliberated a long time over including the denial of monarchical sentiments in his address. To Gerry he wrote, " I had been so abused, belied and misrepresented, for seven years together, without uttering one syllable in my own vindication, and almost without one word in my favor from anybody else, that I was determined to give the lie direct to whole volumes at once, be the consequence what it would." [3]

At this period he was still quite out of touch with the majority of the Federalist leaders. For several weeks after the inaugural every letter to his wife speaks of his isolation, his inability to find where he stood. "And now the world is as silent as the grave,"

---

[1] Schuyler to Hamilton, Albany, Mar. 19, 1797. Hamilton's *Works* (Hamilton, ed.) VI, 212.

[2] Adams' *Works*, I, 504.

[3] Adams to Gerry, April 6, 1797. Adams' *Works*, VIII, 538.

he wrote.[4] Apparently he even began to wonder whether he would have the support of the leaders of the party. " If the federalists go to playing pranks, I will resign the office, and let Jefferson lead them to peace, wealth and Power if he will." He was also concerned over the misrepresentations of his position which appeared in the Republican press.[5]

The cabinet which Adams inherited from Washington was of mediocre ability. Washington had started with a distinguished cabinet which was non-partisan and which was headed by Jefferson and Hamilton. Following the departure of Jefferson from the cabinet, he had attempted to continue the non-partisan character of his advisers with the selection of Edmund Randolph as the Secretary of State. Randolph's term closed under disagreeable circumstances with both the loyalty and integrity of the Secretary of State suspect.[6] This marked the end of efforts to maintain a

[4] Adams to Abigail Adams, March 17, 1797. *Letters to Wife*, II, 252. Same to same, March 9, 1797. *Ibid.*, 247.

[5] Same to same, March 16, 1797. *Ibid.*, 252.

[6] The curious history of Edmund Randolph's tenure as Secretary of State has long been in controversy. The best appraisal of his virtual dismissal by Washington (actually he resigned) is by Dice R. Robinson, in his " Edmund Randolph," in Bemis, Samuel F., ed., *American Secretaries of State and Their Diplomacy*, II, 149-59. On the basis of information in an intercepted dispatch from the French Minister, Fauchet, Randolph was regarded by his colleagues in the cabinet, Wolcott and Pickering, as being guilty of bribery by the French. This hardly seems feasible, although Pickering and Wolcott immediately communicated these charges to Washington. Whether or not this was correct, Washington regarded Randolph as guilty of indiscretions in giving information to Fauchet, and possibly of personal disloyalty to him and the administration in his discussions with Fauchet. Consequently, he permitted Randolph to retire in 1795. The difficult circumstances of a divided cabinet offer extenuation for Randolph's disclosures to Fauchet, but hardly provide an airtight defense.

A separate issue is that of Randolph's accounts as Secretary of State. These are reviewed in U. S. Senate Documents, 50th Congress, 2nd Session, No. 58 (1889).

Irving Brant probably claims too much for Randolph in his " Edmund Randolph, Not Guilty," *William and Mary Quarterly*, 3rd Series, VII, 179-98 (1950). Much of his material (except for re-translation of several phrases in the Fauchet correspondence) follows Conway, Moncure D., *Omitted Chapters of History Disclosed in the Life and Papers of Edmund Randolph* (New York, 1888). Pickering's and Wolcott's positions are stated in Gibbs, *Wolcott*.

broadly representative cabinet. Thereupon other difficulties appeared. By the period of Washington's second administration, the work of the new government had settled down largely to routine. The prestige of a cabinet position was slight. Jay even left the chief-justiceship for the governorship of New York. Cabinet posts were lower yet in the scale. Under these conditions, Washington's attempts to make cabinet appointments met with repeated refusals, and the cabinet that resulted was poor in a number of respects.

The three positions of actual cabinet level were filled by Timothy Pickering as Secretary of State, Oliver Wolcott as Secretary of Treasury, and James McHenry as Secretary of War. All of these had two things in common. First, they were accustomed to consult with Alexander Hamilton on all important matters of policy. Hamilton gave his advice, down to details. They took this advice. Hamilton was the recognized leader of the Federalist party, and there were no secrets from him. In similar fashion he transmitted his advice on legislative matters to such followers as Theodore Sedgwick, Senator from Massachusetts, to Representative Uriah Tracy, of Connecticut, and later to the Speaker, Jonathan Dayton. Thus he was able to integrate the operations of the legislative and executive branches. Adams had no such advantage.

The second common characteristic of the cabinet was that they belonged to the wing of the Federalists known as the High-Federalists. Moreover, when left to themselves, their neglect of public opinion was extremely impolitic. Hamilton himself was the leader of the High-Federalists, but he did think in political terms — how to win elections, how to carry public opinion with him and keep it abreast of strong measures. The members of the cabinet, on the other hand, were inflexible. They were apt, therefore, when not guided by Hamilton, to give advice or take measures which would often be beyond what the public was willing to accept.

In personal characteristics, the members naturally differed.

Timothy Pickering, from Salem, Massachusetts,[7] was a member of the Essex Junto. While lacking the wealth of George Cabot or Stephen Higginson, he fully shared their point of view. As a diplomat he was not a success. As an administrator he was able, industrious, and energetic. As the position of Secretary of State embraced more general duties than at present, this was of some considerable importance despite his lack of capacity where foreign policy was concerned. Pickering was humorless, cold, and harsh. He had no liking for Adams, and not only worked against him when a conflict with Hamilton was concerned, but also opposed him in other matters. To Adams he also acted treacherously, at times withholding information, at times striving to thwart the President by indirection or direct disobedience.

Oliver Wolcott, from Connecticut, had served as auditor in the Treasury Department under Hamilton.[8] After the retirement of Hamilton, Washington appointed Wolcott, who served successfully under both Washington and Adams. Although just as loyal to Hamilton as were Pickering and McHenry, Wolcott succeeded in deceiving Adams to the end. Staying on in the cabinet after the dismissal of Pickering and McHenry in May, 1800, Wolcott was given a federal judgship by Adams when he finally resigned from the cabinet.

James McHenry of Maryland was easily the most incapable member of the cabinet.[9] A former military secretary to Washington, he was offered the secretaryship of war after four others declined the post. When the crisis with France arrived in 1798, both Hamilton and Washington sadly concluded that he was far out of his depth,[10] Washington stating to Hamilton: "Your

[7] Pickering, Octavius and Upham, C. W., *The Life of Timothy Pickering*, 4 vols. (Boston, 1867-1873); Robinson, W. A., "Timothy Pickering," *DAB*, XIV, 565-68.

[8] Gibbs, George, *Memoirs of the Administrations of Washington and Adams from the Papers of Oliver Wolcott*; Purcell, R. J., "James McHenry," *DAB*, XII, 62-63.

[9] Steiner, *McHenry*.

[10] Washington to Hamilton, Mt. Vernon, Aug. 9, 1798. *Writings* (Fitzpatrick, ed.), XXXVI, 394. Also cf. Washington's criticisms to McHenry himself written Sept. 14, 1798 and March 25, 1799. *Ibid.*, XXXVI, 463 and XXXVII, 157.

opinion respecting the unfitness of a certain Gentleman [McHenry] for the office he holds, accords with mine. . . ." McHenry was an amiable and pleasant person. But after the intrigue over naming Hamilton second in command to Washington, when the army was enlarged in 1798 because of the crisis with France, Adams had no doubt but that McHenry was acting against him.

After the creation of the Navy Department in May of 1798, Benjamin Stoddert of Maryland was appointed as secretary. He served capably, and alone of the cabinet was loyal to Adams, ultimately warning Adams of his cabinet's attempted reversal of the President's policy of a peace mission to France in 1799. Had it been possible for Adams to work with a cabinet of men such as Stoddert, and John Marshall, Secretary of State, after the dismissal of Pickering, then the course of Adams' administration would have been vastly different. Unfortunately there was no tradition of the cabinet members submitting their resignations upon the election of a new President. Moreover, because of the delicate relations between Adams and the Hamiltonian wing of the party, a change in the cabinet would have meant a party split. Ultimately that was the result in any event. But for such to have been apparent at the start of the administration in 1797 would have necessitated Adams having the gift of prophecy.

In determining the necessary steps to be taken toward France in 1797, Adams early decided to send a new embassy to that nation. Jefferson arrived in Philadelphia on March 2, and called on Adams that same day. The following day Adams came to see Jefferson. He then, before consulting any of his cabinet, broached the project of the mission to Jefferson and urged that either Jefferson should go himself or that Madison should do so. Jefferson declined on his own account, both because of a disinclination to leave the country and the feeling that his office made it improper for him to go on a mission. Adams was of the same opinion in regard to this feeling about the propriety of the matter. Many others were considered. According to Jefferson a mission made up of Gerry, Madison and Pinckney was preferred by Adams. Jefferson, however, feared that Madison would have so great a disinclination to leaving the country that it would be impossible to secure his permission. He would, however, try to secure his acceptance. Accordingly Adams departed with the agreement that they should again discuss the question.[11]

At this juncture Adams went to one of the heads of departments; Pickering would be the most likely one for Adams to consult at this point, although Wolcott was a possibility. To this head of department Adams broached the project of the new mission, mentioning Madison as one of his choices. The secretary replied, " Sending Mr. Madison will make dire work among the passions of our parties in Congress, and out of doors thro' the States." To this Adams asserts he replied, " Are we forever to be overawed and directed by party passions? " Thereupon the secretary offered his resignation. Adams at once declared that this was not his aim at all, that he had confidence in the cabinet and wished all the members to continue.

Upon consulting the secretaries and certain party leaders, he found that opposition to Madison would be so great as to endanger chances of approval in the Senate. Accordingly he was forced to drop the idea of sending Madison. It had been his intention to couple Hamilton with Madison, he asserts, but this, too, was now abandoned.[12]

Several days later, probably on March 6, Adams and Jefferson met at Washington's. There Jefferson informed him that Madison would be unable to go. Adams answered that he had found it inadvisable to include Madison, " on consultation, some objections to that nomination had been raised which he had not contemplated." Adams seemed somewhat embarrassed, and thereafter did not consult Jefferson on any matters. The impression Jefferson received was that Adams had let his own feelings run away with him in the first instance, and had then been checked by the cabinet. The entire incident Jefferson regarded as an example of the fact that Adams " never acted on any system." [13] It is

[11] *Jefferson's Complete Anas*, 184-85, March 2 ff.

[12] Adams to the *Boston Patriot*, Quincy, May 29, 1809; *Patriot*, June 7, 1809. Also Adams to Gerry, April 6, 1797. *Works* VIII, 538. This gives the date of the conference and informs Gerry of the result of his talk with Jefferson.

[13] *Complete Anas*, 184-85.

certain, at any rate, that he could have avoided a difficult position by not approaching Jefferson until after consulting the cabinet and deciding whether or not he would follow their advice. Commenting on what this incident demonstrated about the possibility of cooperation between the new President and Vice-President, Adams stated, " Party violence soon rendered it impracticable, or at least useless, and this party violence was excited by Hamilton more than any other man." [14] As a matter of fact the three secretaries, Wolcott, Pickering and McHenry were all opposed to any new mission to France, and their position was shared by a respectable number of the Federalists at large. Wolcott wrote to Hamilton that he had opposed the measure, so that for the moment the matter was held in abeyance.[15]

What finally caused a change of cabinet opinion was that Hamilton favored the mission as a means of assuring public support for whatever defense measures would need to be taken. Hamilton had regarded a new embassy as the proper procedure as early as January.[16] Before the opposition to the step was overcome he had to write several times to each secretary. He informed Wolcott that it was necessary he should learn " pliancy " in order to avoid policies which would outstrip public opinion.[17] To William Smith, then an important leader in the house who likewise opposed the project, he wrote in similar vein, " I would accumulate the proofs of French insolence, and demonstrate to all our citizens that nothing possible had been omitted.

[14] *Patriot*, June 7, 1809, *op. cit.* Also Adams to Rush, Quincy, August 23, 1805. *Old Family Letters*, 76.

[15] Wolcott to Hamilton, Mar. 31, 1797. Gibbs, *Wolcott*, I, 485.

[16] Hamilton to Washington, Jan. 22, 1797, Hamilton's *Works* (Hamilton, ed.), VI, 195. Also to Sedgwick, Feb. 26, 1797. *Ibid.*, 209.

[17] Hamilton to Wolcott, April 5, 1797, *Ibid.*, 229. Also Wolcott to Hamilton, March 21, and Hamilton to Wolcott, March 30. Gibbs, *Wolcott*, I, 484-85. Also Pickering to Hamilton, March 25, 1797 and Hamilton to Pickering, March 29, 1797. Hamilton's *Works* (Hamilton, ed.), VI, 215-16. Again, Pickering to Hamilton, April 26, 1797 and Hamilton to Pickering, May 11, 1797. Likewise, Hamilton to McHenry, not dated, and same to same, April 29, 1797. Steiner, *McHenry*, 212-22.

" . . . I would try hard to avoid rupture, and if that cannot be, to unite the opinion of all good citizens of whatever political denominations. This is with me, a mighty object.

". . . My plan is ever to combine energy with moderation." [18]

The composition of the mission he considered would be correct, if made up of two Federalists and one Republican. Pinckney, Madison, and George Cabot were the three he preferred.

Thus it was that by the time Adams propounded questions to the cabinet as to recommendations he should make to the special session of Congress, all had abandoned their earlier opposition and were ready to support the new mission.[19] The call for the special session had been issued on March 25. The idea was that it would only be proper to send the embassy if, hand in hand with this measure, the country were put in a proper state of defense. Adams' acceptance of this second thesis placed him in accord with the desires of the Federalists, and in opposition to the Republicans. Doubtless it was knowledge of this which caused Hamilton to write King on the first of May, stating: Adams is firm, but is he prudently so? [20] Hamilton always felt that if Adams were charting a correct course, even then there was no guarantee but that he would land on a reef when he actually tried to act.

As soon as the President's queries were received by the members of the cabinet, McHenry and Pickering sent a copy of them to Hamilton.[21] In detailed letters Hamilton outlined the policies which should be recommended to Adams. He had already suggested the necessity of calling a special session, though Adams seems to have arrived at the same conclusion independently. Now he proposed a number of measures, most of which were to

[18] Hamilton to Smith, April 5, 1797. Hamilton's *Works* (Hamilton, ed.) VI, 235.

[19] Adams to secretaries, Philadelphia, April 14, 1797. Adams' *Works*, VIII, 540.

[20] Hamilton to King, April 8, 1797. Hamilton's *Works* (Hamilton, ed.) VI, 236.

[21] Steiner, *McHenry*, 212. Also Pickering to Hamilton, April 26, 1797. Hamilton's *Works* (Hamilton, ed.) VI, 238.

be acceptable to the President, who was, of course, ignorant of their true source. First he urged that the President should recommend a day of thanksgiving and prayer. It would also be necessary that adequate steps for the defense of commerce should be taken. These should include the creation of a naval force to provide convoys, and the permission to merchant vessels to arm. A bill should be passed to create a provisional army of 25,000 with permission to start the training of officers as soon as possible. This idea of a provisional army was so far in advance of public opinion that it was not adopted until after the publication of the XYZ dispatches. Any plan of substituting a strengthened militia for the provisional army, he opposed as entirely inadequate.[22] In order to assure proper action in Congress, Hamilton wrote an equally detailed letter to Representative William Smith, laying emphasis upon the provisional army, and recommending that it be given part pay at once. Likewise he pointed out the necessity of seeking additional sources of revenue. He favored the immediate imposition of a property tax.[23]

Congress was called for May 15, but a quorum was not assembled until two days later. This was much better than usual, as a week was often needed before business could be transacted. Adams realized that the policy he was about to outline would be entirely unsatisfactory to the Republicans. On April 24 he wrote his wife, "I warrant you I shall soon be acquitted of the crime of *Chronicle, Argus* and *Aurora* praise. Let it run its rig, however, and say nothing at present." [24]

In many respects the speech was in accord with the sentiments of Hamilton. Adams pointed out that the refusal of France to receive the envoy sent by the United States meant that diplomatic intercourse was suspended. Despite this indignity and the depredations suffered by American commerce, the government was

[22] Hamilton to McHenry, April 29, 1797. Steiner, *McHenry*, 215. Hamilton to Pickering, May 11, 1797, Hamilton's *Works* (Hamilton, ed.) VI, 248.

[23] Hamilton to Wolcott, June 6 and again June 8. Gibbs, *Wolcott*, I, 543; 546. It is well to note that he favored a building tax, not a land tax, at this stage.

[24] *Letters to Wife*, II, 254.

determined again to try negotiation through sending a new mission. Meanwhile it would be advisable to appropriate funds to complete the three frigates, work upon which had been suspended. Further, smaller vessels to serve as convoys should be provided and merchants be permitted to arm their vessels for defense against attack. For land defense, the militia should be reorganized, additional artillery and cavalry provided, and a provisional army established. These measures would entail additional expense. Consequently the house should look into the matter of providing further sources of revenue.[25] In thus setting forth his program, Adams sought to show France that the United States could not be trifled with. Such recommendations met with approval from all of the extreme Federalists.[26] Naturally they met with quite the opposite response on the part of the Republicans, and were in advance of moderate opinion.

However, the idea which Adams had was that these measures were sufficient to meet any eventuality short of declared war. He felt, by going the entire distance at this juncture, it would be possible to clear up the difficulties with France. The later program, as adopted after the publication of the XYZ dispatches, he was not to approve. He considered that the measures as outlined above were what the emergency required, that to go further was to create expense uselessly.

To the Republican press, this was a war speech. Having no faith in the Federalists, Adams' acceptance of their program made the Republicans believe that the President was now for a war with France.[27] The Republicans believed that this was the end which the Federalists had in view. Commenting upon this change, Porcupine headed an article, " Bache's Bow-Wow." " The public must have observed how artfully, how basely this spaniel has been fawning on the President for some time past." Who would ever have thought he would now turn about? [28]

---

[25] *Annals*, VII, 55.

[26] Cabot to Wolcott, May 21, 1797. Lodge, *Cabot*, 139. Iredell to Wolcott, Richmond, June 5, 1797. Gibbs, *Wolcott*, I, 542. Sedgwick to King, Philadelphia, June 24, 1797. King's *King*, II, 192.

[27] *Aurora*, May 17, 18, 1797; *Chronicle*, May 29 ff., 1797.

[28] *Porcupine's Gazette*, May 18, 1797. *Porcupine's Works*, V, 399.

When it came to making up the personnel of the mission, new difficulties arose. While the cabinet desired a mission composed of Federalists, Adams wished to include a moderate. All agreed upon John Marshall and Pinckney, but the cabinet desired George Cabot for the third member. Adams insisted upon Judge Francis Dana or Elbridge Gerry, both supporters of his in Massachusetts. In the meeting, when Gerry was proposed, McHenry, at least voiced open opposition.[29]

When the nominations were transmitted to the Senate, opposition appeared against Gerry. Sedgwick wrote to King that he considered the choice of Gerry a very injudicious one. The vote against confirmation was: Sedgwick (Mass.), Goodhue (Mass.), Read (S. C.), Marshall (Ky.), Ross (Pa.) and Tracy (Conn.).[30]

Just at this time a friend communicated to Adams, from memory, the contents of a circular letter of Jefferson's he had seen evidently criticising the policy being pursued. Adams replied, " It is evidence of a mind soured, yet seeking for popularity and eaten to a honeycomb with ambition, yet weak, confused, uninformed, and ignorant. I have been long convinced that this ambition is so inconsiderate as to be capable of going great lengths." [31]

Gerry was the only member of the commission whom Jefferson felt was close to him. However, he must have regarded Marshall as a satisfactory choice, for he wrote Gerry that he would have a majority to work with in favor of a genuine settlement.[32] On his part, Gerry was afraid that he would be undermined by the cabinet. Adams denied that any such tactics were being used.[33] Perhaps fearing that there might be friction among the commissioners, he wrote to Gerry urging that every effort be made to assure harmony.[34]

---

[29] McHenry to Pickering, Feb. 23, 1811. Steiner, *McHenry*, 224.

[30] Sedgwick to King, Philadelphia, June 24, 1797. King's *King*, II, 192.

[31] Adams to Uriah Foster, June 20, 1797. Philadelphia, Adams' *Works*, VIII, 547.

[32] Jefferson to Gerry, June 21, 1797. Austin, *Gerry*, II, 154-56.

[33] Adams to Gerry, July 17, 1797. Adams' *Works*, VIII, 549.

[34] Adams to Gerry, June 20, 1798. Adams' *Works*, VIII, 548.

The first work of Congress was the preparation of a reply to the address of the President. At this session this stupid business required over two weeks debate in the House. One part of Adams' speech aroused considerable opposition from the Republicans. This was a statement that a part of the address of the Directory to Monroe, " evinces a disposition to separate the people of the United States from the Government." It has already been pointed out that Adams regarded parties as inevitable.[35] However, many of the Federalists were not willing to admit that an opposition to the government should exist. They did not draw the distinction between opposition to the Constitution and opposition to those who administered it. They sought to continue the stigma of Anti-Federalism, to regard the Republicans as being desirous of tearing down the Constitution, if not being absolutely disloyal. Consequently, the echoing of this stock phrase by the President was not agreeable to the Republicans. As a matter of fact what Adams most probably had in mind was that foreign influence should be deprecated, and should not involve appeals to a people against their own government. But for the phrase " separating the people from their government," he might have escaped censure. As it was, the Federalists used the occasion to deplore opposition to the government, and the Republicans answered in kind.[36]

In the course of the debate, the question of the possibility of war entered. In relation to this, Harper, seeking to show that strong measures would intimidate France, introduced a subject which was in the minds of the Federalists throughout this period. He stated, " She [France] knows that in case of war with us Spain and Holland, who must be her allies would be within our grasp. She knows that the Americans could and would lay hold of New Orleans and the Floridas, and that they are well acquainted with the road to Mexico, and she would dread that enterprising valor which formerly led them through barren walks

[35] Adams had written to Gerry on June 20 that there would always be parties in a free country. Adams' *Works*, VIII, 548. Also see Chapter 3, *infra*, on this point.

[36] *Annals*, VII, 91-92; 101; 104; 114.

and frozen mountains to the walls of Quebec." He further stated that she must know such a conflict would drive us to ally with England, which France had been seeking by all means to prevent. Harper was notorious for letting the cat out of the bag in the excitement of debate, and the Republicans enjoyed these statements very much.[37]

As initially reported to the House the temper of the draft reply to the President's address was too strong for the House. As a result two amendments, offered by moderates, Coit of Connecticut and Dayton of New Jersey, were accepted. That Dayton, the speaker, should have taken such a position was no surprise. He had maintained this attitude since he was first elected to Congress. That Coit, a Federalist, should fall away from orthodox Federalism, was, however, a matter of grave concern. He was attacked in the *Centinel*,[38] and in the Connecticut *Courant*.[39] In the latter paper one " Gustavus " demanded that those who were veering to Anti-Federalism should be kept in mind and defeated at the next election. On the other hand he was praised by the *Chronicle*, until finally he inserted a note in the *Centinel* that he did not appreciate plaudits from such a source, and requested that they might stop.[40]

The moderates in this Congress held the balance of power. Most of these came from localities which might be expected to elect such representatives. From western Massachusetts the nominal Federalist, Skinner, who voted consistently with the Republicans, appeared. The three southern Massachusetts districts sent two moderates and a Republican. Virginia contributed a stronger Federalist delegation than had been the case during the previous Congress. The strongest Federalist district in the state, the first, sent General Daniel Morgan, of Revolutionary fame. From the adjacent Third District came James Machir, the most consistent Federalist from the state during this session.

[37] *Annals*, VII, 187.

[38] *Centinel*, July 12, 1797.

[39] Welling, " Connecticut Federalism," *loc. cit.*, 279. Quoting *Courant* of July 10.

[40] *Centinel*, August 8, 1797.

Grove was returned from North Carolina, and South Carolina increased its quota of Federalists to three.

Federalist gains in this Congress appeared also in Pennsylvania and Maryland. On Map 4 the total number voting consistently Federalist is forty-two (also cf. Chart III). Of the twenty-three moderates, there are fourteen Federalists. In addition to those already indicated these include one from Maryland, two from Pennsylvania, and one from Rhode Island. One independent, so-called Federalist, Skinner, voted steadily with the Republicans. Adding Dayton, the speaker, and one who was absent during the session, this gives a total of fifty-eight Federalists, which is in exact agreement with an estimate printed in the *Centinel*.[41] The Federalists had ten more than a majority in the House, which placed the balance of power in the hands of the moderates. It should be observed that in contrast with the twenty-nine moderates in the Fourth Congress the total has been reduced to twenty-three, and that as the Fifth Congress continued, the party lines were drawn even sharper. There is but one case in this session of a member elected by one party but consistently voting with the opposing party. There were four such individuals in the Fourth Congress.

The effect of there still being a large number of moderate Federalists was that no strong measures passed during the first session.[42] Galleys, which were useful only for coast defense and harbor fortifications, received support. On the question of larger vessels the Federalists received an overwhelming defeat. The only measure for increase of the army which reached an advanced stage, that for an additional regiment of artillery, was defeated by a vote of 57 to 39. On this vote, in addition to the moderates, Samuel Lyman of the Third Western Massachusetts District, and Thomas of the Third Pennsylvania District were opposed.

One bill which was defeated presents a very interesting situation. This was a bill to prescribe the mode of expatriation. Many Americans were enlisting in the service of France or taking licenses

[41] *Ibid.*, May 10, 1797.
[42] All the votes referred to will be found in Vote Chart No. III.

as privateers under the French flag. In order to preserve neutrality, it was considered desirable to prescribe the mode of expatriation whereby an American citizen could renounce allegiance and take up arms under another sovereignty. Accordingly a bill was introduced to give to the courts the power of granting the right of expatriation. This, however, caused opposition from two sources when taken up for debate on June 1. On the one hand the Republicans, led by Giles, were unwilling to place any restrictions on expatriation. On the other hand, the moderate Federalists desired to limit and regulate it by law. The High-Federalists, however, led by Samuel Sewall, were opposed to expatriation, except under more stringent terms than the bill provided. They wished that a person might not be able to expatriate himself at his own convenience, but that the right should be strictly limited. Considering the character of the American population, this was a curious stand. At any rate, the tenth and eleventh votes on Vote Chart III show this tendency. On the tenth, those following the doctrine as laid down by Sewall are recorded with an asterisk, on the eleventh with an X. On the eleventh vote the High-Federalists rather than the moderates voted with the Republicans. This is because at the same time the Federalists were striving to secure a stronger bill, the Republicans were voting to take advantage of the Federalist split, and thereby to prevent any bill from passing. In this they were successful.

The vote had an interesting sequel. On February 27, 1797, one Isaac William was indicted for taking the oath of allegiance to France and engaging in privateering under that flag. When brought to trial on September 26, 1799, he pleaded the right of expatriation. Chief Justice Oliver Ellsworth, then on circuit, charged the jury as to the law in the case. He followed an earlier decision of James Iredell in declaring the common law of England a part of the law of the United States. This being the case, it followed that the British doctrine of perpetual allegiance became a part of the law of the United States. As a consequence only express authorization by statute could confer the right of expatriation. The fact that the United States permitted naturalization of foreigners could not operate to create implied consent for expatriation, in opposition to common law.[43] The point is here given attention in demonstrating most clearly the anti-foreign sentiment of the extreme Federalists, which could not be expected to find favor in the expanding sections of the country.

At this session for Congress there was another manifestation of the same outlook. In order to discourage immigration, a tax of twenty dollars on certificates of naturalization was proposed in the revenue bill. This was reduced to five dollars and passed. During the course of this debate Harrison Gray Otis of Boston declared " he did not wish to invite hordes of wild Irishmen, nor the turbulent and disorderly of all parts of the world, to come here with a view to disturb our tranquillity, after having succeeded in the overthrow of their own Governments." [44] As Otis' " Wild Irish Speech " this received considerable notoriety, and was strongly approved by the Federalists.[45]

At the close of the session, the House withdrew from a position it had adopted earlier, in permitting the use of naval vessels as convoys. Previously these had been restricted to waters adjacent to America. One of the last acts of the session — the levying of a duty on salt — was distasteful to the farming sections. This meant that both for personal use and for live stock the tax would have to be paid. The Republican members secured some revenge by reducing the drawback on salt used in the fisheries.

The result of the special session was most disappointing to the Federalist leaders. Sedgwick asserted that though there was a slight majority in the house, not one necessary measure had been taken.[46] William Hindman, of Maryland, was equally disappointed by the failure of the Federalists to vote with their party.[47] Adams, too, felt that the temper of Congress was not sufficiently

---

[43] *Connecticut Courant*, Sept. 30, 1799, gives the charge in full. Also see Brown, William G., *Oliver Ellsworth* (New York, 1905), 257.

[44] *Annals*, VII, 430.

[45] Morison, S. E., *Harrison Gray Otis* (Boston, 1913), I, 108.

[46] Sedgwick to King, June 24, 1797, King's *King*, II, 192.

[47] Hindman to King, Aug. 21, 1797. *Ibid.*, 212.

high.[48] To add to the general dissatisfaction, the depredations upon trade were causing frequent bankruptcies and a general stagnation of trade.[49] Hindman declared that virtually all of the great land speculators were in debtors prison, and that the famous Robert Morris would soon be there.[50] All in all the situation during 1797 was not such as provided a very cheerful outlook to the Federalists. Their majority in the House, due to the disinclination of the representatives of certain non-commercial sections, was not following the party program, which might be expected to provide some redress for their financial difficulties.

[48] Adams to Wolcott, Oct. 27, 1797. Adams' *Works*, VIII, 558.
[49] Bingham to King, Phila., July 10, 1797. King's *King*, II, 199.
[50] Hindman to King, Talbot County, Md., August 21, 1797. *Ibid.*, 213.

Chapter 9

Beginning of the XYZ Session

THE second session of the Fifth Congress was one of the most momentous ever held. On November 23, 1797, Adams delivered the customary opening address. The mission to France, he declared, had landed safely in Holland, but no news had been received from the members. Meanwhile depredations upon the commerce of the United States were continuing. The importance of commerce was such that if it were not given adequate protection all classes and interests would feel harmful results. The interdependence of all industries should be recognized. Consequently, adequate defense measures were necessary, and should receive the serious attention of both houses.

Necessarily such a program would entail additional expense. The size of the debt of the United States made any further increase in this item a question of anxiety. By the abuse of the funding system Great Britain had gone into bankruptcy. Bearing this lesson in mind, all expenses possible should be borne out of current revenue. The House, therefore, should levy taxes adequate to the needs of the country.[1]

From this address it was evident that Adams was determined to follow the policy of resisting France, believing that only in such a manner could the United States secure redress. This was the logical continuation of the policy which was launched during the special session. It was equally acceptable to the Federalists, obnoxious to the Republicans.

At this juncture Adams rewarded another of his friends who was anathema to most Federalists. In this case it was the appointment of Dr. Benjamin Rush, with whom Adams kept up what was probably his most intimate correspondence outside the family, as treasurer or superintendent of the mint. Rush, like

---

[1] *Annals*, VII, 631. Nov. 23, 1797.

Gerry, was a friend of Jefferson as well as of Adams. It was he who, in 1812, effected the reconciliation between the two. Since Rush was of an experimental and philosophical turn of mind, an admirer of the French Revolution, a supporter of McKean and his Republican machine in Pennsylvania, his appointment found little favor with the Federalists. He was regarded as " a wrong headed politician." [2]

More important matters, however, were disturbing the Federalists. Again it was apparent that no important legislation could pass Congress. It was not long before the Federalists gave up in despair so far as action in the House was concerned. Until there was news from the envoys, it was obvious that nothing would be done.[3] Gallatin wrote that the policy of the High-Federalists aimed at deliberately provoking a conflict with France. ". . . We must lay the foundation in the minds of the disinterested and moderate part of their side of the House of a change as to the general policy of our affairs. We must show to the President and his councillors that we understand fully their principles. . . ." [4]

This failure of the Federalists to carry their program did not, however, prevent a tense atmosphere from developing. The tone of the debates became more and more acrimonious. One matter which aroused considerable heat was the charge that the President was the head of a party, and was appointing members of that party alone to office. The idea that the President was the head of a party was denied by Sewall, who declared such a statement sought to degrade the executive. Sewall, however, admitted that an opposition had the right to exist, provided it kept within certain limits.[5] He declared he thought but few of the Republicans were actual enemies of the government itself. Harper took a similar position.[6] On the other hand, certain of the Federalists

---

[2] W. L. Smith to Oliver Wolcott, Lisbon, Feb. 25, 1798. Gibbs, *Wolcott*, II, 55.

[3] Hindman to William Hensley, Jr., Philadelphia, Dec. 3, 1797. King's *King*, II, 250. Ames declared that Congress was divided and debased. Ames to C. Gore, Feb. 25, 1798. Ames's *Works*, I, 221.

[4] Gallatin to Mrs. Gallatin, Jan. 30, 1798. Adams, *Gallatin*, 190.

[5] *Annals*, VII, 942. Jan. 26, 1798.

[6] *Ibid.*, 874. Jan. 19, 1798.

were following a line of attack which soon all would adopt. Chauncey Goodrich of Connecticut stated, ". . . In this manner were the people of the United States to be arranged and marshalled out, and in this manner this Constitution, and these laws were to be endangered, by an attack, which appeared as if it were intended to be the fore-runner of a more serious attack from abroad." [7] John Williams, of New York, took the same line of approach, ". . . If gentlemen can produce proofs of their attachment to the republican cause they will be credited. . . . The minority he regarded as a spark of fire, which if not put out might consume the whole fabric." He declared that those opposing the government were fickle city mobs, degraded by foreign influence; its truest supporters were the sturdy yeomanry. He himself was a representative of a backwoods New York state district of this latter character.[8] In the course of such remarks, Roger Griswold of Connecticut asserted that all appointments should certainly be made from the friends of government, those not of such nature were deplorable. While Adams made but few appointments outside the Federalist ranks, Griswold was dissatisfied, stating that, ". . . He had thought, from some appointments which had been made, that the President had not adopted the determination which every real friend of the Government must wish to see adopted." [9]

At this time the famous Lyon-Griswold affair took place, adding fuel to the flames of party rancor. Representative Matthew Lyon of Vermont, an extreme Jeffersonian, was insulted by the extreme Federalist, Roger Griswold of Connecticut. Lyon then spit in Griswold's face. When Lyon was not expelled, Griswold attacked him with a cane in the House, and Lyon defended himself with the fire tongs which he hastily grasped.[10] Party feeling generally began to tend toward personal enmity among the members. Representative Jonathan Bayard of Delaware, a level-headed member of the House, declared that he looked for blood to be

---

[7] *Ibid.*, 942. Jan. 26, 1798.
[8] *Annals*, VII, 1090. Feb. 27, 1798.
[9] *Ibid.*, 892. Jan. 22, 1798.
[10] McLaughlin, J. F., *Matthew Lyon* (New York, 1900), 209-305 (Ch. V).

let.[11] Strong feeling was manifest both within and without the house.[12]

When the birthday of Washington came around in 1798, the Federalists were faced with a dilemma. It had been the practice to celebrate this date throughout Washington's term of office. What to do now that the Presidency had changed? Celebrate the birthday of the new President, thereby clearly showing that the entire business was a party affair, or continue celebrating the anniversary of the more popular Washington? In February it was decided that, at any event, Washington's should be observed. Accordingly, on February 22, a great ball was held — and the new President did not attend! As a consequence there was considerable adverse comment by the Federalists.[13]

Prior to the reception of the news of a definite rupture with France there was a long debate over the appropriation of money to increase the number of diplomatic representatives in Europe. This came about on a resolution offered by John Nicholas. It gave the Republicans opportunity to comment upon the fact that John Quincy Adams was serving as a minister, and to charge extravagance in the conduct of the government. It was only by a margin of four votes that the Republicans were defeated. (Vote 7 on Chart IV.)

The influence of the moderates in congress was noted by Robert Liston, British minister to the United States. Immediately prior to the XYZ papers being transmitted to Congress, he pointed out that while the Federalists had a small majority of three or four

---

[11] Bayard to Bassett, Feb. 7, 1798. Donnan, *Bayard*, 47.

[12] Same to same, Feb. 16, 1798. *Ibid.*, 48.

[13] Otis to Mrs. Otis, Feb. 24, 1798. Morison, *Otis*, I, 133. Higginson provides a description of the situation in Boston. The question, he declared " has divided our friends more than any such question did before. My own opinion was that it would be improper, unless it was intended to keep the president's birthday also, when it comes round." In this manner it was finally decided, to celebrate both.

" I mention this as an evidence of the proneness there is among our friends to divide upon smaller points, and the difficulty there is to keep them united for want of system and discipline. In this respect the Jacobins have greatly the advantage." Higginson to Pickering, Feb. 22, 1798. *American Historical Association Report, 1896*, I, 801.

in the common course of business, measures of energy were rejected or put off by the same margin.[14]

On March 5, Adams transmitted to Congress a brief dispatch announcing that hope of success for the envoys was at an end; full information would be forthcoming as soon as the entire correspondence could be deciphered.[15] On the 19th he informed Congress that through no fault of the United States, the French had refused to accept the mission. Nothing remained but to prepare measures of defense which would be adequate to protect commerce.[16] The dispatches themselves he decided not to communicate, fearing the effect on the envoys, who were still in France.

This information was regarded by the Federalists as announcing a situation virtually equivalent to war.[17] To the Republicans, however, such a message, without the dispatches, was regarded as an insufficient explanation. They desired, as in the case of the Jay Treaty, to see the dispatches. Similarly, among some of the moderate Federalists, a desire to see the instructions and to hear the reasons advanced by France for not receiving the mission, operated to produce a call for the papers. In most instances, however, the moderate Federalists were satisfied with the judgment of the President, and were willing to act with no further ado. But the news of the insulting treatment of our envoys began to get abroad. Thereupon, the High-Federalists, who had most vehemently opposed the call for dispatches on the Jay Treaty, were now extremely anxious for the papers. On account of the inconsistency, their position was embarrassing. Upon considering the effect that the papers would have, both upon the waverers in Congress and the public at large, they forgot their scruples. Accordingly, on April 2, a combination of Republicans and High-Federalists carried a motion calling upon the President for the communications.

[14] Liston to Grenville, No. 4, Philadelphia, 29 Feb., 1798, *Adams Transcripts* (Library of Congress).

[15] *Annals*, VII, 1200.

[16] *Ibid.*, 1271.

[17] Remarks by Sitgreaves, *Annals*, VII, 1320. March 27, 1798. Also by Sewall, *Ibid.*, 1327.

The vote in question is significant in the highest degree. Commenting upon it, Jefferson wrote to Madison, " This was carried by a great majority. In this case, there appeared a separate squad, to wit, the Pinckney interest, which is a distinct thing, and will be seen sometimes to lurch the President. It is in truth the Hamilton party, whereof P[inckney] is only made the stalking horse." [18]

The erstwhile candidate for the vice-presidency, Thomas Pinckney, was among those joining in the call for papers. Upon the appointment of William Smith as minister to Portugal, Pinckney had been elected to the vacancy from the Charleston District. Rutledge and Harper joined him. From New England, John Allen of Connecticut led the squad. He was the most virulent Federalist in the House, at times becoming incoherent in debate, so exasperated did he become at the Republicans. Bartlett of Essex County, Massachusetts, Wadsworth of the second Maine District, Bayard of Delaware, and Brooks and Hosmer of New York were also included. In the case of Baer and Craik of Maryland, it is a question as to whether there is the same motivation as with the above members.

At this point, however, Adams embarked upon a policy which identified him even more closely with the High-Federalists. In order to provide an outlet for popular demonstrations of confidence, the custom of drawing up and presenting addresses to the President was utilized. Under the system a given meeting would draw up an address and it would be sent to the President. In his answers to these addresses Adams' expressions attained a virulence worthy of such extremists as Pickering and Sedgwick. The electioneering efforts of the French Minister to the United States, Adet, had been a feature of the presidential campaign of 1796 which evidently still lingered in Adams' mind. On top of this came the publication of the dispatches containing assertions that the French party in the United States would be appealed to by France to thwart any measures which the Federalists might take against the Great Nation. Boasting of that " diplomatic

---

[18] Jefferson to Madison, April 5, 1798. Jefferson's *Works*, VII, 230.

skill " which had so aided the French cause in the conquest of Switzerland, Holland, and the Italian States, the French sought to convince the American envoys that it would be impossible for America to make effective resistence, that the only way out was the payment of the *douceur* as a preliminary to negotiation. This added insult to injury. It showed that the French, having twice made a direct appeal to the voters — policies employed by both Genêt and Adet — now proposed a continuation of this policy, and in addition demanded a bribe.

Adams' answers to the addresses were in tones even more belligerent than the threats of the French. The general statements which pervaded the first answers set forth the position of the United States. Adams declared that negotiations had been attempted with pacific intentions. They had been repulsed. It was now the obligation of every citizen to join with the government in opposition to the insults.[19] On parties the position taken by Adams was as follows: " If the American people were, as represented, in opposition to the government of their choice, it would show them ripe for military despotism under foreign influence." [20] Lest there might be any question as to the practical implication of these sentiments, everyone was urged to vote the Federalist ticket: " I sincerely congratulate the town of Weston, on their signal felicity, in having no disorganizers. Two or three of this description of character are sufficient to destroy the good neighborhood, interrupt the harmony, and poison the happiness of a thousand families. A town that is free from them will ever prove their federalism in elections, be firm in the cause of their country, and ready to defend it in all emergencies. . . ." [21]

[19] For example, to Camden Co., N. J., May 1, 1798; to Newark, N. J., May 1, 1798; to Georgetown, Md., April 27, 1798. All from *Gazette of the United States*, May 2, 1798. A selection of these Addresses is in Adams' *Works*, IX, 180-236. Many, of necessity, are omitted from the *Works*, so in most cases reference can be given only to the contemporary press. A complete collection of these addresses and answers would fill a number of volumes. The Republican press refused to publish them, unless they were derogatory to the President.

[20] To the citizens of Philadelphia, May 8, 1798. *Gazette of the United States*, May 15, 1798.

[21] To the citizens of Weston, Mass., Weston, Aug. 8, 1798. *Centinel*, Aug. 15, 1798.

Adams did, however, absolve the opposition from any general imputation of disloyalty, stating, " I am happy to assure you, that as far as my information extends, the opposition to the federal government, in all the states, as well as in New Hampshire, is too small to merit the name of division; it is a difference of sentiments in public measures, not an alienation of affection to their country." [22] For the basis of this opposition he gave a description expressive of his principles as set forth in his works on government: " I believe, however, that the distinction of aristocrat and democrat, however odious and pernicious it may be rendered, by political artifice as particular conjectures, will never be done away, as long as some men are taller, and others shorter, some wiser and others sillier, some more virtuous and others more vicious, some richer and others poorer. The distinction is grounded on unalterable nature, and human wisdom can do no more than reconcile the parties by equitable establishments and equal laws, securing as far as possible to every one, his own." [23]

Hamilton's reaction to the addresses in one instance is interesting. The " soldier citizens " of New Jersey declared, " Let our enemies flatter themselves that we are a divided people. — In New Jersey, Sir, with the exception of a few degraded and a few deluded characters, to whose persons, and to whose services the invading foe shall be welcome, from the moment of their arrival, and whom we shall engage to convey in safety to their lines — In New Jersey, Sir, there is but *one voice.* — . . ." [24] To this portion of the address Adams replied: ". . . The degraded and deluded characters may tremble, lest they should be condemned to the severest punishment an American can suffer — that of being conveyed in safety *within the lines* of an invading enemy." [25]

Referring to this reply, Hamilton wrote, " The answer . . . contains in the close a very indifferent passage. The sentiment is intemperate and revolutionary. It is not for us, particularly for the government, to breathe an irregular or violent spirit. Hitherto

[22] To the Legislature of New Hampshire, June 29, 1798. *Works*, IX, 203.
[23] To the citizens of Harrison Co., Va., Aug. 13, 1798. *Works*, IX, 216.
[24] *Centinel*, May 25, 1798.
[25] May 31, 1798. *Works*, IX, 196.

I have much liked the President's answers, as, in the main, within proper bounds, and calculated to animate and raise the public mind. But there are limits which must not be passed, and from my knowledge of the ardor of the President's mind, and this specimen of the effects of that ardor, I begin to be apprehensive that he may run into indiscretion. This will do harm to the government, to the cause, and to himself. Some hint must be given, for we must make no mistakes." [26] This advice is just, as by virtually everyone, as with Hamilton, the address would be taken as applying to the whole Republican party. Consequently the effect would be quite harmful. It is believed, however, that this is not the outlook held by Adams, as will presently appear.[27]

The temper of Adams' addresses was the subject of the highest praise by the most extreme Federalists.[28] On the other hand they were deplored by the Republicans as being insulting to France and as removing the chances of peace which might still exist.[29]

In anticipation of the measures of defense which would need to be taken, Hamilton had formulated a complete program as early as January, 1798. These measures were now repeated and somewhat enlarged upon in a letter to Pickering. It is evident that, though this was before the communication of even Adams' message of March 19, Hamilton was aware of the general contents of the dispatches at the date of this letter, March 17, 1798. This letter outlined the program of the second session of the Fifth Congress. It involved the following features: First, merchant ships should be permitted to arm. Second, the frigates under construction should be completed. Third, power should be given to the President to build ten ships of the line in case of actual war. Fourth, an actual army of twenty thousand should be provided at once, supplemented by a provisional army of thirty thousand. Fifth, all important ports should be fortified, the ones in question

---

[26] Hamilton to Wolcott, New York, June 5, 1798. Hamilton's *Works*, (Hamilton, ed.) VI, 294.

[27] Chapter XIII, below.

[28] Troup to King, New York, June 3, 1798. King's *King*, II, 228. Cabot to Wolcott, Brookline, June 9, 1798. Lodge, *Cabot*, 158.

[29] Jefferson to Madison, May 3, 1798. Jefferson's *Works*, VII, 246.

being designated in Hamilton's letter. Sixth, new sources of revenue should at once be found. Seventh, treaties with France should be suspended at once by act of Congress. Finally, privateers should be licensed.[30]

At the same time Hamilton wrote a series of articles which ran through the press. These were entitled " The Stand " and appeared over the signature of " Titus Manlius." In this series the adoption of the above measures was strongly urged. A significant passage is that which relates to the importance of raising the army. " The resolution to raise an army, it is to be feared, is that one of the measures suggested which will meet with the greatest obstacle — and yet it is the one which ought to unite opinion. . . .

" The propriety of the measure is so palpable, that it will argue treachery or incapacity in our councils, if it be not adopted. The friends of the government owe it to their characters to press it; its opposers [can prove they are not foreign by concurring in the measure]." [31]

In view of the fact that Adams favored the navy as a means of defense, this last paragraph was regarded as highly exceptionable by the friends of the President.[32]

The scene of interest now returns to Congress, which had the problem of arranging proper steps for defense. The Republican program of giving no further grievance to France now had, of course, no chance of adoption. The Republicans also felt that even the refusal by France to accept our diplomatic representatives did not give reason for war. The merchants should be given the power to protect their own vessels through permission to arm under certain restrictions. Finally fortifications should be erected on the seacoast and adequate measures taken for internal defense.[33] Later developments showed that the Republican plan

[30] Hamilton to Pickering, New York, March 17, 1798. Hamilton's *Works* (Hamilton, ed.) VI, 269.

[31] Hamilton's *Works* (Hamilton, ed.) VII, 675.

[32] See below, Chapter XII.

[33] Sprigg Resolution, *Annals*, VIII, 1319. March 27, 1798.

for internal defense consisted of reorganizing the militia and securing an adequate supply of arms.

Instead of such moderate measures the Federalist program was introduced on April 9, when recommendations from the Secretary of War were communicated through Representative Samuel Sewall of the House Committee of Defense. These were considerably beneath the recommendations of Hamilton and had the support of the President. They were not greatly in advance of the position Adams had taken from the start, as set forth in the recommendation to the special session of May, 1797. They proposed the creation of three additional regiments, one each of cavalry, infantry, and artillery. The three frigates were to be completed and twenty smaller vessels constructed. A provisional army of twenty thousand would be necessary, to be called out by the President in case of danger. Munitions should be supplied and coastal fortifications erected.[34] It will be observed that there is in this recommendation a discrepancy of over seventeen thousand in the size of the army to be raised, as compared with the number desired by Hamilton. Likewise there is a gap of ten thousand in the case of the provisional army.

Strenuous efforts were now made by the High-Federalists to substitute Hamilton's program for the President's. These succeeded to a considerable degree. Increases above the proposed three regiments were continually tacked on, until on July 5 a motion carried by the casting vote of the Speaker raised the total of regiments to be raised from eight to twelve, assuring an army of around twelve thousand (Vote 26, Chart IV).

In the case of the naval force, however, a reduction was obtained. Sixteen vessels were recommended from the Committee. Some of the High-Federalists, including Harper, did not support this measure. Similarly there was, with the relinquishment of pressure upon them, a revolt on the part of the moderates (Vote 9, Chart IV). During the course of the debate on this measure one of these moderates, General John Williams, complained bitterly of the burden being placed upon the farming interests

[34] *American State Papers, Military Affairs* (Washington, 1832), I, 120.

by the demands of the commercial sections for defense. This is the more significant, as he represented a New York district which was undergoing a transition to Republicanism even during the height of the XYZ fervor. General Williams' statement quoted above, in regard to Republicans being a spark which should be extinguished, establishes the fact that he represented orthodox Federalist views in that respect. However he knew that the measures now being demanded were more than the agrarian Federalists voters would support. His statement is as follows:

He knew the landed property of the country was equal to any expense, and in case of war (which God forbid) both money and personal services would be cheerfully afforded; but when farmers were called upon to pay their money, they would inquire into the propriety of this and that appropriation. . . .

. . . he also knew that several seamen of the Eastern States, finding their employment of late precarious, had settled as farmers in his neighborhood, and after a little time were among the best farmers in the country. He thought it probable that others might take the same course.

As to the commerce of this country, he thought it had extended too far. As an agriculturist, he would go all reasonable lengths in the protection of commerce; but when this commerce becomes so unwieldy that it is not possible to protect one-fourth of it, he could not go to the lengths that some gentlemen were desirous of going for the protection of it. . . .

After complaining of the amount of drawbacks from customs allowed during the past year to the shippers for re-export, he continued:

He was ready to meet the commercial gentlemen on assertion, and if twelve vessels were agreed upon, he should propose an additional duty on drawbacks, as well as some articles of luxury imported. He knew that the commercial and agricultural interests were intimately connected, but he wished agriculture not to be too heavily burdened for the support of commerce. If the landed interest was to be called upon for three or four millions of dollars a year to protect commerce, the country had better have no commerce at all.

Mr. W. asked if the strength of the country did not consist in the number of its inhabitants? Does extensive commerce populate the country? It did not; it was mistaken zeal which drove men to pursue commerce instead of agriculture, and to suppose that it was that which served the best interests of the country. He did not believe it. At the close of the late war, in 1783, and 1784, in the part of the country from which he came, the people never saw happier days — their wealth flowed in on all sides; any quantity of money could have been had; but two years afterwards, the people were.drawn off from their own domestic manufactures, to purchase foreign commodities, and their state completely changed. In the Eastern States in particular, manufactories were increasing; but when foreign commodities began to flow in such abundance into the country the home manufactories were annihilated, and the people got into debt.[35]

Several points in relation to this are interesting. In the first place the failure of some of the High-Federalists to support the navy is probably indicative of the superior weight of Hamilton's influence, in his insistence upon the army. Second, the fact that Adams' strongly national spirit brought him to support the navy so ardently served as an additional factor in alienating Federalist agrarian support, particularly outside New England. In this instance his policy was satisfactory neither to the moderates nor to the High-Federalists.

The split in Federalist policy over the Navy developed in the press. Adams' policy of a small army but large navy was defended by the *Commercial Advertiser* (Noah Webster's paper) because: "a navy will prevent all the enormous expense of large land armies. In our present situation, our militia should be disciplined, and our arsenals full — we should be prepared to resist an enemy on our shores." [36] But, representing the opposing views of the High-Federalists, Cobbett urged dependence on British convoys.[37]

[35] *Annals*, VIII, 1464-66. April 19, 1798.

[36] July 27, 1798.

[37] *Porcupine's Gazette*, April 3, 1798. Harold and Margaret Sprout in discussing the program for the navy in their *Rise of American Naval Power, 1776-1918* (Princeton, 1939), Chapter IV, miss this split in the Federalist ranks by failing to compare votes on various phases of the naval program. Compare votes 9 and 11 in Vote Chart IV with their table at p. 48.

The policy which the Federalists followed at this time was avowedly patterned on that of England in constantly keeping up an alarm over impending danger in order to stifle all opposition. As between the actual danger in England on the one hand and in the United States on the other there was considerable difference, but every effort was made to obscure this. The discovery that the French army then being prepared was for the invasion of America, not England, was announced on May 10 to the House by the Speaker, now ardently Federalist.[38] On June 9 the *Gazette of the United States* published " authentic information " from Europe that this was the case.[39] Dayton, Brooks, and endless numbers of other Federalists asserted that all opposition to defense measures showed a disposition to prepare the way for fraternizing with the enemy, or indicated a desire to flee rather than to defend the country.[40] Harper, in the course of remarks concerning a letter from Representative William Findley of Pennsylvania to his constitutents, declared, ". . . I will add, that I should never have troubled the House on the subject of this person's conduct, did not that age, which he dishonors, render him an unfit subject for personal chastisement." [41]

Harper likewise was busily engaged in tracking down conspiracies. He assured the House that he had in his hands certain threads which would lead to discoveries of such a nature as to convict the opposition of treason. There was " a faction leagued with a foreign power to effect a revolution or a subjugation of this country by the arms of that foreign power." [42] Cobbett published information of a conspiracy by the United Irishmen.[43]

[38] *Annals*, VIII, 1679.   May 10, 1798.

[39] *Gazette of the United States*, June 9, 1798.

[40] *Annals*, VIII, 1677.   May 10, 1798.   *Ibid.*, 1751, May 16, 1798.

[41] *Ibid.*, 1415.   April 12, 1798.

[42] *Ibid.*, 2024.   June 21, 1798.   Also *Ibid.*, 1992.   June 17, 1798.

[43] Cobbett, William, *Detection of a Conspiracy formed by the United Irishmen, with the Evident Intention of Aiding the Tyrants of France in Subverting the Government of the United States of America* (Philadelphia, May, 1798).

Someone sent John Adams a letter that Philadelphia was to be burned.[44] The Black Cockade (worn in the hat) was mounted by the Federalists, receiving the designation of British Cockade by the Republicans.[45] It was worn by members of the Federalist party in Congress. In Philadelphia riots took place between those wearing the black, and those wearing the red cockade, which had replaced the tricolour as the badge of Republicanism.[46]

[44] Morison, *Otis*, I, 110-11.
[45] *Gazette of the United States*, May, 1798, passim.
[46] Jefferson to Madison, Philadelphia, May 10, 1798. Jefferson's *Works*, VII, 24.

Chapter 10

The Alien and Sedition Laws;
Defense Legislation; War?

IT was in the tense atmosphere of threatening war against France
and bitter party animosity that the extremist legislation of
the second session of the Fifth Congress was enacted. The seed
which, in the House, grew into the Alien and Sedition Laws had
a harmless appearance at the start.[1] On April 17 Representative
Joshua Coit, the Connecticut moderate Federalist, introduced a
resolution instructing the House Committee for Protection of
Commerce and Defense of the Country to look into the question
of the length of the term of naturalization, which at this time,
stood at five years. When called upon the floor two days later
this was amended to instruct the Committee also to consider
regulations for resident aliens. This passed unanimously.[2] Sewall,
chairman of the Committee, reported on May 1 three recommendations: first, that there should be a longer period for naturalization; second, that a system of report and registry for aliens
should be adopted; third, that legislation should be enacted to
provide for the deportation of aliens of a country with which the
United States was at war.[3] During the course of the debates on
these resolutions Harper proposed that the rights of United
States citizenship should be restricted to the native born.[4] Otis
proposed that none but native born should hold office in the
federal government.[5] In both cases these were withdrawn as

---

[1] The recent work by John C. Miller, *Crisis in Freedom: The Alien and
Sedition Acts* (Boston, 1951) is the fullest and best treatment of the Alien
and Sedition Acts.

[2] *Annals*, VIII, 1427, April 17, 1798; *Ibid.*, 1453. April 19, 1798.

[3] *Ibid.*, 1566. May 1, 1798.

[4] *Annals*, VIII, 1567. May 2, 1798.

[5] *Ibid.*, 1648-70. May 2-3, 1798.

152

being beyond the power of Congress. The latter proposition, however, was recommended as a subject for a Constitutional amendment by several states.[6]

Before proceeding further to trace the legislative progress of the Alien and Sedition Laws, the origin of this legislation should be considered, this being important for an understanding of the views of the High-Federalists. Primarily these laws were a manifestation of the Federalist belief that they alone were fit to rule, and a resentment of all criticism of their policy. Secondly, the extraordinary virulence of the press gave countenance to this feeling, on the ground that it was an extension of the law of libel. The reasoning runs something as follows: There is great danger to public peace and security from the attempts to tear down the character of public officials; consequently, it should be the business of the prosecuting attorneys to protect the officials of the government, without the necessity of the individuals instituting suit on their own behalf. It is obvious, however, that only the most jealous impartiality could prevent such a doctrine from becoming an instrument of oppression; which is another way of saying that it would be impossible.

Such an attitude toward the criticism of the government was taken early by certain of the judges. One such example is recorded in the diary of the Rev. William Bentley, a New England Congregationalist minister, whose comments on this period are generally balanced and enlightening. On November 8, 1796, he states that he attended the opening of the Massachusetts Supreme Court, which was presided over by Chief Justice Francis Dana. "After the usual articles of charge the Chief Justice Dana remarked upon the slanders against great characters in the service of their country. . . ."[7] The following year Dana delivered a charge of like nature.[8]

Further, quite similar to the doctrine set forth by Dana is the position taken by United States Supreme Court Justice James Iredell in 1797. As of this date Supreme Court Justices rode on

---

[6] *Ibid.*, 2132. July 9, 1798.

[7] Bentley, William J., *Diary* (Salem, 1905-15), II, 204.

[8] *Ibid.*, 241.

circuit; Iredell's included Virginia. One of the Republican Virginia Representatives to Congress, Cabell, was presented by the Richmond Grand Jury, following a charge of Iredell strongly condemning the " unsettling tendencies " of certain published letters of Representatives to their constitutents.[9] Iredell denied, later, that he had Cabell in mind, contending that he was concerned with other letters.[10] This has little to do, though, with the principle of the matter. Commenting upon the presentment, Cabell stated, " It has, however, been a regular practice of the federal judges to make political discourses to the grand jurors throughout the United States. They have became a band of political preachers, instead of a sage body to administer the law: — They seem to be making use of their power and influence both personally and officially to control the freedom of opinion, and these things excite a suspicion that the time will come, when men of different political and religious sentiments from the judges will not find that easy access to justice which those of different opinions may expect." [11] This presentment of Cabell has been termed by Randall, the biographer of Jefferson, the first note of the Alien and Sedition Laws.[12] It has likewise been commented upon by Morison.[13] However, it would appear that rather than being an isolated incident, it represented the general view of the Federalists toward the opposition. Further confirmation of this is derived from a letter by Supreme Court Justice Samuel Chase written in December, 1796. Referring to the publication of Adet's notes in the *Aurora*, he stated his opinion that an indictment for libel should be brought against the paper for printing this article.[14]

Another source of the laws in question is to be found in the doctrine that the common law of England was a part of the law of the United States. This doctrine was stated as early as May

[9] *Gazette of the United States*, June 5, 1797.
[10] *Ibid.*, July 6, 1797.
[11] *Aurora*, May 31, 1797.
[12] Randall, H. S., *Life of Jefferson* (New York, 1856), II, 376.
[13] Morison, *Otis*, I, 116, Note 12.
[14] Chase to McHenry, Dec. 4, 1796. Steiner, *McHenry*, 205.

22, 1793 by Chief Justice John Jay in a charge to the Richmond
Federal Grand Jury.[15] In July of this same year, Justice James
Wilson followed the same principle in a charge to the Philadelphia
Federal Grand Jury in the *Case of Gideon Henfield*.[16] Finally,
Justice Peters upheld the same doctrine in *United States* v.
Worrall in 1793,[17] and so did Chief Justice Ellsworth in his charge
to the jury in the *Case of Isaac Williams* in 1799.[18] The general
ground was that without legislation by Congress, the Federal
Courts might mete out punishment for offenses under the common
law when a federal question or federal jurisdiction was involved.
This doctrine ran counter to the Jeffersonian doctrine of federal
jurisdiction being narrowly limited to the powers delegated under
the constitution. It naturally opened the federal courts to many
types of cases. It also permitted the courts to act in a broad area
without waiting for Congress to enact legislation if a precedent
existed in common law. This doctrine was abandoned by the
Supreme Court after the Federalist period.

This doctrine of common law jurisdiction was directly connected
with the Sedition Act, and might even be considered to make
such a statute unnecessary. The earliest federal prosecution for
sedition was brought on the basis of the precedents cited even
before the enactment of the sedition law. Benjamin F. Bache,
editor of the *Aurora*, the leading Jeffersonian newspaper, was

---

[15] Wharton, Francis, *State Trials of the United States during the Administrations of Washington and Adams* (Philadelphia, 1849), 49-59.

[16] *Ibid.*, 59-89.

[17] 2 Dallas, 384-96.

[18] *Connecticut Courant*, Sept. 30, 1799; 29 *Federal Cases*, 1330-34; Brown,
W. G., *Life of Oliver Ellsworth*, 257-59; Anderson, Frank M., " Enforcement of
the Alien and Sedition Laws," *American Historical Association Report*,
1912, 118. This case incorporated the British common law doctrine of perpetual allegiance as a part of the Law of the United States. Ellsworth held
that this common law doctrine prevented expatriation in the absence of a specific federal statute permitting expatriation. Hence Williams, who had accepted
a French commission, had not divested himself of American nationality and
was found guilty of violating American neutrality. Case was in the Federal
Circuit Court for the District of Connecticut. 29 *Federal Cases* 1330-34
reproduces the *Courant* report. Also on the common law origin of the Sedition
Law, and the *Worrall Case*, cf. Carroll, Thomas F., " Freedom of Speech and
Press in the Federalist Period," *Michigan Law Review*, XVIII, 615-51.

arrested on June 26, 1798, while the sedition act was not signed by the President until July 14.[19]

Consequently, it enabled the Federalists to take the position that the Alien and Sedition Laws actually mitigated the common law doctrine on libels, by permitting the admission of the truth in evidence. In the course of a charge to the Jury in 1798 this doctrine was clearly set forth by Judge Francis Dana of Massachusetts. He states very well the attitude of the Federalists toward the opposition, an attitude which aimed at placing the Republicans in the position of the Tories during the Revolution: ". . . He was now prepared to show that they [the Alien and Sedition Laws] were *vastly more moderate* than the provisions which Congress and the several states thought it necessary to establish during our revolutionary contest — The Judge then drew an elegant and striking parallel between the situation at the former and the present period. He observed, that at both periods there existed a daring and desperate faction in the bosom of our country, not only marshalled and organized against the government, but aided and encouraged by a foreign power. If there was any difference between them it it [sic] was in favor of the Tories in 1774 — who were adhering to a government to whom they had owed allegiance. . . . He then proceeded to state that on the 14th March, 1776, the Congress of the then United Colonies recommended to the several assemblies and councils or committees of safety to cause all persons to be disarmed within the United Colonies who are notoriously disaffected to the cause of America, or who have not associated or refuse to associate to defend them by arms.['] " The charge then proceeds to trace the course of all legislation enacted by Massachusetts against Tories, against those giving them aid and comfort, etc.[20]

---

[19] Anderson, " Alien and Sedition Laws," *loc. cit.*, 118; Smith, James Morton, in " The Aurora and the Alien and Sedition Laws," Part I, *Pennsylvania Magazine of History*, LXXII, 3-23, begins a detailed treatment of the *Aurora* case; also in his " The Sedition Law, Free Speech, and the American Political Process," *William and Mary Quarterly*, 3rd ser., IX, 497-511, he notes the connection between the British legislation, the common law precedents, and the American legislation.

[20] *Boston Gazette* (Russell's), Dec. 12, 1798.

Another source of the Alien and Sedition Laws was the press. Even before the introduction of such legislation into Congress, the Federalist press contained demands for restrictions upon the Republican press. On April 24 the *Gazette of the United States* declared that such attacks upon the government as those by Callender should be stopped. The times were too critical to permit them to continue.[21]

A further source of the Alien and Sedition Acts was the great influence which comparable British legislation had in stimulating their adoption.[22] Upon careful scrutiny, the Alien Act is copied from comparable British legislation; and sections of the Sedition Act follow the British common law and other statutes. This fact is of significance, as it suggests a more intimate interconnection between British and American policy than has generally been accepted. It would appear that this connection was in part deliberate and in part simply a product of parallel forces operating in the two countries. In any event the fact that there was such a close connection in policy is worth establishing.

The British laws which strongly influenced those adopted in the United States arose at the time that the Pitt ministry was seeking to consolidate public opinion against the French Revolution and against British organizations friendly to the ideas of the French Revolution. In 1794 Parliament had enacted a statute which authorized the government to imprison those suspected of treason. This act was of limited duration, but was repassed annually thereafter.[23] This legislation did not, however, touch upon one important source of concern to the ministry: the various corresponding societies such as the London Corresponding Society.[24] On October 29, 1795 an attack occurred against the

---

[21] *Gazette of the United States*, April 24, 1798. One of the earliest letters urging the laws is one by Higginson to Pickering, June 9, 1798. *American Historical Association Report, 1895*, I, 806.

[22] Samuel Eliot Morison has briefly noted the influence of the British alien law on the American Alien Act. Cf. *Harrison Gray Otis*, I, iii. Also see Miller, *Crisis in Freedom*, 68.

[23] *Statutes at Large* (Pickering edition), 34 George III, Ch. 54. This act was further strengthened when repassed in 1798, *Ibid.*, 38 George III, Ch. 36.

[24] Hall, Walter P., *British Radicalism, 1791-1797* (New York, 1912); *First*

King while he was driving to Parliament to deliver the speech from the throne. The opportunity was taken by the ministry to enact two laws which became the subject of wide public controversy. The first of these laws was known as the Sedition Act. The first section provided for a broadening of the definition of treason. The second section provided for punishment of anyone writing, publishing, or speaking so as to bring his majesty or the government in contempt or to arouse hatred against them. This was classified as a " high misdemeanor," and punishment might be banishment or transportation for seven years.[25] The second act was one regulating public meetings, establishing a licensing system, and empowering magistrates to adjourn meetings at which exceptional statements were made.[26] Together these acts were known as " The Two Acts," and so intense was public interest concerning them that a compendium of the parliamentary debates and record of petitions and public meetings concerning them was published.[27]

At this time it was the practice of the American papers to publish important foreign debates. Notice of these acts and the developments concerning them was taken in the American press. The leading Hamiltonian organ, the *Gazette of the United States,* noted them with approval, and observed the discomfiture of the American " Jacobins " at the successful results from them. The Republican press predicted riots in England as a protest against the acts. The Federalist press reported that actually England had become more orderly.[28] Subsequently the compendium of the debates and the texts of the laws were imported into the United

---

Report from the Committee of Secrecy appointed by the House of Lords (fourth edition, London, 1794) ; *Second Report from the Committee of Secrecy appointed by the House of Lords* (London, 1794) ; *First Report from the Committee of Secrecy* [House of Commons] (fifth edition, London, 1794) ; *Second Report from the Committee of Secrecy of the House of Commons* (fourth edition, London, 1794) .

[25] *Statutes at Large,* 36 George III, ch. 71.

[26] *Ibid.,* Ch. 8.

[27] *The History of the Two Acts* (London, 1796) .

[28] *Gazette of the United States,* March 25, 1796.

States and were widely advertised under the title, *History of the Treason and Sedition Bills lately passed in Great Britain.*[29]

At an even earlier date England had adopted legislation concerning aliens. In 1793 legislation had been passed providing for a systematic listing of those aliens arriving in England. These were also required to secure upon arrival identification papers which they should carry with them. Any aliens in the country might also be deported, and if they did not leave the country after being ordered to do so, should be transported for life.[30] Later, on June 1, 1798, this act was made more stringent by empowering the Crown to establish a national system of registration and licenses for aliens.[31]

It should also be noted that the President, John Adams, although making no recommendation to Congress concerning the Alien and Sedition Laws, and later writing that they were originated by the Hamilton faction of the party,[32] did contribute materially to the atmosphere which produced this legislation. Never a temperate person, Adams indulged in the most violent language in his replies to the addresses sent him by various groups.

In the course of these addresses Adams delivered statements which could only be interpreted as placing him in agreement with the Federalist sentiment which produced the Alien and Sedition Laws. These laws were not enacted until July. In May Adams declared, " I trust with you, that the spirit of disunion is much diminished; more however by an event which no man could have foreseen, than by our own wisdom — but unless the spirit of libelling and sedition shall be controlled by an execution of the laws, that spirit will again increase." [33] The reference to the laws as already being capable of application refers to the doctrine that the federal courts had general common law jurisdiction. The least that can be said, however, is that such sentiments did

[29] *Porcupine's Gazette*, July 12, 15, 18, August 2, 1798.

[30] *Statutes at Large*, 33 George III, Ch. 4.

[31] *Op. cit.*, 38 George III, Ch. 50.

[32] John Adams to Benjamin Rush, Quincy, November 11, 1806. *Old Family Letters*, 18.

[33] To the citizens of Easton, Pa., May 11, 1798. Boston *Centinel*, May 26, 1798.

yeoman service in preparing the way for the acts of Congress. Jefferson wondered if such remarks were made with an eye to the bills then being discussed.[34] Another of Adams' remarks of this same period is of similar tenor: " I ought not forget the worst enemy we have: — That obloquy, which you have observed, is the worst enemy to virtue, and the best friend to vice; it strives to destroy all distinction between right and wrong, it leads to divisions, sedition, civil war, and military despotism." [35]

To the citizens of Hartford, he wrote: " If the designs of foreign hostility and the views of domestic treachery are now fully disclosed — if the moderation, dignity, and wisdom of government have awed into silence the clamors of faction, and palsied the thousand tongues of calumny, if the spirit of independent freemen is again awakened, and its force is combined, I agree with you that it will be irresistable." [36] To the citizens of Franklin, North Carolina, he declared: " It was indeed high time for the friends of government and good order to exert themselves, and declare their opinions, or in a short time, there might have remained, neither government nor order." [37] Becoming even more specific, he stated to the citizens of Baltimore City and County:

Republics are always divided in opinion concerning forms of governments, and plans and details of administration — these divisions are generally harmless, often salutary, and seldom very hurtful, except when foreign nations interfere and by their arts and agents excite and ferment them into parties and factions: such interference and influence must be resisted and exterminated or it will end in America, as it did anciently in Greece, and in our own time in Europe, in our total distruction as a republican government, and independent power.[38]

Further as early as 1797 he had stated to the citizens of Boston:

Although many of our worthy Citizens may flatter themselves that

---

[34] Jefferson to Madison, May 3, 1798. Jefferson's *Works*, IX, 246.

[35] To the Young Men of Boston, May 22, 1798. Boston *Centinel*, May 30, 1798; *Works*, IX, 194.

[36] May 10, 1798, Boston *Centinel*, May 26, 1798; *Works*, IX, 192.

[37] *Gazette of the United States*, July 3, 1798.

[38] *Ibid.*, May 4, 1798.

calumnies and contempts against the Constituted Authorities will not make a dangerous impression upon a public opinion formed with so much deliberation, intelligence and integrity, as it generally is among us . . . ; yet I cannot but be of the opinion, that the profligate spirit of falsehood and malignity, which has appeared in some, and the unguarded disposition of others, to encourage it, are serious evils, and bear a threatening aspect upon the Union of the States, their Constitution of Government, and the moral character of the Nation.[39]

In others of these addresses Adams made a specific appeal against those who would " separate the people from their government," [40] inveighed against attackers of religion,[41] and indicated that the time had come to unite on military preparations.[42] All of this was hailed with delight by the extreme Federalists,[43] while at the same time censured by the Republicans.[44] Years later Timothy Pickering wrote: ". . . Mr. Adams, in his vigorous answers to the numerous addresses presented to him, enforced by the weight of his high official station, as president of the states, contributed, doubtless, more than any other man to elevate the temper of the nation to that resistance." [45]

The next step in the legislative history of these laws was the beginning of debates in the House on the Alien Law. During the course of these debates the Federalists began to speak of the necessity of an accompanying sedition law for those already citizens. Before the House was ready to consider a sedition law the Senate had acted on its own initiative. In its original form

[39] *Centinel*, August 19, 1797.

[40] *Ibid.*, November 3, 1798; also see *Works*, IX, 95, for another containing this statement in May, 1798.

[41] *Ibid.*, October 16, 1798; also in another address in *Connecticut Courant*, Jan. 21, 1799. The implication against Jefferson is clear in both.

[42] *Centinel*, October 13, 1798 *et seq.*

[43] George Cabot to Oliver Wolcott, June 9, 1798, Lodge, Cabot, 158; Robert Troup to Rufus King, June 3, 1798; King's *King*, II, 328; Fisher Ames to Timothy Pickering, July 10, 1798; Ames, *Works of Fisher Ames*, I, 235.

[44] Jefferson specifically visualized the addresses as demanding the enactment of a sedition law. To Madison, May 3, 1798; Ford, *The Works of Thomas Jefferson*, VII, 246.

[45] Memorandum of April 6, 1819 in the Pickering Manuscripts (Massachusetts Historical Society), 46-75.

the Senate bill contained a section providing that American adherents of France should be liable for the death penalty for treason. The bill itself was entitled " An Act to define more particularly the crime of treason." [46] The text of this bill went far beyond the law as finally enacted. For the first time this text is analyzed here. It is given in full in Appendix IV. The original text is of importance in showing how far the extremists among the Federalists hoped to go.

The bill as originally drawn up declared in the first section that the government and people of France were enemies. It provided the death penalty for anyone owing allegiance to the United States, who should " adhere to the aforesaid enemies of the United States, giving them aid and comfort, within the United States or elsewhere. . . ." [47]

The second section of the bill set up the crime of misprision of treason for those having knowledge of any of the grounds of treason defined in the first section, and provided a penalty of not exceeding blank years for those found guilty.

The third section prohibited any combinations of persons to " oppose any measure or measures of the Government of the United States . . ." and provided for fine or imprisonment, plus, in the case of aliens, banishment. The fourth section was the most sweeping, making it a crime to write, print, publish, or speak, in such a manner as to charge that the government in any law entertained " motives hostile to the constitution, or liberties and happiness of the people thereof; or tending to justify the hostile conduct of the French government to the said United States, or shall, in manner aforesaid, attempt to defame the President of the United States, or any Court or Judge thereof, by declarations directly or indirectly tending to criminate their motives in an official transaction. . . ." [48]

This bill greatly alarmed Hamilton who had an extreme pro-

---

[46] Printed copy of the Bill, Senate Bills, Fifth Congress, 2nd Session (National Archives).

[47] *Ibid.*

[48] Senate Bills, Fifth Congress, 2nd Session (National Archives); CF. Doc. 1, Appendix IV, *Infra.*

gram of his own, but thought that the bill went so far it would alienate support and even precipitate civil war. He wrote to Wolcott:

> I have this moment seen a bill brought into the Senate, entitled " A Bill to define more particularly the crime of Treason, etc." There are provisions in this bill, which, according to a cursory view, appear to me highly exceptionable, and such as, more than anything else, may endanger civil war. I have not time to point out my objections by this post; but I will do it tomorrow. I hope sincerely, the thing may not be hurried through. LET US NOT ESTABLISH A TYRANNY. Energy is a very different thing from violence. If we make no false stop, we shall be essentially united; but if we push things to an extreme, we shall then give to faction body and solidity.[49]

Before passing in the Senate, the bill was amended and the first section providing the death penalty and declaring the French to be enemies was stricken from the bill. A new fourth section was added making the printing of a seditious libel in any paper competent evidence as to the guilt of the editor, publisher, or printer of the paper.[50] In this form the bill passed the Senate on July 3. John Marshall, alone of the Federalists, was critical of the act.[51]

On the tenth of July the bill as sent to the House of Representatives was reported as amended. The essential change was to modify the first and second sections, so that combinations against the law were prohibited, as well as libelous or false statements against any part of the government, or any of its officers. There still remained, however, penalty for exciting against the government or its officers ". . . The hatred of the good people of the

---

[49] Hamilton to Wolcott, June 29, 1793. Hamilton's *Works* (Hamilton, ed.), VI, 307. I disagree with Miller in his statement in *Crisis in Freedom*, 71, that Hamilton disapproved of the Sedition Act. Rather, he disapproved of this version. Actually, he indicated specific approval. See his 1799 letter in my Chapter 12.

[50] Amendments to Sedition Bill, Fifth Congress, Second Session (National Archives). Cf. Doc. 2, Appendix IV, *Infra*.

[51] *Senate Journal*, 417; Fifth Congress, Second Session; Miller, *Crisis in Freedom*, 182-85.

United States, or to stir up sedition within the United States." [52]
Two sections were substituted for the third and fourth sections
which permitted the introduction of the truth of any statements as
a part of the defense against charges, and limited the operation of
the law until March 3, 1801. With these final changes the law
passed the House, the Senate concurred in the amendments, and
the President signed the law July 14, 1798. [53]

The law, as enacted, was a compendium of the various British
common law principles on seditious libel, plus one or two original
features. [54] In certain respects, the law went further than the
existing British practice. The famous *Anti-Jacobin Review* of
London, the British administration organ, hailed the passage of
the sedition act and noted useful features in it which went beyond
the common law. [55] On the other hand, the admission of the truth
in evidence was a mitigation of one feature of the British law.
The Federalists, now convinced that the British common law was
a general part of the federal jurisdiction, argued that in this last
respect what they had done was to lessen the severity of the
common law principles which were in force in any event. Based
on the doctrines of *U. S. v. Worrall*, this may have been the case.
On the other hand now this legislation was explicit, doubt was
removed. In practice the legislation proved open to all the abuses
the Republican opponents had stated during the course of the
debates in the House. It was not long before Republican editors
and all leading Jeffersonian papers began to be prosecuted under
this act, and one member of Congress, Matthew Lyon, also went
to jail. [56]

[52] House of Representatives, Amendments to Sedition Bill, Fifth Congress,
Second Session (National Archives).

[53] *Senate Journal*, 472; Fifth Congress, Second Session, July 14; *Statutes at
Large*, I, 596 (Ch. LXXIII); also Doc. 3, Appendix IV, *Infra*.

[54] Hailsham, Viscount, ed., *Halsbury's Laws of England*, Second edition
(London, 1933), IX, 302-304; Stephens, H. J., *Summary of the Criminal Law*
(London, 1834), 52; Russell, W. O., *A Treatise on Crimes and Misdemeanors*,
1st American ed. by Daniel Davis (Boston, 1824), I, 316 ff.; Stephen, James
F., *History of the Criminal Law of England* (London, 1883), II, Ch. 24,
298-395.   [55] Vol. II, 350 (March, 1799).

[56] Wharton, Francis, " Trial of Matthew Lyon," *State Trials of the United*

In addition to the bias of the judges, the practice of the marshals in empanelling Federalists for jury service converted the law into an engine of the Federalist political machine.[57] For all practical purposes the definition of sedition might have been that taken from the *Gazette of the United States,* " It is Patriotism to write in favor of our government — it is sedition to write against it." [58] The manner in which the leading Republican papers were made the object of prosecution under the sedition law has been pointed out by Anderson in his article on the enforcement of the laws. Another writer of recent date calls the period of the Alien and Sedition Laws " The Blackout of Freedom." [59]

During the session three laws were enacted concerning aliens. The first of these, the Alien Act, followed closely the British Aliens Act of 1793.[60] The United States act provided that the President might, at any time, in peace or war, order from the country an alien he deemed to be dangerous. Federal marshals should execute such presidential orders. Provision for a hearing might stay the deportation, and aliens deemed not dangerous be permitted to receive licenses. Those finally deported might take their property with them. A further provision of the act required masters of all vessels to file lists of entering aliens with collectors of customs. This act was effective for two years.

The second act concerning aliens changed the naturalization provisions by extending the time for naturalization from five to fourteen years. An elaborate system was established whereby clerks of courts handling declarations of intention and naturalization proceedings must file records of such actions with the federal Secretary of State. Most important, a system of registra-

---

States during the Administration of Washington and Adams, 333-44; Anderson, " Enforcement of the Alien and Sedition Laws," *loc. cit.,* 115-30; McLaughlin, *Matthew Lyon,* 306-82.

[57] Anderson, " Alien and Sedition Laws," *loc. cit.*

[58] *Gazette of the United States,* October 10, 1798.

[59] Anderson, " Alien and Sedition Laws," *loc. cit.,* 119; Weyl, Nathaniel, *Treason* (New York, 1950) , 87-109; and Malone, Dumas, *Public Life of Thomas Cooper* (New Haven, 1926) , 111-49.

[60] United States *Statutes at Large,* I, 570-72; *Statutes at Large,* 33 George III, Chapter IV.

tion for all white aliens in the United States was established, whereby all aliens were required to register with clerks of the district court, or if these be more than ten miles distant, registration with federal collectors at ports might be substituted. All such registrations had to be reported monthly to the federal Secretary of State. Provisions for fees and penalties were also included.[61]

The third act applied to alien enemies. It defined alien enemies as those in the United States, citizens of a foreign power, ". . . whenever there shall be a declared war between the United States and any foreign nation or government, or any invasion or predatory incursion shall be perpetrated, attempted or threatened against the territory of the United States, and the President of the United States shall make public proclamation of the event." Upon such proclamation being issued all such enemy aliens should be liable to be apprehended, restrained, and removed from the United States.[62]

The enactment of such sweeping legislation naturally brought about violent opposition. During the course of the debate on the Alien Law the following remarks by Livingston were thereafter pointed out by the Federalists as proof of the revolutionary aims of the Republicans:

If there is, then, any necessity for the system now proposed, it is more necessary to be enforced against our own citizens than against strangers; and I have no doubt, that either in this, or some other shape, this will be attempted. I now ask sir, whether the people of America are prepared for this? Whether they are willing to part with all the means which the wisdom of their ancestors discovered, and their own caution so lately adopted to secure their own persons? Whether they are ready to submit to imprisonment, or exile, whenever suspicion, calumny, or vengeance shall mark them for ruin? Are they base enough to be prepared for this? No, sir, they will, I repeat it, they will resist this tyrannic system! The people will oppose, the States will not submit to its operation. They ought not to acquiesce,

---

[61] United States *Statutes at Large*, I, 566-69, approved June 18, 1798.

[62] United States *Statutes at Large*, I, 577-78 (Chapter LVI), approved July 6, 1798.

and I pray to God they never may. My opinions, sir, on this subject are explicit, and I wish they may be known; they are, that whenever our laws manifestly infringe the Constitution under which they were made, the people ought not to hesitate which they should obey. If we exceed our powers we become tyrants, and our acts have no effect. Thus, sir, one of the first effects of measures such as this, if they be not acquiesced in, will be disaffection among the states, and opposition among the people of your Government; tumults, violations, and a recurrence to first revolutionary principles. If they are submitted to, the consequence will be worse. After such manifest violation of the principles of our Constitution the form will not long be sacred. Presently every vestige of it will be lost and swallowed up in the gulf of despotism; but should the evil proceed no further than the execution of the present law, what a fearful picture will our country present. The system of espionage thus established, the country will swarm with informers, spies, delators, and all that reptile tribe. . . .[63]

Aside from that on the Alien and Sedition Laws, the most bitter debates of this session occurred over the measures relative to the state militia. On June 14, the debate was held over the bill providing arms for the militia. This measure involved no gift to the militia, but would have a good supply furnished from which the militia could buy their own. Dayton moved to strike out the first section of the act. At once Harrison of Virginia charged that the Federalists were trying to keep the South from arming; before, all were traitors who objected to expense, but now excuses were advanced to keep arms out of the hands of the people. Thatcher of Maine joined Dayton in opposing the turning over of arms to the states for sale to the militia. Allen of Connecticut declared in reply to the Republicans that no one in Kentucky would be able to buy arms at any rate. (This had reference to a statement by Davis of Kentucky, who, in opposing the land tax, asserted that when he left the state there was not $10,000 in money in all Kentucky.) W. C. C. Claiborne had advanced the same argument on behalf of Tennessee.[64] Continuing, Allen declared that instead of turning over the arms to the people

[63] *Annals*, VIII, 2014. June 21, 1798.
[64] *Annals*, VIII, 1917. June 13, 1798.

they should be placed in depositories " for safekeeping." This move on the part of the Federalists failed, arms being provided.[65]

A similar spirit of distrust was shown during debates on a proposed bill permitting the President to accept the services of companies of volunteers which would be the nucleus of the provisional army. The officers of these companies would be appointed by the president, not the governors. Moreover, those serving should be exempt from state militia service. In this instance, an effort was made by the Republicans to prevent furnishing free arms for the volunteers. This was defeated.

The direct tax was not resisted by the Republicans. Efforts were made to change the mode of assessment, and with some success. However, the Republicans were, in principle, in favor of a direct tax. They had sought to secure its passage in earlier congresses rather than the excise. Consequently this measure passed by a vote of 62-19. An added factor in securing their acquiescence was the obvious necessity for new revenue. To have opposed it would have been to risk the accusation of attempting to defeat all defense measures. They had, however, made a sufficiently strenuous effort against the mode of levying to enable them to make political capital of its subsequent unpopularity.[66]

The last important measure of the session was an attempt by the Federalists to secure a direct declaration of war despite the absence of any recommendation by the President of such a measure. As early as May 25 Sitgreaves had declared, "If it were known either that our envoys had left the territory of France, or were retained in the country against their will, or if it could in any way be ascertained that this mission was at an end, he gave it as his opinion that the honor, dignity, and interest of this country require that we should make war upon the French Republic, and he believed it would be the duty of Congress to declare it." [67] On June 20 and July 1, articles had appeared in

[65] *Ibid.*, 1927-33. June 14, 1798.

[66] *Annals*, VIII, 1563, 1923. May 1–June 13, 1798. Also *Ibid.*, 2066. July 2, 1798, by which vote the House concurred in the Senate plan of assessment.

[67] *Ibid.*, 1806. May 25, 1798.

the *Gazette of the United States* urging war.[68] On the latter day Sedgwick wrote to King that every Federal member of the Senate except Bingham was for an immediate declaration. The fact, however, that the House would be the test caused them to hesitate before taking action in the Senate. He felt that a declaration of war would assure the Federalists of carrying all the elections. Dayton had just told him that he thought the House would take a vote on the Fourth of July. " Unless among our most reliable friends in the House, there is absolute despair of success, the measure will be brought forward and I presume in the course of two or three days." [69] The news that such a vote would be taken must have spread rapidly. The *Centinel* of July 4 carried a lengthy article asserting that a defensive war was now forced upon the United States. Likewise the following item appeared:

Reports

It was yesterday *reported* that *England* and *Spain* were in pacific negotiation; ———— and that this day is fixed on in Congress for a declaration of war against France.[70]

On the fifth, Allen introduced the following resolution in the House: " Resolved, That a committee be appointed to consider the expedience of declaring, by Legislative act, the state and relation subsisting between the United States and the French Republic." [71] On the following day this resolution was called up for debate. It was obvious, however, that there was no possibility of carrying the resolution. Sitgreaves supported the measure, declaring, " We are now in a state of war." It was opposed by such a staunch Federalist as Sewall. The result was that the motion was voted down without a roll call.[72] It is believed that this sequence of events, ranging from the war caucus to the actual voting on a declaration of war, constitutes the most serious

---

[68] *Gazette of the United States*, June 20 and July 1, 1798.
[69] Sedgwick to King, July 1, 1798. King's *King*, II, 352.
[70] *Centinel*, July 4, 1798.
[71] *Annals*, VIII, 2114. July 5, 1798.
[72] *Ibid.*, 2116-20. July 6, 1798.

attempt in American history to declare war without a recommendation by the President.[73]

Robert Liston, the British Minister to the United States, informed Lord Grenville that a Federalist caucus had shown it was not possible to carry the motion for a declaration of war. ". . . At a meeting of the friends of Government, where the matter was taken into consideration, and the votes calculated as accurately as it was practicable, they were mortified to find that the question was still likely to be carried against them by a small majority. They therefore determined not to bring on the discussion, and it was agreed that the House should adjourn the beginning of next week." [74] The fact that the party could come so close to having the votes for a declaration of war, although this was not requested by the President, is a great tribute to Hamilton's power as opposed to the influence of the President.

Summarizing the effects of this political program on the party alignments, in this session there are only twelve who fall under the classifications of moderates. Five of these were elected as Republicans: T. Davis of Kentucky, Smith of Maryland, Freeman of Massachusetts, Hanna of Pennsylvania, and Tillinghast of Rhode Island. The seven " Half-Federalists " (those elected as

---

[73] This statement is made after comparing materials on later periods as follows: For the 1806-1808 period, Adams, Henry, *History of the United States During the Administration of Thomas Jefferson* (New York, 1930), Book III, Ch. XV, and Book IV, especially Chs. I, IV, V, VII, IX, X, XV, XVIII, and XIX; for the War of 1812, Adams, Henry, *History of the United States During the Administration of James Madison* (New York, 1930), Book VI, Chs. VI-XI and XVIII, and Pratt, Julius W., *Expansionists of 1812* (New York, 1925); for the Mexican War, Smith, Justin H., *The War with Mexico*. 2 vols. (New York, 1919), especially Vol. I, Ch. X, and McCormac, Eugene I., *James K. Polk* (Berkeley, Calif., 1922); for the Civil War, Randall, James G., *Lincoln the President*, 2 vols. (New York, 1945); for the war with Spain, Pratt, Julius W., *Expansionists of 1898* (Baltimore, 1936), and Millis, Walter, *The Martial Spirit* (New York, 1931); for World War I, Paxson, Frederic L., *America at War, 1917-1918* (Boston, 1939), and *Post War Years: Return to Normalcy, 1918-1923* (Berkeley, Calif., 1948); finally, for World War II, Sherwood, Robert, *Roosevelt and Hopkins* (New York, 1948), and Rosenman, Samuel I., *Working with Roosevelt* (New York, 1952).

[74] Liston to Grenville, Philadelphia, 14 July 1798, No. 41, *Adams Transcripts*, 1796-1798 (Library of Congress).

Federalists but who did not vote regularly as such) were: Dent of Maryland, Sprague of New Hampshire, Bullock of the Third Southern Massachusetts district, Williams of New York, Machir and Parker of Virginia, and Grove of North Carolina. Skinner of Massachusetts, of doubtful party affiliation, continued to vote with the Republicans. In April, 1798, Sedgwick counted on 54 Federalists, which included four weak ones, to 52 Republicans.[75] This may be accounted for on the ground that he was discarding one of the weakest. On the other hand, Murray counted the margin as 55 to 51, which agrees with the chart [76] (Vote Chart IV and Map 5). Party lines were drawing much tighter, there being but twelve moderates in this session compared with twenty-nine in the Fourth Congress, and compared also with twenty-three in the first session of this same Fifth Congress.

[75] Sedgwick to King, April 4, 1798, King's *King*, II, 298.
[76] Murray to John Quincy Adams, The Hague, April 13, 1798. Ford, " Murray," *loc. cit.*, 392.

Chapter 11

The Aim of Federalist Foreign Policy

THE important question which remains to be answered is, what motives prompted the program which passed Congress? Also, what were the motives of those responsible for the abortive attempt to declare war against France? First of all, foreign policy will be considered. Next the goal of the Federalists' internal policy will be outlined.

Foreign policy centers about three points: first, the question of an alliance with England, desired by some Federalists as an end in itself; second, the project of Anglo-American cooperation in Francisco de Miranda's scheme for the liberation of South America; third, the acquisition of the Floridas and Louisiana. In 1798 all of these issues were intimately related. Naturally any practical steps toward any of these goals would be based upon an open war with France.

The geographic position of the United States and the disturbed status of European affairs assured a series of intrigues by various foreign powers. The weakening Spanish Empire was fair game for both British and French. This applied to Louisiana and the Floridas as well as to Mexico, Central and South America. In the United States various Americans were in the pay of one or another of the foreign ministers to the United States. George Rogers Clark was in the pay of France.[1] Senator William Blount of Tennessee was expelled from the Senate on July 8, 1797 because of complicity with a plan of the British minister to the United States, Robert Liston, concerning the Louisiana territory.[2] Ira

---

[1] James, J. A., " George Rogers Clark," *Dictionary of American Biography*, 127-30; Kyte, George W., " A Spy on the Western Waters: The Military Intelligence Mission of General Collot in 1796," *Mississippi Valley Historical Review*, XXXIV (Dec. 1947) , 428.

[2] Liston to Grenville, Philadelphia, 25 Jan., 16 March, 10 May, 24 June, and

Allen of Vermont was probably concerned with plans against Canada in cooperation with the French.[3] Even as early as 1797 Aaron Burr was reported by the British to be involved in still another plan concerning the establishment of an independent republic in Canada.[4]

In the Washington Manuscripts there is a letter from Andrew Ellicott, United States Commissioner at Natchez, Mississippi, declaring that Brig. Gen. James Wilkinson, ranking officer in the regular army after the death of Gen. Wayne, and others were in the pay of Spain in 1797.[5] This news came as no surprise to Washington, who had warned Ellicott against both Wilkinson and the Spanish when, as President, he had dispatched Ellicott to start taking over the territory yielded by the Treaty of San Lorenzo of 1795 (Pinckney's Treaty). Under this agreement Spain had started a conciliatory policy towards the United States. This policy reversed the attempts to intrigue with the United

8 July, 1797, Dispatches Nos. 2, 8, private letter of 16 March, Nos. 19, 27, and 30. Frederick J. Turner, ed., " Documents on the Blount Conspiracy, 1795-1797," *American Historical Review*, X (April, 1905) , 574-606; also Turner, " The Policy of France toward the Mississippi Valley in the Period of Washington, and Adams," *American Historical Review*, X (January, 1905), 249-79; *Annals of Congress, Fifth Congress*, I, 34-45, 448-66, 499 ff., 672-99 and II, 2245-2415; and Whitaker, Arthur P., *The Mississippi Question, 1795-1803* (New York, 1934) .

[3] Wilbur, James B., *Ira Allen, Founder of Vermont, 1751-1814*, 2 vols. (Boston, 1928) ; Ludlum, David McW., *Social Ferment in Vermont, 1791-1850* (New York, 1939) ; Liston to Grenville, Philadelphia, 25 Jan., 1797, No. 1, *Adams Transcripts* (Library of Congress); Turner, " Blount Conspiracy," *loc. cit.*, 576-77.

[4] Liston to Grenville, Philadelphia, 1 Nov., 1797, No. 48, *Adams Transcripts* (Library of Congress). For earlier activities also see Bemis, Samuel F., " Relations between the Vermont Separatists and Great Britain, 1789-1791," *American Historical Review*, XXI, 547-60.

[5] Vol. 285 (Manuscripts Division, Library of Congress). Also see Cox, I. J., biography of Wilkinson in *DAB*, XX, pp. 222-26 and Whitaker, Arthur P., *Spanish American Frontier, 1783-1795* (Boston, 1927) and Weyl, Nathaniel, *Treason*, 119 ff. This document in the Washington papers is in the handwriting of Timothy Pickering, Secretary of State. Wilkinson had been connected with the Conway Cabal in the Revolution. As a Brigadier General, he was active in the West, was in the pay of Spain, and at the same time in communication with Hamilton in regard to invasion of Spanish territory.

States settlers in the West for disunion from the United States.
But in Federalist circles the change of heart by the Spanish was
hardly credited. The connection of Spain with France made the
two countries but one in the eyes of the Secretary of State,
Timothy Pickering. Believing that the Jeffersonians were loyal
to France, it was easy for Pickering to feel that the intriguers in
the West might be loyal to Spain. The actual attitude of many in
the West was difficult to determine at this period. Arthur P.
Whitaker has summed up the situation in the statement:
"Neither unionism nor disunionism was deeply rooted in the
West at the end of the century. Patriotism ebbed and flowed
with almost every act of the federal government and every turn
of international affairs."[6] One is almost tempted to say that the
West was loyal to the Mississippi River. Whoever controlled the
Mississippi and the outlet at New Orleans could ultimately find
great strength and support among those west of the Appalachians.
Spain's granting of the right of deposit at New Orleans to the
United States in the Treaty of 1795 helped to solidify Western
adherence to the United States, but many cross-currents were
still at work. With the increase of tension toward France, the
extreme Federalists began to consider the conquest of Louisiana
and the Floridas, and as Hamilton put it, " to squint at South
America."[7] The development of this South American policy becomes the central theme of extreme Federalist aims in 1798.

By the summer of 1798 the crisis in foreign policy had been
reached. After the ratification of Jay's Treaty, relations with
England had improved. Among the cabinet members whom
Adams had carried over from the Washington administration,
Timothy Pickering was at the same time the most narrow, most
opinionated, and the strongest. Like James McHenry, Secretary
of War, and Oliver Wolcott, Jr., Secretary of the Treasury, he
was loyal to Hamilton. But whereas these other two members
of the cabinet drew their opinions from Hamilton, Pickering made

---

[6] *The Mississippi Question*, 25.
[7] Hamilton to McHenry, New York, June 27, 1799, Hamilton's *Works*
(Hamilton, ed.) V, 283.

up his own mind first. His point of view was that of a commercial man from Salem, Massachusetts.

Pickering had been embroiled in a virulent controversy with Adet, the French minister to the United States. Following Adet's recall, the Spanish Minister, the Chevalier d'Yrujo, and Pickering carried on an embittered correspondence. Pickering made no secret of his preference for England, and his distrust of Napoleon and Spain. He managed to put all of this on a personal basis as well as a policy one. Robert Liston, the British Minister, described him as " one of the most violent Anti-gallicans I have ever met." [8]

The progress of the Napoleonic wars had resulted in depredations on American shipping by both the British and the French.[9] The XYZ affair terminated negotiations with France. Commercial intercourse was suspended, our treaty with her was annulled, and a limited naval warfare with that country began.[10] A complete reorientation of American policy was possible, and of all Adams' advisers Pickering wished to make the most sweeping changes. A part of the plan which came to the forefront was that of allying immediately with England to bring about the independence of Latin America. In England, Rufus King, the American minister, held the same relationship to Hamilton as did the members of Adams' cabinet. A New Yorker himself, long a close friend as well as political ally of Hamilton, he became the channel for a three-way correspondence. The focal point of this correspondence was the South American revolutionary leader, Francisco de Miranda, who was seeking to promote independence of South America from Spain. Miranda corresponded with Hamilton by way of King, and with the American government, also by way

[8] Liston to Grenville, Phila., 18 April, 1797, No. 16, *Henry Adams Transcripts* (Library of Congress); Ford, H. J., " Timothy Pickering," in Bemis, S. F., ed., *American Secretaries of State and their Diplomacy* (New York, 1928) II, 161-244; also on relations with England cf. Mowat, R. B., *Diplomatic Relations of Great Britain and the United States* (London, 1925).

[9] For a summary of French spoilations, cf. Bemis, Samuel F., *A Diplomatic History of the United States* (New York, 1936), 114.

[10] Allen, Gardner, W., *Our Naval War with France* (Boston, 1909).

of King. At the same time Miranda was in close touch with the British Prime Minister, Pitt, and the Foreign Secretary, Lord Grenville.

Miranda, when in America in 1783 and 1784, had communicated with many of the leaders of the Revolution. Among those in whom he felt greatest confidence were Hamilton and Knox.[11] Ever since that date he had sought to keep in touch with these two, as well as with others in the United States. So far as Hamilton is concerned, the letters written by Miranda in the 1780's to Hamilton seem to have been the only intercourse between the two until 1798.[12]

Miranda did communicate, however, with many of the Americans who represented their government in Europe at this time. John Trumbull, the artist whose reproduced pictures of the American Revolution now adorn many schoolrooms, had been appointed the fifth commissioner under the seventh article of Jay's Treaty and was serving in London.[13] As early as January 15, 1797, he wrote to President Adams' Secretary of War, Oliver Wolcott, that it would be possible for America to seize the Floridas, New Orleans and the French and Spanish West Indies. Further it would be possible to emancipate South America in cooperation with the British fleet.[14] While there is no evidence to show that Trumbull was in communication with Miranda, this plan is so like the one formulated by him, as to make it likely that Miranda was the source of the idea.

Robert Goodloe Harper, the prominent Federalist representative from South Carolina, spoke of Latin American liberation in the House in the Spring of 1797, as has already been mentioned. He likewise sought to win his district to this program in a letter to his constitutents dated May 25, 1797. There he stated: ". . . if driven into war, we can buy at a price cheap to ourselves the

[11] Robertson, W. S., "Francisco de Miranda and the Revolutionizing of Spanish America," *American Historical Association Report, 1907*, I, 251-52. Cited as "Miranda."

[12] Robertson, "Miranda," 252, 278.

[13] Trumbull, John, *Autobiography* (New York, 1841), 190.

[14] Trumbull to Wolcott, Jan. 15, 1797. Gibbs, *Wolcott*, I, 474.

full cooperation of the British navy. . . ." Further, such a rupture would enable the United States to acquire the Floridas and New Orleans, thus assuring the free navigation of the Mississippi.[15] Mexico had been added to this on the floor of the House. This led the Republicans to pounce upon these statements as an admission that Federalist policy contemplated a British alliance against France and the conquest of Mexico.[16]

As a matter of practical politics this question quieted down in 1797, but with increased tension with France revived strongly in 1798. On January 16 Miranda approached Pitt with an outline of his plan for the liberation of South America. This included a plan for an Anglo-American alliance. In the actual undertaking an American army would cooperate with a British fleet. At this part of the plan Pitt " exclaimed in a note of joyfulness and sincerity: We should much enjoy operating jointly with the United States in this enterprise." [17] At the close of this month and the first of February, Rufus King, American minister to London, had conversations with Miranda and with Grenville on the project.[18] He learned that British countenance of the project would depend upon the attitude which Spain took in regard to France. Should she ally with France it would then be the policy of England to aid Miranda.

Apparently before intimation of this latest development had reached the United States, Hamilton, in a letter to McHenry, had outlined his ideas on the matter of South America. This letter was written in January, and contained the same plans for defense as those in the letter to Pickering just after the news of the XYZ dispatches was received. On the question of the policy to be followed toward England, he stated, ". . . it is believed to be best, in any event, to avoid *alliance*." The mutual interest of the two countries would result in just as effective cooperation should a rupture occur. The proper procedure would be to have Rufus

[15] Harper, *Select Works*, 103-104.

[16] Callender, *History of America for 1796*, viii; also *Sketches of the History of America for 1798*, 52-54.

[17] Robertson, W. S., *Life of Miranda* (Chapel Hill, 1929) I, 168.

[18] King's *King*, III, 555-59.

King " sound out Pitt as to cooperation in case of open rupture, the furnishing us with naval force — the point'g the cooperation to the Floridas, Louisiana, & South American possessions of Spain, if rupture, as is probable, shall extend to her. To prevail on Britain to lodge in her Minister here ample authority for all these purposes; but all this without engagement or commitment in the first instance. All on this side of the Mississippi must be ours including both Floridas." [19] In his recommendations to the President, McHenry specified New Orleans as well, otherwise transmitting this part of the letter without change.

In all probability, before King's dispatches had reached America, Pickering sent Hamilton a detailed account of the XYZ dispatches. Pickering was most concerned about a British alliance, which he now considered both possible and desirable in the light of the dispatches. " What shall we say to the British Government? You hint at nothing. The opposition party have already insinuated that a treaty offensive and defensive has doubtless been already concluded with Great Britain — a friend of mine yesterday told me that he was asked if such a treaty had not arrived. The truth is, that not one syllable has been written to Mr. King or any one else upon the subject. I confess it to have been for some time my opinion that provisional orders should be sent to Mr. King — Mr. King in one of his latest letters desires to be particularly instructed. The dispatch boat may be directed to go from France to England with such instructions. . . ." [20] In writing this, Pickering was fairly certain to know the contents of Hamilton's earlier letter to McHenry, as his instructions to the cabinet were generally passed around. The explanation for his writing again on this point is most likely to be found in Pickering's hope that the situation created by the dispatches would cause Hamilton to change his mind.

[19] Hamilton to McHenry, January, 1798. Steiner, *McHenry*, 291. An excellent appraisal of Hamilton's plans at this period is in Schachner, Nathan, *Alexander Hamilton* (New York, 1946), Ch. XXV, especially, 383-85.

[20] Pickering to Hamilton, March 25, 1797. Hamilton's *Works* (Hamilton, ed.) VI, 485. Higginson was also urging an alliance " offensive and defensive " with England. Higginson to Pickering, June 9, 1798. *American Historical Association Report, 1896*, I, 806.

Hamilton had not materially changed his outlook. Of the XYZ dispatches he stated, " I am delighted with their contents." On the British Alliance he repeated what he had stated to McHenry, with the additional warning, " Public opinion is not prepared for it — it would not fail to be represented as to the *point to which* our previous conduct was directed and in case of offers from France satisfactory to us the public faith might be embarrassed by the calls of the people for accommodation and peace." He was anxious, however, that limited cooperation should be arranged:

The *desideratum* is that Britain could be engaged to lodge with her *Minister here* powers commensurate with such arrangements as exigencies may require & the progress of opinion permit. I see no good objection on her part to this plan—it would be good policy in her to send to this country a dozen frigates to pursue the directions of this government.[21]

In accordance with this view, Pickering did not insist on a British alliance in his conference with Adams, with whom he must have failed in any event. On April 2, he wrote King, ". . . the President does not deem it expedient at this time to make any advances to Great Britain. . . ." Some hope may have been left to King in a succeeding sentence: " In one word, being forced by France into the war, the United States and Great Britain will have a common interest to defeat the unjust and dangerous enterprise of the French Republic. . . ." [22]

King had first written to Pickering about Miranda's plans on February 7.[23] Enclosed in this dispatch was a letter for Hamilton. King, moreover, anticipated that Pickering and Hamilton would consult on the project, as in a direct communication to Hamilton on May 12 and again on May 14 he declared that fuller details would be familiar to Hamilton through the dispatches to the

[21] Hamilton to Pickering, March 27, 1798. Hamilton's *Works* (Hamilton, ed.) VI, 278.

[22] Pickering to King, April 2, 1798. Robertson, " Miranda," *loc. cit.*, 335-36. In part in King's *King*, II, 296.

[23] King to Pickering, Feb. 7, 1798. King's *King*, II, 650.

Secretary of State.[24]   Concerning the letter of February 7 from Miranda to Hamilton, Hamilton wrote:

> Several years ago this man was in America much heated with the project of liberating South America from the Spanish Domination.
> I had frequent conversation with him on the subject and I presume expressed ideas favorable to the object and perhaps gave an opinion that it was one to which the United States would look with interest— He went then to England upon it—Hence his present letter.   I shall not answer because I consider him as an intriguing adventurer.[25]

This endorsement bears a rather Jesuitical aspect in that it could at best be applied with sincerity only to Miranda's project, not to the general idea of participating in the liberation of South America.   The latter had been fully endorsed in the letter to McHenry.   Further, in August, Hamilton wrote to King that he had been interested in the project from the start, and at the same time communicated his approval to Miranda.[26]   Commenting on Hamilton's interest in this entire project, Whitaker correctly states: ". . . there can be no question that Hamilton threw himself heart and soul into the plan of conquest in 1798 and 1799 . . .; there was nothing chimerical about it."   Continuing, he qualifies the aims of Hamilton somewhat more than may be necessary, stating, " Mexico and Peru lay doubtfully on the outer fringe of his designs.   At the heart and center lay Florida and Louisiana." [27]

Pickering had not given up hope that his desire for a British alliance would find favor.   In June he wrote to Hamilton that he thought the position of America much more difficult without an alliance than with one.   If England fell, he declared, this would mean America would be attacked at once.   If she made peace, America, if at war with France, would likewise be made the object of assault.   Then, unless we had a treaty of alliance, England

---

[24] Robertson, *Life of Miranda*, I, 176-77.

[25] Robertson, *Life of Miranda*, I, 176-77.

[26] Hamilton to King, Aug. 22, 1798; same date to Miranda, Hamilton's *Works* (Hamilton, ed.) VI, 347-48.

[27] Whitaker, *Mississippi Question*, 117.

would not re-enter the war to save us. A third possibility, that
America might make peace with France, had completely dropped
out of Pickering's calculations by this time. That the spirit of the
country would look with disfavor upon such an alliance he
deplored: " I think the animosities and hatred engendered in
the American Revolution towards England exist yet, in some
breasts [an obvious reference to Adams] in greater force than our
interest or our safety admit; and these passions will keep us aloof
till any cooperation may become impracticable. We cannot expect
overtures from England. I very much suspect she is waiting to
receive them from us. I wish you were in a situation not only ' to
see all the cards,' but to play them. . . ." [28]

British policy coincided almost exactly with that desired by
Pickering. In 1796 instructions were sent to the British minister
in Washington: ". . . you will consider yourself as distinctly
authorized by His Majesty to assure the American Government
that, if France should commence Hostilities against it, in consequence of the Jay's Treaty concluded with this Country, His
Majesty will be ready to enter into such engagements with the
United States as may appear best calculated to repel an aggression of this nature and to make common Cause against an
Attack. . . ." [29] These instructions were renewed in 1798. It was
emphasized that only a temporary alliance was wanted. At the
same time new instructions were sent to Liston, the administration organ in London, *The Anti-Jacobin Review*, also publicly
urged an alliance with the United States.[30]

England also offered to establish a convoy system to protect
American shipping on the high seas.[31] William Cobbett, spokes-

[28] Pickering to Hamilton, June 9, 1798. Hamilton's *Works* (Hamilton, ed.)
VI, 303.

[29] Draft to Liston, Downing Street, London, March 18, 1796, No. 2. Secret,
Mayo, Bernard, ed., *Instructions to the British Ministers to the United States,
Annual Report of the American Historical Association* (Washington, 1941),
III, 114.

[30] Draft to Liston, Downing Street, London, June 8, 1798, No. 12, Mayo,
Instructions to British Ministers, 155-60; also *Anti-Jacobin Review*, August,
1798, I, 245.

[31] Draft to Liston, Downing Street, London, Jan. 27, 1797, Mayo, *Instructions to British Ministers*, 129.

man for the High-Federalists, correctly pointed out the benefits of convoys and advocated an alliance with England in his paper.[32] Finally, to prevent misunderstandings naval signals were interchanged between the two countries,[33] but that was as far as a detailed settlement went. The actual negotiation of an alliance was left for Liston to take up with the American government. Suggestion was made that Rufus King, American Minister to London, might be given detailed instructions. Meanwhile the British government suggested that the following points should be covered in preliminary conversations: [34]

1. Florida and Louisiana might be conquered by the United States without British objection.

2. England would expect to acquire St. Domingo.

3. War should be conducted by collaborative action which should include:

(a) The chief advantage to be derived from the United States by England would be the recruitment of seamen for British ships. At the moment His Majesty's Naval establishment had a surplus of both officers and ships.

(b) In return the United States would secure the service of a squadron of British ships. The number of ships in this would depend upon the extent of assistance supplied by the United States.

(c) Alternately, England would consider lending or selling ships to the United States, together with lending the services of officers, it being assumed that the United States would lack trained personnel. Such sale or loan would likewise be dependent upon the supply of

---

[32] *Porcupine's Gazette*, April 3, 1798; also cf. Cole, G. D. H., ed., *Letters from William Cobbett to Edward Thornton, 1797-1800* (Oxford, 1937); and Clark, Mary E., *Peter Porcupine in America, 1792-1800* (Philadelphia, 1939).

[33] Benj. Stoddert, Sect. of Navy, to Timothy Pickering, July 14, 1798, Misc. Letters, Dept. of State (National Archives); Pickering to Stoddert, July 23, 1798, Dept. of State, Domestic Letters, Vol. 11, 19 (National Archives); also in *Pickering Manuscripts*, Vol. 9, 84 (Massachusetts Historical Society); Liston to Grenville, Boston, 27 Sept. 1798, No. 57, informs the Foreign Office that the signals transmitted were those of Vice Admiral Vandeput, *Adams Transcripts*, 1796-1798 (Library of Congress).

[34] Draft to Liston, Downing Street, June 8, 1798, No. 12, Mayo, *Instructions to British Ministers*, 155 ff.

American seamen to man British naval vessels, as well as those operated by the United States.

Toward the end of July, 1798, Liston formally broached the proposal for an alliance to the Secretary of State. He found Pickering personally in favor of such an alliance, but deterred by the unreadiness of public opinion and the lack of instructions from the President.[35] Next Liston proceeded north to Boston and saw Adams. Adams talked freely, and declared that personally he was for such an alliance; however, " ' The people of this country (said Mr. Adams) are at present employed in deliberating upon that question; and it would perhaps not be wise to disturb their meditations; no doubt all will come out right by and by. . . .' " [36]

Adams expressed willingness to receive and listen to whatever proposals the British might wish to make. He did not feel that detailed propositions should originate with the American government. Liston took all of this at face value, and indicated that he expected negotiations to be delayed because of the illness of Mrs. Adams and the general separation of government officers during the summer.

Actually, Adams seems to have tried to tell Liston that he was interested only in a temporary alliance in case of actual war with France. Liston quoted Adams as stating:

He has been careful to reject all idea of a permanent Treaty offensive and defensive, but he has represented it as the height of folly for a people on the eve of a war not to secure the assistance and defence that may be derived from another nation engaged in the same common cause. . . .[37]

Moreover, there was a basis for many differences between England and the United States even in the British proposals for

[35] Liston to Grenville, New York, 31 August 1798, No. 52, *Adams Transcripts* (Library of Congress).

[36] Liston to Grenville, Boston, 27 Sept. 1798, No. 55, *Adams Transcripts* (Library of Congress).

[37] Liston to Grenville, Kingston (New Jersey), 7 Novr. 1798, *Adams Transcripts* (Library of Congress). This same view was expressed also by the *Commercial Advertiser*, the paper closest to the Administration. Jan. 21, 1799.

an alliance. Adams' policy of an independent American Navy led to difficulties. Instances of search and impressment even on American Naval vessels continued.[38] While England offered to convoy American ships, she refused to consider waiving the right of search of American vessels in American convoy, even if an alliance were signed.[39] It should be noted that Hamilton's policy of concentrating on the army, while making the navy secondary, minimized these difficulties. As it was, the rise of Adams' Navy ultimately created so many difficulties that the reaction of the British by 1800 was to hail the election of Jefferson as offering one advantage at least, the reduction in size of the U. S. Navy.[40]

With the convening of Congress in December, Liston was forced to conclude that he had been too optimistic. He informed the foreign office that " The President of the United States seems to have been mistaken in his opinion, (expressed in the Conversation I had the Honor to hold with him last autumn) that the people of America were deliberating on the propriety of a connection with Great Britain, and would soon come to adopt favourable sentiments on that subject." [41] Failure was due to the " bias to the public mind " produced by " the violent and artful declamation of the French Party," i. e. the Republicans, plus the failure of a positive policy by the Federalists.

Further, Liston became conscious of the fact that the divisions within the Federalists were stronger than he had previously acknowledged. ". . . those who enroll themselves under the banner of what is called the Federal Party are by no means unanimous in their wish for the adoption of engagements with England whether of a temporary or a permanent nature." Much of this, Liston went on, was due to the rising spirit of American national-ism, and the desire to be dependent on no nation, sentiments to

---

[38] Liston to Grenville, Phila., 16 Jan., 1799 and 5 Feb., 1800, *Adams Tran-scripts* (Library of Congress); Pickering to King, Dec. 13, 1798 and Jan. 12, 1799, Department of State Instructions, 5/8 and 5/52 (National Archives).

[39] Grenville to Liston, Downing Street, London, June 8, 1798, No. 12, Mayo, *Instructions to British Ministers*, 155 ff.

[40] Thornton to Grenville, Washington, 27 Dec. 1800, Separate No. 7, *Adams Transcripts* (Library of Congress).

[41] Liston to Grenville, Phila., 29 Jan., 1799, No. 4, *Adams Transcripts* (Library of Congress).

be specially found ". . . in the younger part of the Society." [42]
Pickering, he reported, was greatly disappointed with the turn
of events, but the administration continued to drive forward with
measures of defense. As yet Liston was not conscious of how
much the President shared the sentiments the British minister
had attributed to the younger part of society.

While these negotiations with the British failed to produce an
alliance, the correspondence with Miranda on the South American
project continued. At one stage Miranda and his collaborators
in the British Foreign Office drew up the preamble to a draft
treaty for a triple alliance among " the United States, the King
of Great Britain, and the Sovereign States of the Spanish People
of America, to act against France." [43] Instructions were likewise
drawn up and this material was taken by one of Miranda's
followers to the United States.

Less definite proposals also continued to be considered. When,
on August 21, Pickering received full dispatches and plans from
Miranda and King, he forwarded the letters addressed to Hamilton, and on the following day wrote Hamilton as follows: " Not
to miss the mail, I wrote you one line today, and inclosed a letter
from, I suppose, General Miranda. If its contents give rise to
any questions which it will be prudent for you to ask, and for
me to answer by the mail, it may be done; otherwise the information may be suspended till we meet." [44] By this time, both
through letters to the cabinet and through conference with them,
Hamilton was trying to bring Adams around to a favorable view
of the South American project. His letters indicate that he now
thought the government was nearing a decision. On August 22 he
wrote: "Are we ready for this undertaking? Not quite. But we
ripen fast, and it may, I think, be rapidly brought to maturity,
if an efficient negotiation for the purpose is at once set on foot
upon this ground. Great Britain cannot alone insure the accom-
plishment of the object. I have some time since advised certain

---

[42] *Ibid.*

[43] Robertson, *Life of Miranda*, I, 171.

[44] Same to same, August 21, 1798. Hamilton's *Works* (Hamilton, ed.) VI,
343.

preliminary steps to prepare the way consistently with national character and justice. I was told they would be pursued, but I am not informed whether they have been or not." [45]

In view of Pickering's expressed views, his failure to write officially to King [46] about the South American project was due to the inability of the cabinet to interest Adams, not to any misgivings of his own. In 1809 Adams stated that he received many suggestions that he should broach the question of an alliance to Liston, the British Minister, and that Liston " in modest and delicate terms " intimated that such an approach would meet with a favorable reception. He and Liston never got so far as to discuss the Latin American plan.[47] Adams wrote to Pickering asking his advice on the overtures from Miranda, but there is no written record of a reply.[48] Among the papers which Adams did receive were:

(1) the full draft of the proposal for independence of Latin America signed by Miranda and his associates. This included the project for a triple alliance to include (a) the new independent Latin American State which should be created, (b) Great Britain, and (c) the United States.

(2) From McHenry, Adams received, early in 1798, advice on foreign policy which corresponded closely with Hamilton's recommendations that had been sent to members of the cabinet. These were:

(a) Recommendation for reliance upon British convoys.

(b) The proposal that ten naval vessels be borrowed from England.

(c) The proposal that, when war might be declared against France, England and the United States should cooperate in a joint series of moves against Florida, Louisiana, and South America.

(d) Recommendation that the British minister be asked to request authority from his government to enter upon immediate agree-

---

[45] Hamilton to King, Aug. 22, 1798. King's *King*, II, 660.
[46] King to Pickering, Oct. 20, 1798. King's *King*, II, 453.
[47] *Boston Patriot,* May 19 and May 24, 1809; Quincy, May 10, 1809.
[48] Adams to Pickering, Quincy, Oct. 3, 1798; Adams' *Works*, VIII, 600.

ments with the United States covering these points in the event of war with France, but that no immediate alliance should be signed.[49]

The effect of this scheme upon Adams will be considered in a later chapter. It was certainly apparent to him by the time Liston took the unusual step of going to Massachusetts to see him, that there was a strange concurrence of opinion, even as to detail, among the ideas of Liston, the views of his cabinet, the recommendations of his minister to England, and the policy advocated by Hamilton in the press.

Hamilton, of course, was even more a part of the planning than Adams might yet conjecture. At the same time that he wrote to King, Hamilton also wrote to Miranda on August 22, 1798. This letter indicates that Hamilton had definite interest in the part he might personally play in the military command. He declared: " The sentiments I entertain with regard to the object have been long since in your knowledge, but I could personally have no participation in it, unless patronized by the government of this country. It was my wish that matters had been ripened for a cooperation in the course of this fall on the part of this country.

" But this can scarcely now be the case. The winter, however, may mature the project, and an effectual cooperation by the United States may take place. In this case, I shall be happy in my official station, to be an instrument of so good a work." [50] It should be noted at this point that Hamilton was the senior field general, and that he always had strong military ambitions.

In a letter to King in October, Hamilton again showed anxiety over the progress being made toward securing the President's endorsement: " Mr. R. delivered me your letter of the 31st of July. The opinion in that and other of your letters concerning a very important point, has been acted upon by me from the very moment that it became unequivocal that we must have a rupture

[49] For McHenry's letter, cf. footnote to p. 516, Vol. I of Adams' *Works*. The copy of the Miranda proposal is in *Ibid.*, 679-84.

[50] Hamilton to Miranda, Aug. 22, 1798. Hamilton's *Works* (Hamilton, ed.) VI, 361.

with France. In some things my efforts succeeded, in others they were disappointed: — in others I have had promises of conformity to lay the foundations of future proceedings; the performance and effect of which promises are not certainly known to me. The effect, indeed, cannot yet be known." [51] A nicer example of a letter from one conspirator to another could hardly be imagined.

One result of the desire to start the expedition to Latin America was to make Hamilton increasingly anxious for a direct rupture with France. In January, 1799, he wrote to Harrison Gray Otis that he would be glad to see a law passed by Congress which should provide that if no negotiation with France were set on foot by August 1, or any in progress had terminated unsuccessfully by then, war should be declared. This law should provide that in such circumstances the President should be given the power to employ the land and naval forces " as shall appear to him most effectual for annoying the enemy, and for preventing and frustrating hostile designs of France, either directly or *indirectly through any of her allies.*"

Moreover, as France might seize Florida and Louisiana, the most effective way of checking her would be to anticipate such action through seizing these territories first. In addition, " If universal empire is still to be the pursuit of France, what can tend to defeat the purpose better than to detach South America from Spain, which is only the channel through which the riches of *Mexico* and *Peru* are conveyed to France? The executive ought to be put in a situation to embrace favorable conjunctures for effecting that separation. 'Tis to be regretted that the preparation of an adequate military force does not advance more rapidly." [52]

As late as the spring of 1799, after the new peace mission to France was announced by Adams, but had not yet sailed,

---

[51] Hamilton to King, Oct. 2, 1798. Hamilton's *Works* (Hamilton, ed.) VI, 362.

I cannot agree with John C. Miller's statement in his *Crisis in Freedom*, 151-52 and 155, that Hamilton was reluctant for there to be war with France. The statement quoted above and the weight of Hamilton's other letters leaves no room for doubt, in my mind.

[52] Hamilton to Otis, Jan. 26, 1799. Hamilton's *Works* (Hamilton, ed.) VI, 390.

Hamilton was still hopeful of success. Correspondence continued between him and King and Miranda. Hamilton himself, when the command of the army was divided, was given command over the troops in the North and the West. Those in the West were directly commanded by General Wilkinson.[53] This placed him in a strategic position in case of operations against Florida and Louisiana. Furthermore he had Wilkinson visit him, and went over the entire situation of the Spanish at New Orleans with Wilkinson.[54] Gradually, though, it became increasingly apparent that there would be no war, with the result that the matter dropped from sight. The frustration of his hopes caused Hamilton to suffer a severe depression of spirits. A letter to William Smith in 1800 contains the following pessimistic passage: ". . . You see I am in a humor to laugh. What can we do better in *this best of all possible worlds*? Should you even be shut up in the seven towers [Smith was going to Constantinople], or get the plague, if you are a true philosopher you will consider this only a laughing matter."[55]

To go forward a bit in the story in order to clarify Pickering's view as to peace, it becomes evident that his rage and despair over the prospect of peace with France were equal to Hamilton's. When the President determined on a new peace mission to France, Pickering sent a series of bitter and resentful letters to William Vans Murray, our emissary to the Hague, concerning this policy. Murray was unfortunate enough to be the channel of communication between the United States and France. Pickering's first letter informed Murray that the President's decision for a third mission had the unanimous opposition of the cabinet and came as a complete surprise.[56] The next letter rebuked Murray sharply.

---

[53] McHenry to Hamilton, Feb. 4, 1799. Hamilton's *Works* (Hamilton, ed.) V, 199; and Hamilton to Wilkinson, Feb. 12, 1799, *Ibid.*, 211. When Washington did not take the field the command was divided between Gen. Pinckney and Hamilton, with Pinckney taking the Southern part of the forces.

[54] Whitaker, *Mississippi Question*, 125.

[55] Hamilton to Smith, March 11, 1800. Hamilton's *Works* (Hamilton, ed.) VI, 432. Also see Henry Lee to Hamilton, March 5, 1800, *Ibid.*, 430. He states, " It gives me pain to find you so despondent . . . Be then more like yourself, and resist to victory all your foes."

[56] Pickering to Murray, July 10, 1799. Ford " Murray," *loc. cit.*, 573.

In the correspondence between Murray and Pichon, who was making the overtures on behalf of France, Murray had expressed his " ' perfect respect and high esteem ' " for Talleyrand. Pickering wanted to know what was meant by using this language toward a " shameless villain." " ' Esteem ' is the sentiment of affection and friendship for moral worth: the profession of it you have constantly and abundantly lavished on me: and I hoped that I was not wholly unworthy of it: But what value am I to place on it when I see that with the like facility it is addressed to one of the most false, hypocritical, and corrupt villains of whom France has produced a bountiful crop." As to the letter which Pichon sent, it is full of " Impudent lies . . . [which] would have justified you in dashing the letter in Citizen Pichon's face." [57]

For the motives which prompted the High-Federalists in their desire for war with France, another letter of Pickering's is of extreme importance. It shows that the idea of neutrality had been abandoned by this group, as was already pointed out in connection with an earlier letter from Pickering to Hamilton. Seeing advantages to be derived from entering the war on the side of Great Britain, and believing that it was necessary to get into the war on one side or the other, they were determined that it should be on the side of the nation which could advance the interest of commerce. Of the results to be anticipated from the new mission, Pickering wrote:

An actual treaty with the French Republic will probably bring us into a war with the combined powers; or if open war be not declared, our commerce will be harrassed and deeply injured, and from the Russian ports (on which we depend for sail cloth and hemp) be probably excluded. In the mean time, the intercourse with France will be renewed, and we shall be cursed with a revolutionary minister to intrigue with the numerous enemies of our government, until it be overturned. These are some of the evils with which this mission is pregnant. When it was intimated to the President, that the negotiation with the French Republic, this time, might lead to war with

---

[57] Same to same, Oct. 4, 1799. *Ibid.*, 600.

Great Britain, would you believe it possible that he should answer, '*Great Britain could not hurt us!*'[58]

For another expression of the reasons for the desire for war, there is an excellent statement in the letters of George Cabot. Cabot was the head of the Junto, and a man not given to pursuing chimeras. On July 2, when there was reason to think that war might be declared before Congress adjourned, he wrote, ". . . It is true that we shall do little more at first than provide for our own defense, but we are capable of greater efforts after we are fully engaged, & a variety of considerations unite to render our association in the war extremely favorable to G. B.; we are at least sufficient for a make weight where the scales are so nearly even. . . . But I am fully persuaded that G. B. in concert with U. S. can command the ocean in opposition to all Europe, Russia alone excepted, and if the war should continue several years, these nations would enjoy exclusively the commerce of all Americas & Africa & the best part of Asia & Europe — the colonies of France and the Nations subject to her power would soon listen to the pleas of necessity & would voluntarily receive the commercial ships of those who alone would supply their wants."[59] After the close of the session Cabot wrote deeply regretting that there had been no declaration of war.[60]

Also at this time, Hamilton's friend Christopher Gore, like John Trumbull one of the United States commissioners in London, sent to Hamilton a long pamphlet which he hoped might be printed and distributed, although it never was. This lengthy document, 142 manuscript pages in length, urges an immediate war against France. The argument is advanced that the continuation of peace permits the opposition to defend France and continually to attack the Federalist party. An immediate war would put a stop to this. Also instead of defense with nothing coming in, there would be offense against both French and Spanish possessions. The immediate result would be an easy victory for the United States. Not

[58] Same to same, Oct. 25, 1799. *Ibid.*, 610.
[59] Cabot to King, July 2, 1798. King's *King*, II, 354.
[60] Same to Wolcott, Oct. 25, 1798. Gibbs, *Wolcott*, II, 109.

over 10,000 troops would be needed for the operation. The South Americans would be liberated from tyranny. A united America would be able to stand against future European invasion. A profitable trade would be opened up for American shipping and manufactures. To the South we would have peaceful and friendly allies. All of this demanded an immediate declaration of war against France and the courageous waging of an offensive war.[61]

In determining the aims of the Federalist program, the expressed views of the leaders are of greatest importance. The views of their followers are of next significance, and those expressed in the press are also of some import. What might be charged by the opposition is not nearly so significant as statements in the press of the party. At this point, the close of 1798 and first part of 1799, the general trend of the Federalist press was to charge that the opposition was disloyal and plotted revolution. Such statements ran through comments of all factions of the Federalist press. The *Gazette of the United States* ran a comment which was copied by Noah Webster's *Commercial Advertiser*, pointing to the fate of Naples and calling for a policy ". . . where there is the smallest reason to suspect a collusion with the enemy, or a strong disposition to favor him, instantly to cashier the guilty person.

". . . Purge your country, but especially all its Public Offices, BEFORE IT IS TOO LATE, OF DOMESTIC TRAITORS." [62] Lest it be augued that such statements might apply only to public officials, Webster's paper warned that because of French influence ". . . the United States are ripening fast for a revolution — as important as that which Rome suffered in the days of Julius Caesar." [63] In general, Webster's position was more moderate than the position taken by the *Gazette of the United States* and *Porcupine's Gazette*. Webster endorsed only a temporary British alliance and supported Adams when he renewed negotiations with the French.[64]

---

[61] Gore to Hamilton, London, 27 Feb. 1799, and inclosure. Hamilton Papers, Vol. 36/4944-5022 (Manuscripts Division, Library of Congress).

[62] *Commercial Advertiser*, June 4, 1799.

[63] *Commercial Advertiser*, March 19, 1800; also see comments for Jan. 21, 1799; April 26, 1800.

[64] *Commercial Advertiser*, March 7 and March 8, 1799.

The Gazette of the United States and *Porcupine* advocated sup-
pression of the opposition, war with France, and a British
alliance.[65] All this was too much for Webster, and after announcement of the third mission to France in 1799, a marked split
developed among the Federalist papers.[66]

Another excellent statement of the thought of this wing of the
Federalist party is that which appeared in March, 1799, in a
statement by John Ward Fenno, editor of the *Gazette of the
United States*.[67] These statements were later elaborated in a
pamphlet in 1800 designed to favor the election of Pinckney over
Adams by setting forth the failures of the latter and the proper
policy which should be followed: [68]

[65] *Porcupine's Gazette*, May 17, 1797; Jan. 25, April 3, April 10, July 13,
July 20, Sept. 7, Nov. 10 and Dec. 3, 1798; Jan. 29, 1799. *Gazette of the United
States*, July 17, 1799; July 18, 1799; July 10, 1799, etc.

[66] *Commercial Advertiser*, March 15 and 16, 1799.

[67] Cf. *Gazette of the United States*, March 4, 1799.

[68] It is well to mention here that in the summer of 1798 the yellow fever
did great damage among newspaper editors. Among those who died was John
Fenno, whereupon his son assumed the editorship of the paper. Fenno, Jr.,
was very indiscreet, and his paper, along with *Porcupine*, broke with Adams
upon the appointment of the new mission. As soon as he assumed the editorship he joined *Porcupine* in advocating an offensive and defensive alliance with
England, and became strongly pro-English. However, his attitude is in harmony with the private letters of the High-Federalists, and the position is taken
here that although regarded as going too far in making statements of Federalist
policy to the public, the views set forth by him throw some light on points of
policy on which there is insufficient elaboration in the correspondence. An
example of this may be taken from a statement of Pickering. Only *Porcupine*
and Fenno, of all the press, criticized the new mission.

Pickering writes, " Without saying any more, I beg leave to refer you to the
enclosed column of a newspaper. Who was the author I know not. The irony
is severe: but it did no more than express the strong feelings of the men whom
you respect and esteem, so far as it regarded a mission to France." Pickering
to Murray, July 10, 1799. Ford, " Murray," *loc. cit.*, 573. Pickering was
referring to Fenno's " A View of the United States of America," which appeared
on March 4, 1799 and on which Cobbett commented on March 9, 1799. This
view of American policy was strongly endorsed by the British *Anti-Jacobin
Review*, II, 563-76. Liston enclosed the pamphlet of 1800 to Grenville with
the comment that these had been published " not . . . without the advice and
consent of some of the leading Federalists in New York. . . ." Liston to
Grenville, Philadelphia, 16 Aug., 1800, No. 34, *Adams Transcripts* (Library
of Congress) .

The measure which most pressingly demands adoption, is a declaration of war against France, and her dependencies, Spain and Holland . . .

The conquest of the remaining possessions of France, Spain and Holland in the West Indies, might be effected by this country, with very little expense or inconvenience. The naval force already extant is fully adequate, and the regular troops lately embodied, though its intervention would have atchieved [sic] the conquest without difficulty. This country possesses such advantages for carrying on expeditions against the West India Islands, as must render her cooperation in the cause very acceptable. In short, the contingent we could bring into the coalition would be such as to entitle us to assume the rank of a first rate power, and to make stipulations, the fulfillment of which could not fail to fix us in a state of prosperity and to extend to our empire and renown. To instance, for our quota of 25,000 troops (which should act separately and independently) and a stipulated quantum of military stores, etc. Great Britain should guarantee to us the island of Cuba, or which would be more convenient to our commerce, that of Porto Rico. Either of these possessions would amply remunerate us for the most expensive exertions which the conquest of them could require. In the East, we might establish ourselves in the possession of Batavia or the Mauritius, and thus to secure a footing in the Indian Ocean, highly essential to us, but now depending on the most precarious tenure.

It is in vain to disguise the truth that America is essentially and naturally a commercial nation; and that from her location on the map of the world she must ever remain so. It ought therefore to be the undeviating care of the Government, whether it be Federal or Jacobinical, or true Columbian, to secure on the most advantageous footing possible, our commercial intercourse with foreign nations. To procure admission to our flag, in ports whence it is now excluded; to obtain it by right where it now rests on the ground of sufferance; and to establish it on a regular and permanent footing; in those cases where it is at present precarious and temporary; is not merely the province of the Government, but a duty, and obligation which its subjects have a right to hold it to.

We have a right to expect and the Government ought to exact it from Spain, the opening of those of her ports in South America the most convenient for refitting our whalers on that coast. For the want of this privilege our people are subjected to needless deprivation and hardships, during voyages of two years duration.

From Portugal through the intervention of Great Britain, it could not be difficult to exact for some adequate compensation which we could offer, the same privileges in Brazil, a station the most convenient to the whaling ground.

Pepper, Spices, Cottons of various kinds, and above all Sugar and Coffee, are, what-ever negro-philanthropists [sic] may assert, undoubtedly, necessaries of life.

This summarizes the views of the Federalist shipping interests with their expanding trade which now included the spice trade of the East Indies. The article then proceeds on the same tune that Hamilton and the Junto played in trying to dissuade Adams from the mission. The Bourbons would be restored in a brief time, would ally with England, and make America suffer for not having joined the coalition.[69]

So far as the actual tactical policy of the Federalists is concerned, the best description of the method by which the policy was supposed to advance is given by Fisher Ames: " Wage war and call it self defense; forbear to call it war, on the contrary, let it be said that we deprecate war, and will desist from our arms as soon as her acts shall be repealed, &c., &c., grounding all we do on the necessity of self preservation &c. . . . tell the citizens of danger & bring them to war gradually."

" My long letter amounts to this, we must make haste to *wage war*, or we shall be lost. . . . My faith is that we are born to high destinies. . . ." Ames also favored an alliance with England.[70]

What change in American policy would have come from following the program of the High-Federalists in 1798? Charles Francis Adams, in his biography of John Adams,[71] has correctly pointed out that the Hamiltonian policy meant the abandonment of the

[69] Fenno, *Desultory Reflections Upon New Political Aspects* (Philadelphia, 1800).

[70] Ames to Pickering, July 10, 1798. Ames's *Works*, I, 234. Also on Federalist aims cf. Brooks Adams, " The Convention of 1800 with France," *Massachusetts Historical Society Proceedings*, XLIV, 401 and 405.

[71] Adams' *Works*, I, 524-25.

neutrality and nonintervention policy advocated by Washington. It meant involvement in foreign adventure. At least a temporary alliance with England would have followed a declaration of war against France, and involvement in South America would probably have made this a more lasting one. Hamilton himself wrote to King that in regard to South America, he hoped the United States would furnish the entire land force. " The command in this case would very naturally fall upon me; and I hope that I should disappoint no favorable anticipations. The independency of the separate territory under a moderate government, with the joint guarantees of the co-operating powers, stipulating equal privileges in commerce, would be the sum of the results to be accomplished." [72] This means nothing more nor less than the permanent involvement of the United States in the alliance system of Europe, and that before the national character of the country had itself been formed. What was projected was a complete change in the position that the United States had held since independence. One cannot but feel that the aim of Hamilton was to change the role of the United States in foreign policy, and as will next appear, there were just as specific aims to remould the domestic character of the country.

In the next century the German liberals were overwhelmed in moulding the character of the rising German state by the policies pursued by Bismarck after 1862.[73] Liberalism in the Germanic states was defeated, and a military character given to the new state. In the United States of 1798, there were many domestic forces in the direction of expanison of popular government. But the situation was fluid. What changes could be wrought in a period of military adventure? These Hamilton sought to experiment with.

The desire for war was, then, quite general on the part of the commercial group who sought to expand their commerce. This does not mean, as is usually stated, that the Federalist program was exhausted, but that there was a widening gap between the

---

[72] Aug. 22, 1798, Hamilton's *Works* (Hamilton, ed.) **VI**, 347.
[73] Kohn, Hans, *The Idea of Nationalism* (New York, 1944), 357.

commercial and agrarian groups of the party on account of the extremes to which the High-Federalists desired to carry their program. The agrarian elements of the party could see no profit in an adventure looking toward empire. They were Federalists so long as the party promised stability in government and finance. But when it proposed a policy of war, of large military expenditures, of higher taxes, this was quite another matter. Taxes were going up under the Adams administration. The direct tax, levied under Adams, has already been discussed. In the last year under Washington, 1796, tax receipts of the Federal government came to $8,377,530. Four years later for 1800, they came to $10,848,749.[74] In 1799 there was a federal deficit of $2,119,642.[75] These figures do not appear too impressive today, but at the time they indicated a sharp rise in government spending. This badly upset the agrarian Federalists.

On the other hand, the commercial elements were winning their place in the carrying trade of the world because of the Napoleonic Wars. They were experiencing benefits from the extreme Federalist policy. Already American tonnage in foreign trade had risen from 124,000 gross tons in 1789 to approximately 500,000 gross tons by 1798 and still further by 1800.[76] This made American tonnage in foreign trade in 1800 equal to England's tonnage as of the year 1794; although only 50 per cent of the British foreign tonnage in 1800. American ships were engaged in the European and South American trade and considerable numbers went even to the Orient. This expansion of shipping also meant an extensive expansion of the shipbuilding industry.[77] With such expanison, why not an American Empire, perhaps comparable to and allied with the British Empire? This was the dream. Could it become reality?

[74] *Historical Statistics of the United States*, 298, Series P 89-98.
[75] *Ibid.*, 306, Series P 132-33.
[76] Hutchins, John G. B., *American Maritime Industries and Public Policy, 1789-1914*, 224-25.
[77] *Ibid.*, 178-87.

Chapter *12*

The Aim of Federalist Domestic Policy

As was the case with foreign policy, the domestic policy of the High-Federalists was quite ambitious. One of the chief reasons for desiring a declaration of war, or for provoking such a declaration from France (which was the policy actually followed) sprang from a desire to place the Republican party in an intolerable position. The best expression of this aim is in a letter written by Theodore Sedgwick:

Our measures in themselves were not only feeble, but taken with that graduation and hesitation, which shewed a want of system, & of spirit & vigor. The extent & shape of our measures were divided, not by comprehensive measures and wisdom, but by the feeble minds of the Tillinghasts, the Bullocks & the Coits of the House of Representatives. We ought at once to have put an end to the cooperation of external & internal enemies — to have at once, as far as is in our power, prevented the possibility of their carrying on that most dangerous species of warfare for the seduction of our people, "diplomatic skill." This could not in my opinion have been done effectually but by a declaration of war. This would have conduced equally to the honor & interest of the U. S. To have taken advantage of that measure, it would have been necessary to consider Spain, as in fact she is, a Colony of France. Besides, acting under the character of Enemy, as such, I would have rendered myself respectable by a prompt and decided blow. The mouth of the Mississippi & the country connected with and dependent on it should have been immediately seized. The immense benefits to have derived from that position, whether for treaty, or for a continuance of the war, are obvious. In the meantime we should have superseded the necessity of alien and sedition laws— without them we might have hanged traitors and exported Frenchmen. This was the policy I would have pursued instantly after the publication of dispatches.

But it was ordered otherwise.[1]

The Secretary of State shared this belief in the disloyalty of the opposition, stating:

. . . some of the leaders of the opposition have explicitly avowed, what their actions had long spoken, their wish to break the *confederation* of the states—*to sever the union.* . . .

[These] . . . unprincipled men and French partisans, who to gratify their selfish and ambitious views, would yield the wealth and independence of their country to France, whose love of plunder and lust of domination are bounded only by the limits of the habitable globe. I speak correctly when I ascribe the measures of the leaders of opposition to *ambition.* We have seen in Holland—Switzerland and Italy, men of such inverted ambition that they have betrayed and laid prostrate their countries rights and independence at the feet of the French Government in order to gain the sad preeminence of ruling their fellow citizens under the patronage, and even under the lash of that despotic power.[2]

James Lloyd declared that:

I fear Congress will close the Session without a Declaration of War, which I look upon as necessary to enable us to lay our hands on traitors. . . .[3]

In like manner Fisher Ames asserted, " Nothing doubtful in the situation of the United States, or in the duty of citizens should have been left." [4] Cabot held a similar idea as to the position in which the opposition should be placed, writing,

---

[1] Sedgwick to King, Jan. 20, 1799, King's *King*, II, 514-15. This point will be considered in some detail on account of its importance. Dodd in his *Nathaniel Macon*, and Henry Adams in his *Life of Albert Gallatin* have taken the same position as is set forth here. More recently, however, the opposite view has been adopted by S. E. Morison in his *Harrison Gray Otis*. Channing does not touch upon this point.

[2] Department of State Instructions to Ed Stevens (San Domingo) 5/1226, May 9, 1799 (National Archives).

[3] Lloyd to Washington, Philadelphia, July 4, 1798, Washington *Papers*, Vol. 289.

[4] Ames to C. Gore, July 28, 1798. Ames's *Works*, I, 237.

It is unfortunate that Congress did not declare war; the danger of French artifice would have been less. It is impossible to make the people feel or see distinctly that we have much more to fear from peace than war; that peace cannot be real . . . But war, open and declared, would not only deprive our external enemy of his best hopes, but would extinguish the hopes of internal foes. The rights and duties of every citizen in a state of war, would be known and regarded; traitors and sedition mongers who are now protected and tolerated, would then be easily restrained or published [punished?]. I hope, therefore, we shall not long persist in pacific war, with one part of our citizens against us, and another part neutral. At this moment it appears to me everything depends on the elections.[5]

One of the most authoritative and important statements as to the precise line of demarcation between the Federalists at this period is to be found in the farewell circular letter of Samuel Lyman to his constituents. Lyman was a good Federalist, voting for virtually every Federal measure in Congress. He did not, however, share the views of the High-Federalists. His statement was never contradicted, though it received wide circulation in the press. Writing from Springfield on July 14, 1800, he stated:

. . . you wish to know how it happens, that the federal interest is divided in the National Councils — This is a *delicate question*, and a short answer is better than a long one: however, I will just observe that the federal interest is not divided *in sentiment*, or in the principles of administering the Government; but there is a division as to men and as to measures, there is a division as to the degree of hatred and animosity necessary to be used in order to destroy all opposition to Government. A small party, I suppose, sincerely believe, that a few bold strokes would silence all opposition; others say no, let it be done by civility and sound argument; so here they are at issue; but their ultimate views are the same, they all wish for peace and tranquillity — this discord is favorable to the opposition. . . .[6]

After the inital part of this statement the declaration that

---

[5] Cabot to Wolcott, Oct. 25, 1798. Gibbs, *Wolcott*, II, 109.

[6] This first appeared in the *Federal Spy*, was copied by the *Boston Gazette* and by the *Aurora* on Oct. 7, 1800.

both groups desired "peace and tranquillity" was obviously intended in a Pickwickian sense. Commenting on this statement Wolcott wrote, " It is known that many federalists are dissatisfied [with Adams]; even Samuel Lyman has ventured to publish this truth, and though he says that both parties are honourable men, yet the President's friends assert that all his measures are perfectly consistent and right; that his opposers are altogether in the wrong — are either Jacobins or factious characters devoted to the British." In like manner Lyman told Adams in 1800 that he was glad of the split in the party, that it would result in bringing into the open the motives of the High-Federalists, and would cause them to be overwhelmed.[7]

There is an interesting piece of doggerel which appeared in the *Gazette of the United States*:

" The Trimmer "

A canting Trimmer *came to me and said,*
  '*I fear, my friend you are too rank a Fed*;
Pity the Jacos, *think how hard their case is,*
  '*By disappointment stretch'd, how long their faces.*
' *Emmollients better suit with our condition,*'
Jack Ketch[8] *said I's an excellent physician.*
  ' *What thirst for blood?* ' — *not I Sirs, as I breathe* —
Why hanging is a fine dry kind *of death.*
  '*We* moderates *are for holding all things even.*'
You *mean like him who hangs twixt earth and heaven.*
' *Pshaw no; the French spill blood enough already*' —
Aye Aye; yet you're *for holding all things steady.*
  Now if the weight is all one sided brother
You trimmers *may to poize it hang on t'other.*
  These neuters *in the middle way of steering*
Are neither black nor white, nor fish nor herring,
  Nor feds nor Jacobins, nor this nor that,
Nor birds nor beasts, but just a kind of bat

---

[7] Wolcott to Ames, Washington, Aug. 10, 1800, Gibbs, *Wolcott*, II, 400; Adams to James Lloyd, Feb. 17, 1815. Adams' *Works*, X, 125.
[8] The famous hangman.

Or twilight reptile, *true to neither cause,*
With FEDERAL *Wings, but* Jacos' *teeth and claws.*

Steady [9]

Exactly what, then, was the domestic program of the Federalists and the method by which it was to be accomplished? Although in a preceding chapter it was pointed out that Hamilton was not in favor of needlessly harsh measures, his program for internal reform is as extreme as any suggestions advanced during this period. In a lengthy letter to Jonathan Dayton, the Speaker, his ideas were set forth. This letter must have been written early in 1799. His first statement is that " Though something may have been gained on the side of men of information and property, more has probably been lost on that of persons of a different description." The opposition now aimed not at the administration but at the Constitution itself. The Virginia and Kentucky Resolutions showed a serious disaffection toward the government. Virginia was now arming, levying taxes for munitions, and disciplining, the militia.[10] " Amidst such serious indications of hostility, the safety and the duty of supporters of the government call upon them to adopt vigorous measures of counteraction. It will be wise in them to act upon the hypothesis, that the opposers of the government are resolved, if it shall be practicable, to make its existence a question of force. Possessing as they now do all the constitutional powers, it will be an unpardonable mistake on their part if they do not exert to surround the Constitution with more ramparts, and to disconcert the schemes of its enemies."

Hamilton proposed the measures to be adopted under three heads: First, to extend the influence and promote the popularity of the government:

A. Extension of the Judiciary:

  1. Subdivision of each state into small districts with a

_____

[9] *Gazette of the United States,* Dec. 28, 1798.

[10] This is correct. The fall session of the Virginia legislature, 1798, passed the famous Virginia Resolution and at the same time provided for an arsenal at Harper's Ferry, the thorough organization of the militia, and additional revenue for this program.

salaried judge. For example, four districts for Connecticut.

2. Appointment in each county of conservators or justices of the peace, with only ministerial functions and only fees for compensation. " The thing no doubt would be a subject of clamor, but it would carry with it its own antidote, and when once established would bring a very powerful support to the government."

B. Improvement of roads.

C. Institutions to encourage arts and sciences.

Second, " Provisions for augmenting the means and consolidating the strength of the government."

A. The direct tax should be continued and additional indirect taxes totalling $1,000,000 be levied.

B. Military measures.

1. A total army of around 18,000 on a five-year enlistment basis is necessary. But if England, France, Spain, and the United States all are at peace, the army shall be reduced to around 6,000.

2. The navy should be enlarged to six ships of the line, twelve frigates, and twenty sloops.

3. The laws pertaining to the presidential volunteer force and the provisional army should be made permanent, and the executive should proceed without delay to organize the latter.

Third: Arrangements for confirming and enlarging the legal powers of the government.

A. The Constitution should be amended so that canals could be constructed by the Federal Government.

B. An amendment governing the admission of new states should be enacted, restricting this privilege to states of at least 100,000 population. Moreover these should be required to assume their share of the antecedent federal debt, with power in the Federal Government to levy the tax in case of delinquency.

C. " *The subdivision of the great states is indispensable to the security of the general government, and with it of the Union.*

" *Great States will always feel a rivalship with the common head, will often be supposed to machinate against it, and in certain situations will be able to do it with decisive effect. The subdivision of such states ought to be a cardinal point in the federal policy; and small states are doubtless best adapted to the purpose of local regulation and the preservation of the republican spirit.* This suggestion, however, is merely thrown out for consideration. It is feared that it would be inexpedient and even dangerous to propose, *at this time,* an amendment of this kind.

" Fourth: Laws for restraining and punishing incendiary and seditious practices. It will be useful to declare that all such writings &c., which at common law are libels, if levelled against any officer whatsoever of the United States, shall be cognizable in the courts of the United States."

1. The non-execution of the alien law is to be deeply deplored. Several editors of Republican papers are aliens. Why are they not deported? One thing that is particularly needed is energy in the executive. Those who can approach Adams should urge the necessity of vigor.[11]

It is well known that this idea of Hamilton, the necessity for strengthening the Constitution, had been in his mind since the adoption of the instrument. He felt that with a favorable situation the time had come when measures should be risked. Later, when action had still not been taken, Hamilton wrote that despite a sizable majority, there was grave risk that the Federalists in the two houses of Congress might not go forward with plans for ". . . the erection of additional buttresses to the Constitution, a

[11] Hamilton to Dayton, 1799. Hamilton's *Works* (Hamilton, ed.) VI, 383.

fabric which can hardly be stationary, and which will retrograde if it cannot advance." [12]

The ideas of Federalist leaders for expansion of the powers of the central government had, at this point, moved forward to a considerable degree. Early attempts of the federal courts to reduce the powers of the state had been partly checked by the Eleventh Amendment, which became effective in 1798. But now the federal courts moved forward on another front. In the Federal Court for the Pennsylvania District, Judge Richard Peters, in the *Worrall Case,* ruled that the federal courts had general common law jurisdiction, extending to criminal cases involving a federal question or federal officials.[13] This doctrine was again enunciated by the Chief Justice, Oliver Ellsworth, in the *Case of Isaac Williams.*[14] The doctrine of federal criminal jurisdiction extending to common law offenses where a federal question or federal official was involved broadened federal jurisdiction more and more rapidly than if this were left to legislative action. As the federal Constitution's supreme law clause meant this expansion of power would sharply limit state jurisdiction, strong attacks were launched against the doctrine in the *Aurora, The Independent Chronicle,* and other Republican newspapers.

In addition to this, there was a strengthening of the federal bureaucracy. The provisional army and recruitment machinery for the new regiments of the regular army greatly increased both the military power of the central government and the machinery under the Secretary of War.[15] With the advent of the direct tax, the treasury began to send in collectors. The Attorney General started the direction of the prosecutions under the Sedition Act, and the Secretary of State began an elaborate system of communication with the various collectors of ports and federal clerks of courts, who were required to register aliens, transmit reports

---

[12] Hamilton to King, Jan. 5, 1800. Hamilton's *Works* (Hamilton, ed.) **VI**, 416.

[13] 2 Dallas, 384-96. This doctrine was specifically over-ruled later by the Federal Supreme Court in *U. S.* v. *Hudson and Goodwin* (1812), 7 Cranch, 32.

[14] *Connecticut Courant,* Sept. 30, 1799; 29 *Federal Cases,* 1330-34.

[15] Steiner, *McHenry,* 309-69 (Ch. XIII).

on those registered, transmit records of naturalization, and perform other duties.[16] While no aliens were ever deported under
the alien act, some prosecutions were directed by Adams or Pickering, but the aliens concerned either left the country or went into
hiding.[17] This did not mean that the alien acts were without
effect. As early as July 26, 1798, Pickering reported to Adams
that large numbers of French aliens were leaving the United
States.[18] In addition Pickering collected information leading to
prosecutions under the Sedition Law.[19]

As Frank Maloy Anderson has pointed out, prosecutions under
the Sedition Act were numerous.[20] Twenty-four or twenty-five
individuals were arrested for violations of the act. Fifteen of these
were indicted, ten or eleven of the cases went to trial, and there
were ten convictions. All four of the leading Republican Papers
were attacked, including the Philadelphia *Aurora*, Boston *Independent Chronicle*, New York *Argus* and Richmond *Examiner*.
Four other lesser papers were also involved in cases. Wharton's
State Trials devotes space to a number of cases under the Sedition
Act, including those of Matthew Lyon,[21] Thomas Cooper,[22]
Anthony Haswell[23] and James Thomas Callender.[24] In addition,
two cases in state courts on charge of political libel or seditious
disturbance are given where Republicans were involved, the cases
of David Frothingham for a libel against Alexander Hamilton,[25]
and the trial of Duane, Reynolds, Moore and Cumming.[26] One
case is recorded of a libel case against a Federalist editor, that
against William Cobbett.[27]

---

[16] Cf. Vol. 11 of *Domestic Letters, Department of State* (National Archives)
for 1798 *et seq.* For example, Timothy Pickering to Joshua Sands, Collector
of the Port of New York, July 27; State Dept. (Wagner) to Clement E. Brown,
Deputy Collector of Customs, Chester, Sept. 13, 1798; to Robert Bogg, Clerk
for the District of New Jersey, Jan. 1, 1800.

[17] Anderson, "Alien and Sedition Laws," *Loc. cit.*, 117-18.

[18] Dept. of State, Domestic Letters, 11/27 (National Archives).

[19] For example, A. McLance, Wilmington, to Timothy Pickering, Feb. 8,
1800. Pickering *Manuscripts*, 26/26.

[20] Miller, John C., *Crisis in Freedom*, Chapter VI ff., treats the enforcement
question in detail.

[21] 333-44.

[22] *Ibid.*, 659-81.

[23] *Ibid.*, 684-87.

[24] *Ibid.*, 688-721.

[25] *Ibid.*, 649-51.

[26] *Ibid.*, 245-391.

[27] *Ibid.*, 322-32.

The collection of the direct tax had unforeseen consequences. In the German counties of Pennsylvania, Northampton, Bucks, and Montgomery, those federal officials surveying for the federal tax were resisted. When arrests of the resisters were made by the federal marshal, his prisoners were rescued by a group under one Amos Fries. Thereupon the Secretary of War, McHenry, had Hamilton send troops from the nearest post. The rebellion was immediately put down. Fries was convicted of treason, but was pardoned by Adams despite his cabinet's opposition.[28] Thus there was repetition by the Adams' government of the immediate mobilization of troops that had been carried out against the Whiskey Rebellion at the time Hamilton was Secretary of the Treasury. The government showed energy and strength, but as Adams himself remarks, the hitherto Federalist district of Pennsylvania comprising the three counties concerned in Fries's Rebellion, never again showed Federalist majorities. (Compare 1796 Pennsylvania election returns in Table 11, p. 108, with the election returns for 1800 in Table 13, p. 258). This tax measure, the necessity for which was regretted by Adams but forced by extreme Federalist policy, converted another conservative agricultural district to the Jeffersonians.

A year earlier, in 1797, former federal Representative Uriah Tracy of Connecticut had written to Alexander Hamilton expressing a myopic view of the state of the nation. The strength of the French influence was so great that Jeffersonian victory threatened in the country at large, especially with the spread of Southern influence. " The southern part of the Union . . . is large and capable of such increases both in population & number of States — that in both houses of Congress, the Northern States will soon be swallowed up. . . ." [29] To prevent this, Tracy proposed a separation of the Union, with the Federalists dominating the Middle and Northern States, and the South left to unite with France and go its own way. This position was again held by Tracy in 1804 when he and Timothy Pickering headed an abortive

[28] Steiner, *McHenry*, 432-37.
[29] Philadelphia, April 6, 1798, Hamilton Papers (Library of Congress), 29/4121.

plot looking toward the secession of New England,[30] a move revived again with the Hartford Convention of 1814.[31]

Hamilton, however, was in sympathy with no such move. His program was to dominate the small enough union which had been created after Independence was won from England. Moreover, by 1798, this plan seemed on the way to succeed. If opposition came from the South, Hamilton had a different remedy. His program became specific as a reaction against the famous Virginia and Kentucky Resolutions, which were adopted by the Jeffersonians in these state legislatures late in 1798. These resolutions were passed in opposition to the Alien and Sedition Laws. The laws were declared to be unconstitutional and inoperative in Kentucky and Virginia. Exactly how far these early States' rights claims were intended to go is somewhat moot. James Madison, author of the Virginia Resolution, later disclaimed agreement of the resolution with Calhoun's doctrines.

Federalists from Virginia were quite alarmed at this time and conveyed to Hamilton the most alarming intelligence of Jeffersonian aims. From Petersburg, Virginia, William Heth wrote to Hamilton:

. . . In my opinion it requires only some great energetic measure like open war, to bring those *deluded* and *imposed* upon, of our fellow citizens to a just sense of their weakness and folly. We now appear to have a most favorable opportunity to give a decided blow to French ambition & cruelty — *War,* — ever brings *peace.* — I need not say more to a man of quickness of comprehension, to convey what I mean.

You ask, 'What do the faction in your state really aim at?' I answer, nothing short of disunity and the heads of JOHN ADAMS and ALEXANDER HAMILTON; some few others perhaps. So take care of yourself.[32]

Four days later Heth again wrote that he feared civil war and himself desired to be called into service and others reported the same.[33]

Hamilton's reaction was immediate. He expressed his ideas to

[30] Morison, *Otis*, I, Ch. XV.   [31] Morison, *Otis*, II, Ch. XXIV.
[32] Jan. 14, 1799, Hamilton Papers (Library of Congress), 33/4726.
[33] Jan. 18, 1799, Hamilton Papers (Library of Congress), 33/4748. A letter

Theodore Sedgwick, his most frequent correspondent in the Senate and a usual channel of communication to the members of the cabinet. His reaction was the same as it had been at the time of the Whiskey Rebellion and Fries's Rebellion. Let Virginia be put " to the test of resistance." Hamilton stated that he had feared what might happen because of the use of militia to subdue the Whiskey Rebellion; but that with regular troops he would not hesitate ". . . to subdue a *refractory and powerful State.*"[34] Hamilton also proposed the outline of a senate resolution to answer those of Virginia and Kentucky. But the full policy of the federalists was soon checked by Adams sending the message to the Senate for a new mission to France.

The entire program outlined offers another example of the fact that the High-Federalist program was far from exhausted. The forces which had dominated in the party since 1789 were desirous of utilizing this golden opportunity to erect an aristocratic system which would be truly satisfactory to them. To this end, the danger of invasion and civil war was emphasized in order that an army might be available. It was hoped first of all that this army, through conquest, would make a war popular against France and Spain. Meanwhile, through centralization of the government and strengthening of one party, Hamilton hoped to overwhelm the opposition. He hoped the army would not be necessary to suppress general domestic opposition, that the opposition would be powerless. Other federalists expected the army would be necessary, and such means as the sending of troops to suppress Fries's Rebellion offered the pattern.

from Benj. Reeder of New Morgantown, Monongalia, reported on March 22, 1799, that insurrection was coming in Harrison and Randolph Cos. in Virginia. Hamilton Papers (Library of Congress) 37/4193. William Moulton, Pittstown, wrote on May 9, 1799, that he was again ready to take up arms in view of the " menacing attitude of the domestic and foreign enemies to our administration." Hamilton Papers, 41/5718. As early as 1794 growth of secession sentiment in Virginia alarmed Edward Carrington. Richmond, Dec. 12, 1794. Hamilton Papers, 23/3231.

[34] Schachner, *Alexander Hamilton*, 387, quoting hitherto unpublished letter of Hamilton. That Jefferson's reaction was also extreme is shown by Adrienne Koch and Harry Ammon, " The Virginia and Kentucky Resolutions," *William and Mary Quarterly*, 3rd Ser., V, 166 (1948); and Koch, Adrienne, *Jefferson and Madison* (New York, 1950), Ch. VII.

On the need for a stronger program Fisher Ames wrote, " The length of this letter, and the fear of being too officious, restrains me from descanting on our prospects, as to our government and as to an alliance with England. As to the former idea, governments are generally lost from bashfulness. Great occasions, like the present, either overturn or establish them. . . ." [35] At the time when the army was being disbanded, Ames wrote in protest to Wolcott, stating, " a few thousand, or even a few hundred, regular troops, well officered, would give the first advantage to government in every contest." [36] Commenting upon this passage Henry Adams states, ". . . this idea was always foremost in the minds of the extreme Federalists as it was among the extreme Republicans. To crush democracy by force was the ultimate resource of Hamilton. To crush that force was the determined intention of Jefferson." [37] Elsewhere he writes, ". . . The essential point to be remembered is that in 1798 the majority in Congress made a deliberate and persistent attempt to place extraordinary powers in the hands of the President, with a view to the possible necessity for the use of such powers in case of domestic difficulties then fully expected to occur. The extreme Federalists hoped that a timely exercise of force on their side might decide the contest permanently in their favor." [38] On the other hand, referring to these statements by Adams, S. E. Morison states, " Another and more serious charge against the Army Acts of 1798 would scarcely be worth refuting, but for its acceptance by an eminent modern historian. This indictment, that the regular and provisional armies were designed primarily to suppress democracy, and not to protect the country against France, is not supported by the slightest evidence." [39] This impasse is naturally incapable of compromise. The point of view held here is in agreement with Henry Adams.

Further evidence of the domestic program of the Federalists is contained in Hamilton's idea of the use to which the Alien Law should be put. To Pickering he wrote:

[35] Ames to Pickering, July 10, 1798.   Ames's *Works*, I, 234.
[36] Ames to Wolcott, Jan. 12, 1800.   Gibbs, *Wolcott*, II, 320.
[37] Adams, *Gallatin*, 170.   [38] *Ibid.*, 199 and 211.
[39] Morison, *Otis*, I, 102.

If an Alien Bill passes I should like to know what policy in execution is likely to govern the *Executive*. My opinion is that while the mass ought to be obliged to leave the country—the provisions in our Treaties in favour of Merchants ought to be observed & there ought to be *guarded* exceptions of characters whose situations would expose them too much if sent away & whose demeanour among us has been unexceptionable. There are a few such. Let us not be cruel or violent.[40]

This is a good illustration of the fact that Hamilton's ideas of what is cruel and violent are relative. To send away the mass of aliens would certainly have involved a great uprooting of population.

At this point there is one feature of the system of domestic reform which was probably in the minds of the High-Federalists, but yet is not mentioned in their letters, i. e., the franchise. The only clue to their ideas on this subject is in the pamphlet by Fenno, *New Political Aspects*, cited in the previous chapter. The writer of this pamphlet, it is believed, was reproducing what he had gained through contact with the extremists. His plan for internal reform embraces several points. In place of the unchecked executive, the president is to be made dependent upon his cabinet in a manner similar to the British system. The present states are to be abolished and replaced by divisions dependent upon the central government. The governors are to be " praefects," appointed by the central executive. These " praefects " are to form the upper house of the national legislature. As to the franchise, " Under the auspices of a wise and prudent ruler the elective franchise might for ever be cut off from all paupers, vagabonds and outlaws, and the Legislation of the country placed in those hands to which it belongs, the proprietors of the country, at present we are the vassals of foreign outlaws. The frequency of elections, those elections being now entrusted to men of sense, men of principle, men having an interest connected with the interests of the country, decline of course; as the folly and danger of annual elections can now be securely remedied." [41]

---

[40] Hamilton to Pickering, June 7, 1798. Hamilton's *Works* (Hamilton, ed.) **VI**, 299-300.   [41] Fenno, *New Political Aspects*, 21-22.

Chapter 13

Adams Prepares to Block the Program

WHAT effect did the Hamiltonian program for the Federalist party have on the President? In the first place he had not recommended the greatly increased army which Congress had approved. Congress, it should be remembered, had gone beyond even the recommendations of Secretary of War McHenry for additional regiments. Commenting in 1805 on the adoption of Hamilton's program, Adams wrote, ". . . The army was none of my work. I only advised a few companies of Artillery to garrison our most exposed forts that a single frigate or Picaroon Privateer might not take them at the first assault. Hamilton's project of an army of fifty thousand, ten thousand of them to be horse, appeared to me to be proper only for Bedlam. His friends however in the Senate and the House embarrassed me with a bill for more troops than I wanted." [1] Unsupported by substantiating contemporary evidence, this would not be fully convincing, but there is evidence that Adams opposed the army from the beginning, and that this opposition received re-enforcement from several events attendant upon raising the army. First Adams recalled Washington to duty to head the army. Adams was glad to make this appointment without question, but the choice of officers to serve under Washington thereby passed from the control of the President.

In the designation of the subordinate officers one blow was struck at Adams which he felt keenly. Adams' son-in-law, Col. William Stevens Smith, had served as aide-de-camp to Washington during the Revolution. Smith volunteered for service in the new army in 1798 and Washington recommended him for a position as brigadier general. [2] Adams already had him in mind

---

[1] Adams to Benjamin Rush, Quincy, Aug. 23, 1805. *Old Family Letters,* 76.
[2] Washington to Hamilton, July 14, 1798. *Writings of George Washington* (Worthington C. Ford, ed.) XIV, 41.

for such a post.[3] Accordingly the nomination was sent to the Senate.

Pickering, however, now interposed. Smith had recently failed for a large sum of money with considerable loss of funds to his creditors. Smith's business had been land speculation, which at this time carried down Robert Morris, Henry Knox, Benjamin Lincoln, and others. There were, however, imputations of dishonesty against Smith. Hearing of these, Adams had required a full explanation from Smith, which convinced him that the failure was very poor business but was not dishonorable. Pickering was certain that it was. Accordingly he went to the Senate, told the Federalists that Smith was bankrupt in character and fame as well as in business, with the outcome that only two or three votes were cast in favor of the appointment.[4]

The popularity of the army with Adams was not increased by the long and involved *intrigue* over securing for Hamilton the post as second in command to Washington. There is nothing to be gained by again unravelling this tangled skein here. It is sufficient to state that this affair occupied the summer of 1798, from July until October 9, on which date Adams capitulated in view of information from the cabinet that unless Hamilton were appointed Washington would resign.[5] One interesting point is that Hamilton was so sure of the result that in his letter of August 22 to Rufus King he wrote that he was second in command, and in that capacity would have charge of the expedition to South America.[6] Another fact is that when this situation was finally cleared up, everyone was embarrassed to find that no steps had yet been taken toward starting enlistments, with the result that much censure fell on the hapless head of Secretary of War James McHenry.

[3] Adams to Smith, Feb. 16, 1798 and same to same, March 2, 1798. The first letter requests a complete explanation, the second expresses satisfaction with it. Adams' *Works*, VIII, 566-67.

[4] Pickering to Washington, Sept. 1, 1798. Pickering Mss. 9/261-70.

[5] Adams to Washington, Oct. 9, 1798. Adams' *Works*, VIII, 600.

[6] Hamilton to King, August 22, 1797. Hamilton's *Works* (Hamilton, ed.) VI, 347.

On top of this, there came to Adams in August the letters from King and Miranda projecting a British alliance. These were accompanied by a missive from Pickering mentioning that other letters by the same boat had been forwarded by him to Hamilton and Knox.[7] Pickering doubtless mentioned this because he thought that it was quite possible Miranda might have referred to his contacts with these two in his letter to Adams. Such information must have had an electric effect upon him and revealed a great deal which he could hardly have suspected before. At any rate, in his letters to the *Boston Patriot* in 1809, he certainly gives this impression.

Adams realized that there would be considerable trouble through the expense involved for the army. To McHenry he wrote:

As to recruiting service, I wonder whether there has been any enthusiasm which would induce men of common sense to enlist for five dollars a month, who could have fifteen, when they pleased, by sea, or for common work on land.

.   .   .   .

There has been no national plan, that I have seen, as yet formed for the maintenance of the army. One thing I know, that regiments are costly articles everywhere, and more so in this country than any other under the sun. If this nation sees a great army to maintain, without an enemy to fight, there may arise an enthusiasm that seems to be little foreseen. At present there is no more chance of seeing a French army here than there is in Heaven.[8]

His reaction to the bugbear of domestic insurrection was equally positive. Some of his replies to the addresses in 1798 may have given the High-Federalists hopes that Adams would welcome the army as a safeguard. But he did not believe it was needed to assure domestic stability. Senator Sedgwick, in February, 1799, doubtless sharing Hamilton's desire for energy in the executive, called upon Adams and dwelt upon the dangers to be expected from Virginia. In answer to Hamilton's letter urging preparation for use of force against Virginia, Sedgwick wrote, " He replied,

[7] Pickering to Adams, August 21, 1798. Adams' *Works*, VIII, 583.
[8] Adams to McHenry, October 22, 1798. Adams' *Works*, VIII, 612.

and nearly in the following words: — As to the Virginians, sir, it is weakness to apprehend anything from them; but, if you must have an army, I will give it to you, but remember, it will make the government more unpopular than all their other acts. They (the people) have submitted with more patience than any people ever did to the burden of taxes, which has been *liberally laid on*, but their patience will not last always!" Sedgwick was greatly astonished to hear such views.[9]

Further information on the policy Adams desired to follow is contained in his attitude toward appointment in the army. Everyone was agreed that no outright Jacobins should receive positions as officers. Washington wrote to McHenry: ". . . My opinion is of the first that you could as soon scrub a blackamour white as to change the principles of a profest Democrat, and that he will leave nothing uninterrupted to overturn the Government of this Country."[10] Similarly, of one prospective appointee Adams wrote to McHenry he had received information of his speaking at a late election " in a manner highly disorganizing and inflammatory." Should this prove true, McHenry would do well to consider carefully making such an appointment.[11] This justified the Federalist press in boasting, " The Federal Officers have it in charge not to inlist any man into the service of the United States, who, within a certain period of time, has had the audacity to mount the French cocade."[12] This attitude lent countenance to the Republican charge, voiced by Senator Stevens Thomas Mason of Virginia " That it has been mentioned on the floor of Congress, by the friends of this government, that it was the intention of the government to arm one half of the people, for the purpose of keeping the other in awe."[13]

[9] Sedgwick to Hamilton, February 7, 1799. Hamilton's *Works* (Hamilton, ed.) VI, 393.

[10] Washington to McHenry, September 30, 1798. Washington's *Writings*, (Ford, ed.), XIV, 104-105. Washington was skeptical of the chances of invasion, as his other letters of this period show. Similarly his only motive in following this policy was that if any invasion or domestic insurrection should occur, it would not be well to have Republicans in the army.

[11] Adams to McHenry, August 18 and September 13, 1798. Adams' *Works*, VIII, 582; 593.   [12] *Centinel*, August 18, 1798.

[13] *Gazette of the United States*, June 27, 1798.

When this policy of proscription of the opposition first became manifest, a friend of McHenry's wrote to him from Baltimore that he delighted in the defensive measures being taken by the government. Some, however, were urging too extreme a policy, advocating a doctrine of extermination. " The doctrine of extermination would be a delightful way to introduce a *civil war*, while, on the other hand, changing the deluded people by degrees from past error, as different dispositions can bear it, will nerve our *union, country*, and *Government* stronger than at any former period." As an example of where to draw the line between whom to consider sincere and whom not to, he mentions one Winchester, a Jefferson elector, whose conversion would appear to be too sudden.[14]

In February, 1799, an interesting correspondence appeared in the press, which is not reproduced in either the *American State Papers*, or in Steiner's *McHenry*. The commandant of the Virginia militia was Gen. William Darke, who had a good record of service both during the Revolution and on St. Clair's ill-fated Indian campaign of 1791. In August, 1798, he wrote to McHenry offering the services of a volunteer company headed by John Oferall. On September 14, McHenry replied in a letter requesting information from some reliable party, known to him, as to Oferall's principles. Darke's own recommendation will be acceptable, he declares. The date of Darke's reply is torn out of the next letter. In it he recounts the services of the Virginia militia, his own record in the Indian wars, and other data. He refuses to guarantee any man other than to state he is a good citizen and officer. Who has the right to question the patriotism of a Virginian? On December 18, 1798, McHenry replied:

Those who do not confide in the government of their country, cannot expect that it should confide in them; and it is surely proper, whenever necessity requires a selection of its defenders, and of the liberty of the country, government should prefer those who have discovered no improper foreign attachments, or prejudices, that might abate their zeal in its service. This is so much the dictate of common

---

[14] James Ash to McHenry, Baltimore, August 24, 1798. Steiner, *McHenry*, 333.

sense, as to intrude itself upon every reflecting mind, in times of common danger.

Our country is threatened from abroad by a nation which has exhibited towards us in the face of the world, the most studied marks of contempt and disrespect, and whose practices aim at the overthrow of our government by the same steps which have been successful in subverting many of the governments of Europe, and from within by a party which has uniformly advocated or countenanced the policy of that nation, by putting the most indiscriminate censure on all occasions upon every measure of their own government, and those who administered it, tending to frustrate the designs of that nation, which can have no other effect than to divide the people or excite in them groundless jealousies and discontents.

It would be folly, McHenry held, to admit such characters into the service of the government. They could not serve zealously. He is familiar with the distinction between

differences of opinion upon political points . . . and that desperate state of party animosity, which, regardless of decorum, and wisdom, and candour, easily approximates to insurrection and revolt.

In the present crisis of our affairs, and state of party in the country, it was, and is deemed important not to accept companies composed of disaffected persons who may for improper motives, be desirous to intrude themselves into the army, under the pretense of patriotic associations; and to guard against it, certificates have been, and are required, from prominent and known characters, or those whose virtues, talents, and usefulness, have given them a weight and respectability in the community, setting forth the principles of the associates, those of the officers elect, especially, and that the company have complied with the conditions prescribed by law. . . .[15]

---

[15] *Gazette of the United States*, February 27, 1799. McHenry would hardly have been assured by Gen. Darke's appointment as Chairman of the Republican Party Corresponding Committee for Berkely Co., Va., January 23, 1800, *Va. Cal. State Papers*, X, 77. William Darke was born in Penn. in 1736. A colonel during the Revolution, he died November 20, 1801. Howe, Henry, *Historical Collections of Virginia* (Charleston, 1852). For the record of Gen. William Darke, see Heitman, Francis B., *Historical Register of Officers of the Continental Army* (Washington, 1914), 185; and Jacobs, James R., *The Beginning of the U. S. Army, 1783-1812* (Princeton, 1947), 107-09.

However, this attitude helped in thwarting a plan Adams had very much at heart. He considered that the pivotal political states were Pennsylvania and New York, in which he was entirely correct. On July 6, he suggested to Washington the following from whom the subordinate officers might be taken: " Lincoln, Morgan, Knox, Hamilton, Gates, Pinckney, Lee, Carrington, Hand, Muhlenberg, Dayton, Burr, Brooks, Cobb, Smith. . . ." [16] This is likewise the approximate order in which he would have liked to have seen the appointments made, though he did not so state in his letter. At any rate, the significant names are John Peter G. Muhlenberg and Aaron Burr. Augustus Muhlenberg, brother of John Peter G. Muhlenberg, had previously applied for the position as Treasurer of the mint. Adams had some misgivings about the propriety of this and had concurred with the cabinet when they opposed it.

Now he felt that a good opportunity was offered to secure the confidence of the Pennsylvania Germans by appointing one of the Muhlenbergs, both of whom were moderate Republicans. On this point he wrote to Rush, " During the half War with France, General Peter Muhlenberg applied to me directly for a commission in the Army and expressly said he would make no conditions or difficulties about Rank. I concluded from this that General Muhlenberg was convinced of the Justice and necessity of the War, and I would have been very happy to have appointed him notwithstanding his party in Politics. Accordingly I proposed him to ·General Washington, who allowed him to be a good officer. But I was only Viceroy under Washington and he was only Viceroy under Hamilton and Hamilton was Viceroy under the Tories as you call them and Peter Muhlenbourg [sic] was not appointed." [17]

In like manner his effort to secure the appointment of Burr as a brigadier, thereby detaching him from Republicanism, was defeated.[18] This latter case is fully confirmed by a letter of Pickering, who wrote, on July 11, 1798, " I have but a moment

---

[16] Adams to Washington, July 6, 1798. Adams' *Works*, VIII, 572.
[17] Adams to Benjamin Rush, September 30, 1805. *Old Family Letters*, 85.
[18] *Ibid.*

to inform you that although strange ideas are entertained by [the President] relative to the general and staff officers, yet Col. B. [Burr] will assuredly not be Q. M. G. [Quarter Master General]. He has mentioned to the President the necessity of an immediate appointment to Q. M. G., to provide everything belonging to that department, but it is impossible that Gen. W. should confide in him, and therefore he cannot be appointed." [19] Adams' analysis of the situation is rather amusing: Hamilton and Burr were both adventurers; Washington took one of them on his staff; why should he object to having another? Hamilton himself wished a slight relaxation of the policy of confining appointments to the Federalists. But he wished to make the departure only in the case of the younger officers in junior ranks. Some of the leading youth of the country he believed could be won to Federalism by being given commissions in the army. [20]

Further evidence of Adams' disagreement with the Federalist program is that drawn from the campaign literature of 1800. At that time the position of Adams was stated by two writers, or possibly twice by the same party, so close is the agreement between the two defenses of his policy. One is the pamphlet by Noah Webster signed "Aristides," which was based on information obtained in a conference with Adams. [21] The other appeared in the *Boston Gazette* prior to Hamilton's pamphlet. It carried all the earmarks of a semiofficial statement.

The *Boston Gazette* statement appeared over the signature of that worthy Roman, "Marcus Aurelius." He declared that Adams was for neither the suspension of treaties with France nor the immediate raising of an army. Adams' views were expressed in the report of the Secretary of War on April 9. It was "Titus Manlius" (Hamilton) who was responsible for the raising of the army and the suspension of the treaties. He continues by quoting Lyman's address to his constituents as demonstrating the purpose

[19] Pickering to Wolcott, July 11, 1798. Gibbs, *Wolcott*, II, 71. Brackets by Gibbs.

[20] Schachner, *Alexander Hamilton*, 386.

[21] Timothy Phelps to Oliver Wolcott, July 15, 1800. Gibbs, *Wolcott*, II, 380, tells of the conference of Webster and Adams.

for which the army was actually raised. Moreover, the object of this measure was expressly stated to be, " ' a precaution for internal security; ' and the friends of the increase have since avowed that one principal object of raising an army, was to overawe and repress the opposition to government."

The increase was opposed by many of the most active and zealous proponents of the government. "But all this availed not — an act passed for raising an army — the President could not effectually oppose it, without hazarding a division of our Councils, which might have crippled all the measures which he approved of. The friends of government were everywhere surprised — they saw no occasion for such a force."

The writer also draws a distinction between Pickering, who wanted a British alliance, and Hamilton, who had vetoed such a plan. This at least, he states, is to Hamilton's credit. The Alien and Sedition Laws are placed as a part of administration policy.[22] As the line of argument in "Aristides" is precisely the same, duplicating every argument outlined above, and the pomposity of style in both is alike (Webster is the only man in this period who is a match for Robert Goodloe Harper in that respect), there is little need for considering the latter work.[23]

It is worth noting that Webster had been in Adams' confidence at least since 1792, and his paper, The New York *Commercial Advertiser*, had been the vehicle of materials in defense of Adams' importance in negotiating the Treaty of 1783, as compared with the credit due to Jay.[24] Further, Webster had broken with Hamilton on his army policy as soon as it was announced. In addition, during 1798, he had revealed the danger of a British alliance, and engaged in controversy with those advocating such a policy.[25] In reply one " Massachusettensis " wrote to him, ". . .

[22] *Boston Gazette*, October 13, 1800.

[23] Aristides, *Letter to General Hamilton . . . By a Federalist*, Second Edition (New York, 1800). The Boston *Independent Chronicle* of November 20 and 24, 1800 identified Aristides as Noah Webster.

[24] Adams to Mrs. Smith, January 2, 1792. DeWindt, *Correspondence of Miss Adams*, II, 114.

[25] *Boston Gazette*, August 16, 1798.

A treaty for mutual defense, a treaty offensive and defensive against the infernal projects of the French Republic, would not only be both honorable and politic in us and in every civilized nation, but may be, what is still more, necessary to our political existence, as well as that of every other independent nation." [26]

Another person who viewed with a jaundiced eye the policy of the extreme Federalists during this period was the Rev. William Bentley. At the close of 1797 he recorded in his *Diary,* " This day was my service to open the Supreme Court with Prayer. In the conversation I discovered such virulence of political prejudices as exceeded even the vulgarity of Jacobinism or what is stigmatized a vile democracy. When the higher orders have such unmanly prejudices, how can a country be safe and well-governed." [27] Also, in 1799 he recorded, " Our common topics are the capture of French vessels. Everything is done to excite our joy upon these events, but we rejoice with trembling. The news of the *Insurrection* in western parts of Pennsylvania is much in the fog & the tale of *the tub* [28] has vanished. We have the story of Brown,[29] a ridiculous fellow in our gaol, for another alarm, & what is more serious the President is to call out his additional *24 regiments.* Political violence in party is not a proof of quiet possession, and this stir makes us fear more from the directed strength than the progress of any party." [30]

It is plain that the program of the extreme Federalists was not receiving great support. Among many of the people there was considerable alarm. Up to this point the aim of this study has been to produce evidence from those who were concerned in the direction of High-Federalist policy, or from those Federalists who would be in an unbiased position. However, some consideration of the views of others may be of value.

[26] *Ibid.,* August 23, 1798.

[27] Bentley, *Diary,* II, 245.   November 14, 1797.

[28] There was considerable excitement at this time over the capture of supposed plotters in Charleston.   Their baggage was supposed to contain papers with plans for revolutionizing the country.   Nothing was found but clothes.

[29] This was a Republican who had erected a liberty pole near Dedham as a protest against the Alien and Sedition Law.

[30] Bentley, *Diary,* II, 298.   March 28, 1798.

Henry Adams refers to the following statement written by Jefferson in 1816 as an essentially correct appraisal of his own situation, though somewhat exaggerated:

The Federalists' usurpations and violations of the Constitution at that period and their majority in both Houses of Congress, were so great, so decided, and so daring, that, after combatting their aggressions inch by inch without being able in the least to check their career, the Republican leaders thought it would be best for them to give up their useless efforts there, go home, get into their respective legislatures, embody whatever of resistance they could be formed into, and, if ineffectual, to perish there as in the last ditch. All therefore retired, leaving Mr. Gallatin alone in the House of Representatives, and myself in the Senate, where I then presided as Vice-President. . . . No one who was not a witness to the scene of that gloomy period can form any idea of the afflicting persecutions and personal indignities we had to brook.[31]

In like manner, John Adams wrote in 1809, in reference to Hamilton's motives in desiring that the government should insist France send a mission to America to reopen negotiations:

No, Hamilton and his associates could not have seriously believed that the French would soon send a minister here. If they had not, or if they had delayed it, Hamilton would have continued as the head of the army—continual provocations and irritations would have taken place between the two nations, till one or the other would have declared war. In the meantime, it was my opinion then, and has been ever since, that the two parties in the United States would have broken out into a civil war; a majority of all the States to the southward of Hudson River, united with nearly half New England, would have raised an army under Aaron Burr; a majority of New England might have raised another army under Hamilton — Burr would have beat Hamilton to pieces, and what would have followed next let the prophets foretell. But such would have been the result of Hamilton's ' enterprises of great pith and moment.'

As a matter of fact, Hamilton would not have had the support of a majority of New England, Adams goes on to say. Rather,

[31] Adams, *Gallatin*, 205.

Adams concluded, had envoys not been sent, the country would have voted unanimously against Federalists in the election of 1800.[32] This conjecture makes Adams' disclaimer of the gift of prophecy appear as the prompting of modesty.

In a more restrained moment, Adams analyzed the situation as follows: " To dispatch all in a few words, a civil war was expected. The party committed suicide, they killed themselves and the national President (not their President) at one shot, and then, as foolishly or maliciously indicted me for the murder. My own mission to France . . . I esteem the most splendid diamond in my crown; or if any one thinks this expression too monarchical, I will say the most brilliant feather in my cap." [33]

In 1800 John Quincy Adams wrote from Berlin, " With the scanty information I can collect I distrust my own opinions upon American affairs. But from what I do see, it is impossible for me to avoid the supposition that the ultimate necessary consequence, if not the ultimate object of both the extreme parties which divide us, will be a dissolution of the Union and a civil war. Your father's policy was certainly to steer between the shoals on one side, and the rocks on the other, but as both factions have turned their arms against him, and the people themselves have abandoned him, there is too much reason to expect that the purpose common to the two opposite factions will be effected. . . ." [34]

Thus it is clear that as the time approached for the opening of the third session of the Fifth Congress, in December, 1798, the crisis was acute. At this time such papers as the Philadelphia Gazette and the Courant contained articles like the following:

Salem, December 11, 1798.

Our government is under a moral obligation formally to declare War against France or the principles upon which their late measures

---

[32] *Patriot*, June 10, 1809, Quincy, June 5, 1809.

[33] Adams to James Lloyd, February 6, 1815. Adams' *Works*, X, 115.

[34] John Quincy Adams to T. B. Adams, Berlin, December 30, 1800. Ford, Worthington C., *Writings of John Quincy Adams*, II, 491; Bemis, Samuel Flagg, *John Quincy Adams and the Foundations of American Foreign Policy* (New York, 1949), Ch. V.

respecting her have been founded, must be abandoned as false. It is true those measures would have been sufficient to have roused any nation, possessing one spark of national honor or self-respect, or feeling and energy in her resources, either to propose an honorable accomodation, or to declare an open and honorable war. But the last act is left for our government. It is true this formality will not much alter our relations to France, but it will very materially affect our internal situation; for until that is done, France will not abandon her hopes here; and divisions will be constantly excited and fomented by them. But that act would take us at once out of our present *amphibious* situation, and crush the *French* party in this country, at the same time it would not create an enemy, but only put us in a situation to act with more energy against the enemy that has already attacked us.—Every measure yet taken by government against France, has been opposed by men who have afterwards been convinced that it ought to have been taken before; and this will undoubtedly share the fate of the rest.[35]

But at the opening of Congress, Adams struck the note which determined that Federalist policy should retreat, not advance.

---

[35] *Gazette of the United States*, December 19, 1798.

Chapter 14

The Party Splits

ACCORDING to his statement in 1809, when Adams arrived in Philadelphia in December, 1798, he found his cabinet anxious that he should recommend a declaration of war.[1] In their letters, however, none of the cabinet except McHenry urged such a step.[2] It was at this time, according to Adams, that the war caucus of the Federal party was held.[3] He recounts that at this caucus the extremists of the party were unable to carry a majority for the measure. That the caucus was held is certain, but Robert Liston's account places it during the preceding July following the introduction of the Allen Resolution into the House.

Whether or not the cabinet sought a declaration of war, the three major members were unanimous in urging that Adams should make a declaration that the United States would send no embassy to France. The only way negotiations could be reopened would be by France sending a mission to America.

Adams, who was already receiving overtures from France, took the position that this showed a desire by the cabinet to continue the rupture until some crisis would bring about an open war. Consequently he disregarded this advice and, on December 8, 1798, stated in his address to the third session of Congress that upon the receipt of adequate assurance that an embassy would be accepted by France, America, anxious for peace, would name envoys. The spirit of the country in connection with the general

---

[1] *Patriot*, June 24, 1809. Quincy, June 10, 1809.

[2] For McHenry's letter, see Adams' *Works*, VIII, 604, note. Also Pickering to Adams, November 27, 1798. Pickering Mss., 9/659. Wolcott to Adams, November, 1798. Gibbs, *Wolcott*, II, 168. Stoddert, the new cabinet officer, Secretary of the Navy, dealt chiefly with his own department. Stoddert to Adams, November 23, 1798. Gibbs, *Wolcott*, II, 115.

[3] *Patriot*, June 24, 1809. Quincy, June 10, 1809. *Complete Anas*, 204. March 24, 1800. Likewise Stoddert to Adams, October 12, 1809. Lodge, *Cabot*, 202.

determination to resist the demands of **XYZ**, he hailed with delight. Pending the opening of any negotiation the only way of assuring the safety of the country would be through a vigorous determination to resist aggression. To this end enlargements in the navy, to a limited extent, would be desirable.[4]

Compared with what had been anticipated the tone of this address was a pleasant surprise to the Republicans, although Gallatin erroneously saw in it the failure of England to sign a treaty offensive and defensive as the cause of the pacific tone.[5] The Federalists of the Hamiltonian wing saw that all was lost. It is significant, in view of the later uproar over the " unexpected " naming of the envoys, that immediately after the speech some of the Federalists anticipated that a third mission to France was what Adams had in mind.[6]

It was now obvious that the Federalist program was to fall between two stools. It would have been possible to maintain an economical system of defense, such as Adams had desired. More-over, with someone in the presidential chair who could have been brought to recommend war, it would have been possible to enter upon the adventuresome program which was actually started. But the expense attendant upon the compromise system put the party in an untenable position, incapable of defense at the polls. The reaction of the War Federalists at this point is well stated in the following letter to Harrison Gray Otis:

ALS

Boston
January 12, 1799

. . . In omitting the declaration of war the last session, we are con-tinually reminded that the Government lost ground. Tho' the French have relaxed in no point: Tho' they daily repeat the most aggravated injuries, rob & despoil us of our property, trample upon our Flag, imprison our seamen, & interfere with our Government — Yet that manly spirit which our country has so lately displayed seems to be succeeded by a general stupor — That the French have not declared

---

[4] *Annals*, IX, 2320. December 8, 1798.

[5] Gallatin to Mrs. Gallatin, December 14, 1798. Adams, *Gallatin*, 223.

[6] Higginson to Pickering, January 1, 1799. *American Historical Association Report, 1896*, I, 817.

war against us instead of producing sorrow in the breast of every
friend to order, has brought forward astonishment and delight from
the most high toned of our Federalists.[7]

In Congress the session was more notable for the amount of
wrangling than for the measures passed during the session. One
of the earliest acts was a Federalist's proposal to print copies of
the Alien and Sedition Laws, so that they could be known to all
in their true form. The Republicans offered an amendment to this
resolution to provide that the Constitution be printed with them.
This placed the Federalists in the embarrassing position of either
voting against distributing the Constitution, or admitting, by
distributing it with the laws included, that there was at least an
argument as to their constitutionality. The point was settled by
defeating the measures for printing the laws and the Constitution.[8]

During the debates on this point Harper asserted the Republicans were plotting rebellion against the laws just as they had in
the case of the Whiskey Rebellion.[9] The best example of the
intolerance of the Federalists occurred in the course of some
remarks by Thatcher of Maine, speaking of the opposition to the
Alien and Sedition Laws in the West:

Mr. Thatcher agreed with the gentleman who had just sat down,
that the people in the Western country were greatly misinformed; but
he did not believe it was either with respect to the Constitution or
the laws, but on moral subjects.

The Speaker said, no remarks of this kind could possibly be in order.

Mr. Thatcher said, he was about to state facts from which he meant
to draw an argument against the publication of the Constitution. If
any conclusion could be drawn from the speeches of their Governors,
and Legislatures, and public meetings, it is evident they are misinformed, and in a state of ignorance, not of the Constitution, or the
laws in question, as, when they quote either, they quote them correctly . . . It was not political information which these people were
in want of, but moral information, correct habits, and regular fixed
characters.[10]

---

[7] T. J. Mason, Boston, Jan. 12, 1799 to Harrison Gray Otis, Otis *Mss.*,
Boston.   [8] *Annals*, IX, 2445 ff., Dec. 14, 1798.
[9] *Ibid.*, 2430. Dec. 12, 1798.   [10] *Ibid.*, 2450. Dec. 28, 1798.

The first important business of the session was the Logan Act, one of the few penal statutes which has received the name of the " criminal " against whom it was aimed. Dr. George Logan, a Jeffersonian, had gone, as a private citizen, on a mission to France with the aim of reopening negotiations between the two countries. To the Federalists this was evidence of the treasonable communications they held were constantly taking place; particularly was this the case in view of Logan's carrying a letter from Jefferson certifying that he was an American citizen. Harper declared that Logan might have gone to arrange for invasion of America. France has stated she has a party here, he said. Further, many admit they desire to procure a change of administration and system, may it not be that they have decided to effect this by insurrection and a foreign force? [11] The Federalists were resolved to put a stop to individual efforts at diplomacy. Hence they proposed and passed a bill to prohibit interference, by an unauthorized private citizen, with the conduct of international negotiation. This act is still in force. One of the high points of the debates on the Logan Act came when, after eight days of discussion on the measure, Allen of Connecticut stated that it was time for debate to close, " . . . if they [the Republicans] continued thus to act, the people ought to drive them from their seats. . . . He hoped his friends [the Federalists] would forbear to lengthen the debate as it would be casting ' pearls before swine.' " [12] Gallatin declared that he was interested in observing this type of appeal to the sovereign people by the Federalists.[13]

With the passage of the Logan Act, which received a large majority, no other important measure was adopted during the session. The bankruptcy bill, which had been before Congress for around six years, was postponed until the next session. Minor increases were effected in the army and navy.

After January petitions began to roll into the House praying for the repeal of the Alien and Sedition Laws, the disbanding

[11] *Annals*, 2530.   Dec. 28, 1798.
[12] *Ibid.*, 2704-2705.   Jan. 17, 1799.
[13] *Ibid.*, 2706.

of the army, and the repeal of the direct tax. The total signing the petitions in Pennsylvania alone came to 18,000.[14] All of these were not voters, but considering that only 20,000 votes had been cast in the election of 1796, this was obviously an overwhelming manifestation of public opinion. Despite this, however, the report of the committee which passed on these petitions was in favor of the continuance of all the measures. Particular attention was paid to a defense of the Alien and Sedition Laws in this committee report. This report was approved in the House by a vote of 52 to 28.[15]

As the session drew to a close Adams was becoming farther and farther separated from the Federalists. In February, during the course of Sedgwick's interview with him, the following conversation occurred: " He asked me what additional authority it was proposed to give the commander-in-chief? I answered none; that all that was proposed to give him was a new title — that of general. ' What,' said he, ' are you going to appoint him general over the President? I have not been so blind but I have seen a combined effort among those who call themselves the friends of government, to annihilate the essential powers given to the President. This, sir, (raising his voice) my understanding has perceived and my heart felt.' " [16]

This feeling on Adams' part was certainly justified. George Cabot, leader of the Essex Junto, likewise made a proposal in regard to the President which is worthy of Fenno's pamphlet, and would have angered Adams to the greatest degree. Adams had been defending the conduct of Gerry, who had remained in France when Pinckney and Marshall returned to the United States. These remarks by the President led to reports quite at variance from the orthodox Federalist reaction to Gerry's conduct. This had the bad effect of undermining the Federalist propaganda about the insincerity of the overtures to Gerry. Accordingly, Cabot and Higginson decided to send Otis, who was always close

[14] *Annals*, IX, 2993., Feb. 25, 1799.

[15] *Ibid.*, 2985 ff., Feb. 25, 1799.

[16] Sedgwick to Hamilton, Feb. 7, 1799. Hamilton's *Works* (Hamilton, ed.), VI, 394.

to Adams, to tell him that he should stop defending Gerry. Further, Cabot suggested, " But my dear sir, must there not be something more done? Must it not become a maxim, never to be violated, that the President shall be always accompanied by those whom he has selected to assist him in carrying on the executive government? If at any time he is absent for the benefit of relaxation, let it be adhered to that he does no business and gives no opinion. If some system like this is not established there will be no order nor consistency in our affairs." [17]

As the Fifth Congress came to a close, Adams prepared a measure which marked the definite end of his connection with the High-Federalists. This was the nomination of the new mission to France. As already indicated, his speech at the start of the session pointed toward such an end. Further, in October he had written to Pickering that he had in mind making nominations for a new mission, which should then be held in abeyance until proper assurances of its being accepted were received. [18] The position of the cabinet had been in complete opposition to this. But it was not long before Adams received assurance that a new mission would be honorably received. On June 21, 1798, shortly after the time of the XYZ communications to Congress, Adams had stated he would not send, " another minister to France without assurances that he will be received, respected and honored as the representative of a great, free, powerful, and independent nation." [19] Talleyrand moved to meet these conditions. There is strong evidence that he was surprised at the violence of the American reaction. He realized that he had over-reached himself in the XYZ proposals. Also he was warned by Jefferson and others in the United States that the situation was critical. Finally he received information of the negotiations for an Anglo-American alliance and the accompanying threat to the Floridas, Louisiana, and South America. Accordingly he was quite anxious to retrieve the situation. On September 18, 1798, Talleyrand sent a letter

---

[17] Cabot to Wolcott, Oct. 10, 1798.   Gibbs, *Wolcott,* II, 110.
[18] Cabot to Wolcott, Oct. 10, 1798.   Gibbs, *Wolcott,* II, 110.
[19] Adams' *Works,* IX, 159.

by Louis Pichon, one of his diplomatic staff, to William Vans
Murray, American Minister to the Hague. This letter quoted
Adams' very words and assured him that "you were right in
asserting that every plenipotentiary whom the Government of
the United States will send to France, to terminate the differences
which subsist between the two countries, will undoubtedly be
received with the respect due to the representative of a free,
independent, and powerful country." [20] Murray sent this dispatch
at once to the Secretary of State, and also sent copies direct to
the President by Thomas B. Adams, son of the President, who
returned with them to the United States in January. [21] Murray
also sent copies to John Quincy Adams, then United States
minister to Prussia. In his work, *John Quincy Adams and the
Foundations of American Foreign Policy,* Samuel Flagg Bemis [22]
has shown how all of these — Murray, T. B. Adams, and John
Quincy Adams — advised the President of the sincerity of Talleyrand's change of heart. Also Murray and J. Q. Adams advised the
Secretary of State, Pickering, that all differences could probably
be settled with France by a new mission. Many private statements to this same end were also received by the President. But
the public assurances were what counted most. They led the
President on February 18, 1799 to nominate William Vans Murray
to the Senate to renew negotiations with France. Along with
the nomination Adams transmitted the Talleyrand-Pichon letter. [23]

But despite earlier warnings this nomination came as a bomb-
shell to the cabinet and to the High-Federalists. In view of the
prior position of the cabinet, Adams had not consulted them again.
In the Senate, there was extreme consternation. Senator Sedgwick

---

[20] *American State Papers, Foreign Relations*, II, 239. For the role of
Jefferson in urging the French to adopt a conciliatory attitude, cf. Morison,
S. E., "Dupont, Talleyrand, and the French Spoilations," *Massachusetts
Historical Society Proceedings*, XLIV, 63-78; for the information concerning
the proposed Anglo-American alliance, cf. Lyon, E. Wilson, "The Directory
and the United States," *American Historical Review*, XLIII, 514-32.

[21] Ford, *Letters of William Vans Murray, Annual Report of American Historical Association, 1912*, 481.

[22] (New York, 1949), 99 ff.

[23] Adams' *Works*, VIII, 690-91.

at once wrote to Hamilton to find out what the Senate should do — negate the nomination, secure a better negotiator, or approve? He stated: "Had the foulest heart and ablest head in the world been permitted to select the most embarrassing and ruinous measures, perhaps it would have been precisely the one which has been adopted." [24] Hamilton replied that it would be inadvisable to negate the entire idea of a mission. Instead two other members should be added, and an agreement reached with the President on the point.[25] Accordingly, a committee called on Adams. Attempts to persuade him against the mission were unavailing. "During the conversation he declared repeatedly that to defend the executive against oligarchic influence, it was indispensible that he should insist on a decision on the nomination." [26] Thereupon the Senate rejected Murray, but then approved a mission to consist of Patrick Henry, Oliver Ellsworth, and Murray. Upon Henry's declining, William R. Davie, Governor of North Carolina, was named in his stead.

Of the entire Federalist press only two papers disapproved the nominations, *Porcupine's Gazette* and the *Gazette of the United States*. Porcupine simply denied it. No Federalist President could do such a thing, consequently it had not happened.[27] Fenno was so overcome that he relinquished the editorship of his paper.[28]

In this manner the Fifth Congress same to a close. In the House the last business of the session was fitting. Since the publication of the XYZ papers the Speaker had conducted himself in an insulting and belligerent manner. Accordingly the Re-

---

[24] Sedgwick to Hamilton, Feb. 19, 1799. Hamilton's *Works* (Hamilton, ed.) VI, 397.

[25] Hamilton to Sedgwick, New York, Feb. 21, 1799. Hamilton's *Works* (Hamilton, ed.) VI, 397.

[26] Sedgwick to Hamilton, Feb. 25, 1799. Hamilton's *Works* (Hamilton, ed.), VI, 399. The day the committee called on Adams was Saturday, Feb. 23. As the nomination was on the 18th, the business was evidently held in abeyance until Hamilton could be notified and his letter of the 21st be received. Two days were usually necessary for transmission of mail from New York to Philadelphia.

[27] *Porcupine's Gazette*, Feb. 19, 1799. *Works*, X, 148.

[28] *Gazette of the United States*, March 4, 1799.

publicans refused him an unanimous vote of thanks. This unanimous vote had been customary since the start of the government.
In this instance the vote was 40 to 22. Thereupon the Speaker
stated: ". . . Permit me to say, that far from being displeased,
I have, on the contrary, been very much gratified at hearing
that the resolution of thanks had not been passed, as a mere
matter of form, unanimously. As in all public bodies, there have
ever been found men whose approbation must be considered by
the meritorious as censure, so in this body, there are, unhappily,
some whose censure must be regarded by all whose esteem I
value, as the highest testimony of merit. . . ." [29]

One feature of the closing session of the Fifth Congress deserves
consideration. There is a higher number of moderates during this
session as compared with the previous one. This tendency is
restricted to the Federalists, and shows a reaction from the first
fervor aroused by the XYZ dispatches. In Maryland and Pennsylvania this tendency is apparent, though in New York where a
comparable change of sentiment was taking place, no such reflection of popular feeling appears in the voting in the House.
The 4th Pennsylvania District chose two representatives. This is
the section of the state where Fries's Rebellion against collection
of the direct tax was soon to break out among the Germans. In
a bye-election Sitgreaves, a strong Federalist, was replaced by
Brown, a strong Republican. Chapman, from the same district,
changed from Federalist to moderate.

The elections for the Sixth Congress extended from the spring
of 1798 to the spring of 1799, in accordance with the variation in
date from state to state. These elections were generally influenced
by publication of the XYZ dispatches but came before there
was the full reaction against the direct tax and the Alien and
Sedition Laws. Due to the aroused public sentiment, the election
resulted in the choice of 63 Federalists to 43 Republicans, although
the great sweep was, in many respects, more than offset by the
losses suffered in certain sections heretofore Federalist and the
fact that some of the new Federalists did not vote with the party.

[29] *Annals*, IX, 3055. March 4, 1799.

This was true of the pivotal states of New York, New Jersey, Pennsylvania, and Maryland. For this election New York was redistricted to give a larger proportion to the rapidly growing West. New Jersey was districted for the only time in the period under consideration (Map 8). In New York, General John Williams was defeated by a Republican, John Thompson, in the 7th District which was on the upper Hudson River. This gave a Republican majority in the delegation from the state, six to four as compared with a Federalist margin of six to four in the previous Congress. In Pennsylvania, General Peter Muhlenberg, after his failure to receive an army appointment, appeared from the 4th District, giving a Republican margin in the Sixth Congress of eight to five, as contrasted with only seven to six in the preceding Fifth Congress. In his memoirs Alexander Graydon, a Federalist active during this period, wrote that the Germans were not so greatly affected by the Alien and Sedition Laws, but, " The tax on real property was the fatal blow to Federalism. Their pockets had hitherto been spared, and wheat had borne a good price. But now their vulnerable part was touched, and they began to look about them." [30] One Federalist gain was registered in Pennsylvania, the City of Philadelphia returning a Federalist instead of a Republican, who had represented the city at the start of the Fifth Congress. This off-set one of the two new Republicans from the 4th District.

In New Jersey, which had previously returned five Federalists, there now appeared three Republicans. One of these (Rep. Linn) was at first claimed by some of the Federalists, while others classified him as a Republican. As he voted with the Republicans he is considered as such here. In Maryland the Republicans gained two members, carrying the formerly Federalist Sixth and Seventh Districts but lost one member in the Second District. This gave the Federalists a five to three majority, a net Republican gain of one.

Noticing the tendency of formerly Federalist sections to turn

[30] Graydon, Alexander, *Memoirs of His Own Times* (Philadelphia, 1846), 390.

toward Republicanism, Hamilton wrote in his memorable letter
to Dayton at the beginning of 1799:

> An accurate view of the internal situation of the United States
> presents many discouraging reflections to the enlightened friends of
> our government and country. Notwithstanding the unexampled suc-
> cess of our public measures at home and abroad, — notwithstanding
> the instructive comments afforded by the disastrous and disgusting
> scenes of the French Revolution—public opinion has not been amelio-
> rated; sentiments dangerous to social happiness have not been dimin-
> ished; on the contrary, there are symptoms which warrant the appre-
> hension that among the most numerous class of citizens, errors of a
> very pernicious tendency have not only preserved but have extended
> their empire. Though something may have been gained on the side
> of men of information and property, more has probably been lost on
> that of persons of a different description. . . . some of the parts of
> the Union which, in times past have been the soundest, have of late
> exhibited signs of a gangrene begun and progressive.[31]

In New England there was a greater trend to Federalism. Only
three Republicans were returned, Lyon of Vermont, and from
Massachusetts, Bishop from the 3rd Southern District and
Varnum from the 2nd Middle District. In the 1st Western District
Theodore Sedgwick ran and assured a strong Federalist from that
region. The chief reason for his leaving the Senate was the
desire of the Federalists for a reliable Speaker of the House,
Dayton having been elected to the Senate from New Jersey.

The South accounted for the great increase in number of Federalists as contrasted with the previous total. In many cases,
however, the gains were of no value when it came to voting.
Georgia sent two so-called Federalists, both the Fifth Congress
representatives being defeated. One of these new Georgia representatives did not vote at all with the Federalists and his voting
was that of a Republican. Only General Thomas Sumter of the
South Carolina Republicans survived, giving the Federalists a
total of five out of six representatives. In North Carolina only five
Republicans were returned, while the same number of Feder-

---

[31] Hamilton to Dayton, 1799. Hamilton's *Works* (Hamilton, ed.), VI, 383.

alists were elected. In like manner Virginia increased her number of Federalists from four to eight. These eight were Evans, Goode, Gray, Lee, Marshall, Page, Parker, and Powell. The Republicans chosen totalled eleven. Further, according to Jefferson, only the fact that the election was not held until March, 1799, prevented the defeat of the entire group of far western Republicans, the two Triggs and Holmes.[32] The influences at work in this Western region may be observed in the letter General Daniel Morgan wrote to his constituents:

> However unnatural it may appear, and however difficult to be believed, yet, it is a dreadful melancholy truth, that we have a considerable party among ourselves, who, instead of supporting and rendering respectable our government, would divide and distract it, and I believe, lay it prostrate at the feet of *France*, notwithstanding her insulting aggressions.
>
> I would that this was not the case — I wish the proceedings of the majority in our State Legislature, at the late session, was not too indicative of such a disposition. My God? Can it be possible!
>
> .   .   .   .
>
> The crisis is arrived — . . . . You are now to determine whether you will support your nation . . . or dwindle to a state of Tributary vassalage.
>
> . . . We may (I fear) experience the same dreadful calamities which have afflicted *Ireland* for some time. —— French influence has destroyed that country, and drenched it in blood; if we are not guarded, the same causes will produce the same effects in our own.[33]

By the time of the election for the Sixth Congress, Washington himself had started to play a fairly strong role in Virginia Federalist circles. He urged John Marshall[34] to run for the House in 1798, and after the elections hailed with delight the victories

---

[32] Jefferson to Tench Coxe, Monticello, May 21, 1799. Jefferson's *Works*, VII, 378.

[33] *Centinel*, May 4, 1799. This was an electioneering letter, but took some time to get to New England.

[34] Washington to Marshall, Mt. Vernon, Dec. 30, 1798, *Writings* (Fitzpatrick, ed.), XXXVII, 75.

of the eight Virginia Federalists.[35] Commenting on parties at this time he declared his full sympathies with the Federalists, or at least that branch represented by Marshall. He remarked upon the increasing virulence of the party struggle. As a result, the presidential office was no longer to be considered as above politics. Whoever was president would now be regarded as a party president.[36]

This appeal to the feeling that the union was in danger, brought back, in the coastal and western portions of the South, the same support which had resulted in the adoption of the Constitution. In Virginia and the states to the south, the Virginia and Kentucky Resolutions were regarded as a threat to the Union. The voters in these areas reacted against such extreme measures and returned moderate Federalists. However, in many instances, the extent of this Federalism was limited to the above feeling alone. Consequently, when the scope of the High-Federalist program began to be felt in the shape of taxes and the repression of the Alien and Sedition Laws, this momentary support dwindled. On the other hand, the northern states, where there was no feeling that the union was endangered, showed practically no change from the Fifth Congress. Including Pennsylvania and all states to the north thereof, the Sixth Congress shows, in that north central and New England area, practically the same number of Federalists and Republicans as does the Fifth Congress.

[35] Washington to John Trumbull, Mt. Vernon, June 25, 1799, *Ibid.*, 249.
[36] *Ibid.*

Chapter 15

Closing the Administration

IT is probable that had Adams been unable to control the policy of the party in regard to reopening negotiations with France he would have resigned the presidency, and at the same time have delivered a denunciation of his party. He wrote:

The nomination of Murray has had one good effect at least. It has shown to every observing and thinking man the real strength and weakness of the Constitution and where one part of that weakness resides. It has also produced a display of the real spirit of the parties in this country and the object they have in view. To me it has laid open character. Some of these will do well to study a little more maturely the spirit of their station. . . . Arrogance shall be made to feel a curb. If anyone entertaining the idea that, because I am a President of three votes only, I am in the power of a party, they shall find that I am no more so than the Constitution forces upon me. If the combination of Senator, General and Head of Department shall be formed as I cannot resist, and measures are demanded of me that I cannot adopt, my remedy is plain and certain. I will try my own strength at resistance first however.[1]

Adams' threat to resign if the Senate blocked a new mission may have been all that deterred the Federalists. The British minister wrote to his government:

that the " Altercations " . . . between Mr. Adams and the leading members of the Senate . . . have been carried to a greater height than is generally known. I am assured in confidence that, after an indignant rejection of their interference, he went so far as to threaten to resign and to leave the Government in the hands of Mr. Jefferson, who would of course in to [under] the American Constitution hold the

---

[1] Adams to —————, March 29, 1799. *Quarterly Magazine of the Sons of the Revolution of the State of Virginia*, II, No. 2, 35. Also Adams to Lloyd, March 30, 1815. Adams' *Works*, X, 151.

office of President during the remainder of the term for which Mr. Adams and he were jointly chosen at the last election.

The federal party have felt the necessity of temporary forbearance, and seem determined, for the sake of the Country, to continue to give the Chief Magistrate their support.[2]

That the President should have been driven to the possible necessity of holding up the High-Federalists to public scorn, dramatizing this by his own resignation, would certainly have wrecked the party. However, that relations between the two wings of the party could be conducted only on the basis of such recriminations, is an obvious commentary on the chances of success in the forthcoming election. But despite the temporary restoration of a working basis between the two wings of the party, a worse situation soon followed.

Retiring to Quincy at the close of the Fifth Congress in 1799 Adams there began to receive warnings that all was not well. From Georgetown he received a letter from a friend, Uriah Forrest, warning him that close supervision over the Secretaries was needed. Adams had been elected, not they. He should stay in Philadelphia to supervise their activities.[3]

A letter written to Pickering at this time clearly sets forth the policy Adams intended to follow. The overtures from France, while possibly reflecting a mere desire to intrigue, would be acted upon in good faith by the American Government. ". . . They shall find, as long as I am in office, candor and integrity, and, as far as there can be any confidence or safety, a pacific and friendly disposition. . . . In this spirit I shall pursue the negotiations, and I expect the cooperation of the heads of departments." There shall, however, be no weakening of the system of defense. " Our operations and preparations by sea and land are not to be relaxed in the smallest degree. On the contrary, I wish them to be animated with fresh energy." [4] Adams also directed immediate steps

---

[2] Liston to Grenville, Phil., 11 March 1799. *Adams Transcripts* (Library of Congress) Vol. 42.

[3] Forrest to Adams, April 28, 1799. Adams' *Works*, VIII, 637.

[4] Adams to Pickering, Sept. 6, 1799. Adams' *Works*, IX, 10.

to send the envoys to France. He directed that the navy should prepare a ship to take them across immediately.

Shaken by statements of the unreliability of his cabinet, Adams hastened his departure from Quincy to Trenton, where the offices of Government had been removed during the periodic epidemic of yellow fever in Philadelphia. He received a letter from Benjamin Stoddert, Secretary of the Navy, informing him that a conspiracy was afoot to defeat the plans for sending the envoys. Moreover, plans were being formulated to prevent Adams from receiving full Federalist support at the next election.[5] Accordingly he went to Trenton, there to find Hamilton astray from his army, and seeking to prevent the envoys from sailing. The arguments advanced to dissuade Adams have been recounted in a preceding chapter: the Restoration of the Bourbons was likely. Therefore for America to risk making peace with France under these circumstances would entail great danger. Moreover, just at this time, the affairs of France were so unsettled, that pending this expected outcome, there could be no assurance of a lasting agreement from the unstable government. These arguments fell on deaf ears. On October 16 the Secretary of State was ordered to supply the envoys with copies of the instructions,[6] and at the same time Stoddert was instructed to hold a government vessel in readiness for their departure. Under this close supervision by the President the mission to France at last sailed on November 3, 1799 aboard the frigate " United States." [7]

To the British the curious results produced by the foreign policy of the United States showed an unsound government. Liston conjectured at the time of the new mission to France that the President might be in his dotage.[8] There was some disposition to delay settlement of American claims against the British, based on the theory that a breakup in the government

[5] Stoddert to Adams, Sept. 13, 1799. *Ibid.*, 18.

[6] Adams to Pickering, Oct. 16, 1799. Adams' *Works*, IX, 39.

[7] Adams to Stoddert, Oct. 16, 1799, *Ibid.*; Lyon, E. Wilson, " The Franco-American Convention of 1800," *Journal of Modern History*, XII, 309.

[8] Liston to Grenville, Phila., 4 March 1799, No. 17, *Adams Transcripts* (Library of Congress).

and the Union was possible, but Liston advised that matters were not that critical.[9] Grenville may have been reassured, but he had stated:

" [The] . . . whole system of the American Government seems to me to be tottering to its foundations, and so far from being able to enforce upon the country good faith towards foreign powers, I much doubt their power of maintaining internal tranquility." So much did Grenville consider this to be possible that he thought it might be desirable to reconsider the entire policy toward the United States.[10]

Leaving the field of foreign policy, several features of Adams' domestic policy are of significance in showing a growing division from the Hamiltonians. Any extensive reforms in the financial system of the country, such as he had hinted at in letters to his wife, notably the desire to restrict the use of paper money and the functions of the Bank of the United States, were necessarily precluded by the enforced preoccupation of the administration with foreign affairs, and the expense entailed by the defense operations. The danger from the taxation measures he clearly perceived and regretted, at a time when Hamilton was clamoring for further levies.

Certain steps were taken to prevent further concentration of powers in the hands of the Treasury Department. Adams complained to Wolcott that there seemed to be a tendency to make this department independent of the executive.[11] The greatest effort he made in opposition to Wolcott's policy was an attempt to have the interest rate of the $5,000,000 loan placed at six per cent rather than at eight per cent, which Wolcott contended was necessary in order to secure the money. Hamilton, it should be noted, supported the eight per cent rate.[12] Earlier, Adams had

[9] Liston to Grenville, Phila., 7 May, 1800, Private, *Adams Transcripts* (Library of Congress).

[10] Grenville to R. Liston, Feb. 28, 1800, *Manuscripts of J. B. Fortescue . . . at Dropmore* (Historical Manuscripts Commission, London, 1892-1927), VI, 146.

[11] Adams to Wolcott, Oct. 20, 1797. *Ibid.*, VIII, 554.

[12] Hamilton to Wolcott, Dec. 28, 1798, Hamilton *Papers* (Library of Congress) 33/4641.

written to Wolcott complaining of the bad effect on public credit from the fluctuation of the paper money, and likewise denouncing the tendency of state legislatures to set up new banks, under the plea of the advantages to be derived by agriculture.[13] Of the eight per cent loan he wrote, " The rate of interest is a subject of great anxiety to me. . . . I cannot but suspect that some advantage is taken of this government by demanding exorbitant interest." [14] Wolcott won his point, with the result that the loan became a prominent issue in the campaign of 1800.

In a few instances toward the close of his administration, Adams yielded to pressure from the Federalists. One case where he did so was in removals from office, for political reasons. He yielded to pressure from the New Hampshire Federalists, and against his better judgment displaced two Portsmouth " Jacobins." [15] This action brought violent attacks from the Republicans. But in most decisions he continued to go against the advice of the extreme Federalists. In the Fries case Adams' action in pardoning Fries brought a storm of criticism from the Hamiltonian Federalists in the campaign. His idea of the case shows that he saw the danger of the lengths to which party violence was being carried. In a list of questions to the cabinet he asked, " Is there not great danger in establishing such a construction of treason, as may be applied to every sudden, ignorant, inconsiderate heat, among a part of the people, wrought up by political disputes, and personal or party animosities? " [16] So far as the Alien Law was concerned, the fact that no deportation took place under it was in part caused by Adams' refusal to sign warrants in blank which Pickering might execute.[17] However he was in favor of utilizing the measure, as he wrote to Pickering in regard to the supposed foreign origin of Duane, who succeeded Bache as editor of the *Aurora* after the death of the latter: " If Mr. Rawle does not

---

[13] Adams to Wolcott, June 21, 1799. Adams' *Works*, VIII, 660.

[14] Same to same, May 17, 1800. *Ibid.*, IX, 57.

[15] Adams to Benjamin Lincoln, March 10, 1800. *Ibid.*, 46.

[16] Adams to Heads of Departments, May 20, 1800. *Ibid.*, 57. Hamilton's criticism is expressed in his pamphlet in 1800.

[17] Adams to Pickering, Oct. 16, 1798. Adams' *Works*, VIII, 606.

think this paper libelous, he is not fit for his office; and if he does not prosecute it, he will not do his duty."

" The matchless effrontery of this Duane merits the execution of the Alien law. I am very willing to try its strength upon him." [18] Duane was, however, prosecuted under the Sedition Law instead. Three warrants for deportation of aliens were signed by Adams. By the time they were sent from Quincy to Philadelphia, the individuals had left the country; or, as in one case, Pickering's anxiety to follow clues further in order to find other suspects, provided time for the alien to leave.[19]

Turning from the consideration of the growing split between Adams and his cabinet to a consideration of the legislation adopted by the new Sixth Congress, it is obvious that the temper of the Federalist majority was directly affected by the division in party councils. At the time of its election in 1798 and 1799 great things had been expected of the Sixth Congress. But when it actually convened the circumstances were vastly different. The new mission to France had sailed. Adams' address of December 3, 1799 to the opening session struck a calm and pacific note. While recommending continued defense efforts, he at the same time urged the House to examine the expenditures with an eye to " beneficial retrenchments." [20] Congress, as a consequence of the mission and the recommendation for economy, suspended further enlistments for the army.[21] In regard to this Adams wrote to Jay, " The last mission to France and the consequent dismission of the twelve regiments, although an essential branch of my system of policy has been to those who have been intriguing and laboring for an army of fifty thousand men an unpardonable fault." [22] There is an amusing incident in connection with Federalist policy at this period. Ames wrote to Pickering that the Junto had just seen the Massachusetts governor's message of thanksgiving in time to prevent God being thanked for the mission to France.

[18] Adams to Pickering, July 24, 1799. Adams' *Works*, IX, 5.
[19] Same to same, Aug. 13, 1799. *Ibid.*, 14.
[20] Adams' *Works*, IX, 140.
[21] *Annals*, X, 425. Jan. 24. 1799.
[22] Adams to Jay, Washington, Nov. 24, 1800. Adams' *Works*, IX, 90.

This passage had been at once removed from the gubernatorial address.[23]

The recognition by the first session of the Sixth Congress of the trend in public sentiment is evident from lack of productivity of the House. The disbanding of any of the soldiers in service was first prevented by the Federalists, but then was authorized on May 14, the last day of the session. Another measure, the Bankruptcy Act, finally secured a majority through the casting vote of the Speaker. On the other hand the Republicans were able to carry a postponement of the Judiciary Act until the next session. (Vote 5 on Chart No. VI.) This act sought to reorganize and increase the number of federal courts, as well as to increase the number of federal judges.

The most interesting piece of legislation during the session was the Ross Bill. This provided for the creation of a commission, composed of six members of each house, and presided over by the Chief Justice. After the President of the Senate received the electoral votes, the state certifications were to be turned over to this commission which would have absolute power to examine the circumstances surrounding the choice of each elector, to determine the validity of the votes, then to count the votes and report who was elected.[24] The measure was chiefly aimed at the Pennsylvania vote.[25] In that state a deadlock between the Republican House and Federalist Senate had prevented the passage of the usual law calling a popular election. It was the intention of the Federalists either to prevent any Pennsylvania electoral votes being cast, or to reject Republican electors. The absolute powers proposed for the commission, by which Congress abdicated all control, have never been explained on any other basis. The House changed the measure to require a joint vote of both houses for the acceptance of the commission's report. In this form the bill was less harmful, but was still resisted by the Republicans (Vote Chart VI). The House version of the bill did not please the Senate, with the result that the session closed with the two bodies in disagreement.

[23] Ames to Pickering, Oct. 19, 1799, Ames's *Works*, I, 258.
[24] *Aurora*, February 19, 1800, prints the bill in full.
[25] King's *King*, III, 284 n.

Despite their majority of twenty in the House of Representatives, the Federalists could not count on a steady majority; ten of those elected as Federalists voted as moderates (Vote Chart VI and Table 20). Only one of these moderates came from New England, and an additional one was from Pennsylvania. The remaining eight were Southern Federalists. In addition, one of the Georgia Federalists voted steadily with the Republicans (Vote Chart VI and Table 20). On the other hand, there was only one Republican moderate. Clearly the Republicans were consolidating their position while the program of the extreme Federalists was proving distasteful to a number of the party.

Chapter **16**

The Election of 1800

SOON after the mission to France sailed, the Hamiltonian Federalists began to take the position that Adams should not be supported in the coming presidential election. Pickering, in October, 1799, was convinced that the party should have another candidate. He wrote, ". . . This fatal error will subvert the present administration & with them the government itself. Mr. Adams has not by this mission gained one friend among the democrats; to their former *hatred* will now be added *another sensation*: while among the federalists he has forfeited the support of his best friends and our most estimable citizens." [1] The only remedy would be ". . . for the P. at the close of next session of Congress, publicly to decline the presidency after the expiration of his term. This alone can unite the federalists and save our country. . . ." However Pickering is afraid Adams will not step aside voluntarily, and it would be impossible to persuade him to do so. [2]

The actions of Adams' friends at this time added to the ire of the Federalists. In Massachusetts Gerry ran for Governor on the Republican ticket in the election early in 1800. The result was a very close contest, in which Gerry actually carried Boston, and came near winning the entire state. Of this election Higginson declared, ". . . much has been done by holding up Gerry as the friend of Adams & of peace, as well as of the people & the rights of man. The P's patronage has been indeed very efficacious, & his friends have been in favour of Gerry. . . ." [3]

Gerry explained his motives to Adams as follows:

[1] Pickering to Bingham, Oct. 29, 1799, Pickering *Mss.* 12/262.

[2] Pickering to Ames, Trenton, Oct. 24, 1799. Pickering *Mss.* 12/275.

[3] Higginson to Pickering, Apr. 26, 1800. *American Historical Association Reports, 1896,* 836. Original in Pickering *Mss.* 26/85.

[It] has been unfortunate for this country, that the new constitution has divided the people, & enabled those who were disaffected to the revolution, & who only supported the constitution as a stepstone to monarchy, to avail themselves of the denomination of a party & stiling themselves federalists, to destroy the distinction between themselves and real federalists, whereby they have had an opportunity incessantly to rail against the republican federalists, or the antifederalists as they were reproachfully called, & to continue the scism, so fortunately for our enemies produced by the constitution. God grant that the eyes of true friends to this country. . . . [may be opened to the fact that one may give]. . . . unequivocal proof of the virtue of patriotism by cordial support, when sanctioned by the voice of the people; as real a proof of his virtue & patriotism as if he had been a *zealot*, from the purest motives for its adoption.

The remainder of the letter is a justification of Anti-Federalism on the ground that those who opposed ratification of the Constitution for certain reasons have had their course approved by the adoption of amendments covering these points.[4] This part of the letter was doubtless a reflection of the nature of the campaign waged against Gerry, who had opposed adoption of the Constitution.

In New Hampshire a similar situation existed. There the Republicans followed the plan that if banks were to be instituted, it would be proper to support a measure for an agrarian bank. This resulted in the desertion from the Federalist party of a number of Federalist legislators who voted for the charter. When the election was held for governor, one of Adams' electors in 1796, Judge Walker, performed a service similar to that of Gerry in Massachusetts.[5] Of this election Benjamin Russell, Editor of the *Centinel*, wrote to Otis, " In New Hampshire the Devil has been riding in the whirlwind: — for fear Walker should be chosen we have dubbed him a Federalist; in order, as he is a perfect go-betweenity, he may become Federalist if chosen, and to lessen the effect of a Jacobin triumph on this State." [6]

[4] Gerry to Adams, Cambridge, April 13, 1800, *Mss.* (Boston).
[5] *Centinel*, March 22, 1800.
[6] Russell to Otis, Boston, March 14, 1800. Otis *Mss.*

Despite his assuming the leadership of the Massachusetts Republicans, Gerry continued to support Adams. To Jefferson he wrote, " I must candidly acknowledge that I tho't it the best policy to re-elect Mr. Adams & yourself; because in that event, you would have united your exertions & respective parties in suppressing the feudalists & in the next choice there was little reason in my mind to doubt, that Mr. Adams would retire, &, with his friends support your election to the chair & administration: whereas there is danger now, that many of his adherents will unite with the Hamiltonians & embarrass your administration, if you should succeed him, to avenge what they consider as an act of ingratitude to the object of their choice, but every friend to this country, in this event, will double his exertions to support you. . . ." [7]

This idea of Gerry's had evidently been anticipated by one of the moderate Republicans, Samuel Smith of Baltimore. Early in 1800 it appeared uncertain that the Republicans would be able to carry the election. Consequently the idea of a coalition with Adams appeared as one method of preventing the influence of Hamilton from continuing. Smith approached Stoddert, Adams' Secretary of the Navy, on the question, both being natives of Maryland and doubtless having known each other for some time. He declared that except for some of the measures of the administration, for which Adams was not responsible, he approved of the course which had been followed. Should Stoddert think it advisable, he would like to approach Adams.

Before any further steps could be taken, however, the news of the Republican success in the New York elections for the legislature so buoyed up the hopes of the Republicans that there was no further mention of the plan. Stoddert conjectured that the basis of the proposal would have been a reorganization of the cabinet, and the agreement that after the next term Adams should step aside in favor of Jefferson.[8]

[7] Gerry to Jefferson, Jan. 15, 1801. *New England Historical and Genealogical Register*, XLIX, 439.

[8] Stoddert to Adams, Oct. 27, 1811. Adams' *Works* X, 4. This letter is apparently the first intimation of the proposal which Adams received.

While these ideas were abroad in the Republican camp the Hamiltonians were determined that another candidate should replace Adams. The efforts that were made probably had the support of Hamilton. Washington was urged by John Trumbull to accept another term as President. Trumbull asserted that the country was divided by factions at a critical period. Washington alone could reunite the country. Much the same sentiments were also voiced by his brother, Jonathan Trumbull, the Governor of Connecticut.[9] These statements did not move Washington. He replied that the only event that could recall him to service would be actual military attack by an enemy. Moreover, the Trumbulls were mistaken if they believed that Washington would be able to poll a single vote more than Adams or any other strong Federalist could receive. Early in the beginning of the new government it had been possible to have a non-partisan administration. Now this could not happen. The cleavage between parties was too deep. Consequently Washington would not even consider such an idea.[10] Apparently unconvinced, Jonathan Trumbull replied that if Washington would not run, then others would have to be considered.[11] Gouverneur Morris also wrote to Washington, just before the death of the latter, urging him to run again in order to reunite the party.[12] This letter did not reach Mount Vernon in time for Washington to reply.

With this possibility removed, the efforts of the High-Federalists were concentrated on securing an agreement which would enable the election to be thrown into the House in the event of a Federalist victory, or to permit the detached South Carolina vote to give a greater number for their candidate. With this in view C. C. Pinckney became the candidate for the vice-presidency, and, at Hamilton's instigation, a caucus of the members of the

[9] Washington to John Trumbull, Mt. Vernon, June 25, 1799, *Writings* (Fitzpatrick, ed.), XXXVII, 249, and to Jonathan Trumbull, July 21, 1799. *Ibid.*, 312.

[10] *Ibid.*

[11] Jonathan Trumbull to Washington, Lebanon, Aug. 10, 1799, Washington *Papers* (Library of Congress), Vol. 297.

[12] Morris to Washington, Dec. 9, 1799, Sparks, Jared, *Life of Gouverneur Morris* (Boston, 1832), III, 127.

party in Congress pledged all to support both equally.[13] If necessary Hamilton stated that he would attend himself, but trusted that Sedgwick and the others would be able to arrange matters without the necessity for his participation.

Following the defeat of the Federalist legislators in New York it was apparent that if the method usually adopted in that state were continued, the Federalists would lose the state. Accordingly, Hamilton wrote to Jay, pointing out that Pennsylvania would be deadlocked by the Federalists so as to prevent that state from casting any vote. In order to salvage something from New York, he urged convening the old legislature to district the state and have the electors chosen by popular vote. Jay, Governor of New York, noted on the back of the letter, " Proposing a measure for party purposes which it would not become me to adopt," and that ended the matter.[14]

Other states were making changes in the method of choice in order to secure an advantage. In Massachusetts the district method was abandoned, not so much to assure an unanimous Federal vote, as to make certain that electors would not be chosen who would vote for Adams alone. Had the electors been chosen by popular vote, it is likely that in a number of districts only those would have been selected who were pledged to vote for Adams and throw away votes from Pinckney. Adams' proponents opposed this change, but without avail.[15]

In Maryland a similar effort to change from district to legislative choice was thwarted, and, in fact, the issue enabled the Republicans to secure a majority in that body.[16] In Pennsylvania the deadlock between House and Senate continued upon the convening of the new legislature. Apparently the Federalists were to effect their aim in that state.

For a time it appeared that the campaign might continue

---

[13] Hamilton to Sedgwick, Feb. 22 and May 4, 1800. Hamilton's *Works* (Hamilton, ed.) VI, 429; 436.

[14] Hamilton to Jay, May 7, 1800. Hamilton's *Works* (Hamilton, ed.) VI, 438.

[15] Ames to King, July 15, 1800. King's *King*, III, 275.

[16] Harper to Otis, Oct. 10, 1800. Morison, *Otis*, I, 197.

without an open rupture between the two wings of the Federalist party. This was not to be. On May 6 Adams requested the resignation of McHenry and received it at once. On the 10th he asked for that of Pickering. Upon Pickering's refusal to comply he was removed on the 12th.[17] At once the campaign changed into a Donnybrook Fair with the two wings of the party more bitter in their denunciation of each other than even of the Republicans.

There is no evidence to show that Adams had any negotiations with the Republicans. However, the charge was at once made by the High-Federalists that this was the case. Apparently there were some rumors from Samuel Smith's direction, probably arising from discussions before he had abandoned his attempts for a Jefferson–Adams coalition during the election of 1800. In 1811 both Smith and Adams denied having even seen each other during the spring of 1800.[18] On the other hand Pickering collected a heterogeneous mass of rumors on this point, continuing his activity to the time he died.[19] Immediately after his dismissal he attributed his removal to a bargain between Adams and Jefferson. Several days before the removal Adams told Pickering that Jefferson would probably win, and would be as little inclined to go to war as he would.[20]

Reflecting this belief or suspicion that Adams had entered into a bargain, and desiring to use the dismissals as ammunition in their campaign to lessen the exclusive support for him, the High-Federalists inspired an interesting article, which appeared in the *Trenton Federalist* of June 2. From this paper it was copied throughout the country. The item stated that the dismissals were

[17] McHenry to Adams, May 6, 1800; Adams to Pickering, May 10, 1800; Pickering to Adams, May 12, 1800; Adams to Pickering, May 12, 1800. Adams' *Works*, IX, 53-55.

[18] Adams to R. Smith, Nov. 25, 1811; Adams to S. Smith, Nov. 25, 1811; R. Smith to Adams, Nov. 30, 1811; S. Smith to Adams, Dec. 1, 1811. Adams' *Works*, X, 7-9.

[19] E. B. Caldwell to Timothy Pickering, Apr. 3, 1810; Pickering *Mss.*, 43/294. Hazen Kimball to Timothy Pickering, Dec. 29, 1803. *Ibid.*, 43/13. Memorandum of Apr. 6, 1819. *Ibid.*, Vol. 46.

[20] Pickering to Timothy Williams, Philadelphia, May 19, 1800. Pickering *Mss*, 13/516.

the result of a bargain between Jefferson and Adams. The purity of Adams' motives was not to be questioned, but he had been deceived by the Virginia Philosopher. On his part Jefferson had pledged himself to abandon the extremists of his own party, Gallatin, Giles, Burr, Livingston and Nicholas. More sacrifices of Federalists would be made by Adams, but other Federalists would secure positions and promotions. Hamilton would become Secretary of State, being included, as later commentators on the article pointed out, for the purpose of diverting suspicion from the group which had inspired the story. The people, however, would save Adams in spite of himself from a bargain which could end only in the " Disappointment, if not disgrace, of these great politicians." The voters would support him and General Pinckney.[21] When the article was shown to Adams, he denied its truth at once.[22]

Hamilton's attitude towards Adams during the campaign is illustrated best in a statement to Sedgwick: " I will never more be responsible for him by my direct support. . . . The only way to prevent a fatal error in the Federal party, is to support General Pinckney in good earnest." [23] This support for Pinckney was never openly avowed. It became apparent that such a policy would only divide the party. Ames regarded the partisans of Adams as being comparatively weak in force and influence, but realized that an open opposition would cost many votes. He stated, " I scorn, as much as my friends do, duplicity or timidity in politics; yet, while I avow my opinions and expectations as much as any enquirer has a right to know them, I think myself bound to exercise that discreet reserve, [without which] we might divide the votes, and mar the success of good measures." [24] Accordingly the attitude pursued was the old one of emphasizing the closeness of the election, and the consequent necessity of supporting both candidates.

[21] *Courant*, June 9, 1800; *Centinel*, June 14, 1800, June 11, 1800.

[22] C. C. Pinckney to McHenry, June 19, 1800. Steiner, *McHenry*, 401.

[23] Hamilton to Sedgwick, May 10, 1800. Hamilton's *Works* (Hamilton, ed.) VI, 441.

[24] Ames to Goodrich, Jan. 12, 1800. Gibbs, *Wolcott*, II, 367. Brackets by Gibbs.

Developments did not, however, take the course that was expected. There was apparently more force in the support for Adams than was previously anticipated. Hamilton felt it necessary to go on a tour of the Eastern states, ostensibly to inspect military bases. This visit, on which Hamilton made a number of indiscreet speeches,[25] brought down a torrent of abuse on his head.[26] An open controversy was begun between the factions. Returning to New York, Hamilton wrote an analysis of the situation which is essentially correct. ". . . The greatest number of strong minded men in New England are not only satisfied of the expediency of supporting *Pinckney*, as giving the best chance against Jefferson, but even prefer him to Adams, yet in the body of the people there is a strong personal attachment to this gentleman, and most of the leaders of the second class are so anxious for his re-election that it will be difficult to convince them that there is as much danger of failure as there unquestionably is. . . ." [27] This phrase, the " leaders of the second class," recurs through Hamilton's letters of this period, and is significant of the difference between Adams' supporters and the Hamiltonians.

There was some mention during the campaign of the formation of a third party, which should unite impartial men disgusted with the extremes of both the old parties. The chief advocate of this in the press was one Everett, who appeared as " Junius Americanus " in the *Boston Gazette*.[28] He was only one of the proprietors of that paper, but apparently struck a popular chord. This was indicative of the position held by Adams and the moderates. But the solution was the transfer of this group to the Republicans.

The most frequently used pieces of ammunition that appeared in the press attacks against the Federalist extremists were Fenno's pamphlet, *Political Aspects*;[29] Lyman's reference to the party

---

[25] Hale to King, July 9, 1800. King's *King*, III, 269.

[26] *Boston Gazette*, June 26, 1800, and following.

[27] Hamilton to Charles Carroll, July 1, 1800. Hamilton's *Works* (Hamilton, ed.) VI, 445.

[28] *Boston Gazette*, July 21, 1800 ff. Ames to Wolcott, Aug. 3, 1800. Gibbs, *Wolcott*, II, 396. The party name was to be " Constitutionalists."

[29] " Massasoit," and " Adams Federalist," *Boston Gazette*, Sept. 11, 1800. *Aurora*, Aug. 5, 1800; and Oct. 18, 1800.

desiring to use "bold strokes"[30] and after its appearance, Hamilton's pamphlet.[31] The *Aurora* and *Chronicle* writers, on behalf of the Republicans, pointed out that those who voted for the Federalists would not know who would be President. Half of the Federalists admitted that the other part of the party could not be trusted; yet they could offer no assurance as to which of the candidates would be President if elected. Could voters take the risk of such chances? Look at the admission of the Federalists as to what the program of the High-Federalists represented. Under such circumstances how could they expect voters to take the risk of putting such a faction in the chair?[32]

Adams' attitude during the campaign was that the danger from the extreme Federalists was greater than that from the Republicans. Remarks of this nature were frequently quoted as coming from him. Likewise the Junto noticed that he was placing increasing reliance on the record he had made during the Revolution. Furthermore in July, probably at the July 4th celebration, he gave the following toast at a banquet in Fanueil Hall, " The proscribed patriots, Hancock and Adams," referring, of course, to Samuel Adams.[33]

The chief explanation for Hamilton's pamphlet is that the attack launched against his wing of the party threatened to overwhelm the High-Federalists. Certainly it threatened in New England the program of equal support for Pinckney and Adams. Finally Hamilton wrote: " It is plain that unless we give our reasons in some form or other, Mr. Adams' personal friends, seconded by the Jacobins, will completely *run us down in the public opinion.*"[34] Adams was assuredly doing considerable talking, so much so that full reports reached the ears of those he was denouncing as a " damned faction."[35] The Hamiltonians were

---

[30] *Aurora*, Oct. 7, 1800; Webster, *Letter to General Hamilton.*

[31] A citizen of the States, *A Letter to Major General Hamilton* (Salem, 1800).

[32] *Aurora*, Aug. 5, 15, 18 and Dec. 12, 1800. " Old South " (Benjamin Austin) in *Independent Chronicle*, Nov. 20 and 24, 1800.

[33] Cabot to King, July 19, 1800. King's *King*, III, 278.

[34] Hamilton to Wolcott, Aug. 3, 1800. Hamilton's *Works* (Hamilton, ed.) VI, 449.

[35] Cabot to King, July 19 and Aug. 9, 1800. King's *King*, III, 278, 291.

equally extreme in their attitude. Troup wrote to King that Hamilton " makes no secret of his opinion that Jefferson should be preferred to Adams." [36]

Be this as it may, the pamphlet, published as " Letter Concerning the Public Conduct and Character of John Adams " did not live up to the expectations of Hamilton's friends. In many respects it was felt that he had not driven home enough charges to warrant writing the pamphlet. Written to be circulated privately, it was intercepted and published by the delighted Republicans. The points advanced were the disregard of the cabinet, the assertion that the honor of the country had been damaged by the new mission to France, and the disturbing tendency of such measures as the pardon of Fries and such laxity as the nonenforcement of the Alien Laws. Cabot wrote to Hamilton that the frank opinion of many was that he had exhibited as much vanity as he had accused Adams of having.[37]

Among those who supported Adams, as opposed to Pinckney, were Gerry and Otis from Massachusetts, as has already been noticed. Further, in Connecticut the Trumbulls helped to offset the opposition of the Dwights.[38] In Rhode Island, Adams attributed the preference given him to the influence of Fenner.[39] Rutledge gained the impression that Representative Champlin of Rhode Island was also for Adams.[40] Rutledge was likewise familiar with the Maryland situation, declaring that there the influence of Carroll against Adams was offset by the Chases, Craik, Stoddert, and the Republicans Samuel Smith and Dent. Both of these last, though Republican moderates, preferred Adams to Pinckney and would be in a position to thwart any attempt to deflect votes from Adams in Maryland. The general trouble with the plan to find a state where votes could be dropped from Adams arose from the source which Hamilton outlined. Many of the leaders could

[36] Troup to King, Dec. 31, 1800. King's King, III, 358.

[37] Cabot to Hamilton, Nov. 29, 1800. Hamilton's Works (Hamilton, ed.) VI, 482.

[38] Adams to Trumbull, Aug. 12, 1800. Adams' Works, IX, 74.

[39] Ibid., VI, 544.

[40] Rutledge to Hamilton, Newport, R. I., July 17, 1800, Steiner, McHenry, 463 n.

be satisfactorily convinced that such a step should be taken. When, however, an effort at execution was made, some of the less prominent seem to have thwarted the attempt. Certain noteworthy exceptions, such as Justice Chase, were due in no small part to friendship for Adams. In like manner Otis in Massachusetts never felt completely bound to the Junto.

At the last moment a compromise was reached in the Pennsylvania legislature, with the result that the Republicans secured eight electors, the Federalists seven. As the returns came in, it became evident that South Carolina was the pivotal state. Federalist Representative John Rutledge, Jr. of South Carolina was in close communication with Robert Goodloe Harper and with Ames and Cabot. All were working to put Pinckney ahead of Adams.[41] At first it was believed that there was a Federalist legislature. Soon a rude awakening came with the news that the eight votes of this state were for Jefferson and Burr, assuring the selection of one of these.[42]

Despite the close result of the presidential election, public sentiment was considerably stronger for Republicanism than the electoral vote in Table 12, following, would indicate. This table of electoral votes is, in this instance, much less representative than the columns showing the results of the elections for the House. The reason is to be found in the difference between the methods of choosing electors and that of voting for representatives. One example of this discrepancy is the state of Pennsylvania. There the available returns for representatives show the extent to which the Federalists were in the minority. Only three Federalists out of thirteen representatives were chosen. (This includes Albert Gallatin, who did not serve. Cf. footnote 3 to Vote Chart VIII.) Northampton, Bucks, and Montgomery, the 4th District, were now overwhelmingly Anti-Federal. These were the counties in which opposition to the district tax had led to Fries's Rebellion.

---

[41] Cometti, Elizabeth, " John Rutledge, Jr., Federalist," *Journal of Southern History*, XIII, 196-97.

[42] Wolfe, *Jeffersonian Democracy in South Carolina*, 155 ff. For a good analysis holding that the parties were so sharply divided in South Carolina that it would hardly have been possible to secure support for C. C. Pinckney, even had Adams been abandoned by the Federalists, cf. *Ibid.*, 158 ff.

TABLE 12

THE ELECTION OF 1800 [43]

State	Jefferson	Burr	Adams	Pinckney	Jay	Seventh Congress, 1st session, House of Representatives	
						F	R
New Hampshire			6	6		4	0
Vermont			4	4		1	1
Massachusetts			16	16		8	6
Rhode Island			4	3	1	0	2
Connecticut			9	9		7	0
New York	12	12				3	7
New Jersey			7	7		0	5
Pennsylvania	8	8	7	7		4	9
Delaware			3	3		1	0
Maryland	5	5	5	5		3	5
Virginia	21	21				2	17
North Carolina	8	8	4	4		5	5
South Carolina	8	8				3	3
Georgia	4	4				0	2
Kentucky	4	4				0	2
Tennessee	3	3				0	1
	73	73	65	64	1	41	65

In 1796 these counties had shown a Federalist majority of 749 (Table 11, p. 108). In 1800, according to available election returns, this had become a Jeffersonian majority of 3,102. These were counties peopled by the agrarian conservatives whose support was necessary to the continued success of the Federalists. This reversal of sentiment in favor of the Republicans was one of the results of the policy of adventure pursued by the High-Federalists who were governed by the point of view of commercial sections. For another example, the state of New Jersey is similarly unrepresentative. The members of the United States House of Representatives, chosen at large by popular vote, were all Republican. On the other hand, the old New Jersey Legislature, representing previous elections, chose the electors, who were for Adams.

[43] Stanwood, Edward, *History of the Presidency*, 63; and figures on Representatives elected, taken from Vote Chart VIII, Appendix III.

TABLE 13

PENNSYLVANIA ELECTION RETURNS FOR U. S. HOUSE OF REPRESENTATIVES,
ELECTION OF 1800 [44]

County	Federalist	Republican
City of Philadelphia	1,634	1,698
County of Philadelphia	765	2,742
York	629	2,382
Berks	44	2,542
Delaware	752	546
Chester	1,980	2,738
Montgomery	1,242	2,015
Bucks	491	614
Northampton	138	2,344
Northumberland	0	2,860
Allegheny	944	1,937
Washington	345	1,690
	8,964	24,108

The party strength in the House of Representatives, 64 or 65 (*q. v.* Taliaferro of Ga.) Republicans and 41 or 42 Federalists, gives the truest picture of public sentiment, as contrasted with the electoral vote in which Jefferson's margin is only eight electoral votes (cf. Table 12 and Vote Chart VIII). At the same time this compares with the previous Congress which, at the time of election, had 63 Federalists and 43 Republicans.[45] Further, it should be noted that in contrast with the Sixth Congress, the Seventh Congress had few moderates. When the Seventh Congress met there were but six moderates, only two of whom were elected as Republicans. In addition, three elected as Federalists voted consistently Republican (Vote Chart VIII). Thus, those elected to the Seventh Congress were strong party men. There were 29 moderates in the Fourth Congress. This number had dwindled to but six moderates by the time the Seventh Congress met in 1801.

[44] *Aurora*, Oct. 17 — Nov. 3, 1800. The returns given are the highest number of votes received by the candidates for the respective parties.
[45] Cf. Vote Chart VI.

Following the election, the closing scenes of the Sixth Congress do not require great attention. Two measures left over from the first session constituted the main legislation. The Judiciary Act was passed, in no small measure deriving more support than at the previous session because it offered the possibility of jobs which would survive the election. After modifications of the Bankruptcy Act were accepted, this measure was also assured a majority.[46]

When, early on March 4 Adams left Washington prior to the inauguration of Jefferson, his conduct was censured. Never one to accept defeat with equanimity, he still felt deeply the bitterness of the charges made during the election. In large measure, the disintegration of the Federalist party was well on its way. The failure of Adams to stem the tide of the commercial influences in the party caused the transition of most moderates to Republicanism. This, in the very nature of the forces at play was to be expected. The two expanding economic forces in the country were agriculture and commerce. The party battle represented a contest between these two for supremacy. It was natural, that when the demands of the commercial group should become too great, the agrarian forces would become united. A program of forbearance, which alone might have enabled the alliance that secured the passage of the Constitution to continue, was not satisfactory to the commercial groups. As a consequence, the Federalist party became a minority, concentrated politically in the sections of the country where commerce or sectional factors in their favor were strongest.

[46] Cf. Vote Chart VII and Maps 9-10, App. III.

Chapter **17**

Conclusion

AFTER 1800 Adams found himself alienated from most of those remaining in the Federalist Party. This was hardly surprising. Many of his friends, such as Gerry and Rush, went with the Jeffersonians. It was not long before his son, John Quincy Adams, traveled the same road.[1] Again, it is not unnatural that he should renew friendly relations with Jefferson and John Taylor. A recent writer on Taylor states that " The greater part of his [Taylor's] work which deals with contemporary political thought is opposed to the monarchal apologia of Adams and to the nationalism of the *Federalist,* each of which advocated a dangerous consolidation of power."[2] But this statement seems to miss a main point. It is perfectly true that Adams was a nationalist, Taylor an advocate of States' rights. But the assumption that Taylor was a greater advocate of popular government is a doubtful one. Properly considered he is a rather strong proponent of agrarian aristocracy. Taylor favored self-government, but with aristocratic agrarian leadership. Such a program is one of the central themes of Taylor's book, *Inquiry into the Principles and Policy of the*

---

[1] Bemis, Samuel Flagg, *John Quincy Adams and the Foundation of American Foreign Policy.*

[2] Mudge, *Social Philosophy of John Taylor of Caroline,* 29. Although not the case in Mudge, in many of the treatments of Taylor's political thought there is confusion, which follows Taylor, between advocacy of agrarianism and advocacy of popular government. As a matter of fact, Taylor, while a strong agrarian, is actually a proponent of aristocracy. His protest is much more that of a displaced aristocracy, seeking to ally itself with the rising tide of popular government, than a genuine expression of opposition to all aristocracy. It is interesting to examine, for example, his *Arator* (Georgetown, 3d ed., 1817) at pp. 30, 31, 35 and 37 in the light of some of the generalizations of Gaetano Mosca in *The Ruling Class* (New York, 1939), especially at chapter XV. Cf. Manning J. Dauer and Hans Hammond, " John Taylor, Democrat or Aristocrat? ", *Journal of Politics,* VI, 381-403 (1944).

Government of the United States.[3] Taylor found Adams in agreement with many of the strictures he made on the economic policies of the government. At the same time Adams was rather amused at the criticism of his (Adams') presentation of the subject of aristocracy.[4] Adams thought he had merely made a realistic set of observations; he had not advocated that the aristocracy should dominate. Out of the active political arena he could consider the whole matter more objectively than was the case while he was in politics. He replied to Taylor in a friendly letter and prepared a longer series as a reply, but never published it.[5]

On the other hand, the relations of both John and John Quincy Adams with the Federalists of Massachusetts grew worse. It was not long before a series of bitter public controversies developed with the members of the " Essex Junto." [6] It was possible to make peace with the agrarians; with the commercial group he could not long remain on good terms. As a matter of fact, the mid-position which Adams desired to achieve was adopted, in the main, by Jefferson and his successors. But even they were unable to check the rising tide of banks and the increasing influence of finance capitalism. This economic trend overwhelmed the dogmas of the opposition.

The success of the Jeffersonians constituted a refutation of another of Adams' cherished principles. The party which achieved " moderation " did so as a political party. Adams' plan for an independent executive was an abstraction never achieved. In reality, the practice of Adams, as well as his personal choice of policies, was dictated all along by the wishes of the moderates

---

[3] (Fredericksburg, 1814.)   Page proof was sent to Adams by Taylor as the book was in press. A copy of the final work is in Adams' library, as is Taylor's *Arator.*

[4] Adams to Jefferson, Sept. 13, 1813, *Works*, X, 69-71.

[5] Published in *Works*, VI, 445 *et seq.* Adams praised the *Arator* as the best American work on agriculture; to George Jeffreys, in *American Farmer*, II, 93; Simms, Henry H., *Life of John Taylor* (Richmond, 1932).

[6] Cf. *Boston Patriot*, 1809 for Adams' letters reviewing his administration and also see *Correspondence between John Adams and W. Cunningham, Esq.* (Boston, 1823).

among whom he found his greatest support; but he was hardly conscious of this. Influenced by various writings on the British Constitution, Adams stated in his *Defense of American Constitutions* (1787) and other writings of the post-revolutionary period, that an independent executive was necessary. In this belief he followed the most widely accepted interpreters of the British system, including Montesquieu and De Lolme. He thought his independent executive was patterned after the British monarch. The rich and poor of the commonwealth would be represented in the Senate and House, respectively. The executive would hold the balance between these groups.

Actually this was a misinterpretation of the operation of the British parliamentary system. George III attempted such a role, but most effectively when acting through the existing parties. Moreover, the prime minister, head of the majority party and responsible to Parliament, exercised the executive power in fact. But the theory of the independent executive was a commonplace among members of the Constitutional Convention. Organized national political parties were not fully foreseen. Washington launched his administration under such a conception of the presidency, appointing his heads of departments from all factions, including both Jefferson and Hamilton in the original group. But before his second administration closed, this theory had been abandoned of necessity. His cabinet was a Federalist cabinet. The party was headed by Hamilton, even though Hamilton had left the cabinet for New York.

The trend in this direction is perfectly clear in the party press of the period. The *Aurora*, national organ of the Republicans, hailed Washington's retirement with delight. In 1799, when Washington was urged to run for a third term, among reasons he gave for declining was that he clearly saw the growth of parties had prevented universal acceptance of the President.[7] The country would be no more united under him than under some other president, he maintained.

[7] Washington to John Trumbull, June 25, 1799, *Writings* (Fitzpatrick, ed.), XXXVII, 279.

Adams was not as clear on the connection which had developed between the presidency and the parties by 1799 as was Washington. He still hoped, throughout his administration, for the President to be regarded as above party, as representing the national interest. At the same time, he sometimes acted on the opposite theory, that he needed to take steps to build a party interest around himself. This becomes the impression when one considers part of his plans and his relationship to Elbridge Gerry, Benjamin Rush, the Muhlenbergs, the Fenners, and others. Here he seemed to be trying to build a faction or party of his own, or to take over the Federalist party himself. But in the main, Adams acted on his theory of the independent executive.

The force which actually proved strongest in the development of American politics was the growth of parties. The authority of the President rested upon political power [8] as represented by these parties. The question next arises, why did these parties grow up? The answer is found in terms of the economic, social, religious, cultural, and geographic influences of the period. These factors divided the people into divergent groups. These groups coalesced into two major combinations — the commercial (Federalist) and the agrarian (Republican). But the economic elements named are merely those which dominated in each party. A considerable portion of farmers who grew cash crops supported the Federalists until 1800 or shortly thereafter. Artisans in the cities were generally Republican. But once a stable central government was established, the dominance of agriculture in the American economy assured that the Jeffersonians would triumph if they could develop a moderate program. They did so. They drew off the middle class of farmers from the Federalists. They modified sufficiently their opposition to banks to assure a banking program for the expanding economy of the country. In contrast, Federalist policy, while ambitious, was designed increasingly for commercial groups alone. Except where some extraordinary factor like the Congregational Church entered, as it did in the state of Connecticut, this program was too extreme to hold the farm

[8] Cf. Merriam, Charles E., *Political Power* (New York, 1934).

support to the party. The result was the split in policy in 1799-1800, peace with France, the election of Jefferson, the ultimate extinction of the Federalist party.

There is another matter of importance. With the growth of political parties an important extension of the principles of free speech and free press occurred. The idea of an opposition political party having the right to exist had necessarily received a set-back because of the strife between Whigs and Tories during the American Revolution. Civil war at home accompanied the war with England. With the growth of political parties under the new constitution there were two immediate dangers after 1789. One was that organized political parties might not be granted the right to exist. This danger was typified by the Alien and Sedition Laws. The other danger was that the splitting off process of the American Revolution might be continued, perhaps through the program possibly suggested by the Virginia and Kentucky Resolutions, or the secession plans of the extreme Federalists for New England.

But the constitutional government established, through the medium of political parties, proved capable of bringing the divergent groups representing political power into an adjustment with one another that was acceptable to the great majority. This was achieved through the legislative process. Protest and change came through the electoral process. To some degree Adams contributed to this. But his major contribution was probably not ideological, not his idea of an independent executive and a balance. His major contribution, instead, was made because he thought with the moderates. It was in that way that his great decision — peace with France, no foreign adventure, an end to domestic extremism — contributed greatly to the development of ultimate national well-being. He also contributed to the establishment of a peaceful method whereby change could take place within the framework of constitutional republican government, which ultimately became democratic government.

A question may be raised concerning the political leadership exercised by Adams. It has already been suggested that Jefferson came close, after his inaugural, to moulding together the rather disparate groups which had opposed extreme Federalist policy. Had it been possible for Adams to follow, from 1797 on, the policy which he did after his break with the cabinet, he might have had a comparable reception. Honesty and forthrightness he had in abundance. He was motivated by an intense sense of trusteeship on behalf of his countrymen. In this respect he sought, like Washington, to be impartial. He stood against the extremists of his own party. But, impetuous in temperament, he lacked the ability of great political leaders like Jefferson and Lincoln to carry with him the groups necessary to political success. Probably from the Federalist position this could not have been done in any event. But Adams also lacked that characteristic of the great political leaders of the United States, the capacity to act as a mediator among groups and bring eventual agreement. Despite this, and despite his angry departure from Washington before the inauguration of his successor, his decisions in the period of critical relations with France were important in prolonging peace until the new United States government had reached a period of greater stability. Added to his service in the Revolution he could well feel that his contribution had been great.

Appendix I

CONGRESSIONAL DISTRICTS FROM 1793–1803

I.
CONNECTICUT
Not Districted

II.
DELAWARE
One representative

III.
GEORGIA
Not Districted

IV.
KENTUCKY

Election at large for Fourth through Sixth Congresses.

Districts for Seventh Congress:

Northern Districts: All of the state north of the Kentucky River plus Franklin and Gallatin Counties.

Southern District: Remainder of the State.

> Littell, William—*Statute Law of Kentucky* (Frankfort, 1810). Cf. Act of June 26, 1792 and Ch. 222, Sect. 14, vol. II, 348.

V.
MARYLAND
Eight Districts

1. Saint-Mary's, Charles and Calvert.
2. Prince-George's and Anne Arundel, including Annapolis.
3. Montgomery and that part of Frederick adjacent, as far as the mouth of the Monocacy River, and thence to the Pennsylvania State line.
4. The remainder of Frederick, Washington and Alleganey.
5. Baltimore town and county.
6. Harford, Cecil and Kent.

7. Queen Anne's, Caroline, and Talbot.

8. Dorchester, Somerset, and Worcester.

Elections to be the first Monday in October, 1792, and every two years thereafter.

> Laws of Maryland, Revised and Collected by William Kilty, (Annapolis, 1800). II, Chapter LCII. November session, 1790.

VI. MASSACHUSETTS DISTRICTS, 1794–1801
Fourth, Fifth, Sixth, and Seventh Congresses

First Western: Berkshire Co., together with the town of Rowe, Cummington, Plainfield, Worthington, Hawley and Charlemont in Hampshire Co.

Second Western District: Following towns in Hampshire Co.: Westfield, Russell, Hatfield, Deerfield, Northampton, Blandford, Southampton, Greenfield, Gill, Granville, Chesterfield, Conway, Ashfield, Southwick, Williamsburgh, Whately, Norwich, West Springfield, West Hampton, Montgomery, Colerain, Barnardston, Shelburne, Goshen, Leyden, Northfield, Montague, Sunderland, Hadley, Chester, Buckland, Heath, Middlefield, and East Hampton.

Third Western District: Towns in Hampshire Co.: Brimfield, Pelham, Palmer, New Salem, Greenfield, Amherst, Monson, Belchertown, Shutesbury, Ware, Springfield, South Brimfield, Holland, Warwick, Orange, Wilbraham, Granby, Leverett, Wendell, Longmeadow, South Hadley, Ludlow; and the following in Worcester Co.: Western, Petersham, New Braintree, Barre, Sturbridge, Athol, Templeton, Toyalston, Gerry, Winchendon, Gardner and Hardwick.

Fourth Western District: Towns in Worcester Co.: Mendon, Brookfield, Oxford, Worcester, Leicester, Rutland, Sutton, Uxbridge, Shrewsbury, Dudly, Grafton, Upton, Holden, Leominster, Lancaster, Douglass, Spencer, Charlton, Oakham, Paxton, Hubbardton, Westminster, Princeton, Northbridge, Ward, Milford, Sterling, and Boylston.

First Southern District: Barnstable Co., Dukes Co., Nantucket Co.; towns in Plymouth Co.: Wareham and Rochester; towns in Bristol Co.: New Bedford and Dartmouth.

Second Southern District: Towns in Plymouth, all except the two
in the first Southern District; towns in Suffolk: Hingham and
Hull; towns in Norfolk: Cohasset, Braintree, Quincy, Randolph,
Weymouth, Milton.

Third Southern District: Towns in Bristol, all except the two in
first Southern District; towns in Norfolk; Foxborough, Wren-
tham, Franklin, Medfield, Dover, Walpole, Stoughton, and
Bellingham.

First Middle District: Town of Boston in Suffolk Co., towns in
Norfolk Co.; Roxbury, Dorchester, Brookline, Sharon, Dedham,
Needham, and Medway; towns in Middlesex Co.; Newton,
Weston, East Sudbury, Natick, Sherburne, Hopkinton and
Holliston.

Second Middle District: Towns in Middlesex; Charlestown, Cam-
bridge, Watertown, Concord, Sudbury, Groton, Marlboro',
Framingham, Dunstable, Stow, Lexington, Littleton, Westford,
Townsend, Acton, Dracut, Chelmsford, Waltham, Shirley,
Pepperel, Lincoln, Ashby, Carlisle, Boxboro' and Tinsboro';
Towns in Worcester: Ashburnham, Fitchburgh, Lunenburgh,
Harvard, Westboro', Bolton, Berlin, Northboro' and Southboro'.

Third Middle District: Towns in Essex Co.; Salem, Marblehead,
Lynn, Lynnfield, Danvers, Middleton, Beverly, Manchester;
towns in Middlesex; Reading, Stoneham, Medford, Malden,
Tewksbury, Wilmington, Woburn, Bedford, Billerica; with town
of Chelsea in Suffolk Co.

Fourth Middle District: Towns in Essex Co.: Salisbury, Almesbury,
Methuen, Haverhill, Andover, Bradford, Boxford, Newbury,
Newbury Port, Rowley, Ipswich, Hamilton, Wenham, Glou-
cester and Topsfield.

Maine Districts of Massachusetts.

First Eastern District: Hancock Co., Washington Co., Lincoln Co.
(Except such towns and plantations in the county of Lincoln
as are hereafter made a part of the second Eastern District).

Second Eastern District: Cumberland Co., (Except the towns of
Bridgeton, Standish and Flintstown); towns in Lincoln Co.:
Topsham, Winthrop, Readfield, Bath, Bowdoin, Green, Monmouth, Mount Vernon, Sandwich, Livermore and Rocomecko,
mouth of Sandy River, Sandy River No. 1, Sandy River No. 2,

Sandy River No. 3, and seven mile brook, Twenty-five mile pond, Titcombtown & Little River & all other towns and plantations which lie wholly on the Western side of Kennebeck River (except Bowdoinham, Sidney and Fairfield which are made part of the first Eastern District).

Third Eastern District: York Co.; and following towns in Cumberland Co.: Bridgetown, Standish and Flintstown.

The election shall be held the first Monday in November next, and biennially thereafter.

Acts and Laws of the Commonwealth of Massachusetts, 1794–5 (Boston, 1896). Acts, 1794—chapter 24 (May Session, ch. 18) pp. 60-5.

VII.   NEW HAMPSHIRE
                        Not Districted

VIII.   NEW JERSEY
            Districted for Sixth Congress only, 1799–1801

Eastern District: Bergen, Essex and Middlesex.
Northern District: Morris and Sussex.
Western District: Hunterdon and Burlington.
Middle District: Monmouth and Burlington.
Southern District: Gloucester, Salem, Cumberland, and Cape May.

Acts of the Twenty-Second General Assembly, second session (Burlington, 1798), chapter DCCV, pp. 310-2.

IX.   NEW YORK
        A. For Third, Fourth, and Fifth Congresses, 1793–99

1. City and County of New York.
2. Suffolk, Queens, and Kings.
3. Westchester and Richmond.
4. Orange and Ulster.
5. Dutchess.
6. Columbia.
7. Rensselaer and Clinton.

8. City and County of Albany.

9. Washington and Saratoga.

10. Montgomery, Otsego, Tioga, Herkimer, and Ontario.

Election to be held on the fourth Tuesday in January, 1793; thereafter, on the second Tuesday in December, 1794; and biennially. Numbers of districts not given in act. Numbers supplied in order as listed in act, following contemporary newspaper practice.

B. For Sixth and Seventh Congresses, 1799–1803.

1. Suffolk, Queens, Kings, and Richmond.

2. City of New York except the seventh ward.

3. Westchester, seventh ward of New York City, and the following part of Orange County: Orange Town, Clarkes Town, Hempstead and Haverstraw.

4. Ulster, Delaware, and the remainder of Orange.

5. Dutchess.

6. Columbia and Rensselaer.

7. Washington, Saratoga and Clinton.

8. City and County of Albany and Schoharie County.

9. Montgomery and Herkimer.

10. Otsego, Tioga, Ontario, Onondaga, and Steuben.

Laws of the State of New York (Albany, 1887), IV, 85. The districts are numbered in the law.

X. NORTH CAROLINA, 1793–1803

1. Burke, Wilkes, Lincoln, Rutherford and Buncombe.

2. Rowan, Mecklenberg, Cabarrus, Iredell, and Montgomery.

3. Stokes, Surry, Rockingham, Caswell, and Guilford.

4. Orange, Person, Randolph, and Chatham.

5. Franklin, Wake, Warren, Nash and Granville.

6. New-Hanover, Brunswick, Duplin, Bladen, Onslow, and Sampson.

7. Anson, Moore, Richmond, Cumberland, and Robeson.

8. Chowan, Perquimans, Pasquotank, Camden, Currituck, Gates, Tyrrell, Bertie, and Hertford.

9. Edgecombe, Halifax, Martin, Pitt, Beaufort, Northampton.
10. Jones, Carteret, Craven, Lenoir, Glasgow, Wayne, Johnston, Hyde.

Elections shall be held on the second Thursday and Friday in February, and on the same day every two years after. Districts not numbered in the law.

> Iredell, James—*Laws in the State of North Carolina* (Edenton, 1791). Appendix: Session Laws of . . . 1792, Chap. XVII, pp. 10-11. Photostat, Illinois State Library.

XI.   PENNSYLVANIA

1. City of Philadelphia.
2. County of Philadelphia.
3. Chester and Delaware.
4. (Two members from this district) Bucks, Northampton and Montgomery.
5. Berks and Luzerne.
6. Dauphin and Northumberland.
7. Lancaster.
8. York.
9. Cumberland and Mifflin.
10. Bedford, Franklin and Huntingdon.
11. Westmoreland and Fayette.
12. Washington and Allegheny.

Elections to be held on the second Tuesday of October, 1794, and every two years thereafter.

Districts not numbered in the act.

> Mitchell, James T., and Flanders, Henry—*Statutes at Large of Pennsylvania* (Harrisburg, 1908), XIII, 171-4.

XII.   RHODE ISLAND
                                  Not Districted

XIII.   South Carolina
               Districted by Court Districts, 1793–1803

Charleston District.

Beaufort and Orangeburg.

Georgetown and Cheraw.

Camden.

Ninety-Six.

Washington and Pinckney.

Election shall be held on the first Monday in February, 1793.

> Cooper, Thomas—*Statutes at Large of South Carolina*, V,
> 212-4 (Columbia, 1839).

XIV.   Tennessee

                         One Representative

XV.   Vermont

Eastern District: Windham, Windsor, and that part of the state
  heretofore included in Orange and Caledonia.

Western District: Bennington, Rutland, Addison, and that tract of
  country heretofore included in the Counties of Chittenden and
  Franklin.

The first election under this act was held in September, 1798. The
previous act, for earlier Congresses, provided for practically the
same districts.

> *Laws of the State of Vermont* (Randolph, Vt., 1808), II, 101.

XVI.   Virginia

  1. Frederick and Berkeley.
  2. Augusta, Rockingham, Shenandoah, Rockbridge and Bath.
  3. Hampshire, Hardy, Pendleton, Randolph, Harrison, Monon-
     galia, and Ohio.
  4. Wythe, Greenbriar, Kanawha, Lee, Russell, Montgomery, Gray-
     son, and Washington.
  5. Franklin, Bedford, Botetourt, Henry, and Patrick.

6. Halifax, Pittsylvania, and Campbell.
7. Prince-Edward, Charlotte, Buckingham, Cumberland, and Powhatan.
8. Brunswick, Mecklenburg, Lunenburg and Greensville.
9. Dinwiddie, Amelia, Nottoway, and Chesterfield.
10. Sussex, Southampton, Surry, and Prince George.
11. Norfolk, Princess Anne, Isle of Wight, and Nansemond.
12. York, Accomac, Northampton, Elizabeth City, Warwick, Gloucester, Mathews.
13. Henrico, Hanover, New Kent, Charles City, James City.
14. Albemarle, Amherst, Fluvanna and Goochland.
15. Orange, Spotsylvania, Louisa, Madison.
16. King and Queen, King William, Essex, Middlesex, and Caroline.
17. Loudoun, Fairfax and Prince William.
18. Culpepper, Fauquier, and Stafford.
19. Richmond, Westmoreland, King George, Lancaster and Northumberland.

Election to be held on the third Monday in March of 1793, and every two years thereafter. Districts not numbered in the act.

Henning, William Henry—*Statutes at Large . . . of Virginia* (New York, Richmond, Philadelphia, 1823), XIII, 331 ff.

Appendix II

THE ALIGNMENT OF POLITICAL PARTIES IN 1796

This study of the Federalist party from 1796 to 1800 attempts to find the relationship between the political measures advanced by the Federalists and the support accorded these measures on account of economic, social, and geographical factors. The line of divergence, in both theory and practice, which separated the Adams Federalists from the Hamiltonian wing of the party is the chief matter under consideration. The aim is to show the origin of this split and the cause of it. Further, the leaders on each side are considered, and, insofar as possible, the rank and file of the party are classified on one side or the other.

To a considerable extent this study is based upon the vote charts and maps, which cover the fourth through the first session of the seven Congresses, 1795–1803. It will be observed that these extend both before and after the dates marked out for more intensive treatment. This is for the purpose of comparison, with the aim of providing a fuller opportunity to observe the various trends which developed than would be possible if the period covered were too restricted.

A brief explanation of the manner in which these maps and charts have been prepared may be of service. For the eight sessions under consideration the yea and nay votes on the principal measures have been charted. A Federalist vote is indicated by an asterisk, a Republican vote by capital x. 0 indicates the member in question was absent when the vote was taken. The record of each member's votes is then totalled both for the session and for the entire Congress.

Where the total of votes cast for Federalist measures, as against the total cast for Republican measures, is greater than four to one, the members are classified as Federalists. Where the same ratio is maintained in regard to the total for Republican measures, the members are classified as Republicans. In mapping the votes the Federalists and Republicans are indicated in accordance with the legend shown before Map 1, cf. p. 332. There remain to be considered those representatives whose votes on measures do not fall under

275

either the Federalist or the Republican classification. On the maps, these are indicated by a separate code, cf. p. 332. It also remains to secure a term which will distinguish them. Non-partisans or neutrals is erroneous, as generally they secured their election under the label of one party or the other. In most cases, though this predominance is not so strongly marked in the Fourth Congress as in the succeeding ones, these men were Federalists. Moreover, it is to the Federalists of this type, rather than the Republicans, that closest attention is given. Therefore in most instances the term, " Half-Federalist," [1] will be used. This term was originated by Fisher Ames, long the Federalist leader in the House. Where the entire group, both Half-Federalists and Half-Republicans, is referred to, the term " moderate " will be used. This still carries more of an implication of non-partisanship than is actually the case. There was in use at the time a word which best expresses the actual situation, " Betweenites." [2] As, unfortunately, this never came into good grammatical usage, it is probably best not to adopt it.

An example or two will be given in order to complete this explanation. During the first session of the Fourth Congress Andrew Gregg represented the 9th Pennsylvania District (Map 1), consisting of Cumberland and Mifflin Counties (Appendix I). During this session he voted for six Republican and two Federalist measures, and was absent once (Vote Chart I). As this ratio is not greater than four to one, Gregg is represented as a moderate on Map 1. It will be observed on vote 3 on Vote Chart I, which is the vote on the appropriation for Jay's Treaty, that Gregg was in favor of the appropriation. It was through securing the support of such Half-Republicans as him that this appropriation was granted. It so happens that during the second session Gregg maintained the same ratio (Vote Chart II); consequently he appears again as a moderate on Map 2, representing the second session, and on Map 3, representing the entire Congress. On the other hand, Andrew Moore, of the 2nd Virginia district (Map 1), consisting of Augusta, Rockingham, Shenandoah, Rockbridge and Bath Counties in the upper Shenandoah Valley (Appendix I), had the following record: first session, Republican by eight to one; second session, Republican by seven to two. In the first session his

---

[1] Ames to Timothy Pickering, Dedham, Oct. 10, 1799; Ames, Seth, *Works of Fisher Ames*, I, 258.

[2] Boston *Columbian Centinel*, June 28, 1800.

ratio is greater than four to one, as, of course, is the total for the Congress. Consequently Moore is represented as a Republican on Maps 1 and 3. On the other hand his vote for the second session is less than four to one and he is represented as a moderate on Map 2.

The advantage of this system, when considered in connection with election returns for important elections, is that it provides a better measure of the sentiment of the various sections on certain measures in the party programs than a straight mapping of each yea and nay vote. This is particularly true of a party made up of diversified interests. When the material from the charting of votes is studied in connection with the speeches, the correspondence of political leaders, and the arguments presented in the newspapers of the period, the pattern of party alignment becomes clearer. That is the chief purpose of the narrative part of this work—to tie the voting pattern together with the political events.

As already indicated in Chapter 1, the main pattern of Federalist leadership in the Hamiltonian wing of the party is commercial. The main pattern of the Jeffersonian group is agrarian. However, there is insufficient strength numerically in the commercial group to form a majority. For the Federalists to succeed they must join together the commercial groups with the wealthier farming sections which are not self-sufficient but which grow crops for export. There is likewise need for support from the pioneering western sections, which might be won because of the need for national defense establishments against the Indians, and because a strong foreign policy would offer a way of securing the Mississippi territory and the right to navigate the river.

With the general characteristics of the Federalist and Republican parties set forth (cf. Ch. 1 and Ch. 2), it will now be well to give a more detailed survey of some sectional and local factors which operated to modify or strengthen the general trend. Starting with the South, Georgia, as a section in an exposed position both as regards the Indians and the Spanish, did not fully share the orthodox Republican doctrine of a decrease of military strength to virtual nullity. In the Fourth Congress her two representatives, Baldwin and Milledge, were Republicans. In accordance with this feeling, therefore, they did not vote with the party on matters of economy, which accounted for a considerable number of votes in the second session of the Fourth Congress. Therefore these representatives appear as moderates on Map 2.

In South Carolina Federalism was strongest in the coastal plain and shipping sections. But a word of explanation is necessary in regard to Robert Goodloe Harper, the representative of the district of Ninety-Six, in the Piedmont area. He had been originally chosen as a violent Republican, a member of a Democratic Society, and a firm believer in the rights of man.[3] In Congress, however, he had changed under the influence of the reaction against France and was rapidly becoming an extreme Federalist. Although this was hardly in accord with the viewpoint of his constituents, his rapid rise to prominence and ability as an orator and pamphleteer, together with the lack of a strong Republican party before 1800 in South Carolina, enabled him to retain his seat.

In Charleston there was a sharp division of parties between the poor and the rich. The leader of the Charleston radicals was Charles Pinckney, cousin of the Federalist Pinckneys, Thomas and Charles Cotesworth. By the conservatives he was called " Blackguard Charlie " to distinguish him from his reputable kinsmen.[4]

North Carolina, with less interest in commercial matters than South Carolina, was correspondingly stronger in its Republicanism. Republicanism was strongest in the Piedmont section, back from the coast. The large plantations were in the Wilmington section on the Cape Fear, and in the Edenton and Washington sectors (District 8 on the Maps), in the extreme north-eastern coastal and river area. In the first two Congresses these last two districts had been represented by a Federalist. In the redistricting after the census of 1790 they had been separated in a manner which added Republican agrarian counties to overbalance the Federalists. This resulted in the curious arrangement of the eighth, ninth, and tenth districts to be observed in Map 1. It has, with justice, been termed an early Gerrymander.[5] In the Wilmington district, the radicals under Timothy Bloodworth, a blacksmith, kept this section safe for the Republicans. Bloodworth was a

---

[3] Cobbett, W., *Porcupine's Works*, IX, 327. Cobbett's paper represented the extreme Anglo-Federal viewpoint. However, Harper incurred his animosity by his failure to defend successfully a libel suit brought against Cobbett by the Republicans, McKean and Rush. Of Harper he wrote that he was " seduced from the Jacobin Club by the good dinners, and gay parties of the merchants of Philadelphia." Also *Porcupine's Gazette*, Mar. 25, 1797, giving Harper's letter of Mar. 24, 1797, explaining his change. *Gazette* extracts in *Porcupine's Works*, V, 139.

[4] Phillips, U. B., " South Carolina Federalists," *loc. cit.*, 542, note 37.

[5] Gilpatrick, D. H., *Jeffersonian Democracy in North Carolina* (New York, 1931), Chapter I, 59.

partisan of the famous Willie Jones of Halifax, leader of the movement that delayed the ratification of the Constitution by North Carolina. For the Fourth Congress (1795) Bloodworth was chosen to the federal Senate for North Carolina. In the western section of the state, sectional differences from the rest of the state, combined with a desire for defense measures, produced a stronger Federalist trend than in the central portion. These factors produced a strong Federalist from this section in the election of 1798 (Cf. Maps 8, 9, and 10 covering the Sixth Congress) to be considered hereafter.

One other portion of North Carolina deserves special treatment. This is the Seventh, or Fayetteville district on the upper Cape Fear, which was steadily Federalist in elections.[6] The principal reason for the situation is to be found in the character of the inhabitants of this sector. They were Highland Scots, who had been loyalists during the Revolution. From this territory had come the forces which opposed the Whigs in the battle of Moore's Creek Bridge during the Revolution. Consequently, in line with the general tendency of Tories to support the Federalists, this heavy concentration in the Seventh District produced North Carolina's lone Federalist in the Fourth and Fifth Congresses, William Barry Grove.[7] He voted, however, with the Republicans on many issues, not being from a commercial district.

Turning to Virginia, a variety of influences produced Federalism in several sections of the state, although the state was generally Republican. In the first place, the Norfolk sector (District 11, Map 1) showed a Federalist tendency. The representative of this district during the Fourth Congress, Josiah Parker, had started as a Republican, but was now tending towards Federalism, in which camp he stayed. The agrarian tide-water territory was also closely contested. A sector which is generally different from the rest of the state is the Northern Neck, that tract lying between the Potomac and Rappahannock Rivers, one of the oldest and wealthiest portions of the state. This together with the counties along the Potomac to the Shenandoah Valley was the scene of conflict between Federalists and Republicans.

A third region of the state which always produced one or more Federalists was the Shenandoah Valley, lying between the Blue Ridge

[6] Grove to M. Hogg, Phil., Jan. 21, 1795, in Wagstaff, H. M., "Letters of William Barry Grove," *Sprunt Historical Monographs* (Chapel Hill, 1910), IX, No. 2, 59. Also same to same, Phil., April 20, 1792, *Ibid.*, 49.

[7] Dodd, William E., *Life of Nathaniel Macon* (Raleigh, 1903), 18-19.

and Alleghenies. This was an important trade route, and was fairly rich farming country. Further it showed a stronger nationalism and a sectional differentiation from the more provincial farmers to the east of the Blue Ridge. These sectional differences likewise operated to make the entire part of the state which is now West Virginia a region where Federalism showed strength.[8]

In Maryland, much the same influence which operated in the Shenandoah and trans-Allegheny counties' territory influenced the western portion of the state for Federalism.[9] The eastern part was Federalist for a different reason. In that part of the state, the closeness to water transportation made it possible to carry crops readily to market and the growing of money crops was widespread. This produced Federalist strength in the farming territory.[10] In Baltimore City the Republicans were generally in the majority, due in part to resentment over the location of the capital on the Potomac,[11] and also the general trend of city masses, when enfranchised, toward Jeffersonian Republicanism.

Pennsylvania, by virtue of strongly organized democratic societies among the poorer classes of the metropolis, generally returned Republicans from the First and Second Districts, Philadelphia City and County, respectively.[12] The surrounding counties of thrifty farmers, York (District 3), Lancaster (District 7), and Chester and Delaware (District 8), were conservative and Federalist. District 4, Montgomery, Bucks, and Northampton, was populated by Germans, whose antipathy to the ideas of the French Revolution and general prosperous condition, caused them to elect Federalists until the direct tax of 1798–99 provoked both a literal revolution in the shape of the Fries's Rebellion and a corresponding change of sentiment at the polls. After that these counties became Republican (Cf. Maps 8 and 9 and compare with Map 5).

Further to the west the region of the Whiskey Rebellion was

[8] Jefferson to Tench Coxe, May 21, 1799, Jefferson's *Works,* VII, 380; Ammon, Harry, *The Republican Party in Virginia, 1789-1824* (Alderman Library, University of Virginia, doctoral dissertation, 1948, unpublished), 163-64.

[9] Libby, Orin G., *Geographical Distribution of the Vote of The Thirteen States on the Federal Constitution,* 49.

[10] Paullin, Charles O., *Atlas of the Historical Geography of the United States.* Plate 67 B and C.

[11] Luetscher, G. D., *Early Political Machinery in the U. S.,* 60.

[12] *Ibid.,* 55-60; Tinkcom, Harry M., *Republicans and Federalists in Pennsylvania, 1790-1801.*

strongly Republican, and the surrounding counties were of similar complexion. The exception came in 1799 when the Federalists swept the extreme West with the upsurge of national feeling which has already been noticed (Chs. 1 and 2) in the case of western North Carolina, Virginia, and Maryland. This shows only in the state elections, not on any of the maps showing Federalist votes, but will be treated in the proper place.

Two regions which were exceptions to the Republican trend of the Pennsylvania west were Luzerne County in the north, the territory of the Connecticut immigrants, who brought their politics with them, and Huntingdon County in the west. This latter had been the Tory center of Western Pennsylvania during the Revolution.[13] In Delaware much the same situation existed as in Pennsylvania. Wilmington in New Castle County was Republican, while the stable farming country of Kent and Sussex was Federalist.[14]

The party majorities in New York State after 1792 represented almost a complete geographic reversal from the sectional alignment which had brought about the adoption of the Constitution. This was due to a shift in the balance of power between the parties. As a result, New York City and the surrounding counties were Republican by 1795 in Congressional elections, although these very sections had produced the vote for adoption of the Constitution. This had been brought about by the rise in importance of the vote of the mechanic (or labor) interests, which the Federalists were no longer able to control.[15] Of great importance, also, was the influence of Burr, working through Tammany Hall; and the accession of Livingston to Republicanism, influenced by the unwillingness of Hamilton to share the spoils.[16] This was of considerable importance in the counties surrounding New York City, where the Livingstons, Clintons and Van Cortlandts wielded great power. In Albany City and County the Van Rensselaers and Schuylers were able to hold this prosperous

[13] Luetscher, *Early Political Machinery*, 155.

[14] *Gazette of United States*, October 12, 1796. Also see Donnan, Elizabeth, *Papers of James A. Bayard* (Vol. II of *American Historical Association Report* for 1915), 116.

[15] Hamilton to Rufus King, New York, May 4, 1796, *Works of Alexander Hamilton*, edited by Henry Cabot Lodge (New York, 1886), VIII, 395. Same to same, New York, December 10, 1796, *Ibid.*, 43-46.

[16] Henry Livingston to Samuel Blachley Webb, New York, March 29, 1791; Ford, Worthington, C., *Correspondence and Journals of Samuel Blachley Webb* (New York, 1893–1914), III, 172. Same to same, New York, February 10, 1792, *Ibid.*, 175. Also Benjamin Walker to Joseph Webb, New York, July 24, 1795, *Ibid.*, 197.

sector for Federalism.[17] The rest of the western part of New York was Federalist on account of the great influx of New England immigrants to this territory,[18] a situation which could not be expected to have a permanent effect, unless the Federalist policy considered the agrarian interest.

By the time of the elections of 1798 and 1800 western New York began to leave the Federalist party. The same general situation as in the rest of the country is apparent in New England. The concentration of commerce in this sector operated to intensify its Federalism. Above all, however, the influence of the Congregational clergy, backed by the traditions of a century and a half, prevented the general spread of Republicanism until a later date. The Rev. Jedidiah Morse, D. D., in his *American Geography,* wrote of the state of Connecticut, " The Clergy, who are numerous and respectable, have hitherto preserved a kind of aristocratical balance in the very democratical government of this state; which has happily operated as a check on the overbearing spirit of republicanism." [19] And Dr. Morse, in the course of his activities as Congregational minister, Federalist politician, orator, pamphleteer and newspaper editor, should have known whereof he spoke.

This does not, however, mean that the poorer agrarian sections of New England departed from the general trend. They were Republican. On the other hand the broad stretch of the Connecticut River Valley, extending through Connecticut, Massachusetts, Eastern Vermont and Western New Hampshire was an area of almost unbroken Federalism.[20] With prosperous farms and a fairly equable distribution of wealth, it formed a stronghold of Congregationalism and Federalism which delighted the heart of Dr. Timothy Dwight,[21] himself. Throughout New England, as in the rest of the country, the banks were used as engines of Federalism which were of great service to the cause.[22]

---

[17] Hammond, Jabez D., *History of Political Parties in the State of New York,* fourth edition (Buffalo, 1850), I, 20.

[18] Hockett, Homer C., *Western Influences on Political Parties to 1825 (Ohio State University Bulletin,* XXII, No. 3, August, 1917), 63. Also Hammond, *op. cit.,* I, 52, 99.

[19] Quoted by Callender, James T., *History of the United States for 1796* (Philadelphia, 1797), 67. The quotation is from Morse's *American Geography* (London edition, 1792).

[20] Robinson, W. A., *Jeffersonian Democracy in New England* (New Haven, 1916), 167.

[21] Bidwell, " Rural Economy in New England," *loc. cit.,* 370; Dwight, Timothy, *Travels in New England and New York,* II, 254.

[22] Robinson, *Jeffersonian Democracy in New England,* 103.

The State of Massachusetts was the largest state and provided many important Federalist leaders. It will be observed, in examining Federalist areas on Maps 2, 3, and 4, that there is a fair correspondence between Republicanism and the poorer counties in per capita wealth as shown in Table 14. Upon the resignation of the strongly

TABLE 14 [23]

POPULATION AND LAND TAX IN MASSACHUSETTS COUNTIES, 1796.

County	Population	Tax	Tax per capita
Norfolk & Suffolk	44,875	$22,264.70	$.50
Essex	57,913	19,023.58	.33
Middlesex	42,727	15,582.11	.36
Worcester	56,807	18,798.11	.33
Hampshire	59,681	16,406.14	.28
Berkshire	30,291	7,625.42	.25
Plymouth	29,535	8,490.08	.29
Bristol	31,709	7,699.09	.24
Barnstable	17,354	3,009.19	.17
Dukes	3,265	751.39	.23
Nantucket	4,620	965.47	.21

Federalist Theodore Sedgwick after the first session of the Fourth Congress a moderate who voted Republican appears from Berkshire (District 1 W, or First Western). Similarly the three southern districts are represented by moderate Federalists throughout much of the period (see Maps 3 and 4). The Cape Cod Counties, Dukes, Nantucket, and Barnstable, on account of the fishing industry, had a somewhat greater proportion of wealth than appears in Table 14. Also they naturally were influenced favorably by the Federalist commercial program. The Second Middle District, which was Republican, consisted of the western part of Middlesex and the eastern townships of Worcester, which is the highest ground in these counties, the poorest

[23] The table is compiled from the census of 1790 and the Massachusetts Assessment Act of 1796, *Acts and Laws of the Commonwealth of Massachusetts, 1796* (Boston, 1896), Ch. 61.

farming country, and the area in the east least affected by shipping and shipbuilding.

The representative from the Second Middle District, J. B. Varnum, stressed in his campaign the fact that he was a farmer, while his opponent, Samuel Dexter, who served during the Third Congress, was a lawyer.[24]

In Boston, as in all the American cities, there was a strong Republican organization among the poorer citizens, with the result that the race in the First Middle District was always closely contested. Until 1800, however, the Boston seat was always held by a Federalist. The town of Salem, in Essex County, formed a Republican oasis in an otherwise strongly Federal Congressional District, designated the Third Middle District.[25] The Maine counties (1st, 2nd, and 3rd Eastern Districts) influenced by the background of the inhabitants and their interest in shipbuilding and shipping, remained dominantly Federalist until after 1800.

Connecticut was by far the strongest state for Federalism. It has been pointed out that the rule of this state was chiefly in the hands of the aristocracy.[26] With a number of shipyards in the towns on Long Island Sound, and the prosperous condition of the Connecticut Valley,[27] the state was perfectly satisfied in its Federalism. Furthermore the grip of the Congregational clergy was here almost unshaken. Timothy Dwight came to the presidency of Yale in 1795. To the Republicans he became " Pope Dwight." At the commencement exercises each year the politicians gathered and agreed on nominations under his sanction. It is not necessary to consider Republican areas in this state until 1800.

Rhode Island, as the last state to ratify the Constitution, was in a different category from the rest of New England. Here the weakness of Congregationalism was strongly felt. The agrarian part of the state was Republican. On the other hand, Providence, mindful of the long struggle between the city and the back country which had even brought forth a threat of secession on the part of Providence, was strongly Federalist.[28] The Governor, Arthur Fenner, steered a middle

---

[24] Robinson, *Jeffersonian Democracy in New England*, 115.

[25] *Ibid.*, 101.

[26] Welling, J. C., " Connecticut Federalism," in *Addresses, Paper and Other Essays*, 307 ff.

[27] Purcell, Richard J., *Connecticut in Transition* (Washington, 1918), 113.

[28] Field, Edward, *State of Rhode Island and Providence Plantations . . . a History* (Boston, 1902), I, 291.

course in politics, though his sympathies were with the Republicans, in which camp he definitely settled after 1800.[29] In the 1794 elections for Representative, the Federalist candidates won by a 750 majority out of 3000 votes.[30]

In New Hampshire a strong Republican and personal organization supporting John Langdon, Senator from the State, was the only group whose opposition to Federalism was noteworthy in 1796.[31] The Federalists acquiesced in the election of Langdon rather than run the risk of having him active throughout the state. The farming part of the state was generally Federalist.[32]

Vermont presented a sharp division between the East and the West. In the eastern section which included the Connecticut Valley there were virtually no Republicans; but on the western side of the Green Mountains, the Republicans were in complete sway among the more self-sufficient farmers of this area.[33] The western portion was newly settled, chiefly from Connecticut, it is true. But the strong sectional opposition against the East, which had always existed in this state, engulfed the newcomers.

With the survey of the East complete, the West is now deserving of consideration. In recapitulation, a generalization may be made concerning the more western sections of the seaboard states (except for New England). In each case it was pointed out that whereas the more orthodox of the Republican doctrines found their strongest support in the central agricultural section, a stronger national feeling in the western sections is manifest, especially where defense from Indian attack is a factor. The region in question, stretches from New York to Georgia, and includes the state of Georgia in its entirety. At the present time no analysis of the reaction of this region to particular measures will be undertaken. But the generalization is pointed out, in order to provide a basis for future references.

The only New England State with characteristics of the West at this date is Vermont. Berkshire County, Massachusetts, and part of the Maine area, might be included, but hardly with accuracy. Western Vermont, however, agrees in characteristics more with Tennessee and

---

[29] *Ibid.*, 288.

[30] *Ibid.*, 283.

[31] *Columbian Centinel*, Mar. 22, 1800 traces the rise of the Republican party in New Hampshire.

[32] *Ibid.*

[33] *Connecticut Courant*, Nov. 4, 1799. Also McLaughlin, J. F., *Mathew Lyon* (New York, 1900). *Passim.*

Kentucky than with any part of New England proper. In all of these western states the feeling of kinship with the rest of the Union was but slight. Tennessee and Kentucky were primarily interested in gaining free access to the Mississippi. Pinckney's Treaty had demonstrated that the Union was of some value, but it was not until the Louisiana Purchase that they were to feel definitely cemented to it and a sense of nationalism was to grow strong. Meanwhile the benefits of protection from the Indians were perhaps overbalanced by restrictions placed upon them in the shape of treaty lines on which they must not encroach. Politically, they found most in common with the Republicans, although one of the Kentucky Senators, Marshall, was a Federalist and had voted for Jay's Treaty.

It has already been asserted that no detailed survey of the measures of the Fourth Congress will be undertaken. One or two points in connection with the maps and charts of this Congress (Map 1, 2, and 3 and Vote Charts I and II) deserve notice, however. In the first place the number of moderates of both parties is striking. As of that date there was still considerable latitude within the parties, still room for the exercise of independent judgment. Moreover, some states, as in the case of New Hampshire with John Langdon, still clung to a prominent Revolutionary leader.

In some instances the members voted so regularly with the party opposite to that which elected them, as to fall under the classification not of moderates, but of the opposition. Rutherford of the 1st Virginia District, Grove of the 7th North Carolina District, and T. J. Skinner [34] and W. Lyman [35] of the 1st and 2nd Western Massachusetts Districts, were chosen as Federalists but voted with the Republicans (Cf. Map 3). With the exception of Grove, who somewhat redeemed himself by voting for Jay's Treaty, there was widespread dissatisfaction among the Federalists who had chosen them. In the elections for the Fifth Congress, Skinner was able to secure re-election with the aid of the Republicans, and Grove was accorded full Federalist support in his district. The others of the group, however, were not returned, being replaced in the Fifth Congress by firmer Federalists.[36]

---

[34] Morse, Anson E., *Federalist Party in Massachusetts to the Year 1800* (Princeton, 1913), 164.

[35] Ames to C. Gore, Phil., Nov. 18, 1794, Ames's *Works*, I, 182; Ames to Dwight Foster, Dedham, Jan. 4, 1796, *Ibid.*, 182.

[36] Cf. Maps 4, 5, and 6 and Vote Charts IV–V.

On the other side, one Republican, Samuel Smith of the Baltimore, Maryland District, voted with the Federalists. Smith was a wealthy merchant who, in debate, prided himself on his moderation. He was in favor of Jay's Treaty.

Of those who fall under the classification of moderates, there are a total of twenty-nine for this Congress who appear as such on Map 3 (also cf. Table 15, p. 297). Two districts are included which were represented by a member of one party but then, upon the resignation of this member during Congress, by a man elected by the opposing party. In the Fifth Pennsylvania District Daniel Hiester (R) was followed by George Ege (F). In the Massachusetts 1st Western District Sedgwick was followed by a moderate, Skinner, who proved satisfactory to the Republicans. It should also be noted that party ties were sufficiently loose that in addition to the twenty-nine, there were three who were elected as Federalists but appear as moderates on Map 3 because they voted with the Republicans, and one elected as a Republican who voted with the Federalists also indicated as a moderate.

Appendix III

A. VOTE CHARTS

I. Abbreviations in Column 1.

The state is first given, followed by the district, if the state is divided into districts. For South Carolina the full names of the districts are as follows: Cheraw and Georgetown, Washington and Pinckney, Orangeburg and Beaufort, Ninety-Six, Charleston, Camden. For Vermont they are East and West.

II. Abbreviations in Column 2.

The party affiliation in column 2 is that claimed by the member at time of election. This is based on biographies, newspapers, and correspondence. Where not known, this column is blank.

III. Abbreviations in Column 3.

The name is given. Next, in parentheses, the date of service is indicated provided the member did not serve out the full term, or came in after the session began. The number, instead of the name of the month, is used. Of the letters, r. stands for resigned, a. for the date a member took his seat, d. for died.

IV. The votes are then given, a small capital x for Republican, and an asterisk for Federal; an 0 indicates not voting.

V. Over the total column, F—indicates Federalist; R, Republican.

LEGEND TO VOTE CHART I

Votes charted during the Session of House, Fourth Congress,
First session, March-May, 1796.

1. Call for papers on Jay's Treaty, March 24, 1796, 5 *Annals*, 759. Yeas (R) 62; Nays (F) 37. *House Journal*, 4th Congress, 480-481.

2. Asserting the power of the House to withhold appropriation for a treaty. April 7, 1796, *Ibid.*, 782. Yeas (R) 57; Nays (F) 35. *House Journal*, 4th Congress, 500-501.

3. Granting apropriation for Jay's Treaty, April 30, 1796, *Ibid.*, 1291. Yeas (F) 51; Nays (R) 48. *House Journal*, 4th Congress, 531.

4. To finish only three instead of all frigates, April 8, 1796, *Ibid.*, 886. Yeas (R) 55; Nays (F) 36. *House Journal*, 4th Congress, 504.

5. To strike out section of bill forfeiting western lands in Indian Territory, April 11, 1796, *Ibid.*, 905. Yeas (R) 36; Nays (F) 47. *House Journal*, 4th Congress, 508-509.

6. To increase salaries of executive officials, May 9, 1796, *Ibid.*, 1337. Yeas (F) 51; Nays (R) 34. *House Journal*, 4th Congress, 546-547.

7. To retain Horse Dragoons, May 21, 1796, *Ibid.*, 1419. Yeas (F) 22; Nays (R) 58. *House Journal*, 4th Congress, 567-568.

8. To retain the office of major general, May 21, 1796, *Ibid.*, 1422. Yeas (F) 34; Nays (R) 49. *House Journal*, 4th Congress, 568-569.

9. Admission of Tennessee, May 28, 1796, *Ibid.*, 148. Yeas (R) 48; Nays (F) 30. *House Journal*, 4th Congress, 587-588.

VOTE CHART No. I
FOURTH CONGRESS, FIRST SESSION

State & Dist.	Party	Name & Date of Service	1	2	3	4	5	6	7	8	9	F—R
Conn.	F	Coit, J.	*	*	*	x	*	*	*	*	*	8 — 1
	F	Goodrich, C.	*	*	*	0	*	*	*	*	*	8 — 0
	F	Griswold, R.	*	*	*	*	*	*	*	*	*	9 — 0
	F	Hillhouse, J. (R-1796)	*	*	*	*	*	*	0	0	0	6 — 0
	F	Davenport, J. (S-12-5-96)	0	0	0	0	0	0	0	0	0	0 — 0
	F	Smith, N.	*	*	*	*	*	*	*	x	*	8 — 1
	F	Swift, Z.	*	*	*	*	*	0	x	x	*	6 — 2
	F	Tracy, U. (R-10-13-1796)	*	*	*	0	*	*	*	*	*	8 — 0
		Dana, S. (S-1-3-97)	0	0	0	0	0	0	0	0	0	0 — 0
Del.	R	Patten, J.	x	x	0	x	x	0	0	0	0	0 — 4
Ga.	R	Baldwin, A.	x	x	x	x	x	*	x	x	x	1 — 8
	R	Milledge, J.	x	x	x	x	x	*	x	*	x	2 — 7
Ky.	R	Greenup, C.	x	0	x	0	0	x	x	x	x	0 — 6
	R	Orr, A.	x	x	x	*	x	*	0	0	0	2 — 4
Md. 6	R	Christie, G.	x	x	*	x	*	*	x	x	0	3 — 5
3		Crabb, J. (R-1796)	0	x	*	x	*	*	x	x	x	3 — 5
3	F	Craik, W. (S-12-5-96)	0	0	0	0	0	0	0	0	0	0 — 0
2	R	Duvall, G. (R-3-28-96)	x	0	0	0	0	0	0	0	0	0 — 1
2	R	Sprigg, R. (S-5-5-96)	0	0	0	0	0	x	x	x	x	0 — 4
1	F	Dent, G.	x	x	*	*	*	*	x	x	*	5 — 4
7	F	Hindman, W.	*	*	*	*	*	*	*	*	*	9 — 0
5	R	Smith, S.	x	x	*	0	0	*	*	*	0	4 — 2
4	R	Sprigg, T.	x	x	x	*	*	*	x	x	x	3 — 6
8	F	Murray, Wm. V.	*	*	*	*	*	*	*	*	*	9 — 0
Mass. 1M	F	Ames, F.	0	*	*	0	*	*	0	*	0	5 — 0
4M	F	Bradbury, T.	*	*	*	*	*	*	*	*	*	9 — 0
1E	R	Dearborn, H.	x	x	x	0	*	0	0	0	0	1 — 3
4W	F	Foster, D.	*	*	*	*	*	*	*	*	*	9 — 0
1S	F	Freeman, N.	*	0	0	0	0	0	0	0	0	1 — 0
3M	F	Goodhue, B. (R-6-96)	*	*	*	*	*	*	0	0	0	6 — 0
3M	F	Sewall, Sam. (S-12-7-96)	0	0	0	0	0	0	0	0	0	0 — 0
3S	F	Leonard, Geo.	0	0	*	0	0	*	0	0	0	2 — 0
3W	F	Lyman, S.	*	*	*	x	*	*	*	*	*	8 — 1
2W	R	Lyman, W.	x	x	x	x	x	x	x	x	x	0 — 9
2S	F	Reed, J.	*	*	*	x	*	*	x	*	0	6 — 2
1W	F	Sedgwick, T. (R-6-96)	*	*	*	*	*	0	0	0	0	5 — 0
1W	F	Skinner, T. J. (S-1-27-97)	0	0	0	0	0	0	0	0	0	0 — 0
3E	F	Thatcher, G.	*	*	*	*	*	*	*	*	*	9 — 0
2M	R	Varnum, J. B.	x	x	x	x	0	0	0	0	0	0 — 4
2E	F	Wadsworth, P.	*	*	*	*	*	*	*	*	*	9 — 0
N. H.	F	Foster, A.	*	*	*	*	*	*	x	x	*	7 — 2
	F	Gilman, N.	*	x	*	*	*	*	x	0	*	6 — 2
	R	Sherburne, J. S.	x	x	0	x	*	0	0	0	0	1 — 3
	F	Smith, J.	*	*	*	x	*	*	x	*	*	7 — 2

VOTE CHART No. I—Continued

State & Dist.		Party	Name & Date of Service	1	2	3	4	5	6	7	8	9	F—R
N. J.		F	Dayton, J. (Speaker)	0	0	0	0	0	0	0	0	0	0 — 0
		F	Henderson, T.	0	*	*	*	*	x	x	x	0	4 — 3
		F	Kitchell, A.	x	0	*	0	0	x	x	x	0	1 — 4
		F	Smith, Isaac	*	0	*	x	*	*	*	*	*	7 — 1
		F	Thomson, M.	*	*	*	*	*	0	0	0	*	6 — 0
N. Y.	5	R	Bailey, T.	x	x	*	x	x	x	x	x	x	1 — 8
	10	F	Cooper, W.	*	*	*	*	*	*	*	*	*	9 — 0
	6	F	Gilbert, E.	*	*	*	*	*	*	*	*	*	9 — 0
	8	F	Glen, H.	*	*	*	*	*	*	*	*	*	9 — 0
	4	R	Hathorn, J.	x	x	x	x	*	x	x	x	x	1 — 8
	2	R	Havens, J.	x	x	x	x	x	x	x	x	x	0 — 9
	1	R	Livingston, E.	x	x	x	*	0	0	0	0	0	1 — 3
	7	F	Van Alen, J. E.	*	*	*	*	*	*	x	*	*	8 — 1
	3	R	Van Cortlandt, P.	x	x	*	x	*	0	x	x	x	2 — 6
	9	F	Williams, J.	*	*	*	x	*	*	x	x	*	6 — 3
N. C.	9	R	Blount, T.	x	x	x	x	x	x	x	x	x	0 — 9
	10	R	Bryan, N.	x	x	x	x	x	x	x	x	x	0 — 9
	8	R	Burges, D.	x	x	x	x	x	x	x	x	0	0 — 8
	3	R	Franklin, J.	x	x	x	x	x	x	x	x	x	0 — 9
	6	R	Gillespie, J.	x	0	x	x	x	x	0	0	x	0 — 6
	7	F	Grove, W. B.	x	x	*	x	x	*	x	x	x	2 — 7
	1	R	Holland, J.	x	0	x	x	x	x	x	x	x	0 — 8
	2	R	Locke, M.	x	x	x	x	x	x	x	x	x	0 — 9
	5	R	Macon, N.	x	x	x	x	x	x	x	x	x	0 — 9
	4	R	Tatom, A. (R-6-1-96)	x	x	x	x	x	x	x	x	x	0 — 9
	4		Strudwick, W. (S-12-13-96)	0	0	0	0	0	0	0	0	0	0 — 0
Pa.	10	R	Bard, D.	x	x	x	x	x	0	x	0	x	0 — 7
	11	R	Findley, W.	x	x	0	x	0	*	x	x	x	1 — 6
	12	R	Gallatin, A.	x	x	x	x	x	x	x	x	x	0 — 9
	9	R	Gregg, A.	x	x	*	x	x	x	x	*	0	2 — 6
	8	F	Hartley, T.	*	*	*	*	0	*	*	*	0	7 — 0
	5	R	Hiester, D. (R-7-1-96)[1]	0	x	x	*	x	x	0	0	x	1 — 5
	5	F	Ege, G. (S-12-8-96)	0	0	0	0	0	0	0	0	0	0 — 0
	7	F	Kittera, J. W.	*	*	*	*	0	*	*	*	*	8 — 0
	6	R	Maclay, S.	x	x	x	x	x	x	x	x	x	0 — 9
	2	R	Muhlenberg, F.[1]	x	x	*	*	x	0	x	*	0	3 — 4
	4	R	Richards, J.[1]	x	x	*	0	0	0	x	x	x	1 — 5
	4	F	Sitgreaves, S.	*	0	*	0	0	*	*	*	*	6 — 0
	1	R	Swanwick, J.	x	x	x	*	0	*	x	*	x	3 — 5
	3	F	Thomas, R.	*	*	*	*	*	0	x	*	0	6 — 1
R. I.		F	Malbone, F.	*	*	*	*	*	*	*	*	*	9 — 0
		F	Bourne, B. (R-1796)	*	*	*	*	*	*	*	*	*	9 — 0
		F	Potter, E. R. (R-12-19-96)	0	0	0	0	0	0	0	0	0	0 — 0
S. C.	Che.	R	Benton, L.	x	x	x	x	x	x	0	x	x	0 — 8
	Wash.	R	Earle, S.	x	x	x	x	*	x	x	x	x	1 — 8
	Or.	R	Hampton, W.	x	x	x	x	x	x	x	x	x	0 — 9
	96	F	Harper, R. G.	*	*	*	x	*	0	x	*	*	6 — 2

VOTE CHART No. I—Continued

State & Dist.		Party	Name & Date of Service	1	2	3	4	5	6	7	8	9	F—R
	Ch.	F	Smith, Wm. L.	*	*	*	*	*	*	0	*	*	8 — 0
	Ca.	R	Winn, R.	x	x	x	0	0	0	x	x	x	0 — 7
Tenn.		R	Jackson, Andrew	0	0	0	0	0	0	0	0	0	0 — 0
Vt.	E.	F	Buck, D.	*	*	*	*	*	0	0	0	0	5 — 0
	W.	R	Smith, Israel	x	x	x	0	*	x	0	x	x	1 — 6
Va.	17	R	Brent, R.	x	0	x	x	x	0	x	x	x	0 — 7
	14	R	Cabell, S. J.	x	x	x	x	x	x	0	x	x	0 — 8
	8	R	Claiborne, T.	x	0	x	x	x	x	x	x	x	0 — 8
	13	R	Clopton, J.	x	x	x	x	0	x	0	0	0	0 — 5
	6	R	Coles, I.	x	x	x	x	x	x	x	x	x	0 — 9
	9	R	Giles, W.	x	x	x	x	0	*	x	x	x	1 — 7
	5	F	Hancock, G.	x	x	*	*	0	x	x	*	x	3 — 5
	10	R	Harrison, C. B.	x	x	x	x	x	*	x	x	x	1 — 8
	19	R	Heath, J.	x	x	x	*	*	*	x	x	x	3 — 6
	3	R	Jackson, Geo.	x	x	x	x	x	x	x	x	x	0 — 9
	15	R	Madison, James	x	x	x	x	0	*	0	0	x	1 — 5
	2	R	Moore, A.	x	x	x	x	x	*	x	x	x	1 — 8
	16	R	New, A.	x	0	x	x	x	x	x	x	x	0 — 8
	18	R	Nicholas, J.	x	x	x	x	0	x	x	x	x	0 — 8
	12	F	Page, J.	x	x	x	x	x	*	0	0	0	1 — 5
	11	F	Parker, J.	x	x	x	x	x	0	x	x	0	0 — 7
	4	R	Preston, F.	x	x	x	x	0	x	0	0	x	0 — 6
	1	F	Rutherford, R.	x	x	x	x	*	*	x	*	x	3 — 6
	7	R	Venable, A.	x	x	x	x	x	*	x	x	x	1 — 8

[1] Note on the part affiliation of the Pennsylvania delegation to the Fourth Congress. The classification of three of the Pennsylvania representatives to the Fourth Congress in Vote Chart I differs from that by Harry M. Tinkcom in his *Republicans and Federalists in Pennsylvania, 1790-1801*, 142. The reason for this is briefly presented below.

Frederick A. Muhlenberg (2nd Pennsylvania District) is classified by me as a Republican at the time of his election in 1794; Tinkcom considers him to be a Federalist. Either position might be justified. My conclusions are based on the fact that Muhlenberg in 1794 was endorsed by Benjamin Franklin Bache, editor of the *Aurora*, the principal Jeffersonian organ, cf. *General Advertiser*, October 13, 1794. He voted most of the time with the Republicans in the first three Congresses. On the other hand, he voted in the Fourth Congress for the appropriation for Jay's Treaty, this caused the Republicans to abandon him; and he was defeated for election to the Fifth Congress in 1796 by a Republican. Also cf. Paul A. W. Wallace, *The Muhlenbergs of Pennsylvania* (Philadelphia, 1950). From 1796-1799 Muhlenberg remained in the Federalist camp; but before his death in 1801 he returned to Republicanism, supporting McKean and Jefferson. George H. Grenzmer, "F. A. C. Muhlenberg," DAB, XIII, 307-308

Daniel Hiester, of the 5th Pennsylvania District was regarded by Bache as a Republican, voted as such, and is listed as a Republican by J. H. Peeling in DAB, IX, 8-10.

John Richards, one of the two representatives from the Fourth Pennsylvania District was in an election contest with James Morris. *Pennsylvania Archives*, 4th Ser., *Papers of the Governors*, IV, 330-337. When the election contest came before the House there was considerable debate on seating him, although a formal vote was not taken. *Annals of Congress*, 4th Congress, 1st Session, Jan. 18, 1796, pp. 249-252. The Federalists opposed seating him, while the Republicans argued he was entitled to the seat. The first report of the committee had been adverse. After being seated he voted with the Republicans. On this evidence he has been listed as a Republican by me.

LEGEND TO VOTE CHART NO. II

(For abbreviations see legend to Vote Chart No. I)

Votes Charted

House, Fourth Congress, 2nd Session, Dec. 1796-March 1797.

1. To approve federal amendment to the answer of the House to the President's Address, December 15, 1796, 6 *Annals* 1666. Yeas (F) 30; Nays (R) 49. *House Journal,* 4th Congress, 2nd Session, 616-617.

2. To reduce number of regiments from four to three, January 24, 1797, *Ibid.,* 1982. Yeas (R) 44; Nays (F) 39. *House Journal,* 4th Congress, 2nd Session, 657-658.

3. To strike out raise of pay for cabinet officers, January 27, 1797, *Ibid.,* 2010. Yeas (R) 39; Nays (F) 49. *House Journal,* 4th Congress, 2nd Session, 662.

4. To strike out further military reductions, Febuary 7, 1797, *Ibid.,* 2094. Yeas (F) 50; Nays (R) 44. *House Journal,* 4th Congress, Second Session, 683-684.

5. To strike out raise of pay for House, Senate, and other government officials, February 9, 1797, *Ibid.,* 2105. Yeas (R) 58; Nays (F) 38. *House Journal,* 4th Congress, 2nd Session, 687-688.

6. Not to man naval vessels, February 11, 1797, *Ibid.,* 2148. Yeas (R) 63; Nays (F) 28. *House Journal,* 4th Congress, 2nd Session, 692-693.

7. To restrict naval appropriations to funds from the surplus, Febuary 18, 1797, *Ibid.,* 2208. Yeas (R) 59; Nays (F) 25. *House Journal,* 4th Congress, 2nd Session, 705-706.

8. Granting power to the Secretary of Treasury to remit fines, February 25, 1797, *Ibid.,* 2292. Yeas (F) 50; Nays (R) 34. *House Journal,* 4th Congress, 2nd Session, 720.

9. Not to itemize appropriations for the War Department, March 3, 1797, *Ibid.,* 2361. Yeas (F) 36; Nays (R) 52. *House Journal,* 4th Congress, 2nd Session, 742-743.

VOTE CHART No. II
FOURTH CONGRESS, SECOND SESSION

State & Dist.	Party	Name & Date of Service	1	2	3	4	5	6	7	8	9	$F-R$	F^1-R^1
Conn.	F	Coit, J.	*	*	*	*	*	x	x	*	*	7—2	15—3
	F	Goodrich, C.	*	*	*	*	*	*	*	*	*	9—0	17—0
	F	Griswold, R.	*	*	*	*	*	x	*	*	*	8—1	17—1
	F	Hillhouse, J. (R-1796)	0	0	0	0	0	0	0	0	0	0—0	6—0
	F	Davenport, J. (S-12-5-96)	*	*	*	*	*	*	*	*	*	9—0	9—0
	F	Smith, N.	*	*	*	*	* ∘	*	x	*	*	8—1	16—2
	F	Swift, Z.	*	x	*	x	*	x	x	*	*	5—4	11—6
	F	Tracy, U. (R-10-13-1796)	0	0	0	0	0	0	0	0	0	0—0	8—0
	F	Dana, S. (S-1-3-97)	0	0	*	*	*	*	*	*	*	7—0	7—0
Del.	R	Patten, J.	x	*	*	*	x	x	x	x	x	3—6	3—10
Ga.	R	Baldwin, A.	x	x	*	*	x	x	x	*	x	3—6	4—14
	R	Milledge, J.	0	x	x	*	x	x	x	*	x	2—6	4—13
Ky.	R	Greenup, C.	x	x	0	x	x	x	x	x	x	0—8	0—14
	R	Orr, A.	0	*	x	*	x	x	x	*	x	3—5	5—9
Md. 6	R	Christie, G.	x	*	*	*	x	x	0	0	x	3—4	6—9
3		Crabb, J. (R-1796)	0	0	0	0	0	0	0	0	0	0—0	3—5
3	F	Craik, W. (S-12-5-96)	*	*	*	*	*	*	0	*	*	8—0	8—0
2	R	Duvall, G. (R-3-28-96)	0	0	0	0	0	0	0	0	0	0—0	0—1
2	R	Sprigg, R. (S-5-5-96)	x	x	*	x	x	x	x	x	x	1—8	1—12
1	F	Dent, G.	x	*	*	*	*	*	x	*	*	7—2	12—6
7	F	Hindman, W.	*	0	*	*	*	*	*	*	*	8—0	17—0
5	R	Smith, S.	0	*	*	*	*	*	*	*	0	7—0	11—2
4	R	Sprigg, T.	0	0	0	*	x	x	x	*	0	2—4	5—10
8	F	Murray, Wm. V.	0	*	*	*	*	*	*	*	0	7—0	16—0
Mass. 1M	F	Ames, F.	*	*	*	*	*	0	0	*	0	6—0	11—0
4M	F	Bradbury, T.	*	*	*	*	*	*	*	*	*	9—0	18—0
1E	R	Dearborn, H.	x	0	*	*	0	x	x	0	x	2—4	3—7
4W	F	Foster, D.	*	*	*	*	*	*	*	*	x	9—0	18—0
1S	F	Freeman, N.	x	x	*	x	x	x	x	*	x	2—7	3—7
3M	F	Goodhue, B. (R-6-96)	0	0	0	0	0	0	0	0	0	0—0	6—0
3M	F	Sewall, Sam. (S-12-7-96)	*	0	*	*	*	*	*	0	*	7—0	7—0
3S	F	Leonard, Geo.	0	0	0	*	0	x	x	*	*	3—2	5—2
3W	F	Lyman, S.	*	x	*	*	*	*	x	*	*	7—2	15—3
2W	R	Lyman, W.	x	*	x	0	x	x	x	x	x	1—7	1—16
2S	F	Reed, J.	*	*	*	0	*	x	*	*	x	6—2	12—4
1W	F	Sedgwick, T. (R-6-96)	0	0	0	0	0	0	0	0	0	0—0	5—0
1W	F	Skinner, T. J. (S-1-23-97)	0	x	x	x	x	x	x	x	x	0—8	0—8
3E	F	Thatcher, G.	*	x	*	x	*	*	*	*	*	7—2	16—2
2M	R	Varnum, J. B.	x	x	x	x	x	x	x	0	x	0—8	0—12
2E	F	Wadsworth, P.	*	*	*	*	*	x	*	*	*	8—1	17—1
N. H.	F	Foster, A.	*	*	*	*	*	*	*	*	*	9—0	16—2
	F	Gilman, N.	x	0	0	x	*	*	0	0	*	3—2	9—4
	R	Sherburne, J. S.	x	x	x	x	x	x	x	x	x	0—9	1—12
	F	Smith, J.	0	x	x	x	*	x	x	*	0	2—5	9—7

State & Dist.	Party	Name & Date of Service	1	2	3	4	5	6	7	8	9	$F-R$	F^1-R^1

VOTE CHART No. II—Continued

State & Dist.	Party	Name & Date of Service	1	2	3	4	5	6	7	8	9	F−R	F¹−R¹
N. J.	F	Dayton, J. (Speaker)	0	0	0	0	0	0	0	0	0	0−0	0−0
	F	Henderson, T.	x	*	x	*	x	0	0	*	0	3−3	7−6
	F	Kitchell, A.	x	0	x	0	0	0	0	0	0	0−2	1−6
	F	Smith, Isaac	*	0	*	*	*	*	x	*	*	7−1	14−2
	F	Thomson, M.	*	*	x	*	x	*	0	*	0	5−2	11−2
N. Y. 5	R	Bailey, T.	x	x	*	x	x	x	x	x	x	1−8	2−16
10	F	Cooper, W.	0	*	*	*	*	*	x	0	*	6−1	15−1
6	F	Gilbert, E.	*	*	*	*	*	*	x	*	*	8−1	17−1
8	F	Glen, H.	*	*	*	*	*	*	x	*	0	7−1	16−1
4	R	Hathorn, J.	0	x	x	x	x	x	x	*	x	1−7	2−15
2	R	Havens, J.	x	x	x	0	x	x	x	x	x	0−8	0−17
1	R	Livingston, E.	x	0	0	0	*	x	x	x	x	1−5	2−8
7	F	Van Alen, J. E.	*	*	*	*	*	*	0	*	*	8−0	16−1
3	R	Van Cortlandt, P.	x	0	0	0	x	x	x	x	0	0−5	2−11
9	F	Williams, J.	*	x	*	x	*	x	x	*	*	5−4	11−7
N. C. 9	R	Blount, T.	x	x	x	x	x	x	x	x	x	0−9	0−18
10	R	Bryan, N.	x	x	x	x	x	x	x	x	x	0−9	0−18
8	R	Burges, D.	0	x	*	x	x	x	x	x	*	2−6	2−14
3	R	Franklin, J.	x	x	x	x	x	x	x	x	x	0−9	0−18
6	R	Gillespie, J.	x	0	x	x	x	x	x	*	x	1−7	1−13
7	F	Grove, W. B.	x	x	x	x	x	0	0	0	0	0−5	2−12
1	R	Holland, J.	x	x	x	x	x	x	x	x	x	0−9	0−17
2	R	Locke, M.	x	x	x	x	x	x	x	x	x	0−9	0−18
5	R	Macon, N.	x	x	x	x	x	x	x	*	x	1−8	1−17
4	R	Tatom, A. (R-6-1-96)	0	0	0	0	0	0	0	0	0	0−0	0−9
4		Strudwick, W. (S-12-13-96)	x	x	x	0	x	x	0	x	x	0−7	0−7
Pa. 10	R	Bard, D.	x	0	0	x	x	x	x	x	x	0−7	0−14
11	R	Findley, W.	0	0	x	x	x	x	x	0	x	0−6	1−12
12	R	Gallatin, A.	x	x	x	x	x	x	x	x	x	0−9	0−18
9	R	Gregg, A.	x	*	x	*	x	x	x	0	x	2−6	4−12
8	F	Hartley, T.	*	*	*	*	0	*	*	*	*	8−0	15−0
5	R	Hiester, D. (R-7-1-96)	0	0	0	0	0	0	0	0	0	0−0	1−5
5	F	Ege, G. (S-12-8-96)	*	0	0	*	*	0	*	*	*	6−0	6−0
7	F	Kittera, J. W.	0	*	*	*	0	0	x	*	*	5−1	13−1
6	R	Maclay, S.	x	x	x	x	x	x	x	x	x	0−9	0−18
2	R	Muhlenberg, F.	x	*	*	*	x	0	*	*	x	5−3	8−7
4	R	Richards, J.	x	0	*	x	x	x	x	x	x	1−7	2−12
4	F	Sitgreaves, S.	*	*	*	*	*	*	x	*	*	8−1	14−1
1	R	Swanwick, J.	x	x	x	x	0	0	*	x	x	1−6	4−11
3	F	Thomas, R.	*	*	*	*	*	*	0	*	*	8−0	14−1
R. I.	F	Malbone, F.	*	*	0	*	*	*	*	*	*	8−0	17−0
	F	Bourn, B. (R-1796)	0	0	0	0	0	0	0	0	0	0−0	9−0
	F	Potter, E. R. (R-12-19-96)	0	*	*	*	*	x	0	*	x	5−2	5−2
S. C. Che.	R	Benton, L.	0	0	0	0	0	0	0	0	0	0−0	0−8
Wash.	R	Earle, S.	0	0	0	0	0	0	0	0	0	0−0	1−8
Or.	R	Hampton, W.	0	x	0	x	x	0	0	0	x	0−4	0−13

State & Dist.	Party	Name & Date of Service	1	2	3	4	5	6	7	8	9	F−R	F¹−R¹

VOTE CHART No. II—Continued

State & Dist.		Party	Name & Date of Service	1	2	3	4	5	6	7	8	9	F—R	F¹—R¹
	96	F	Harper, R. G.	*	*	0	*	*	*	*	*	*	8—0	14—2
	Ch.	F	Smith, Wm. L.	*	*	*	*	*	*	*	*	*	9—0	17—0
	Ca.	R	Winn, R.	0	x	x	x	x	x	x	x	x	0—8	0—15
Tenn.		R	Jackson, Andrew	x	x	x	x	x	x	x	x	x	0—9	0—9
Vt.	E.	F	Buck, D.	0	x	*	x	*	x	*	*	*	5—3	10—3
	W.	R	Smith, Israel	x	x	*	x	x	x	x	x	0	1—7	2—13
Va.	17	R	Brent, R.	0	x	0	0	x	x	0	0	x	0—4	0—11
	14	R	Cabell, S. J.	0	x	x	x	x	x	0	x	x	0—7	0—15
	8	R	Claiborne, T.	x	x	x	x	x	x	x	x	x	0—9	0—17
	13	R	Clopton, J.	x	x	x	x	x	x	x	0	x	0—8	0—13
	6	R	Coles, I.	x	x	x	x	x	x	x	x	x	0—9	0—18
	9	R	Giles, W.	x	0	x	0	0	0	0	0	0	0—2	1—9
	5	F	Hancock, G.	0	*	x	*	x	0	0	0	0	2—2	5—7
	10	R	Harrison, C. B.	x	x	*	x	x	x	x	0	0	1—6	2—14
	19	R	Heath, J.	x	0	0	*	x	x	*	x	x	2—5	5—11
	3	R	Jackson, Geo.	x	x	x	x	x	x	0	x	x	0—8	0—17
	15	R	Madison, James	x	0	0	*	x	0	x	0	x	1—4	2—9
	2	R	Moore, A.	x	x	*	x	x	x	x	*	x	2—7	3—15
	16	R	New, A.	0	x	x	x	x	x	x	x	x	0—8	0—16
	18	R	Nicholas, J.	x	0	*	x	x	x	x	x	x	1—7	1—15
	12	F	Page, J.	x	*	*	*	x	x	x	x	*	4—5	5—10
	11	F	Parker, J.	x	*	x	*	x	*	*	*	*	6—3	6—10
	4	R	Preston, F.	0	*	0	*	x	x	0	0	0	2—2	2—8
	1	F	Rutherford, R.	0	x	x	x	x	x	x	x	x	0—8	3—14
	7	R	Venable, A.	x	x	x	x	x	x	0	x	x	0—8	1—16
State & Dist.		Party	Name & Date of Service	1	2	3	4	5	6	7	8	9	F—R	F¹—R¹

[1] Summary of both sessions of Fourth Congress.

TABLE 15

Summary of Regular Party Members and Moderates, by States, Fourth Congress, 1st and 2nd Sessions

1	2	3 Party electing		4	5	6	7	8	9	10
Seats	State	F	R	F	FM	F(ex R)	R	RM	R(ex F)	Absent
7	Conn.	7	0	6	1					
1	Del.	0	1					1		
2	Ga.	0	2					2		
2	Ky.	0	2				1	1		
8	Md. (1) ?	3	4	2	2	1	1	2		
14	Mass.	11	3	7	4		2	1		
4	N. H.	3	1	1	2		1			
5	N. J.	5	0	3	1				1	
10	N. Y.	5	5	4	1		4	1		
10	N. C.	1	9	0	0		9		1	
13	Penn.	4	9	4	0		5	4	0	
2	R. I.	2	0	2						
6	S. C.	2	4	2	0		4			
1	Tenn.	0	1				1			
2	Vt.	1	1		1		1			
19	Va.	4	15		3		13	2	1	
106	(1) ?	48	57	31	15	1	42	14	3	

Explanation of headings to columns: 1. Number of seats, 2. State, 3. Party alignment at time of election, 4. Voting Federalist during the congress, one Republican from Maryland voted regularly with the Federalists, 5. Voting as Federalist-moderate during the congress, 6. Voting Federalist although elected as Republican, 7. Voting as Republican during the congress, 8. Voting as Republican-moderate during the congress, 9. Elected as Federalist but voting regularly Republican during the congress. 10. Absent.

LEGEND TO VOTE CHART NO. III

Fifth Congress, 1st Session

(For abbreviations see Legend to Vote Chart No. I)

Votes Charted

House, Fifth Congress, 1st Session, June 1797-July 1797.

1. Coit Amendment to the Address of the House in answer to the President, Yeas (R) 48; Nays (F) 46, June 1, 1797. *Annals,* 210. *House Journal,* 5th Congress, 15-16.

2. Sitgreaves Amendment to Dayton Amendment to same, Nays (R) 50; Yeas (F) 49, June 1, 1797. *Ibid.,* 216. *House Journal,* 5th Congress, 16-17.

3. Dayton Amendment to same, Yeas (R) 58; Nays (F) 41, June 2, 1797. *Ibid.,* 231. *House Journal,* Fifth Congress, 19-20 (only 40 Nays listed by name).

4. Republican Amendment to strike out last clause of sixth paragraph, Yeas (R) 45; Nays (F) 53. *House Journal,* 5th Congress, 20-21.

5. Vote on the address, Yeas (F) 62; Nays (R) 36, June 2, 1797. *Ibid.,* 233. *House Journal,* 5th Congress, 22-23.

6. President authorized to employ galleys for defense, Yeas (F) 68; Nays (R) 21, June 10, 1797. *Ibid.,* 297. *House Journal,* 5th Congress, 29.

7. Approve amendment raising amounts in defense measure, Yeas (F) 48; Nays (R) 41, June 15, 1797. *Ibid.,* 323, *House Journal,* 5th Congress, 34.

8. Fortifications pass third reading, Yeas (F) 54; Nays (R) 35, June 16, 1797. *Ibid.,* 324. *House Journal,* 5th Congress, 35-36.

9. Approving committee of whole defeat of bill for additional artillery, Yeas (R) 57; Nays (F) 39, June 20, 1797. *Ibid.,* 347. *House Journal,* 5th Congress, 39-40.

10. Striking out provisions to prescribe mode of expatriation, Yeas 34; Nays 57 (not a direct party vote), June 21, 1797. *Ibid.,* 355. *House Journal,* 5th Congress, 40-41. This vote is omitted from total as party issues did not determine the vote.

11. Postponement of expatriation bill, Yeas 52; Nays 44 (In a few cases not a direct party vote), June 21, 1797. *Ibid.,* 356. *House Journal,* 5th Congress, 41-42.

12. Setting date for adjournment, Yeas (R) 51; Nays (F) 47, June 22, 1797. *Ibid.,* 358. *House Journal,* 5th Congress, 42-43.

13. Prohibiting use of naval vessels as convoys, Yeas (R) 50; Nays (F) 48, June 23, 1797. *Ibid.,* 374. *House Journal,* 5th Congress, 44-45.

14. Striking out nine vessels to reduce the number, Yeas (R) 72; Nays (F) 25, June 23, 1797. *Ibid.,* 374. *House Journal,* 5th Congress, 45-46.

15. Limiting bill for naval establishment to one year, Yeas (R) 53; Nays (F) 43, June 23, 1797. *Ibid.,* 376. *House Journal,* 5th Congress, 48-49.

16. Permitting navy to be used as convoys, Yeas (F) 51; Nays (R) 47, June 29, 1797. *Ibid.,* 409. *House Journal,* 5th Congress, 57-58.

17. Imposing naturalization fee of $5, Yeas (F) 46; Nays (R) 42, July 1, 1797. *Ibid.,* 431. *House Journal,* 5th Congress, 60-61.

18. Resolution to consider salt tax, Yeas (F) 47; Nays (R) 41, July 4, 1797. *Ibid.,* 443. *House Journal,* 5th Congress, 66-67.

19. Limits to draw-backs upon re-exports, Yeas (R) 47; Nays (F) 43, July 5, 1797. *Ibid.,* 446. *House Journal,* 5th Congress, 68.

VOTE CHART No. III
FIFTH CONGRESS, FIRST SESSION

State & Dist.	Party	Name	1	2	3	4	5	6	7	8	9	10[16]	11	12	13	14	15	16	17	18	19	F–R
Conn.	F	Allen, John	*	*	*	*	*	x	*	x	*	*	0	*	*	*	*	*	*	*	*	17–0
	F	Coit, J.[1]	x	*	*	*	*	x	x	x	x	*	x	x	x	x	*	x	x	*	*	6–12
	F	Dana, S.	*	x	x	*	*	*	*	0	*	x	*	x	*	*	*	x	x	*	*	15–2
	F	Smith, N.	*	*	*	*	*	*	*	*	*	*	x	*	*	*	*	*	0	*	*	16–2
	F	Davenport, J.[2]	*	*	*	*	*	*	*	*	*	0	0	*	*	*	*	*	*	*	*	16–0
	F	Goodrich, C.	*	*	*	*	*	*	*	*	*	*	x	*	*	*	*	*	*	*	*	17–1
	F	Griswold, R.	*	*	*	*	*	x	x	*	*	*	x	*	*	x	*	*	*	*	*	14–4
Del.	F	Bayard, J. A.	*	*	*	*	*	*	*	*	*	*	*	*	*	*	*	*	*	*	*	18–0
Ga.	R	Baldwin, A.	x	x	x	x	*	*	*	*	x	x	x	x	x	x	x	x	x	x	x	4–14
	R	Milledge, J.	0	x	x	x	*	*	*	*	x	x	x	x	x	x	x	x	*	x	x	4–13
Ky.	R	Davis, T. T.	x	x	x	*	x	0	x	*	x	*	*	x	x	x	*	x	*	x	x	4–13
	R	Fowler, J.	x	*	*	x	x	*	x	*	x	0	x	x	x	x	*	x	x	x	x	3–15
Md. 4	F	Baer, G.	*	*	0	*	*	*	*	*	*	*	x	*	*	*	*	*	*	*	*	16–1
3	F	Craik, Wm.	*	*	*	*	*	*	*	*	*	*	*	*	*	*	*	*	*	*	*	18–0
8	F	Dennis, J.	*	*	*	*	*	*	x	*	*	x	*	*	*	x	x	*	x	*	*	16–2
1	F	Dent, G.	x	x	*	*	*	*	0	*	*	x	*	*	*	x	*	*	x	x	x	11–7
7	F	Hindman, Wm.	*	*	*	*	*	*	*	*	*	0	*	*	*	*	*	*	x	*	*	18–0
6	F	Matthews, Wm.	*	*	*	0	0	*	*	*	*	x	*	*	*	x	0	0	0	0	0	14–1
5	R	Smith, S.	x	x	x	x	x	*	*	*	x	x	x	x	x	0	x	x	x	x	*	4–9
2	R	Sprigg, R.	x	x	x	x	x	x	*	x	x	x	x	x	x	x	x	x	x	x	x	0–18
Mass. 4M	F	Bradbury, T.[3]	*	0	0	0	0	*	*	0	0	0	0	0	0	0	0	0	0	0	0	16–0
3S	F	Bullock, S.	0	0	*	0	0	*	x	*	*	*	x	*	*	x	*	*	*	*	*	2–1
4W	R	Foster, D.	*	*	*	*	0	*	0	x	*	*	x	*	0	x	0	x	0	0	0	15–2
1S	R	Freeman, N.	x	x	x	x	*	x	x	x	x	0	x	*	*	x	x	x	0	0	0	1–14
3W	F	Lyman, S.	*	*	*	*	*	*	*	*	x	x	*	0	*	x	*	*	*	*	*	16–2
1M	F	Otis, H. G.	*	*	x	*	0	0	*	*	*	x	*	*	*	*	*	*	*	*	*	15–2

VOTE CHART No. III—Continued

State & Dist.	Party	Name	1	2	3	4	5	6	7	8	9	10[16]	11	12	13	14	15	16	17	18	19	F–R
1E	F	Parker, I.[4]	0	0	0	0	0	0	0	0	0	0	0	0	0	0	0	0	0	0	0	0—0
2S	F	Reed, J.	*	*	x	*	*	*	x	*	*	x	*	x	*	x	x	*	*	*	*	13—5
3M	F	Sewall, S.	*	*	*	*	*	*	*	*	*	*	x	x	*	x	*	*	*	*	*	16—2
2W	F	Shepard, W.	*	*	*	x	*	*	*	x	*	x	x	x	*	x	*	*	*	*	*	17—1
1W	F	Skinner, T.[5]	x	x	x	x	x	x	x	x	x	x	x	x	x	x	x	x	x	x	x	2—16
3E	F	Thatcher, G.	x	x	x	x	*	0	x	x	x	x	x	x	x	x	x	x	x	x	x	17—0
2M	R	Varnum, J. B.	x	x	x	x	x	x	0	x	x	x	x	x	x	x	x	x	x	x	x	1—17
2E	F	Wadsworth, P. O.	0	*	*	*	*	*	*	*	x	x	*	*	*	x	*	*	*	*	*	17—0
N. H.																					
	F	Foster, A.	*	*	*	*	*	*	*	x	*	x	*	*	*	*	*	*	*	*	*	18—0
	F	Freeman, J.	*	*	*	*	*	*	0	x	0	*	*	*	*	*	*	*	0	*	*	15—1
	F	Gordon, Wm.	*	*	*	*	*	*	*	*	*	*	x	*	*	*	x	*	x	x	*	15—2
	F	Smith, J.[6]	*	*	*	*	*	*	0	x	x	x	x	*	*	x	x	*	0	*	*	15—1
N. J.																					
	F	Dayton, J. (Speaker)	0	0	0	0	0	0	0	x	0	0	0	0	0	0	0	0	0	0	0	0—0
	F	Imlay, J. H.	*	*	*	*	*	*	*	x	x	x	*	*	*	x	*	*	0	*	*	17—0
	F	Schureman, J.	*	x	x	*	*	*	x	x	*	x	*	*	*	x	*	*	x	*	*	14—3
	F	Sinnickson, T.	*	*	*	*	*	*	0	x	*	x	*	*	*	x	*	*	x	*	*	16—1
	F	Thomson, M.	*	*	*	*	*	*	0	*	*	*	*	*	*	x	*	*	0	*	*	16—1
N. Y. 5	F	Brooks, David	*	*	*	*	*	x	*	x	*	x	*	*	*	x	x	x	*	*	*	17—1
10	F	Cochran, J.	*	*	*	*	*	*	*	x	*	*	*	*	*	x	x	x	*	*	*	17—1
4	R	Elmendorf, L. C.	x	x	x	x	x	*	x	x	x	x	x	x	x	x	x	x	x	x	x	1—17
8	F	Glen, Henry	*	x	x	x	x	x	x	x	x	x	x	x	x	x	x	x	x	0	x	16—1
2	R	Havens, J.	x	x	x	x	x	x	x	0	x	x	x	x	x	x	x	x	x	x	x	0—18
6	F	Hosmer, H.	*	*	*	*	*	*	*	0	*	x	0	*	*	*	*	*	x	x	0	17—0
1	R	Livingston, Ed.	x	x	x	x	x	x	0	0	0	0	0	0	0	x	0	x	x	0	0	1—7
7	F	Van Alen, J.	*	*	*	*	*	*	*	x	x	*	*	*	*	x	*	*	x	x	x	17—1
3	R	Van Cortlandt, P.	x	x	x	x	x	*	x	x	x	*	x	x	x	x	x	x	x	x	x	1—17
9	F	Williams, J.	*	*	x	x	x	0	*	0	x	x	*	*	*	x	x	x	*	*	x	12—6
N. C. 9	R	Blount, T.	x	x	x	x	x	x	x	x	x	x	x	x	x	x	x	x	x	0	x	0—17
10	R	Bryan, N.[7]	x	x	0	0	0	0	0	0	0	*	*	0	x	x	x	0	*	x	x	2—16
10	F	Spaight, R. D.[8]	0	0	0	0	0	0	0	0	0	0	0	0	0	0	0	0	0	0	0	0—0

State & Dist.	Party	Name	1	2	3	4	5	6	7	8	9	10[16]	11	12	13	14	15	16	17	18	19	F–R
8	R	Burges, D.	o	o	o	x	x	x	*	*	x	x	x	x	x	x	x	x	x	x	*	3–9
6	R	Gillespie, J.	x	x	x	x	x	x	x	x	x	x	x	x	x	x	x	x	x	x	x	2–16
7	F	Grove, Wm. B.	*	*	*	*	*	o	o	o	x	*	x	*	x	x	*	*	*	x	o	10–4
2	R	Locke, M.	x	x	x	x	x	x	o	x	x	x	x	x	x	x	x	x	x	x	x	0–17
5	R	Macon, N.	x	x	x	x	x	x	x	x	x	x	x	x	x	x	x	x	x	x	x	0–18
1	R	McDowell, J.	x	x	x	x	x	x	x	x	x	x	x	x	x	x	x	x	x	x	x	0–18
4	R	Stanford, R.	x	x	x	x	x	x	x	x	x	x	x	x	x	x	x	x	x	x	x	1–17
3	R	Williams, R.	x	x	x	x	x	x	x	x	x	x	x	x	x	x	*	x	x	x	x	2–16
Pa. 10	R	Bard, D.	x	x	x	x	x	x	x	x	*	x	x	x	x	x	x	x	x	x	x	1–16
4	F	Sitgreaves, S.[9]	*	*	*	*	*	o	o	o	x	*	*	*	*	*	*	*	*	*	*	16–1
4	F	Chapman, J.	*	*	*	*	*	x	x	*	x	x	x	x	x	x	o	o	o	x	x	8–5
12	R	Gallatin, A.	x	x	x	x	x	o	x	x	x	o	x	x	x	x	x	x	x	x	x	3–15
11	R	Findley, W.	o	x	x	x	x	x	o	x	x	x	x	x	x	x	o	o	o	o	o	2–7
9	R	Gregg, A.	x	x	x	x	x	x	o	o	*	x	x	x	x	x	x	x	x	x	x	0–15
6	R	Hanna, J. A.	*	*	*	*	*	*	*	*	*	x	x	x	*	x	x	x	x	*	x	4–13
8	F	Hartley, T.	*	*	*	*	*	o	o	x	*	x	*	x	*	*	*	o	o	*	o	15–2
5	F	Ege, G.[10]	x	x	x	x	x	x	x	o	*	o	*	*	*	*	x	*	*	o	x	10–2
7	F	Kittera, J.	*	*	*	*	*	*	*	*	*	*	x	*	*	x	*	x	*	*	x	12–4
2	R	McClenachan, B.	*	x	x	x	x	x	x	x	o	o	x	x	*	*	x	x	x	x	x	1–16
1	R	Swanwick, J.[11]	x	x	x	x	x	x	x	x	*	x	x	x	x	x	x	x	x	x	x	2–14
3	F	Thomas, R.	*	*	*	*	*	o	x	o	x	o	*	x	*	*	*	*	*	*	o	15–2
R. I.	F	Champlin, C. G.	*	*	*	*	*	*	*	*	x	x	*	*	*	*	*	*	*	*	*	17–1
	F	Potter, E.[12]	x	x	x	x	x	x	x	x	x	x	*	*	*	x	x	*	*	*	*	11–7
S. C. Che.	R	Benton, L.	o	o	o	o	o	o	o	o	o	o	o	o	o	o	o	x	x	x	x	0–4
96	F	Harper, R. G.	o	*	*	*	*	*	*	*	*	*	*	*	*	x	x	x	*	*	x	14–2
Or.	F	Rutledge, J.	*	x	x	x	x	*	*	*	*	x	x	x	x	*	*	*	o	*	*	14–2
Ch.	F	Smith, Wm. L.[13]	*	*	*	*	*	*	*	*	*	x	*	*	*	*	*	*	*	*	*	18–0
Wash.	R	Smith, Wm.	x	x	x	x	x	x	x	x	x	x	x	x	x	x	x	x	x	x	x	2–16
Ca.	R	Sumter, T.	x	x	x	x	x	x	x	x	x	x	x	x	x	x	x	x	x	x	x	0–17
Tenn.[14]																						

VOTE CHART No. III—Continued

State & Dist.		Party	Name	1	2	3	4	5	6	7	8	9	10[16]	11	12	13	14	15	16	17	18	19	F–R
Vt.	W.	R	Lyon, M.	X	X	X	X	X	X	X	X	X	X	X	X	X	X	X	X	X	X	X	0–18
	E.	F	Morris, L.	0	0	0	0	0	0	0	0	0	0	0	0	0	0	0	*	*	*	*	4–0
Va.	17	R	Brent, R.	X	X	X	X	X	X	X	0	X	X	X	X	X	X	X	X	0	X	X	0–16
	14	R	Cabell, S. J.	X	X	X	X	X	*	X	X	X	*	X	X	X	X	X	X	X	X	X	1–17
	8	R	Claiborne, T.	X	X	X	X	X	X	X	X	X	X	X	X	X	X	X	X	X	X	X	0–18
	6	R	Clay, M.	X	X	X	X	X	*	X	X	X	X	X	X	X	X	X	X	*	X	X	2–16
	13	R	Clopton, J.	X	X	X	X	X	*	X	X	X	X	X	X	X	X	X	X	X	X	X	1–17
	15	R	Dawson, J.	X	X	X	X	X	X	X	X	X	X	X	X	X	X	X	X	X	X	X	0–18
	9	R	Giles, Wm.	X	X	X	X	X	X	X	X	X	X	X	X	X	X	X	X	0	0	0	0–14
	9	R	Eggleston, J.[15]	0	0	0	0	0	0	0	0	0	0	0	0	0	0	0	0	0	0	0	0–0
	12	F	Evans, T.	*	*	X	*	*	*	*	*	*	X	*	*	*	X	X	*	X	X	*	13–5
	10	R	Harrison, C. B.	X	X	X	X	X	*	X	X	X	X	*	X	X	X	X	X	X	X	X	3–12
	2	R	Holmes, D.	X	X	X	X	*	*	*	*	X	X	X	X	X	X	X	X	X	X	X	5–13
	19	R	Jones, W.	X	X	X	X	X	X	X	*	X	X	X	X	X	X	X	X	X	X	X	1–17
	3	F	Machir, J.	*	*	X	*	*	*	*	*	*	X	*	*	*	X	*	*	X	*	X	13–4
	1	F	Morgan, D.	*	*	X	X	X	*	X	*	X	X	*	*	*	X	X	*	*	*	X	11–6
	16	R	New, A.	X	X	X	X	X	X	X	X	X	X	X	X	X	X	X	X	X	X	X	0–18
	18	R	Nicholas, J.	X	X	X	X	X	X	X	*	X	X	X	X	X	X	X	X	X	X	X	3–15
	11	F	Parker, J.	X	X	X	X	X	*	X	*	X	X	X	X	X	X	*	X	X	X	X	5–11
	4	R	Trigg, A.	X	X	X	X	X	0	0	0	X	X	X	X	X	X	X	X	X	0	0	2–15
	5	R	Trigg, J.	X	X	X	X	X	0	X	X	X	X	X	X	X	X	X	X	X	X	X	0–16
	7	R	Venable, A.	X	X	X	X	X	X	0	X	X	X	X	X	X	X	X	X	X	X	X	0–17

NOTES: [1] d. 9-5-98.   [2] d. 8-3-98.   [3] r. 7-24-97.   [4] s. 11-15-97.

[5] With the election of Theodore Sedgwick to the Senate, T. J. Skinner ran against Ephraim Williams and one other candidate. Skinner campaigned as a moderate Federalist in his race against the more orthodox candidate. He is not classified here as a Federalist because he defeated the regular candidate and his program was republican—nor is he classified as a republican. Cf. *Hampshire Gazette*, October 2, 1796.

[6] r. 7-26-97.   [7] d. 6-4-98.   [8] s. 12-10-98.   [9] r. in 1798.   [10] r. 10-97.   [11] d. 8-1-98.   [12] r. in 1798.

[13] r. 7-10-97.   [14] W. C. C. Claiborne did not take his seat until the second session.   [15] s. 12-3-98.

[16] Vote 10 is omitted in this summary because the party vote was split for other than party reasons.

TABLE 16

Summary of Regular Party Members and Moderates, by States, Fifth Congress, 1st Session

1	2	3		4	5	6	7	8	9	10
Seats	State	Party electing		F	FM	F(ex R)	R	RM	R(ex F)	Absent
		F	R							
7	Conn.	7		5	2					
1	Del.	1		1						
2	Ga.		2					2		
2	Ky.		2				1	1		
8	Md.	6	2	5	1		1	1		
14	Mass. (1)?	11	2	8	2		2		1	1
4	N. H.	4		4						
5	N. J.	5		5						
10	N. Y.	6	4	5	1		4			
10	N. C.	1	9		1		8	1		
13	Penn.	6	7	4	2		5	2		
2	R. I.	2		1	1					
6	S. C.	3	3	3			3			
1	Tenn.		1							1
2	Vt.	1	1	1			1			
19	Va.	4	15		4		13	2		
106	(1)?	57	48	42	14		38	9	1	2

LEGEND TO VOTE CHART NO. IV

House, Fifth Congress, 2nd Session, December 1797-July 1798.

1. Permission to report a bill for the further protection of commerce, Yeas (F) 45; Nays (R) 45, carried by speaker. Dec. 11, 1797. 7 *Annals,* 700. *House Journal,* 5th Congress, 10.

2. Expelling Matthew Lyon, Yeas (F) 52; Nays (R) 44, two-thirds required, Feb. 12, 1798. *Ibid.,* 1008. *House Journal,* 5th Congress, 178.

3. To disagree to Senate amendment to bill on Tennessee land, Yeas (R) 46; Nays (F) 48, Feb. 21, 1798. *Ibid.,* 1061. *House Journal,* 5th Congress, 189-190.

4. To put question of reprimand for Lyon and Griswold, Yeas (R) 47; Nays (F) 48, Sitgreaves voted twice, but the count is correct counting him Nay, Feb. 23, 1798. *Ibid.,* 1067. *House Journal,* 5th Congress, 201-202.

5. Instructing committee of whole to report a bill for repeal of the Stamp Act, Yeas (R) 52; Nays (F) 36, Feb. 26, 1798. *Ibid.,* 1083. *House Journal,* 5th Congress, 206.

6. Repeal of Stamp Act, Yeas (R) 51; Nays (F) 42, Feb. 28, 1798. *Ibid.,* 1098. *House Journal,* 5th Congress, 208-209.

7. Nicholas Amendment to foreign intercourse bill, Yeas (R) 48; Nays (F) 52, March 5, 1798. 8 *Annals,* 1234. *House Journal,* 5th Congress, 214.

8. To designate places for fortifications, Yeas (R) 32; Nays (F) 54, April 11, 1798. *Ibid.,* 1402. *House Journal,* 5th Congress, 258-259.

9. Reducing vessels from 16 to 12, Yeas (R) 45; Nays (F) 37, April 20, 1798. *House Journal,* 5th Congress, 266-267.

10. Prohibiting convoys, Yeas (R) 32; Nays (F) 50, April 20, 1798. *Ibid.,* 1521. *House Journal,* 5th Congress, 267-268.

11. Creating Department of Navy, Yeas (F) 47; Nays (R) 41, April 25, 1798. *Ibid.,* 1553. *House Journal,* 5th Congress, 272-273.

12. Prohibiting foreign ministers from receiving presents, Yeas (R) 49; Nays (F) 37, May 4, 1798. *Ibid.,* 1593. *House Journal,* 5th Congress, 285.

13. To commit petition of Captain Magnien's Grenadiers, Yeas (R) 46; Nays (F) 43, May 15, 1798. *Ibid.,* 1704. *House Journal,* 5th Congress, 294-295.

14. Reduce provisional army to ten thousand, Yeas (R) 56; Nays (F) 35, May 17, 1798. *Ibid.,* 1769. *House Journal,* 5th Congress, 298-299.

15. To substitute militia for provisional army, Yeas (R) 39; Nays (F) 51, May 17, 1798. *Ibid.,* 1770. *House Journal,* 5th Congress, 299-300.

16. Restricting duration of provisional army bill to time of next session, Yeas (R) 53; Nays (F) 35, May 17, 1798. *Ibid.*, 1768. *House Journal*, 5th Congress, 296-297.

17. Provisional army, Yeas (F) 51; Nays (R) 40, May 18, 1798. *Ibid.*, 1772. *House Journal*, 5th Congress, 301-302.

18. Recommitting Alien Bill, Yeas (R) 46; Nays (F) 44, May 23, 1798. *Ibid.*, 1796. *House Journal*, 5th Congress, 309-10. In 8 *Annals* 1796, N. Freeman is listed as not voting, in *Journal* he voted Jeffersonian.

19. Call for X Y Z papers, Yeas 65; Nays 27 (not a party vote), April 2, 1798. *Ibid.*, 1371. *House Journal*, 5th Congress, 249-250 (omitted in count of vote).

20. Permission to navy to capture French vessels privateering, Yeas (F) 50; Nays (R) 40, May 26, 1798. *Ibid.*, 1834. *House Journal*, 5th Congress, 315-316.

21. Suspending commercial intercourse with France, Yeas (F) 55; Nays (R) 25, June 1, 1798. *Ibid.*, 1868. *House Journal*, 5th Congress, 320-321.

22. Granting letters of marque and reprisal, Yeas (F) 41; Nays (R) 42, June 8, 1798. *Ibid.*, 1890. *House Journal*, 5th Congress, 329-330.

23. Prescribing valuation for direct tax, Yeas (F) 69; Nays (R) 19, June 13, 1798. *Ibid.*, 1925. *House Journal*, 5th Congress, 335-336.

24. Senate Alien Bill, Yeas (F) 46; Nays (R) 40, June 21, 1798. *Ibid.*, 2028. *House Journal*, 5th Congress, 346-347.

25. Limiting interest on loan, Yeas (R) 34; Nays (F) 48, June 25, 1798. *Ibid.*, 2048. *House Journal*, 5th Congress, 353-354.

26. To raise number of regiments from eight to twelve, Yeas (F) 40; Nays (R) 40, carried by Speaker, July 5, 1798. *Ibid.*, 2092. *House Journal*, 5th Congress, 368-369. In 8 *Annals*, 2092, M. Thompson is listed as not voting, in *Journal* he voted Federalist.

27. Abrogate treaties with France, Yeas (F) 47; Nays 37 (R), July 6, 1798. *Ibid.*, 2127. *House Journal*, 5th Congress, 373-374.

28. Sedition Act, Yeas (F) 44; Nays (R) 41, July 10, 1798. *Ibid.*, 2171. *House Journal*, 5th Congress, 379-380.

29. Bounty to privateers on captured guns, Yeas (F) 40; Nays (R) 41, July 14, 1798. *Ibid.*, 2181. *House Journal*, 5th Congress, 390.

VOTE CHART No. IV

FIFTH CONGRESS, SECOND SESSION

(17)

State & Dist.	Party	Name	1	2	3	4	5	6	7	8	9	10	11	12	13	14	15	16	17	18	19	20	21	22	23	24	25	26	27	28	29	F–R
Conn.	F	Allen, J.	*	0	*	*	*	*	*	*	*	*	*	*	*	*	*	*	*	*	*	*	*	*	*	*	*	*	*	*	*	27–0
	F	Coit, J.[1]	x	*	*	*	*	*	*	x	*	*	*	*	*	*	*	*	*	*	x	*	*	x	*	*	*	x	*	x	*	22–5
	F	Dana, S.	*	*	*	*	*	*	*	*	*	*	*	*	*	*	*	*	*	*	*	*	*	*	*	*	*	*	*	*	*	28–0
	F	Smith, N.	*	*	*	0	*	*	*	*	*	*	*	*	*	*	*	*	*	*	*	*	*	*	*	*	x	*	*	*	*	26–1
	F	Edmond, W.[2]	*	0	0	0	0	0	0	0	0	0	*	*	*	*	*	x	*	*	0	*	*	*	*	*	*	*	*	*	*	18–0
	F	Goodrich, C.	*	0	*	0	0	0	*	*	*	*	*	*	*	*	*	*	*	*	*	*	*	*	*	*	*	*	*	*	*	28–0
	F	Griswold, R.	*	0	*	0	0	*	0	*	*	*	*	*	*	*	*	*	*	*	*	*	*	*	*	*	*	*	*	*	*	26–0
Del.	F	Bayard, J.	0	*	*	*	*	*	*	*	*	*	*	*	*	*	*	*	*	*	*	0	*	*	*	*	*	*	*	*	*	23–0
Ga.	R	Baldwin, A.	x	x	x	x	x	x	x	x	x	x	x	x	x	x	x	x	x	x	x	x	x	*	x	x	x	x	x	x	x	2–26
	R	Milledge, J.	0	x	x	x	x	x	x	*	x	x	x	x	x	x	*	x	*	x	x	x	x	x	*	x	*	0	0	x	0	4–19
Ky.	R	Davis, T.	x	*	x	x	x	x	x	x	x	x	x	x	x	x	x	x	x	x	x	x	*	x	x	*	*	0	0	0	*	5–19
	R	Fowler, J.	0	x	x	x	x	x	x	*	x	x	x	x	x	x	x	0	x	0	0	x	0	0	x	x	x	0	0	x	x	0–24
Md. 4	F	Baer, G.	*	*	*	x	x	*	*	0	0	0	0	x	*	*	*	*	*	x	x	*	x	*	*	0	*	*	*	*	*	21–4
3	F	Craik, Wm.	*	*	*	x	x	*	*	*	0	0	0	0	*	x	x	x	x	x	x	*	*	*	*	0	0	*	0	0	x	25–1
8	F	Dennis, J.	*	*	*	0	0	0	*	0	0	x	x	x	x	*	x	x	x	x	x	x	x	x	0	0	0	0	0	x	x	16–3
1	F	Dent, G.	x	*	*	*	*	*	*	*	0	*	*	*	*	*	*	*	*	*	x	0	x	0	*	x	*	*	0	*	*	15–11
7	F	Hindman, W.	x	*	*	*	*	x	*	x	*	*	*	*	*	x	x	x	x	x	x	x	x	x	x	x	x	x	x	x	*	28–0
6	F	Matthews, W.	*	*	*	0	*	*	*	x	0	*	*	*	*	*	0	0	0	0	x	0	0	0	0	0	x	x	*	0	*	22–5
5	R	Smith, S.	x	x	x	x	x	x	*	x	0	x	x	x	x	x	x	x	x	x	0	x	0	0	*	x	x	0	x	x	x	6–13
2	R	Sprigg, R.	x	x	x	x	x	x	x	0	0	x	x	x	x	x	x	x	x	x	x	x	x	x	*	x	0	x	x	x	x	1–24
Mass. 4M	F	Bartlett, B.[3]	*	*	*	*	*	*	*	*	*	*	x	*	*	*	*	*	*	x	x	*	*	x	x	*	*	*	*	*	*	27–1
3S	F	Bullock, S.	*	*	*	*	*	*	*	x	x	x	x	x	*	0	x	x	x	x	x	x	x	x	x	0	x	x	x	x	x	18–10
4W	F	Foster, D.	*	*	*	*	*	*	*	*	*	*	*	*	*	0	0	0	*	*	*	*	*	*	*	0	*	*	*	*	*	27–1
1S	R	Freeman, N.	0	x	x	*	*	x	x	*	0	0	0	0	0	0	0	0	0	x	x	x	0	0	0	0	0	0	0	0	0	5–5
3W	F	Lyman, S.	*	*	*	*	*	*	*	*	*	*	*	*	x	x	*	*	*	*	*	*	*	*	*	*	*	*	0	*	*	26–2
1M	F	Otis, H. G.	*	*	*	*	*	*	*	*	*	*	*	*	*	*	*	*	*	*	*	0	*	*	*	*	*	*	*	*	*	28–0
1E	F	Parker, I.	*	*	0	*	*	*	*	*	*	*	*	*	*	*	*	*	*	*	*	*	*	*	*	*	*	*	*	*	*	14–0

State & Dist.	Party	Name	F–R
2S	F	Reed, J.	22–5
3M	F	Sewall, S.	28–0
2W	F	Shepard, W.	22–3
1W	F	Skinner, T.[5]	1–16
3E	F	Thatcher, G.	28–0
2M	R	Varnum, J. B.	1–27
2E	F	Wadsworth, P.	27–0
N.H.	F	Foster, A.	28–0
	F	Freeman, J.	24–0
	F	Gordon, W.	16–0
	F	Smith, J.[6]	0–0
	F	Sprague, P.[7]	12–3
N.J.	F	Dayton, J.	2–0
	F	Imlay, J. H.	27–0
	F	Schureman, J.	24–2
	F	Sinnickson, T.	25–1
	F	Thomson, M.	25–1
N.Y. 5	F	Brooks, D.	27–0
10	F	Cochran, J.	19–0
4	R	Elmendorf, L.	0–19
8	F	Glen, H.	28–0
2	R	Havens, J.	0–28
6	F	Hosmer, H.	28–0
1	R	Livingston, E.	3–13
7	F	Van Alen, J.	28–0
3	R	Van Cortlandt, P.	1–22
9	F	Williams, J.	14–7
N.C. 10	R	Bryan, N.[8]	0–17
9	R	Blount, T.	1–27
10	F	Spaight, R.[9]	0–0

Vote columns: 1 2 3 4 5 6 7 8 9 10 11 12 13 14 15 16 17 18 19 20 21 22 23 24 25 26 27 28 29   (17)

VOTE CHART No. IV—Continued

State & Dist.	Party	Name	1	2	3	4	5	6	7	8	9	10	11	12	13	14	15	16	17	18	19	20	21	22	23	24	25	26	27	28	29	F–R
8	R	Burges, D.	x	0	x	x	x	x	x	x	x	x	0	x	x	x	x	x	x	x	x	x	x	x	x	x	x	x	x	x	x	1–25
6	R	Gillespie, J.	x	x	x	x	x	x	x	x	0	0	x	x	x	x	x	x	x	x	x	x	*	x	x	x	x	x	x	x	x	3–22
7	F	Grove, Wm.	*	x	x	*	x	x	*	x	0	*	*	x	x	x	x	0	x	x	x	*	x	x	x	*	x	*	*	*	x	18–10
2	R	Locke, M.	x	x	x	x	x	x	x	x	x	x	x	x	x	x	x	x	x	x	x	x	x	x	x	x	x	x	x	x	x	0–27
5	R	Macon, N.	x	x	x	x	x	x	x	x	x	x	x	x	x	x	x	x	x	x	x	x	x	x	x	x	x	x	x	x	x	0–28
1	R	McDowell, J.	x	x	x	x	x	x	x	x	0	x	x	x	x	x	x	x	x	x	x	x	x	x	x	x	x	x	x	x	x	0–27
4	R	Stanford, R.	x	x	x	x	x	x	x	x	x	0	*	x	x	x	x	x	x	x	x	x	x	x	x	x	x	x	x	x	x	2–26
3	R	Williams, R.	x	x	x	x	x	x	*	x	0	0	x	x	x	x	x	x	x	x	x	x	*	x	x	x	x	x	x	x	x	2–24
Pa. 10	R	Bard, D.	x	x	x	x	x	x	x	x	x	x	x	x	x	x	x	x	x	x	x	x	x	x	x	x	x	x	x	x	x	1–27
4	F	Sitgreaves, S.[10]	*	*	*	*	*	*	*	0	*	*	*	*	*	*	*	*	*	*	*	*	*	*	*	*	*	*	*	*	*	25–0
4	F	Chapman, J.	x	*	x	x	x	x	x	x	0	0	x	x	x	x	x	0	x	x	x	0	x	0	x	x	x	x	x	x	x	17–4
12	R	Gallatin, A.	x	x	x	x	x	x	x	x	x	x	x	x	x	x	x	x	x	x	x	x	x	x	x	x	x	x	x	x	x	1–27
11	R	Findley, W.	x	x	x	*	x	x	x	x	x	0	*	x	x	x	x	x	x	x	x	0	x	0	x	x	x	x	x	x	x	1–16
9	R	Gregg, A.	x	x	x	x	x	x	x	x	x	0	0	x	x	x	x	x	x	x	x	0	x	0	x	*	x	x	x	x	x	2–22
6	R	Hanna, J.	0	*	x	x	0	0	x	0	0	0	x	0	x	x	x	x	x	x	x	x	x	x	*	0	x	x	x	x	x	6–16
8	F	Hartley, T.	0	*	*	0	0	x	*	*	*	*	x	x	x	x	x	*	*	x	*	*	*	*	*	*	*	*	*	*	*	20–0
5	R	Hiester, J.[11]	x	0	*	x	x	0	0	0	*	0	x	x	x	x	x	x	x	x	x	0	x	0	x	0	x	x	x	x	x	1–24
7	F	Kittera, J.	0	0	*	0	0	0	*	0	*	*	x	x	x	x	x	*	*	x	*	*	x	*	x	*	x	*	*	x	*	16–0
2	R	McClenachan,[F]B.	x	x	x	x	x	x	x	x	x	x	x	x	x	x	x	x	x	0	0	0	x	x	0	0	x	x	x	x	x	0–28
1	R	Swanwick, J.[12]	0	0	0	0	0	0	0	0	*	0	0	0	0	0	0	0	0	0	0	0	0	0	0	0	0	0	0	0	0	0–0
3	F	Thomas, R.	0	x	0	x	x	0	*	x	x	x	*	0	0	*	*	*	*	*	*	*	*	*	*	*	*	*	*	*	*	22–0
R.I.	F	Champlin, C. G.	*	0	0	x	x	*	*	*	0	*	0	*	*	x	*	*	*	*	0	*	*	*	*	*	*	*	*	*	*	24–3
	R	Potter, E.[13]	0	0	0	0	0	x	0	0	0	*	0	0	0	0	0	0	0	0	0	0	0	0	0	0	0	0	0	0	0	0–0
	R	Tillinghast, T.[14]	*	x	*	x	x	x	x	x	x	x	x	x	x	x	x	x	x	x	*	*	*	x	*	x	*	*	0	*	x	19–9
S.C. Che.	R	Benton, L.	0	x	x	x	0	0	x	0	0	0	*	x	x	x	x	x	x	x	0	x	x	x	x	0	x	0	x	0	x	0–20
96	F	Harper, R.	*	*	*	*	*	*	x	x	*	*	*	x	*	*	*	x	x	x	*	*	*	*	*	*	x	*	*	*	x	24–4
Or.	F	Rutledge, J.	*	x	x	x	*	*	*	*	*	*	x	*	0	0	0	0	x	x	0	0	0	0	x	0	0	0	0	0	x	23–2
Ch.	F	Pinckney, T.	*	0	x	x	0	0	x	*	0	*	*	x	x	x	0	x	0	0	x	x	x	0	x	0	x	0	0	0	x	5–0
Wash.	R	Smith, W.	x	x	x	x	x	x	x	x	x	x	x	x	x	x	x	x	x	x	x	x	x	x	x	x	x	x	x	x	x	2–24
Ca.	R	Sumter, T.	x	x	x	x	x	x	x	x	x	x	x	x	x	x	x	x	x	x	x	x	x	x	x	x	x	x	x	x	x	0–28

State & Dist.	Party	Name	1	2	3	4	5	6	7	8	9	10	11	12	13	14	15	16	17	18	19	20	21	22	23	24	25	26	27	28	29	F–R
Tenn.	R	Claiborne, W.[15]	x	x	x	x	x	x	x	x	x	x	x	x	x	x	x	x	*	x	x	x	x	x	x	x	x	x	x	x	x	1–27
Vt. W.	R	Lyon, M.	x	0	0	*	*	x	x	x	x	x	x	x	x	x	0	0	0	*	x	0	0	x	x	x	x	x	x	0	x	0–25
Vt. E.	F	Morris, L.	*	x	*	*	*	*	*	*	*	*	*	*	*	*	*	*	*	*	*	*	*	*	*	*	*	*	*	0	0	24–0
Va. 17	R	Brent, R.	x	x	0	x	x	x	x	x	x	x	x	x	x	x	x	x	*	x	x	x	x	x	x	x	x	x	x	x	x	1–21
Va. 14	R	Cabell, S.	0	0	x	x	x	x	x	x	x	x	x	x	x	x	x	x	*	x	x	x	x	x	x	x	x	x	x	x	x	0–7
8	R	Claiborne, T.	x	x	0	x	x	x	x	x	x	x	x	x	x	x	x	x	*	x	x	x	x	x	x	x	x	x	x	x	x	3–24
6	R	Clay, M.	x	x	x	x	x	x	x	x	x	x	x	x	x	x	x	x	*	x	x	x	x	x	x	x	x	x	x	x	x	0–9
13	R	Clopton, J.	x	x	x	x	x	x	x	x	0	x	x	x	x	x	x	x	*	x	x	x	x	x	x	x	x	x	x	x	x	1–23
15	R	Dawson, J.	x	x	x	x	x	x	x	0	*	x	x	x	x	x	x	x	*	x	x	x	x	x	x	x	x	x	x	x	x	2–26
9	R	Giles, W.[16]	0	x	x	x	x	x	x	x	x	x	x	x	x	x	x	x	*	x	x	x	x	x	x	x	x	x	x	x	x	0–4
12	F	Evans, T.	*	*	*	*	*	*	*	*	*	0	0	0	0	0	0	0	*	0	0	0	0	0	0	0	0	0	0	0	0	23–3
10	R	Harrison, C.	x	x	x	x	x	*	x	x	x	x	x	x	x	x	x	x	*	x	x	x	x	x	x	x	x	x	x	x	x	2–26
2	R	Holmes, D.	x	x	x	x	x	x	x	x	x	x	x	0	0	0	0	0	*	x	x	x	x	x	x	x	x	x	x	x	x	5–23
19	R	Jones, W.	x	x	x	x	x	x	x	x	x	x	x	x	x	x	x	x	*	x	x	x	x	x	x	x	x	x	x	x	x	1–24
3	F	Machir, J.	x	x	x	*	0	0	0	0	0	0	0	0	0	0	0	0	*	0	0	0	x	x	x	x	x	x	x	x	x	16–4
1	F	Morgan, D.	*	0	0	0	0	*	*	*	0	0	*	*	0	*	*	*	0	*	0	0	0	0	0	0	0	0	0	0	0	15–0
16	R	New, A.	x	x	x	x	x	x	x	x	x	x	x	x	x	x	x	x	*	x	x	x	x	x	x	x	x	x	x	x	x	1–26
18	R	Nicholas, J.	x	x	x	x	x	x	x	x	x	x	x	x	0	0	0	0	*	0	x	x	x	x	x	x	x	x	x	x	x	0–12
11	F	Parker, J.	*	*	x	x	x	0	0	0	0	0	0	0	0	0	0	0	*	x	x	x	x	x	x	x	x	x	x	x	x	9–9
4	R	Trigg, A.	x	x	x	x	x	x	x	x	x	x	x	x	x	x	x	x	*	x	x	x	x	x	x	x	x	x	x	x	x	0–22
5	R	Trigg, J.	x	x	x	x	x	x	x	x	x	x	x	x	x	x	x	x	*	x	x	x	x	x	x	x	x	x	x	x	x	1–26
7	R	Venable, A.	x	x	x	x	x	x	x	x	x	x	x	x	x	x	x	x	*	x	x	x	x	x	x	x	x	x	x	x	x	1–24

(17)

NOTES: [1] d. 9-5-98.   [2] s. 11-13-99.   [3] s. 11-27-97.

[4] Lyman came in after the roll call and requested to be recorded in the negative. This was not granted. However, as his intention is clear, on the chart this is counted as though he had voted.

[5] With the election of Theodore Sedgwick to the Senate, T. J. Skinner ran against Ephraim Williams and one other candidate. Skinner campaigned as a moderate Federalist in his race against the more orthodox candidate. He is not classified here as a Federalist because he defeated the regular candidate and his program was republican—nor is he classified as a republican. Cf. *Hampshire Gazette*, October 2, 1796.

[6] r. 7-26-97.   [7] s. 12-15-97.   [8] d. 6-4-98.   [9] s. 12-10-98.   [10] Resigned at the close of the second session.

[11] s. 12-1-97.   [12] d. 8-1-98.   [13] Resigned at the close of the first session.   [14] s. 11-13-97.

[15] s. 11-27-97.   [16] r. 10-98.   [17] Call for X Y Z papers, not a direct party vote; consequently omitted from summary.

TABLE 17

SUMMARY OF REGULAR PARTY MEMBERS AND MODERATES, BY STATES, FIFTH CONGRESS, 2ND SESSION

1	2	3		4	5	6	7	8	9	10
Seats	State	Party electing		F	FM	F(ex R)	R	RM	R(ex F)	Absent
		F	R							
7	Conn.	7		7						
1	Del.	1		1						
2	Ga.		2				2			
2	Ky.		2				1	1		
8	Md.	6	2	5	1		1	1		
14	Mass. (1̇)	11	2	10	1		2	1		
4	N. H.	4		3	1					
5	N. J.	5		5						
10	N. Y.	6	4	5	1		4			
10	N. C.	1	9		1		9			
13	Penn.	5	8	5			6	1		1
2	R. I.	1	1	1				1		
6	S. C.	3	3	3			3			
1	Tenn.		1				1			
2	Vt.	1	1	1			1			
19	Va.	4	15	2	2		15			
106	(1̇)	55	50	48	7		45	5		1

LEGEND TO VOTE CHART NO. V

House, Fifth Congress, 3rd Session, Jan. 1799-March 1799.

Votes Charted

1. To recommit Logan Act, Yeas (R) 49; Nays (F) 44, Jan. 11, 1799. 9 *Annals*, 2648. *House Journal*, 5th Congress, 430-431.

2. To postpone Bankruptcy Bill, Yeas (F) 44; Nays (R) 47, Jan. 15, 1799. *Ibid.*, 2676. *House Journal*, 5th Congress, 433-434.

3. Logan Act, Yeas (F) 58; Nays (R) 36, Jan. 17, 1799. *Ibid.*, 2721. *House Journal*, 5th Congress, 439-440.

4. To exempt Mississippi from restrictions on commercial intercourse, Yeas (R) 55; Nays (F) 34, Jan. 25, 1799. *Ibid.*, 2790. *House Journal*, 5th Congress, 449-450.

5. Further suspension of commercial intercourse with France, Yeas (F) 55; Nays (R) 37, Jan. 28, 1799. *Ibid.*, 2791. *House Journal*, 5th Congress, 451-452.

6. Four per cent stamp tax, Yeas (F) 49; Nays (R) 40, Jan. 31, 1799. *Ibid.*, 2814. *House Journal*, 5th Congress, 458-459.

7. Increase of navy, Yeas (F) 54; Nays (R) 42, Feb. 11, 1799. *Ibid.*, 2883. *House Journal*, 5th Congress, 470-471.

8. Call for papers on relations with France, Yeas 52; Nays 38 (Not a party vote), Feb. 14, 1799. *Ibid.*, 2915. *House Journal*, 5th Congress, 476-477.

9. To reject bill for bounty on captured guns, Yeas (R) 52; Nays (F) 48, Feb. 20, 1799. *Ibid.*, 2953. *House Journal*, 5th Congress, 487-488.

10. Expelling Matthew Lyon, Yeas (F) 49; Nays (R) 45, Feb. 22, 1799. *Ibid.*, 2993. *House Journal*, 5th Congress, 487-488.

11. Approval of Report on Alien and Sedition Laws, Yeas (F) 52; Nays (R) 48, Feb. 25, 1799. *Ibid.*, 3016. *House Journal*, 5th Congress, 493-494.

12. Salary increases, Yeas (F) 52; Nays (R) 40, Feb. 27, 1799. *Ibid.*, 3020. *House Journal*, 5th Congress, 500-501.

13. Army increase, Yeas (F) 54; Nays (R) 41, March 1, 1799. *Ibid.*, 3044. *House Journal*, 5th Congress, 509-510.

14. Not to confine service for volunteers to one state, Yeas (R) 51; Nays (F) 44, March 1, 1799. *Ibid.*, 3042. *House Journal*, 5th Congress, 507, 508.

VOTE CHART No. V
FIFTH CONGRESS, THIRD SESSION

State & Dist.		Party	Name	1	2	3	4	5	6	7	8²	9	10	11	12	13	14	F²−R²	F³−R³
Conn.		F	Allen, J.	*	*	*	x	*	*	*	*	x	*	*	*	*	*	12−1	56−1
		F	Coit, J.	0	0	0	0	0	0	0	0	0	0	0	0	0	0	0−0	28−17
		F	Brace, J.	*	*	*	x	*	*	*	*	*	*	*	*	*	*	12−1	12−1
		F	Dana, S.	*	*	*	0	0	0	*	*	*	*	*	*	*	*	10−0	53−2
		F	Smith, N.	*	x	*	0	0	0	0	*	*	*	*	*	*	*	8−1	50−4
		F	Davenport, J.	0	0	0	0	0	0	0	0	0	0	0	0	0	0	0−0	16−0
		F	Edmond, W.	*	*	*	*	*	*	*	*	*	*	*	*	*	*	13−0	31−0
		F	Goodrich, C.	*	*	*	*	*	*	*	*	*	*	*	*	*	*	13−0	58−1
		F	Griswold, R.	*	*	*	*	*	*	*	*	*	*	*	*	*	*	13−0	53−4
Del.		F	Bayard, J.	*	*	*	0	*	*	*	*	x	*	*	*	*	*	12−0	53−0
Ga.		R	Baldwin, A.	x	x	x	x	x	x	x	x	x	x	x	x	x	x	0−13	6−53
		R	Milledge, J.	0	0	0	0	0	0	0	0	0	0	0	0	0	0	0−0	8−32
Ky.		R	Davis, T.	x	0	*	0	x	0	x	0	x	x	x	x	0	0	1−7	10−39
		R	Fowler, J.	0	0	0	0	0	0	x	x	x	x	x	x	x	x	0−7	3−46
Md.	4	F	Baer, G.	x	x	*	x	*	0	*	x	x	x	*	0	*	x	5−6	42−11
	3	F	Craik, Wm.	*	*	*	*	*	*	*	*	*	*	*	*	*	*	13−0	56−1
	8	F	Dennis, J.	*	*	*	x	*	*	*	*	*	*	*	*	*	*	12−1	44−6
	1	F	Dent, G.	x	*	*	x	*	*	*	*	x	x	x	*	*	x	7−6	33−24
	7	F	Hindman, W.	*	*	*	*	*	*	*	*	*	*	*	*	*	*	13−0	59−0
	6	F	Matthews, W.	x	*	*	x	*	x	*	x	*	*	*	*	*	x	9−4	45−10
	5	R	Smith, S.	x	*	*	x	*	*	*	x	x	x	x	*	*	x	7−6	17−28
	2	R	Sprigg, R.	x	x	x	x	x	*	x	x	x	x	x	x	x	x	1−12	2−54
Mass.	4M	F	Bartlett, B.	x	*	*	x	*	*	*	*	*	*	*	*	*	*	11−2	38−3
	4M	F	Bradbury, T.	0	0	0	0	0	0	0	0	0	0	0	0	0	0	0−0	16−0
	3S	F	Bullock, S.	*	x	*	x	*	*	*	x	*	0	*	*	*	*	10−2	30−13
	4W	F	Foster, D.	*	x	*	*	*	*	*	*	*	*	*	*	*	*	12−1	54−4
	1S	R	Freeman, N.	x	0	*	0	*	*	0	x	x	x	x	*	0	0	4−4	10−23
	3W	F	Lyman, S.	*	x	*	*	*	*	*	*	*	*	*	*	*	*	12−1	53−5
	1M	F	Otis, H. G.	*	*	*	*	*	*	*	*	*	*	*	*	*	*	13−0	56−2
	1E	F	Parker, I.	*	*	*	*	*	*	*	*	*	*	*	*	*	*	13−0	27−0
	2S	F	Reed, J.	*	x	*	x	*	0	*	*	*	0	*	*	*	*	9−2	44−12
	3M	F	Sewall, S.	*	*	*	*	*	*	*	*	*	*	*	*	*	*	13−0	57−2
	2W	F	Shepard, W.	*	*	*	*	*	*	*	0	*	*	*	*	*	*	13−0	52−4
	1W	(1)	Skinner, T. J.	x	x	x	x	x	x	x	x	x	x	x	x	x	x	0−13	3−45
	3E	F	Thatcher, G.	*	*	*	*	*	*	*	*	*	*	*	*	*	*	13−0	58−0
	2M	R	Varnum, J. B.	x	x	x	x	x	x	x	x	x	x	x	x	x	x	0−13	2−57
	2E	F	Wadsworth, P.	*	*	*	*	*	*	*	0	*	0	*	*	*	*	12−0	56−0
N. H.		F	Foster, A.	*	*	*	*	*	*	*	*	*	*	*	*	*	*	13−0	59−0
		F	Freeman, J.	*	x	*	x	*	*	*	*	*	*	*	*	*	*	11−2	50−3
		F	Gordon, W.	*	x	*	*	0	*	*	*	*	*	*	*	*	*	11−1	42−3
		F	Smith, J.	0	0	0	0	0	0	0	0	0	0	0	0	0	0	0−0	15−1
		F	Sprague, P.	*	x	*	*	*	*	*	*	x	*	*	x	*	x	9−4	21−7
State & Dist.		Party	Name	1	2	3	4	5	6	7	8²	9	10	11	12	13	14	F²−R²	F³−R³

VOTE CHART No. V—Continued

State & Dist.	Party	Name	1	2	3	4	5	6	7	8²	9	10	11	12	13	14	F^2-R^2	F^3-R^3
N. J.	F	Dayton, J.	0	0	0	0	0	0	0	0	0	0	0	0	0	0	0−0	2−0
	F	Imlay, J. H.	*	*	*	*	*	*	*	*	*	*	*	*	*	*	13−0	57−0
	F	Schureman, J.	*	*	*	*	*	*	*	x	*	*	*	*	*	x	12−1	50−6
	F	Sinnickson, T.	*	*	*	*	*	*	*	*	*	*	*	*	*	x	12−1	53−2
	F	Thomson, M.	*	x	*	x	*	x	0	0	*	*	*	*	*	*	9−3	50−5
N. Y. 5	F	Brooks, D.	*	*	*	*	*	*	*	*	*	*	*	*	*	*	13−0	57−1
10	F	Cochran, J.	*	*	*	*	*	*	*	*	*	*	*	*	*	*	13−0	49−1
4	R	Elmendorf, L.	x	x	x	x	x	x	x	x	x	x	x	x	x	x	0−13	1−49
8	F	Glen, H.	*	*	*	*	*	*	*	*	*	*	*	*	*	*	13−0	57−1
2	R	Havens, J.	x	x	x	x	x	x	x	x	x	x	x	x	x	x	0−13	0−59
6	F	Hosmer, H.	*	*	*	*	*	*	*	*	*	*	*	*	*	*	13−0	58−0
1	R	Livingston, E.	0	*	x	x	x	x	x	x	x	x	x	*	x	x	2−10	6−30
7	F	Van Alen, J.	*	*	*	*	*	*	0	*	*	*	*	*	*		13−0	58−1
3	R	Van Cortlandt, P.	0	0	0	0	x	0	x	0	x	x	x	0	x	x	0−7	2−46
9	F	Williams, J.	*	x	*	*	*	*	*	*	*	*	*	0	*	*	11−1	37−14
N. C. 9	R	Blount, T.	x	x	x	x	x	x	x	0	0	0	x	0	x	x	0−10	1−54
10	R	Bryan, N.	0	0	0	0	0	0	0	0	0	0	0	0	0	0	0−0	2−33
10	F	Spaight, R.	x	0	*	x	*	x	*	x	x	0	0	*	*	x	5−5	5−5
8	R	Burges, D.	0	0	0	0	0	0	0	0	0	0	0	0	0	0	0−0	4−34
6	R	Gillespie, J.	x	*	x	x	x	x	x	x	x	x	x	x	x	x	1−12	6−50
7	F	Grove, Wm.	x	x	*	*	*	*	*	x	x	*	*	*	*	*	10−3	38−17
2	R	Locke, M.	x	x	x	x	x	x	x	x	x	x	x	x	x	x	0−13	0−57
5	R	Macon, N.	x	x	x	x	x	x	x	x	x	x	x	x	x	x	0−13	0−59
1	R	McDowell, J.	x	x	x	x	0	x	x	x	x	x	x	x	x	x	0−12	0−57
4	R	Stanford, R.	x	x	x	0	0	x	x	x	x	x	x	x	x	x	0−11	3−54
3	R	Williams, R.	x	x	0	x	*	x	x	x	x	x	x	x	0	0	1−9	5−49
Pa. 10	R	Bard, D.	x	x	x	x	x	x	x	x	x	x	x	x	x	x	0−13	2−56
4	R	Brown, R.	x	x	x	x	x	x	x	x	x	x	x	x	x	x	0−13	0−13
4	F	Sitgreaves, S.	0	0	0	0	0	0	0	0	0	0	0	0	0	0	0−0	41−1
4	F	Chapman, J.	*	*	*	x	*	0	0	x	x	*	*	x	0	0	6−3	31−12
12	R	Gallatin, A.	x	x	x	x	x	x	x	x	x	x	x	x	x	x	0−13	4−55
11	R	Findley, W.	x	x	x	x	x	x	x	x	x	x	x	0	x	x	0−12	3−35
9	R	Gregg, A.	x	x	x	x	x	x	x	x	x	x	x	x	x	x	0−13	2−50
6	R	Hanna, J.	x	*	x	x	x	x	x	x	x	x	x	x	x	x	1−12	11−41
8	F	Hartley, T.	0	0	0	*	*	*	*	0	*	*	*	*	*	*	10−0	45−2
5	F	Ege, G.	0	0	0	0	0	0	0	0	0	0	0	0	0	0	0−0	10−2
5	R	Hiester, J.	0	x	x	x	x	x	x	x	x	x	x	x	x	x	0−12	1−36
7	F	Kittera, J.	*	*	*	*	*	*	*	*	*	*	0	0	*	*	11−0	39−4
2	R	McClenachan, B.	x	*	x	0	0	0	x	x	x	x	x	x	x	x	1−9	2−53
1	R	Swanwick, J.	0	0	0	0	0	0	0	0	0	0	0	0	0	0	0−0	2−14
1	F	Waln, R.	*	*	*	*	*	*	*	*	*	*	*	*	*	*	13−0	13−0
3	F	Thomas, R.	*	*	*	*	0	*	*	*	*	*	*	*	*	*	12−0	49−2
R. I.	F	Champlin, C. G.	*	*	*	*	*	*	*	*	*	*	*	*	*	*	13−0	54−4
		Potter, E.	0	0	0	0	0	0	0	0	0	0	0	0	0	0	0−0	11−7
	R	Tillinghast, T.	0	0	*	x	*	x	*	*	*	*	*	0	*	x	7−3	26−12

State & Dist.	Party	Name	1	2	3	4	5	6	7	8²	9	10	11	12	13	14	F^2-R^2	F^3-R^3

VOTE CHART No. V—Continued

State & Dist.	Party	Name	1	2	3	4	5	6	7	8²	9	10	11	12	13	14	F²−R²	F³−R³
S. C. Che.	R	Benton, L.	0	0	0	0	0	0	0	0	0	0	0	0	0	0	0−0	0−24
96	F	Harper, R.	x	*	*	*	*	*	*	x	*	*	*	*	*	*	12−1	50−7
Or.	F	Rutledge, J.	*	*	*	*	*	*	*	*	*	*	*	*	0	0	11−0	48−4
Ch.	F	Smith, Wm.	0	0	0	0	0	0	0	0	0	0	0	0	0	0	0−0	18−0
Ch.	F	Pinckney, T.	*	*	*	x	*	*	*	x	*	*	*	*	*	*	12−1	17−1
Wash.	R	Smith, W.	x	x	x	x	x	x	x	x	x	x	x	x	x	x	0−13	4−53
Ca.	R	Sumter, Th.	0	0	0	0	0	x	x	x	x	x	x	x	x	x	0−8	0−53
Tenn.	R	Claiborne, Wm.	x	x	x	x	x	x	x	x	x	x	x	0	x	x	0−12	1−39
Vt. W.	R	Lyon, M.	0	0	0	0	0	0	0	0	x	0	x	x	x	x	0−5	0−48
E.	F	Morris, L.	*	*	*	*	*	*	*	*	*	*	*	*	*	*	13−0	41−0
Va. 17	R	Brent, R.	x	0	x	0	x	0	x	0	x	0	x	0	x	x	0−8	1−45
14	R	Cabell, S.	0	x	0	x	x	x	x	x	x	x	x	x	x	x	0−11	1−35
8	R	Claiborne, T.	x	x	x	x	x	x	x	x	x	x	x	x	x	x	0−13	3−55
6	R	Clay, M.	x	x	x	x	x	x	0	x	x	x	x	x	x	x	0−12	2−37
13	R	Clopton, J.	x	x	x	x	x	x	x	x	x	x	x	x	x	x	0−13	2−53
15	R	Dawson, J.	x	x	x	x	x	x	x	x	x	x	x	x	x	x	0−13	2−57
9	R	Giles, W.	0	0	0	0	0	0	0	0	0	0	0	0	0	0	0−0	0−18
9	R	Eggleston, J.	x	x	x	x	x	x	x	x	x	x	x	x	x	x	0−13	0−13
12	F	Evans, T.	x	*	*	x	*	*	*	*	*	*	*	*	*	*	11−2	47−10
10	R	Harrison, C.	x	x	x	x	x	x	x	x	x	x	x	x	x	x	0−13	5−51
2	R	Holmes, D.	x	x	x	x	x	x	x	x	x	x	x	x	x	x	0−13	10−49
19	R	Jones, W.	x	x	x	x	x	0	x	0	x	x	x	x	x	x	0−12	2−53
3	F	Machir, J.	x	*	*	x	*	*	*	*	*	*	*	*	*	*	11−2	40−10
1	F	Morgan, D.	*	0	*	x	*	*	*	0	0	0	*	0	0	0	6−1	32−7
16	R	New, A.	x	x	x	x	x	0	x	x	x	x	x	x	x	x	0−12	1−56
18	R	Nicholas, J.	x	x	x	x	x	x	x	x	x	x	x	x	0	0	0−11	3−38
11	F	Parker, J.	x	x	*	x	*	x	*	x	x	*	x	*	*	x	6−7	20−27
4	R	Trigg, A.	x	x	x	0	x	x	x	x	x	x	x	x	x	x	0−12	2−49
5	R	Trigg, J.	x	x	0	x	x	x	x	x	x	x	x	x	x	x	0−12	1−54
7	R	Venable, A.	x	x	x	x	x	x	x	x	x	x	x	x	x	x	0−13	1−54
State & Dist.	Party	Name	1	2	3	4	5	6	7	8²	9	10	11	12	13	14	F²−R²	F³−R³

[1] With the election of Theodore Sedgwick to the Senate, T. J. Skinner ran against Ephrain Williams and one other candidate. Skinner campaigned as a moderate Federalist in his race against the more orthodox candidate. He is not classified here as a Federalist because he defeated the regular candidate and his program was republican—nor is he classified as a republican. Cf. *Hampshire Gazette*, October 2, 1796.

[2] Call for papers in relation to France; not a direct party vote so this vote is omitted from summary. These columns summarize vote for third session of Fifth Congress only.

[3] Summary of vote on all three sessions of Fifth Congress.

TABLE 18

Summary of Regular Party Members and Moderates, by States, Fifth Congress, 3rd Session

1	2	3		4	5	6	7	8	9	10
		Party electing		F	FM	F(ex R)	R	RM	R(ex F)	Absent
Seats	State	F	R							
7	Conn.	7	0	7						
1	Del.	1	0	1						
2	Ga.	0	2				2			
8	Md.	6	2	3	3		1	1		
14	Mass. (1)?	11	2	11			1	1	1	
4	N. H.	4	0	3	1					
5	N. J.	5	0	3	1					Speaker did not vote
10	N. Y.	6	4	6			4			
10	N. C.	2	8		2		7			1
13	Penn.	5	8	4	1		8			
2	R. I.	1	1	1				1		
6	S. C.	3	3	3			2			1
1	Tenn.	0	1				1			
2	Vt.	1	1	1			1			
19	Va.	4	15	3	1		15			
106	(1)?	56	49	46	9		44	3	1	2

TABLE 19

SUMMARY OF REGULAR PARTY MEMBERS AND MODERATES, BY STATES, FIFTH CONGRESS, 1ST, 2ND, AND 3RD SESSIONS

1	2	3		4	5	6	7	8	9	10
Seats	State	Party electing		F	FM	F(ex R)	R	RM	R(ex F)	Absent
		F	R							
7	Conn.	7	0	6	1					
1	Del.	1	0	1						
2	Ga.	0	2				1	1		
2	Ky.	0	2				1	1		
8	Md.	6	2	4	2		1	1		
14	Mass. (1)?	11	2	9	2		2	1		
4	N. H.	4	0	4						
5	N. J.	5	0	5						
10	N. Y.	6	4	5	1		4			
10	N. C.	1	9		1		9			
13	Penn.	6	7	3	3		5	2		
2	R. I.	1	1	1				1		
6	S. C.	3	3	3			3			
1	Tenn.	0	1				1			
2	Vt.	1	1	1			1			
19	Va.	4	15	2	2		15			
106	(1)?	56	49	44	12		43	7		

LEGEND TO VOTE CHART, NO. VI

House, Sixth Congress, 1st Session, Jan.-May, 1800.

1. To disagree to reduce army, Yeas (F) 60; Nays (R) 39, Jan. 10, 1800. 10 *Annals*, 369. *House Journal*, 6th Congress, 556-557.

2. To discharge part of officers, Yeas (R) 38 (only 37 names listed in *Annals*); Nays (F) 57, Jan. 23, 1800. *Ibid.*, 403. *House Journal*, 6th Congress, 565-566.

3. Bayard Amendment to repeal the Alien and Sedition Laws, Yeas (F) 51; Nays (R) 47, Jan. 23, 1800. *Ibid.*, 423. *House Journal*, 6th Congress, 567-568.

4. Bankruptcy Act, Yeas (F) 48; Nays (R) 48, carried by speaker, Feb. 21, 1800. *Ibid.*, 504. *House Journal*, 6th Congress, 599.

5. Postponement of Judiciary Act, Yeas (R) 48; Nays (F) 46, April 14, 1800. *Ibid.*, 606. *House Journal*, 6th Congress, 663.

6. Territorial governor to have power to prorogue legislature, Yeas (F) 42; Nays (R) 49, April 24, 1800. *Ibid.*, 682. *House Journal*, 6th Congress, 680-681.

7. Pasage of House Disputed Elections Bill, Yeas (F) 52; Nays (R) 37, May 2, 1800. *Ibid.*, 647. *House Journal*, 6th Congress, 692-693.

VOTE CHART No. VI
SIXTH CONGRESS, FIRST SESSION

State & Dist.		Party	Name & Date of Service	1	2	3	4	5	6	7	F — R
Conn.		F	Brace, J. (R-in-1800)	*	*	*	*	*	*	*	7 — 0
		F	Smith, J. C. (S-11-17-1800)	0	0	0	0	0	0	0	0 — 0
		F	Dana, S. W.	*	*	*	*	*	*	*	7 — 0
		F	Davenport, J.	*	*	*	0	x	*	*	5 — 1
		F	Edmond, W.	*	*	*	*	*	*	*	7 — 0
		F	Goodrich, C.	*	*	*	*	*	*	*	7 — 0
		F	Goodrich, E.	*	*	*	*	*	*	*	7 — 0
		F	Griswold, R.	*	*	*	*	*	*	*	7 — 0
Del.		F	Bayard, J.	*	*	*	*	*	*	*	7 — 0
Ga.		F	Jones, J.	x	x	x	x	x	x	x	0 — 7
		F	Taliaferro, B.	*	*	x	x	x	x	0	2 — 4
Ky.		R	Davis, T. T.	x	x	x	x	x	x	*	1 — 6
		R	Fowler, J.	x	x	x	x	x	x	0	0 — 6
Md.	4	F	Baer, G.	*	*	*	*	*	*	*	7 — 0
	6	R	Christie, G.	x	x	x	x	x	0	x	0 — 6
	3	F	Craik, W.	0	*	*	*	0	0	0	3 — 0
	1	F	Dent, G.	*	*	x	*	x	x	*	4 — 3
	8	F	Dennis, J.	*	*	*	0	*	x	*	5 — 1
	7	R	Nicholson, J.	x	x	x	0	x	x	0	0 — 5
	5	R	Smith, S.	*	*	x	*	x	0	*	4 — 2
	2	F	Thomas, J.	*	*	*	*	*	*	*	7 — 0
Mass.	4M	F	Bartlett, B.	*	*	*	*	*	*	*	7 — 0
	3S	R	Bishop, P.	x	x	x	x	x	x	x	0 — 7
	4W	F	Foster, D. (R-6-6-00)	*	0	0	x	x	*	*	3 — 2
	1E	F	Lee, S.	*	*	*	*	*	*	*	7 — 0
	3W	F	Lyman, S. (R-11-6-00)	*	*	*	x	*	*	*	6 — 1
	3W	F	Mattoon, E. (S-2-2-01)	0	0	0	0	0	0	0	0 — 0
	1M	F	Otis, H.	*	*	*	*	0	0	0	4 — 0
	3M	F	Read, N. (S-11-25-00)	0	0	0	0	0	0	0	0 — 0
	2S	F	Reed, J.	*	*	*	*	*	*	*	7 — 0
	1W	F	Sedgwick, T.	0	0	0	*	0	0	0	1 — 0
	3M	F	Sewall, S. (R-1-10-00)	*	*	*	*	*	*	*	7 — 0
	2W	F	Shepard, W.	*	*	*	*	x	*	*	6 — 1
	3E	F	Thatcher, G.	*	*	*	*	*	*	*	7 — 0
	2M	R	Varnum, J. B.	x	0	x	x	x	x	*	1 — 5
	2E	F	Wadsworth, P.	*	*	*	*	*	*	*	7 — 0
	1S	F	Williams, L.	*	*	*	*	*	*	*	7 — 0
N. H.		F	Sheafe, J.	*	*	*	*	*	*	*	7 — 0
		F	Freeman, J.	*	*	*	0	x	*	*	5 — 1
		F	Foster, A.	*	*	*	*	*	*	*	7 — 0
		F	Gordon, W. (R-6-12-00)	*	*	*	*	0	0	0	4 — 0
N. J.	E	R	Condit, J.	x	x	x	x	0	x	x	0 — 6
	S	F	Davenport, F.	*	*	*	*	*	*	*	7 — 0
State & Dist.		Party	Name & Date of Service	1	2	3	4	5	6	7	F — R

VOTE CHART No. VI—Continued

State & Dist.		Party	Name & Date of Service	1	2	3	4	5	6	7	F−R
	M.	F	Imlay, J.	*	*	*	*	*	*	*	7−0
	N.	R	Kitchell, A.	x	x	x	x	x	x	x	0−7
	W.	R	Linn, J.	*	x	x	x	x	x	x	1−6
N. Y.	5	R	Bailey, T.	x	x	x	x	x	x	x	0−7
	6	F	Bird, J.	*	*	*	*	0	0	0	4−0
	10	F	Cooper, Wm.	*	*	*	*	*	*	0	6−0
	4	R	Elmendorf, L. C.	x	x	x	x	x	x	x	0−7
	8	F	Glen, H.	*	*	*	*	*	*	*	7−0
	1	R	Havens, J. (D-10-25-99)	0	0	0	0	0	0	0	0−0
	1	R	Smith, J.	0	0	0	0	x	x	x	0−3
	2	R	Livingston, E.	0	0	0	*	0	0	0	1−0
	9	F	Platt, J.	*	*	*	0	*	*	*	6−0
	7	R	Thompson, J.	x	x	x	x	x	x	x	0−7
	3	R	Van Cortlandt, P.	x	x	x	x	0	0	0	0−4
N. C.	9	F	Alston, W.	*	*	x	x	x	x	x	2−5
	1	F	Dickson, J.	*	*	*	*	*	x	*	6−1
	7	F	Grove, W. B.	*	0	0	x	*	0	*	3−1
	2	F	Henderson, A.	*	0	x	*	*	0	0	3−1
	6	F	Hill, W. H.	*	*	*	x	*	x	*	5−2
	5	R	Macon, N.	x	x	x	x	x	x	x	0−7
	10	R	Spaight, R. D.	0	0	0	x	x	0	0	0−2
	4	R	Stanford, R.	x	x	x	x	x	x	x	0−7
	8	R	Stone, D.	x	0	x	x	x	x	x	0−6
	3	R	Williams, R.	x	x	x	x	x	x	x	0−7
Pa.	4	R	Brown, R.	*	x	x	x	x	x	x	1−6
	12	R	Gallatin, A.	x	x	x	x	x	x	x	0−7
	9	R	Gregg, A.	x	x	x	*	x	x	x	0−7
	6	R	Hanna, J. A.	x	x	x	x	0	x	x	0−6
	8	F	Hartley, T. (D-12-21-00)	*	*	x	*	x	x	x	3−4
	5	R	Hiester, J.	x	x	x	x	0	x	x	0−6
	7	F	Kittera, J. W.	*	*	*	*	0	0	0	4−0
	2	R	Leib, M.	x	x	x	x	x	x	x	0−7
	4	R	Muhlenberg, P.	x	x	x	x	x	x	x	0−7
	11	R	Smilie, J.	x	x	x	x	x	x	x	0−7
	3	F	Thomas, R.	*	*	*	*	*	*	*	7−0
	1	F	Waln, R.	*	*	*	*	*	*	*	7−0
	10	F	Woods, H.	*	*	*	*	*	*	*	7−0
R. I.		F	Brown, J.	x	*	*	*	*	*	*	6−1
		F	Champlin, C.	*	*	*	*	*	*	*	7−0
S. C.	96	F	Harper, R. G.	*	*	*	*	*	*	*	7−0
	Che.	F	Huger, B.	*	*	*	0	*	x	*	5−1
	Wash.	F	Nott, A.	*	*	*	*	*	x	*	6−1
	Ch.	F	Pinckney, T.	0	0	0	*	*	*	*	4−0
	Or.	F	Rutledge, J.	*	*	*	*	*	*	*	7−0
	Ca.	R	Sumter, T.	x	x	x	x	x	0	0	0−5
State & Dist.		Party	Name & Date of Service	1	2	3	4	5	6	7	F−R

VOTE CHART No. VI—Continued

State & Dist.		Party	Name & Date of Service	1	2	3	4	5	6	7	F−R
Tenn.		R	Claiborne, W. C.	x	x	x	0	x	x	x	0−6
Vt.	W.	R.	Lyon, M.	x	0	x	x	x	x	0	0−5
	E.	F.	Morris, L. R.	*	*	*	*	*	*	*	7−0
Va.	14	R	Cabell, S. J.	0	x	x	x	x	x	x	0−6
	6	R	Clay, M.	x	0	0	x	x	x	x	0−5
	15	R	Dawson, J.	x	x	x	x	x	x	x	0−7
	9	R	Eggleston, J.	x	x	x	x	x	x	x	0−7
	12	F	Evans, T.	*	*	*	*	*	*	*	7−0
	8	F	Goode, S.	*	x	x	x	0	0	0	1−3
	10	F	Gray, E.	x	*'	*	x	x	x	x	2−5
	2	R	Holmes, D.	x	x	x	x	x	x	x	0−7
	3	R	Jackson, G.	x	x	x	x	x	x	x	0−7
	19	F	Lee, H.	*	*	*	*	*	*	*	7−0
	13	F	Marshall, J. (R-6-7-00)	*	*	x	*	*	*	*	6−1
	13	R	Tazewell, L. W. (S-11-26-00)	0	0	0	0	0	0	0	0−0
	16	R	New, A.	x	x	x	x	x	x	x	0−7
	18	R	Nicholas, J.	x	x	x	x	x	x	x	0−7
	1	F	Page, R.	*	*	*	x	*	*	*	6−1
	11	F	Parker, J.	*	*	*	0	*	x	*	5−1
	17	F	Powell, L.	*	*	*	*	*	*	*	7−0
	7	R	Randolph, J.	x	x	x	x	x	x	x	0−7
	4	R	Trigg, A.	x	x	x	x	x	x	x	0−7
	5	R	Trigg, J.	x	x	x	x	x	x	x	0−7
State & Dist.		Party	Name & Date of Service	1	2	3	4	5	6	7	F−R

TABLE 20

SUMMARY OF REGULAR PARTY MEMBERS AND MODERATES, BY STATES,
SIXTH CONGRESS, 1ST SESSION

1	2	3		4	5	6	7	8	9	10
Seats	State	Party electing		F	FM	F(ex R)	R	RM	R(ex F)	Absent
		F	R							
7	Conn.	7		7						
1	Del.	1		1						
2	Ga.	2			1				1	
2	Ky.		2				2			
8	Md.	5	3	4	1		2	1		
14	Mass.	12	2	11	1		2			
4	N. H.	4		4						
5	N. J.	2	3	2			3			
10	N. Y.	4	6	4			5			1
10	N. C.	5	5	1	4		5			
13	Penn.	5	8	4	1		8			
2	R. I.	2		2						
6	S. C.	5	1	5			1			
1	Tenn.		1				1			
2	Vt.	1	1	1			1			
19	Va.	8	11	6	2		11			
106		63	43	52	10		41	1	1	1

LEGEND TO VOTE CHART NO. VII

House, Sixth Congress, 2nd Session, Jan.-March, 1801.

1. Amendment to Judiciary Act, Yeas (R) 55; Nays (F) 35, Jan. 13, 1801. 10 *Annals*, 909. *House Journal*, 6th Congress, 760-761.

2. Duties on licenses, Yeas (F) 46; Nays (R) 31, Jan. 16, 1801. *Ibid.*, 911. *House Journal*, 6th Congress, 764.

3. Judiciary Bill, Yeas (F) 51; Nays (R) 43, Jan. 20, 1801. *Ibid.*, 915. *House Journal*, 6th Congress, 767-768.

4. Resolution to continue Sedition Act, Yeas (F) 48; Nays (R) 48, carried by chairman, Jan. 23, 1801. *Ibid.*, 975. *House Journal*, 6th Congress, 772-773.

5. Jefferson-Burr, vote was by states, but on most votes the totals were as given here, so far as the individual members were concerned. On the first ballot Jefferson received more votes from individual members than is represented here, Jefferson 51; Burr 52, Feb. 2-11, 1801. *Ibid.*, 1032. Also see *Gazette of U. S.*, Feb. 20, 1801. Votes for Jefferson are charted as Republican; those for Burr as Federalist.

6. To repeal certain sections of Sedition Act, first reading, Yeas (R) 50; Nays (F) 49, tied by chairman, Feb. 19, 1801. *Ibid.*, 1038. *House Journal*, 6th Congress, 808-809.

7. To repeal part of the Sedition Act but continue rest in force, Yeas (F) 49; Nays (R) 53, Feb. 22, 1801. *Ibid.*, 1049. *House Journal*, 6th Congress, 816-817.

8. To engross the Bankruptcy Act, Yeas (F) 49; Nays (R) 42, Feb. 27, 1801. *Ibid.*, 1061. *House Journal*, 6th Congress, 832-833.

9. To recommit the Bankruptcy Act for amendments, Yeas (R) 50; Nays (F) 42, Feb. 28, 1801. *Ibid.*, 1065. *House Journal*, 6th Congress, 833-834.

10. Vote of thanks to speaker, Yeas (F) 40; Nays (R) 35, March 3, 1801. *Ibid.*, 1079. *House Journal*, 6th Congress, 847.

VOTE CHART No. VII

SIXTH CONGRESS, SECOND SESSION

State & Dist.	Party	Name & Date of Service	1	2	3	4	5	6	7	8	9	10	F^1-R^1	F^2-R^2
Conn.	F	Brace, J. (R-1800)	0	0	0	0	0	0	0	0	0	0	0–0	7–0
	F	Smith, J. C. (S-11-17-00)	*	*	*	*	*	*	*	*	*	*	10–0	10–0
	F	Dana, S. W.	*	0	*	*	*	*	*	*	*	*	9–0	16–0
	F	Davenport, J.	*	*	*	*	*	*	*	*	*	*	10–0	15–1
	F	Edmond, W.	*	*	*	*	*	*	*	*	*	*	10–0	17–0
	F	Goodrich, C.	*	*	*	*	*	*	*	*	*	*	10–0	17–0
	F	Goodrich, E.	x	*	*	*	*	*	*	*	0	0	7–1	14–1
	F	Griswold, R.	*	*	*	*	*	*	*	*	*	*	10–0	17–0
Del.	F	Bayard, J.	*	0	*	*	*	0	*	*	*	*	8–0	15–0
Ga.	F	Jones, J.	0	0	0	0	0	0	0	0	0	0	0–0	0–7
	F	Taliaferro, B.	0	*	x	x	x	x	x	x	x	0	1–7	3–11
Ky.	R	Davis, T. T.	x	0	x	x	x	x	x	0	x	x	0–8	1–14
	R	Fowler, J.	0	0	0	0	x	0	x	x	x	x	0–5	0–11
Md. 4	F	Baer, G.	x	*	*	0	*	*	*	*	x	*	7–2	14–2
6	R	Christie, G.	x	0	x	x	x	x	x	0	x	x	0–8	0–14
3	F	Craik, W.	x	0	*	*	*	*	*	*	*	*	8–1	11–1
1	F	Dent, G.	x	*	x	x	x	x	x	*	x	x	2–8	6–11
8	F	Dennis, J.	x	*	*	*	*	*	*	*	*	*	9–1	14–2
7	R	Nicholson, J.	x	0	x	x	x	x	x	x	x	0	0–8	0–13
5	R	Smith, S.	x	x	x	x	x	x	x	*	x	x	1–9	5–11
2	F	Thomas, J.	x	*	*	*	*	*	*	*	*	*	9–1	16–1
Mass. 4M	F	Bartlett, B.	x	*	*	*	*	*	*	*	*	*	9–1	16–1
3S	R	Bishop, P.	x	x	x	x	x	x	x	x	x	0	0–9	0–16
4W	F	Foster, D. (R-6-6-00)	0	0	0	0	0	0	0	0	0	0	0–0	3–2
1E	F	Lee, S.	*	*	*	*	*	*	*	*	*	*	10–0	17–0
4W	R	Lincoln, L. (S-2-6-01)	0	0	0	0	x	x	x	x	x	0	0–5	0–5
3W	F	Lyman, S. (R-11-6-00)	0	0	0	0	0	0	0	0	0	0	0–0	6–1
3W	F	Mattoon, E. (S-2-2-01)	0	0	0	0	*	*	*	0	0	0	3–0	3–0
1M	F	Otis, H.	*	*	*	*	*	*	*	*	*	0	9–0	13–0
3M	F	Read, N. (S-11-25-00)	x	0	*	*	*	*	*	*	*	*	8–1	8–1
2S	F	Reed, J.	*	0	*	*	*	*	*	*	*	*	9–0	16–0
1W	F	Sedgwick, T.	0	0	0	*	*	*	0	0	0	0	3–0	4–0
3M	F	Sewall, S. (R-1-10-00)	0	0	0	0	0	0	0	0	0	0	0–0	7–0
2W	F	Shepard, W.	*	0	*	*	*	*	*	*	*	*	9–0	15–1
3E	F	Thatcher, G.	*	0	*	*	*	*	*	*	*	*	9–0	16–0
2M	R	Varnum, J. B.	x	x	x	x	x	x	x	x	x	x	0–10	1–15
2E	F	Wadsworth, P.	*	*	*	*	*	*	*	*	*	0	9–0	16–0
1S	F	Williams, L.	*	*	*	*	*	*	*	*	*	*	10–0	17–0
N. H.	F	Sheafe, J.	*	*	*	*	*	*	*	*	*	*	10–0	17–0
	F	Freeman, J.	*	0	*	*	*	*	*	*	*	0	8–0	13–1
	F	Gordon, W. (R-6-12-00)	0	0	0	0	0	0	0	0	0	0	0–0	4–0
	F	Tenney, S. (S-12-8-00)	*	*	*	*	*	*	*	*	*	*	10–0	10–0
	F	Foster, A.	*	*	*	*	*	*	*	*	*	*	10–0	17–0
State & Dist.	Party	Name & Date of Service	1	2	3	4	5	6	7	8	9	10	F^1-R^1	F^2-R^2

VOTE CHART No. VII—Continued

State & Dist.	Party	Name & Date of Service	1	2	3	4	5	6	7	8	9	10	F^1-R^1	F^2-R^2
N. J. E	R	Condit, J.	x	*	x	x	x	x	x	x	x	0	1−8	1−14
S	F	Davenport, F.	*	*	*	*	*	*	*	*	*	*	10−0	17−0
M	F	Imlay, J. H.	*	*	*	*	*	*	*	*	*	*	10−0	17−0
N	R	Kitchell, A.	x	x	x	x	x	x	x	x	x	0	0−9	0−16
W	R	Linn, J.	x	x	x	x	x	x	x	x	x	x	0−10	1−16
N. Y. 5	R	Bailey, T.	x	x	x	x	x	x	x	x	x	x	0−10	0−17
6	F	Bird, J.	*	x	*	*	*	*	0	*	*	0	7−1	11−1
10	F	Cooper, W.	*	*	*	*	*	*	*	*	*	0	9−0	15−0
4	R	Elmendorf, L. C.	x	x	x	x	x	x	x	0	0	0	0−7	0−14
8	F	Glen, H.	*	*	*	*	*	*	*	*	*	*	10−0	17−0
1	R	Smith, J. (S-2-2-00)	x	x	x	x	x	x	x	x	x	x	0−10	0−13
2	R	Livingston, E.	0	0	0	0	x	x	x	*	x	x	1−5	2−5
9	F	Platt, J.	*	*	*	*	*	*	*	*	*	*	10−0	16−0
7	R	Thompson, J.	x	x	x	x	x	x	x	x	x	0	0−9	0−16
3	R	Van Cortlandt, P.	x	0	x	x	x	x	x	0	0	0	0−6	0−10
N. C. 9	F	Alston, W.	x	*	x	x	x	x	x	x	x	x	1−9	3−14
1	F	Dickson, J.	x	*	*	*	*	*	*	*	*	x	9−1	15−2
7	F	Grove, W. B.	x	*	*	*	*	*	*	0	x	*	7−2	10−3
2	F	Henderson, A.	0	*	*	*	*	*	*	*	0	*	8−0	11−1
6	F	Hill, W. H.	0	*	*	*	*	*	*	*	x	0	7−1	12−3
5	R	Macon, N.	x	x	x	x	x	x	x	x	x	x	0−10	0−17
10	R	Spaight, R. D.	x	0	x	x	x	x	x	x	x	x	0−9	0−11
4	R	Stanford, R.	x	x	x	x	x	x	x	x	x	x	0−10	0−17
8	R	Stone, D.	0	0	0	x	x	x	x	x	x	x	0−7	0−13
3	R	Williams, R.	x	*	x	x	x	x	x	0	x	0	1−7	1−14
Pa. 4	R	Brown, R.	x	x	x	x	x	x	x	x	x	x	0−10	1−16
12	R	Gallatin, A.	x	x	x	x	x	x	x	x	x	x	0−10	0−17
9	R	Gregg, A.	x	*	x	x	x	x	x	x	x	x	1−9	1−16
6	R	Hanna, J. A.	x	*	x	x	x	x	x	x	x	x	1−9	1−15
8	F	Hartley, T. (D-12-21-00)	0	0	0	0	0	0	0	0	0	0	0−0	3−4
8		Stewart, J. (S-2-3-01)	0	0	0	0	x	x	x	x	0	0	0−4	0−4
5	R	Hiester, J.	x	x	x	x	x	x	x	x	x	x	0−10	0−16
7	F	Kittera, J. W.	0	*	*	*	*	*	*	*	*	*	9−0	13−0
2	R	Leib, M.	x	x	x	x	x	x	x	x	x	x	0−10	0−17
4	R	Muhlenberg, P.	x	x	x	x	x	x	x	x	x	x	0−10	0−17
11	R	Smilie, J.	x	x	x	x	x	x	x	x	x	x	0−10	0−17
3	F	Thomas, R.	*	0	*	*	*	*	*	0	0	0	6−0	13−0
1	F	Waln, R.	*	*	*	*	*	*	*	*	*	0	9−0	16−0
10	F	Woods, H.	*	*	*	*	*	*	*	*	*	*	10−0	17−0
R. I.	F	Brown, J.	*	*	*	*	*	*	*	*	*	*	10−0	16−1
	F	Champlin, C.	*	0	*	*	*	*	*	*	*	*	9−0	16−0
S. C. 96	F	Harper, R. G.	*	*	*	*	*	*	*	*	*	*	10−0	17−0
Che.	F	Huger, B.	x	*	*	x	?	x	x	*	*	*	5−4	10−5
Wash.	F	Nott, A.	x	*	0	x	0	0	0	0	0	0	1−2	7−3
Ch.	F	Pinckney, Th.	*	0	*	*	*	*	*	*	*	*	9−0	13−0
State & Dist.	Party	Name & Date of Service	1	2	3	4	5	6	7	8	9	10	F^1-R^1	F^2-R^2

VOTE CHART No. VII—Continued

State & Dist.		Party	Name & Date of Service	1	2	3	4	5	6	7	8	9	10	$F^1 - R^1$	$F^2 - R^2$
	Or.	F	Rutledge, J.	*	*	*	*	*	*	*	*	0	0	0	7−0	14−0
	Ca.	R	Sumter, T.	x	x	x	x	0	0	x	x	0	x	0−7	0−12
Tenn.		R	Claiborne, W.	x	x	x	x	x	x	x	x	x	x	0−10	0−16
Vt.	W.	R	Lyon, M.	0	x	x	x	x	x	x	x	x	x	0−9	0−14
	E.	F	Morris, L. R.	*	*	*	*	*	*	*	*	*	*	10−0	17−0
Va.	14	R	Cabell, S. J.	0	0	0	0	x	x	x	x	x	x	0−6	0−12
	6	R	Clay, M.	x	x	x	x	x	x	x	x	x	0	0−9	0−14
	15	R	Dawson, J.	*	x	x	x	x	x	x	x	x	x	1−9	1−16
	9	R	Eggleston, J.	x	x	x	x	x	x	x	x	x	x	0−10	0−17
	12	F	Evans, T.	x	*	*	*	*	*	*	*	*	*	9−1	16−1
	8	F	Goode, S.	x	*	*	x	x	0	x	0	0	0	2−4	3−7
	10	F	Gray, E.	x	x	x	x	x	x	x	x	x	0	0−9	2−14
	2	R	Holmes, D.	x	x	x	x	x	x	x	x	x	x	0−10	0−17
	3	R	Jackson, G.	x	x	x	x	x	x	x	x	x	0	0−9	0−16
	19	F	Lee, H.	*	*	*	*	*	*	*	0	0	*	8−0	15−0
	13	F	Marshall, J. (R-6-7-00)	0	0	0	0	0	0	0	0	0	0	0−0	6−1
	13	R	Tazewell, L. W. (S-11-26-00)	0	0	0	0	x	x	x	x	x	0	0−5	0−5
	16	R	New, A.	x	x	x	x	x	x	x	x	x	x	0−10	0−17
	18	R	Nicholas, J.	x	x	x	x	x	x	x	x	x	x	0−10	0−17
	1	F	Page, R.	x	*	*	*	*	*	*	0	x	*	7−2	13−3
	11	F	Parker, J.	0	0	0	x	*	x	x	*	*	0	3−3	8−4
	17	F	Powell, L.	x	0	*	*	*	*	*	*	*	*	8−1	15−1
	7	R	Randolph, J.	x	0	x	x	x	x	x	x	x	x	0−9	0−16
	4	R	Trigg, A.	x	x	x	x	x	x	x	x	x	x	0−10	0−17
	5	R	Trigg, J.	x	x	x	x	x	x	x	x	x	x	0−10	0−17
State & Dist.		Party	Name & Date of Service	1	2	3	4	5	6	7	8	9	10	$F^1 - R^1$	$F^2 - R^2$

[1] Summary of second session only.

[2] Summary of first and second sessions of Sixth Congress.

TABLE 21

SUMMARY OF REGULAR PARTY MEMBERS AND MODERATES, BY STATES,
SIXTH CONGRESS, 1ST AND 2ND SESSIONS

1	2	3		4	5	6	7	8	9	10
Seats	State	Party electing		F	FM	F(ex R)	R	RM	R(ex F)	Absent
		F	R							
7	Conn.	7	0	7						
1	Del.	1	0	1						
2	Ga.	2	0		1				1	
2	Ky.	0	2				2			
8	Md.	5	3	4	1		2	1		
14	Mass.	12	2	11	1		2			
4	N. H.	4	0	4						
5	N. J.	2	3	2			3			
10	N. Y.	4	6	4			5	1		
10	N. C.	5	5	2	2		5		1	
13	Penn.	5	8	4	1		8			
2	R. I.	2	0	2						
6	S. C.	5	1	3	2		1			
1	Tenn.	0	1				1			
2	Vt.	1	1	1			1			
19	Va.	8	11	4	3		11		1	
106		63	43	49	11		41	2	3	

LEGEND TO VOTE CHART NO. VIII

House, Seventh Congress, 1st Session, Jan.-May, 1802.

1. To recommit bill for apportionment of representatives, Yeas (F) 34; Nays (R) 56, Jan. 6, 1802. 11 *Annals*, 403. *House Journal*, 7th Congress, 32-33.

2. Resolution calling for information on internal duties, Yeas (F) 37; Nays (R) 57, Jan. 25, 1802. *Ibid.*, 457. *House Journal*, 7th Congress, 65-66.

3. Postponement of Judiciary Act, Yeas (F) 35; Nays (R) 61, Feb. 15, 1802. *Ibid.*, 518. *House Journal*, 7th Congress, 98-99.

4. Repeal of Judiciary Act, Yeas (R) 59; Nays (F) 32, March 3, 1802. *Ibid.*, 982. *House Journal*, 7th Congress, 119-120.

5. Reducing time for naturalization, Yeas (R) 59; Nays (F) 27, March 10, 1802. *Ibid.*, 993. *House Journal*, 7th Congress, 129-130.

6. Judiciary Act, Yeas (R) 46; Nays (F) 30, only 29 names listed, April 23, 1802. *Ibid.*, 1236. *House Journal*, 7th Congress, 218-219.

7. To recommit Report on Disbursements, Yeas (F) 22; Nays (R) 46, May 1, 1802. *Ibid.*, 1285. *House Journal*, 7th Congress, 235-236.

VOTE CHART No. VIII
SEVENTH CONGRESS, FIRST SESSION

State & Dist.	Party	Name & Date of Service	1	2	3	4	5	6	7	F−R
Conn.	F	Dana, S. W.	*	*	*	*	*	*	*	7−0
	F	Davenport, J.	*	*	*	*	*	*	*	7−0
	F	Griswold, R.	*	*	*	*	*	*	*	7−0
	F	Goddard, C.	*	*	*	*	*	*	*	7−0
	F	Perkins, E.	*	*	0	0	0	0	0	2−0
	F	Smith, J. C.	*	*	*	0	*	0	0	4−0
	F	Tallmadge, R.	*	*	*	*	*	*	*	7−0
Del.	F	Bayard, J. A.	*	*	*	0	x	*	*	5−1
Ga.[1]	R	Milledge, J.	x	x	x	x	x	x	x	0−7
Ky.	R	Davis, T. T.	x	x	x	x	x	*	x	1−6
	R	Fowler, J.	0	x	x	x	x	x	x	0−6
Md. 6	R	Archer, J.	x	*	x	x	x	x	x	1−6
1	F	Campbell, J.	*	*	0	*	*	*	*	6−0
8	F	Dennis, J.	*	0	*	*	x	*	0	4−1
3	F	Plater, T.	x	*	*	*	*	*	0	5−1
5	R	Smith, S.	x	x	x	x	x	x	0	0−6
2	R	Bowie, W. (S-3-24-02)	0	0	0	0	0	x	0	0−1
2	R	Sprigg, R. (R-2-11-02)	x	x	0	0	0	0	0	0−2
4	R	Hiester, D.	x	x	x	0	0	x	x	0−5
7	R	Nicholson, J.	x	x	x	x	x	x	x	0−7
Mass. 1W	R	Bacon, J.	x	x	x	x	x	x	x	0−7
3S	R	Bishop, Ph.	x	x	x	x	x	x	x	0−7
4M	F	Cutler, M.	*	*	*	*	*	*	*	7−0
3E	R	Cutts, R.	x	x	x	x	0	x	x	0−6
1M	R	Eustis, W.	x	x	x	*	x	0	x	1−5
4W	F	Hastings, S. (S-1-11-02)	0	*	*	*	0	*	*	5−0
1E	F	Lee, S.	0	0	0	0	0	0	0	0−0
4W	R	Lincoln, L. (R-3-5-01)	0	0	0	0	0	0	0	0−0
3W	F	Mattoon, E.	*	*	*	0	*	0	0	4−0
3M	F	Read, N.	*	*	*	*	*	*	*	7−0
2W	F	Shepard, W.	*	*	*	0	0	0	0	4−0
2S	R	Smith, J.	x	x	x	x	*	0	0	1−4
2M	R	Varnum, J. B.	x	x	x	x	x	0	x	0−6
2E	F	Wadsworth, P.	*	*	*	*	*	*	0	6−0
1S	F	Williams, L.	*	*	*	*	*	*	*	7−0
N. H.	F	Foster, A.	*	*	*	*	*	*	*	7−0
	F	Pierce, J. (R-in-1802)	*	*	*	*	*	0	0	5−0
	F	Tenney, S.	*	*	*	*	*	*	*	7−0
	F	Upham, G.	*	*	*	*	*	*	*	7−0
N. J.	R	Condit, J.	x	x	x	x	x	x	x	0−7
	R	Elmer, E.	x	x	x	x	x	*	0	1−5
	R	Helms, W.	x	x	x	x	x	x	0	0−6
State & Dist.	Party	Name & Date of Service	1	2	3	4	5	6	7	F−R

VOTE CHART No. VIII—Continued

State & Dist.	Party	Name & Date of Service	1	2	3	4	5	6	7	F−R
	R	Mott, J.	x	x	x	x	0	*	x	1−5
	R	Southard, H.	x	0	x	x	x	x	x	0−6
N.Y. 6	R	Van Ness, J. P. (S-12-7-01)	x	x	0	x	x	x	x	0−6
4	R	Elmendorf, L.	x	x	x	x	x	x	x	0−7
2	R	Mitchill, S. L.	x	x	x	x	x	0	x	0−6
10	F	Morris, T.	*	*	*	0	0	*	*	5−0
1	R	Smith, John	x	x	x	x	x	x	x	0−7
5	R	Tillotson, T. (R-12-10-01)	0	0	0	0	0	0	0	0−0
5	R	Bailey, Th. (S-12-7-01)	x	0	x	x	x	x	x	0−6
7	R	Thomas, D.	x	x	x	x	x	0	x	0−6
3	R	Van Cortlandt, P.	x	x	x	x	x	x	x	0−7
8	F	Van Rensselaer, K. K.	*	*	*	*	*	0	0	5−0
9	F	Walker, B.	*	*	*	*	*	0	0	5−0
N.C.[2] 9	F	Alston, W.	*	x	x	x	x	x	x	1−6
7	F	Grove, W. B.	*	*	*	*	x	0	0	4−1
2	F	Henderson, A.	0	*	*	*	*	*	*	6−0
6	F	Hill, W. H.	*	*	*	*	*	0	0	5−0
1	R	Holland, J.	x	x	x	x	x	x	x	0−7
4	R	Stanford, R.	x	x	x	x	x	x	x	0−7
10	F	Stanly, J.	*	*	*	*	*	*	*	7−0
3	R	Williams, R.	0	x	x	x	x	x	x	0−6
8	R	Johnson, C. (D-in 1802)	0	x	x	x	0	0	0	0−3
Pa. 4	R	Brown, R.	x	x	x	x	x	x	x	0−7
7	F	Boude, T.	*	0	*	*	x	*	*	5−1
9	R	Gregg, A.	x	x	x	x	x	0	0	0−5
6	R	Hanna, J. A.	x	x	x	0	0	x	x	0−5
5	R	Hiester, J. J.	x	x	x	x	x	0	x	0−6
3	F	Hemphill, J.	*	*	*	*	x	0	0	4−1
12	F	Hoge, W.[3]	x	x	x	x	x	0	0	0−5
1	R	Jones, W.	x	x	x	x	x	0	0	0−5
2	R	Leib, M.	x	x	x	x	x	x	x	0−7
11	R	Smilie, J.	x	x	x	x	x	x	x	0−7
8	R	Stewart, J.	x	x	0	x	x	x	0	0−5
4	R	Van Horne, I.	x	x	x	x	x	x	0	0−6
10	F	Woods, H.	*	*	*	*	x	*	*	6−1
R.I.	R	Stanton, J.	x	x	x	x	x	x	x	0−7
	R	Tillinghast, T.	x	*	*	*	x	*	0	4−2
S.C. 96	R	Butler, W.	x	x	x	x	x	x	0	0−6
Che.	F	Huger, B.	*	*	*	*	*	0	*	6−0
Ch.	F	Lowndes, Th.	*	*	*	*	*	*	0	6−0
Wash.	R	Moore, Th.	x	x	x	x	x	0	x	0−6
Or.	F	Rutledge, J.	*	*	*	*	*	0	0	5−0
Ca.	R	Sumter, Thomas (res 12-15-01)	0	0	0	0	0	0	0	0−0

| State & Dist. | Party | Name & Date of Service | 1 | 2 | 3 | 4 | 5 | 6 | 7 | F−R |

VOTE CHART No. VIII—Continued

State & Dist.		Party	Name & Date of Service	1	2	3	4	5	6	7	F−R
Tenn.		R	Dickson, W.	0	x	x	x	x	x	x	0−6
Vt.	E.	F	Morris, L. R.	*	*	*	*	*	*	*	7−0
	W.	R	Smith, I.	x	x	x	0	x	x	0	0−5
Va.	17	R	Brent, R.	0	x	x	x	0	x	x	0−5
	14	R	Cabell, S. J.	0	0	x	x	x	0	0	0−3
	8	R	Claiborne, T.	x	0	x	x	x	x	0	0−5
	6	R	Clay, M.	x	x	x	x	x	x	x	0−7
	13	R	Clopton, J.	0	0	x	x	x	x	x	0−5
	15	R	Dawson, J.	0	0	x	x	x	x	0	0−4
	9	R	Giles, W. B.	0	x	x	x	x	x	0	0−5
	10	F	Gray, Ed.	0	x	x	x	0	x	x	0−5
	2	R	Holmes, D.	x	x	x	x	x	x	x	0−7
	3	R	Jackson, G.	x	x	x	x	x	0	0	0−5
	16	R	New, A.	x	x	x	x	0	x	x	0−6
	11	R	Newton, Th.	x	x	x	x	x	0	x	0−6
	7	R	Randolph, J.	x	x	x	x	0	0	x	0−5
	1	R	Smith, John	x	x	x	x	x	x	x	0−7
	12	F	Stratton, J.	x	*	0	0	0	*	0	2−1
	19	R	Taliaferro, J.	x	x	x	x	0	x	x	0−6
	18	R	Thompson, P. R.	x	x	x	x	x	x	x	0−7
	4	R	Trigg, A.	x	x	x	x	x	x	x	0−7
	5	R	Trigg, J.	x	x	x	x	x	x	x	0−7
State & Dist.		Party	Name & Date of Service	1	2	3	4	5	6	7	F−R

[1] Benjamin Taliaferro of Georgia did not attend this session.

[2] N. Macon, Republican, of the 5th North Carolina District was Speaker of the House.

[3] W. Hoge, 12th Pennsylvania District, succeeded to the seat of Albert Gallatin. Gallatin was elected in 1800 by a large margin. The vote in the three counties (Allegheny, Greene, and Washington), was (*Aurora*, October 27, 1800; November 3, 1800):

	Allegheny	Greene	Washington
Albert Gallatin	1937	622	1690
P. Nevill	944	239	345
	993	383	1345
Total majority for Gallatin = 2,721			

In May, 1801, Gallatin resigned to take the Secretaryship of the Treasury under Jefferson. Thereupon there was a bye-election in 1801 in which W. Hoge (Federalist) defeated the Republican candidate. Actually W. Hoge was an extremely moderate Federalist, his brother was a Republican and they cooperated. Tinkcom, *Republicans and Federalists in Pennsylvania, 1790-1801*, 257, considers W. Hoge to be a Republican. I do not and have followed the press and the material in Russell J. Ferguson, *Early Western Pennsylvania Politics* (Pittsburgh, 1936), 173-174, 201; 212-213.

TABLE 22

SUMMARY OF REGULAR PARTY MEMBERS AND MODERATES, BY STATES,
SEVENTH CONGRESS, 1ST SESSION

1	2	3		4	5	6	7	8	9	10
Seats	State	Party electing		F	FM	F(ex R)	R	RM	R(ex F)	Absent
		F	R							
7	Conn.	7		7						
1	Del.	1		1						
2	Ga.		2				1			1
2	Ky.		2				2			
8	Md.	3	5	2	1		5			
14	Mass.	8	6	7			5	1		1 Fed.
4	N. H.	4		4						
5	N. J.		5				5			
10	N. Y.	3	7	3			7			
10	N. C.	5	5	3	1		5		1	
13	Penn.	4	9	2	1		9		1	
2	R. I.		2				1	1		
6	S. C.	3	3	3			2			1 Rep.
1	Tenn.		1				1			
2	Vt.	1	1	1			1			
19	Va.	2	17		1		17		1	
106		41	65	33	4		61	2	3	3

B. MAPS

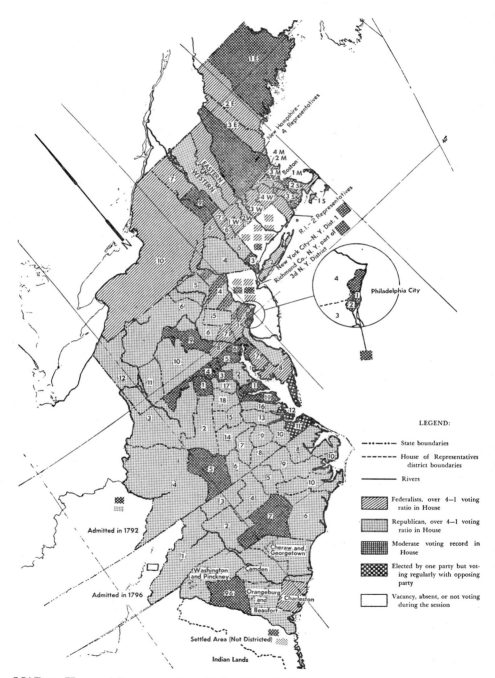

MAP 1: House of Representatives Voting Record, Fourth Congress, First Session, 1796 *

* Fourth Pennsylvania District has two representatives on all maps.

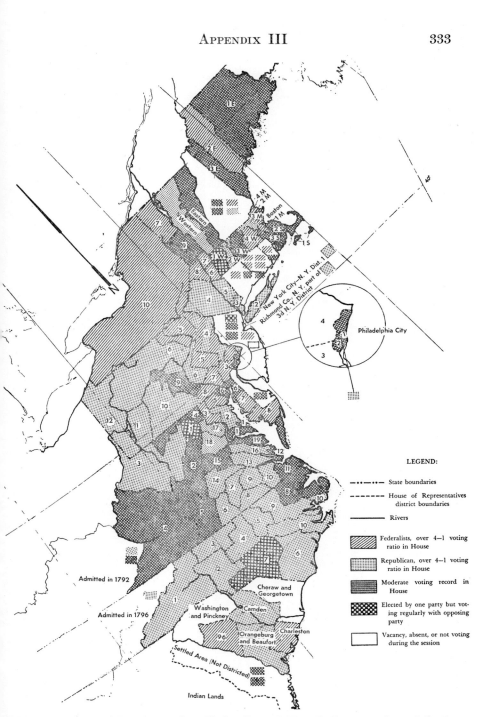

MAP 2: House of Representatives Voting Record, Fourth Congress, Second Session, 1796–1797

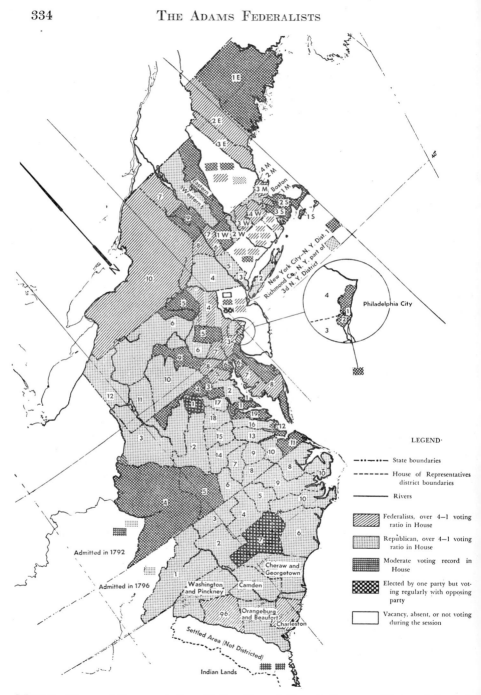

MAP 3: House of Representatives Voting Record, Fourth Congress, First and Second
Sessions, 1796–1797

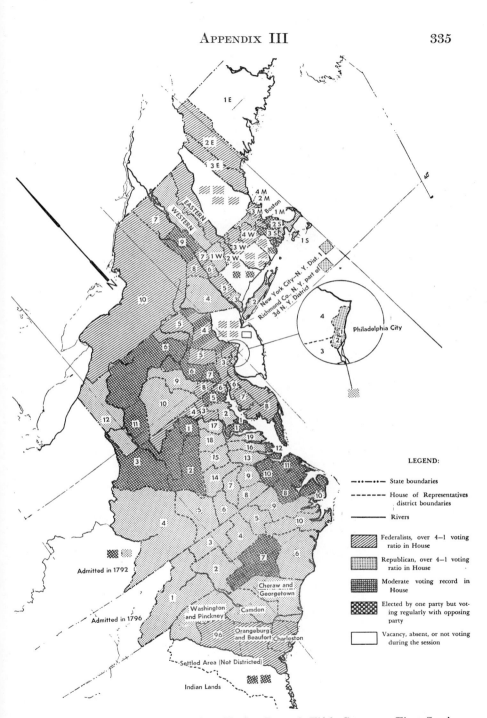

MAP 4: House of Representatives Voting Record, Fifth Congress, First Session
(Special), 1797

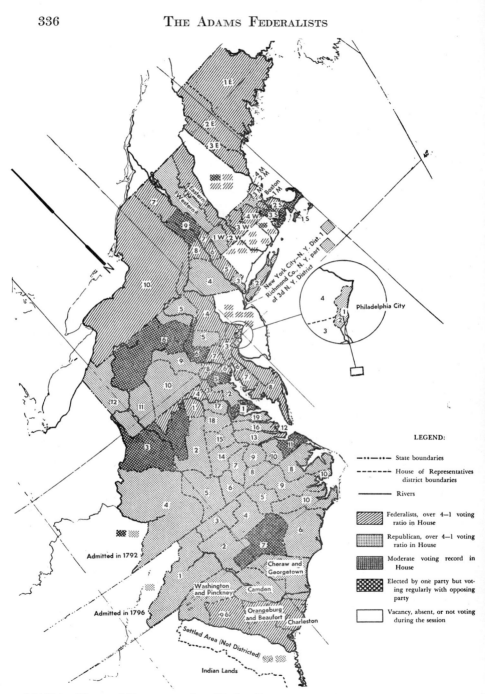

MAP 5: House of Representatives Voting Record, Fifth Congress, Second Session,
1797–1798

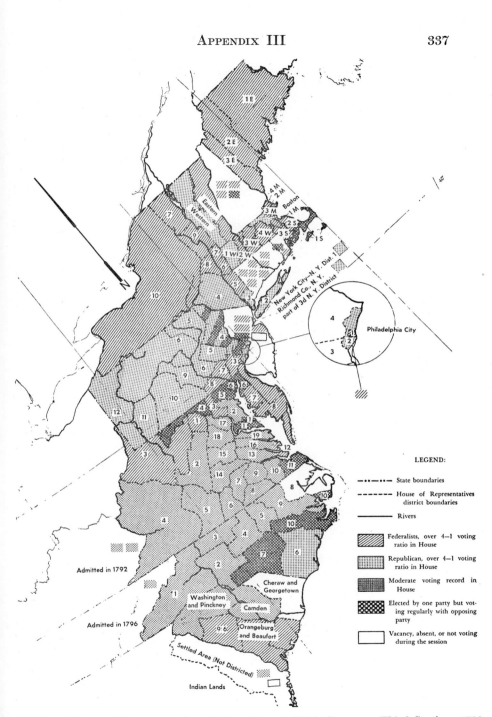

LEGEND:

—··—··— State boundaries

–––––––– House of Representatives
              district boundaries

———————— Rivers

Federalists, over 4–1 voting
ratio in House

Republican, over 4–1 voting
ratio in House

Moderate voting record in
House

Elected by one party but voting regularly with opposing
party

Vacancy, absent, or not voting
during the session

MAP 6: House of Representatives Voting Record, Fifth Congress, Third Session, 1799

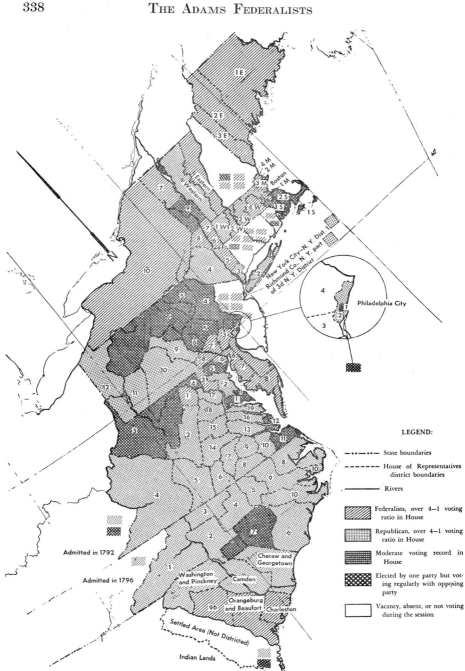

MAP 7: House of Representatives Voting Record, Fifth Congress, First, Second, and
Third Sessions, 1797–1799

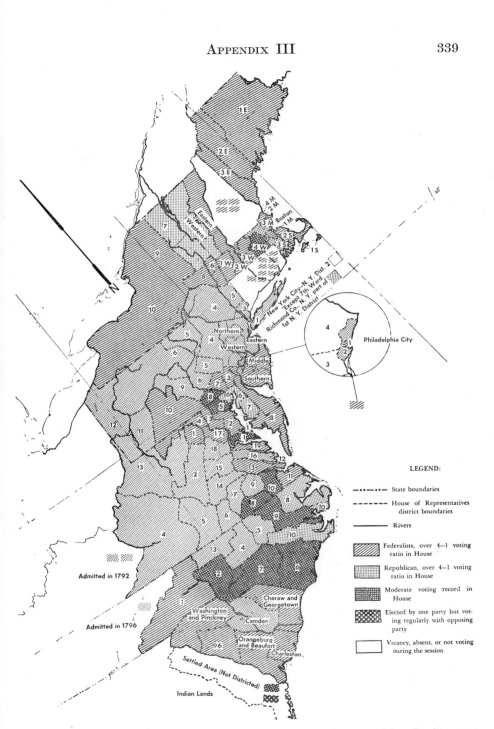

LEGEND:

—··—··— State boundaries

—————— House of Representatives
           district boundaries

—————— Rivers

Federalists, over 4–1 voting
ratio in House

Republican, over 4–1 voting
ratio in House

Moderate voting record in
House

Elected by one party but voting regularly with opposing
party

Vacancy, absent, or not voting
during the session

MAP 8: House of Representatives Voting Record, Sixth Congress, First Session, 1800

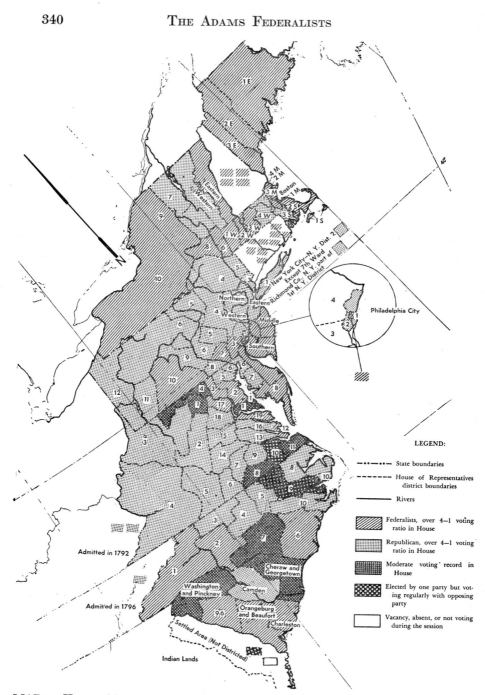

MAP 9: House of Representatives Voting Record, Sixth Congress, Second Session, 1801

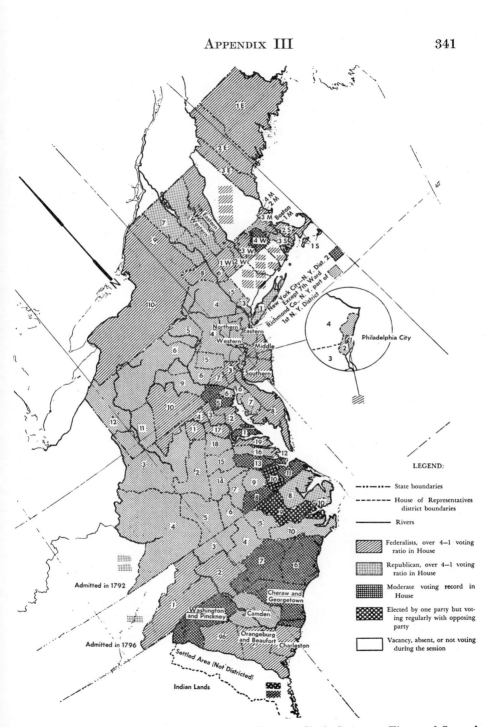

MAP 10: House of Representatives Voting Record, Sixth Congress, First and Second
Sessions, 1800–1801

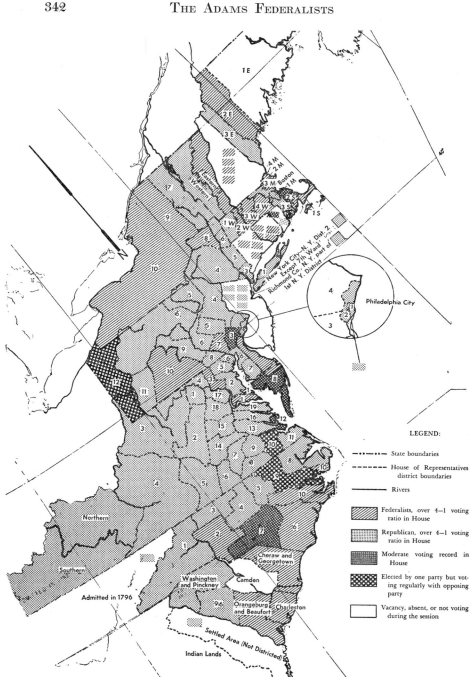

MAP 11: House of Representatives Voting Record, Seventh Congress, First Session, 1802

Appendix IV

DOCUMENTS

1. Original Draft of Sedition Act as Reported to the Senate, June 26, 1798.

A BILL

To define more particularly the crime of Treason, and to define and punish the crime of Sedition

1 Sect. 1. *Be it enacted by the Senate and House of Representatives*
2 *of the United States of America in Congress assembled,* That the govern-
3 ment and people of France and its colonies and dependencies, in conse-
4 quence of their hostile conduct towards the United States, shall be, and
5 they hereby are, declared to be enemies to the United States and the
6 people thereof; and any person or persons owing allegiance to the United
7 States, who shall adhere to the aforesaid enemies of the United States,
8 giving them aid and comfort, within the United States or elsewhere, and
9 shall be thereof convicted, in the manner prescribed by the first section
10 of a statute law of the United States, entitled, "An act for the punish-
11 ment of certain crimes against the United States," shall suffer death.

1 Sect. 2. *And be it further enacted,* That if any person or persons,
2 having knowledge of the commission of any of the treasons aforesaid,
3 shall conceal, and not as soon as may be, disclose and make known the
4 same to the President of the United States, or some one of the Judges
5 thereof, or to the Governor or some one of the Judges or Justices of
6 the state or states in which the same shall have been committed, such
7 person or persons, on conviction thereof, shall be adjudged guilty of
8 misprision of treason, and shall be imprisoned for a term not exceeding
9   years, and fined in a sum not exceeding
10 dollars.

[end of p. 1]

1   Sect. 3. *And be it further enacted,* That if any persons, whether
2 citizens or aliens, shall combine or conspire together with intent to
3 oppose any measure or measures of the government of the United
4 States, which are or shall be directed by the proper authority, or to
5 defeat the operation of any law of the United States, or to discourage or
6 prevent any person holding a place or office in or under the government
7 of the United States, from undertaking, performing or executing his
8 trust or duty; and if any person with intent as aforesaid, shall, by any
9 writing, printing or speaking, threaten such officer or person in public
10 trust, with any damage to his character, person or property, or shall
11 counsel, advise or attempt to procure any insurrection, riot, unlawful
12 assembly or combination, whether such conspiracy, threatening, counsel,
13 advice or attempt shall have the proposed effect or not, he shall, on con-
14 viction thereof before any court of the United States having jurisdiction
15 thereof, be punished by a fine not less than   dollars,
16 and by imprisonment during a term not less than   years;
17 and further, at the discretion of the court trying the same, may be
18 obliged to find sureties for his good behavior in such sum as the said
19 court may direct. And if the person so convicted be an alien, he may
20 be further adjudged and sentenced by the court to be banished and re-
21 moved from the territory of the United States.

1   Sect. 4. *And be it further enacted,* That if any person shall, by
2 writing, printing, publishing or speaking, attempt to defame or weaken
3 the government and laws of the United States, by any seditious or in-
4 flammatory declarations or expressions, tending to induce a belief in the
5 citizens thereof, that the said government, in enacting any law, was in-
6 duced so to do by motives hostile to the constitution, or liberties and hap-
7 piness of the people thereof; or tending to justify the hostile conduct of
    [end of p. 2]

8 the French government to the United States; or shall, in manner
9 aforesaid, attempt to defame the President of the United States, or any
10 Court or Judge thereof, by declarations directly or indirectly tending to
11 criminate their motives in an official transaction, the person so offending
12 and thereof convicted, before any court of the United States having
13 jurisdiction thereof, shall be punished by fine not exceeding
14 dollars, and imprisonment not exceeding   years.

1   Sect. 5. *And be it further enacted,* That the Circuit courts of the
2 United States shall have jurisdiction in all cases within the purview of
3 this act.

Printed by Way and Groff, No. 27, Arch Street

(Original endorsed)

Bill
Reported by Mr. Lloyd
Define and punish
      Treason

June 26. read 1st & passed to 2nd

5th Con
2nd Sess

                  Printed copy endorsed
                    June 27th, 1798
                    Committed
                    Report amend^t
                    To 3rd Reading
                    July 11 considered
                    and passed
                    5th Congress
                    2nd Session

2. Senate Amendments to Sedition Act.

SENATE AMENDMENTS

The Committee to whom was referred the bill " to define more particularly the Crime of Treason, and to define and punish the crime of Sedition," are of opinion that the said bill ought to pass, with the following amendment, viz.

After the word " that," in the second line of the first section of the bill, strike out the remainder of the bill, and insert what follows:

" If any persons shall unlawfully combine or conspire together, with " intent to oppose any measure or measures of the government of the

" United States, which are or shall be directed by proper authority,
" or to impede the operation of any law of the United States, or to
" intimidate or prevent any person, holding a place or office in or
" under the government of the United States, from undertaking, per-
" forming or executing his trust or duty; and if any person or persons,
" with intent as aforesaid, shall, by any writing, printing, or speaking,
" threaten such officer or person in public trust, with any damage to
" his character, person or estate, or shall counsel, advise or attempt to
" procure any insurrection, riot, unlawful assemblege, or combination,
" whether such conspiracy, threatening, counsel, advice, or attempt
" shall have the proposed effect or not, he or they shall be deemed
" guilty of a high misdemeanor, and on conviction, before any court of
" the United States having jurisdiction thereof, shall be punished by a
" fine not exceeding (5000)   dollars, and by imprisonment during
" a term not less than (six months nor exceeding five years); and
" further at the discretion of the court may be holden to find sureties
" for his good behavior in such sum, and for such time as the said
" court may direct.

" Section 2. *And be it further enacted*, That if any person shall, by
" any libellous or scandalous writing, printing, publishing, or speaking,
" traduce or defame the Legislature of the United States, by seditious
" or inflammatory declarations or expressions, with intent to create a
" belief, in the citizens thereof, that the said Legislature in enacting
" any law, was induced thereto by motives hostile to the constitution
" or liberties and happiness of the people thereof; or shall, in manner
" aforesaid, traduce or defame the President of the United States, or
" any Court or Judge thereof, by declarations, tending to criminate
" their motives in any official transaction; the person so offending and
" thereof convicted before any court of the United States, having
" jurisdiction thereof, shall be punished by a fine not exceeding (2000)
" dollars, and by imprisonment not exceeding   (two) years.

" Section 3. *Provided, And be it further enacted*, That if any alien
" or aliens shall be convicted by virtue of this act, the court before
" whom such conviction is had, ~~shall~~ (may at their discretion) in lieu
" of fine, imprisonment   and binding with sureties,
" sentence and adjudge such alien or aliens to be banished and removed
" from the territory of the United States; and to be imprisoned until
" such sentence shall be carried into effect.

" Section 4. *And be it further enacted,* That if any editor, printer
" or publisher of any public newspaper, within the United States, shall
" be prosecuted under this act, for any libellous or scandalous matter
" contained in such paper, the paper containing such libellous or scan-
" dalous matter published in the name of such editor, printer or pub-
" lisher, shall be deemed competent evidence of the fact of printing
" and publishing the same."

" A bill in addition to the act entitled, An act for the punishment of
certain crimes against the United States."

The above is proposed by the Committee as the title of the bill,
if it should pass.

PRINTED BY WAY & GROFF, NO. 27, ARCH-STREET.

3. HOUSE AMENDMENTS TO SEDITION ACT.

Congress of the United States.

In the House of Representatives,

Tuesday, the 10th of July, 1798

The bill sent from the Senate, entitled, "An act in addition to the
act, entitled, An act for the punishment of certain crimes against the
United States," was read the third time.

Resolved, That the said bill do pass, with the following amendments:

Section 1st.

Lines 7th, 8th, & 9th, Strike out the words " *by any writing, printing*
" *or speaking, threaten such officer or person in public trust,*
" *with any damage to his character, person or estate, or shall.*"

Section 2nd,

Strike out from the word " by " in the first line, to the word " thereof " in the ninth line, inclusive; and, in lieu thereof, insert " write,
" print, utter, or publish, or shall cause or procure to be written,
" printed, uttered, or published, or shall knowingly and willingly assist
" or aid in writing, printing, uttering, or publishing any false, scan-
" dalous and malicious writing or writings against the government of
" the United States, or either House of the Congress of the United
" States, or the President of the United States, with intent to defame

" the said government, or either House of the said Congress, or the said
" President, or to bring them, or either of them into contempt or dis-
" repute; or to excite against them, or either or any of them, the
" hatred of the good people of the United States, or to stir up sedition
" within the United States, or to excite any unlawful combinations
" therein, for opposing or resisting any law of the United States, or
" any act of the President of the United States, done pursuance of any
" such law, or of the powers in him vested by the constitution of the
" United States, or to resist, oppose, or defeat any such law or act, or
" to aid, encourage or abet any hostile designs of any foreign nation
" against the United States, their people or government, then such
" person, being thereof convicted before any court of the United States,
" having jurisdiction thereof."

Strike out the 3rd and 4th sections, and in lieu thereof insert two
new sections as follows:

"And be it further enacted and declared, That if any person shall be
prosecuted under this act, for the writing or publishing any libel aforesaid, it shall be lawful for the defendant, upon the trial of the cause,
to give in

[end of page 1]

[on back of page one]

evidence in his defence, the truth of the matter contained in the publication charged as a libel. And the jury who shall try the cause, shall
have a right to determine the law and the fact, under the direction of
the court, as in other cases."

And be it further enacted, That this act shall continue and be in
force until the third day of March, one thousand eight hundred and
one, and no longer: *Provided,* That the expiration of the act shall not
prevent or defeat a prosecution and punishment of any offence against
the law, during the time it shall be in force.

Attest.

JONATHAN W. CONDY, *Clerk*

PRINTED BY WAY & GROFF, No. 27, ARCH STREET.

5th Congress   2 e/sp

Amends to Bill
Sedition
July 11th
1798

Appendix V

COMMENT ON SUMMARY OF CAUSES FOR PARTY ALIGNMENT

(Chapter II, p. 32)

There were 424 different elections of members of the House of Representatives on either a state-wide or district basis for the Fourth through the Seventh Congresses (four general elections for 106 members at each election). This omits bye-elections, which are, however, considered in the text elsewhere.

A summary considering the agreement of the voting behavior of these representatives with the economic, social, and other factors in their districts is presented on page 32. The figures given are the result of superimposing over-lays on the maps of voting behavior summarized for each Congress (Maps 3, 7, 10, and 11, Appendix III). This procedure is not as exact as the presentation of the numbers given would imply. This is because in some cases of border-line districts my judgment as to the composition of the district might be challenged; or another student might come to a different conclusion in some of these. I doubt, however, that this difference would result in a change in over 10% of the districts. Consequently, I have decided to present this numerical summary as I have arrived at it. But it should be understood that some changes might be introduced by securing additional data; or if another did the computing. I do not think the changes would be major. It is within these limits that the paragraph on p. 18 should be read.

Bibliography

PART I

BIBLIOGRAPHY FOR MAPS AND CHARTS

A. State Laws

Laws of Maryland, revised and collected by William Kilty. 2 vols. (Annapolis, 1800).

Acts and Laws of the Commonwealth of Massachusetts. 13 vols. (Boston, 1890-98).

Acts of the Twenty-Second General Assembly of New Jersey, second session (Burlington, 1798).

Laws of the State of New York. 5 vols. (Albany, 1886-7).

Laws of the State of North Carolina, by James Iredell. Appendix, *Session Laws of 1792* (Edenton, 1791).

Statutes at Large of South Carolina, edited by Thomas Cooper. 10 vols. (Columbia, 1836-41).

Statutes at Large of Pennsylvania, edited by James T. Mitchell and Henry Flanders. 13 vols. (Harrisburg, 1906-8).

Statutes at Large . . . of Virginia, edited by William Henry Hening. 13 vols. (Richmond, Philadelphia, New York, 1823).

Laws of the State of Vermont (Randolph, Vt., 1808).

B. Atlases and Geographies

Bureau of Census, *A Century of Population Growth* (Washington, 1909).

Carey, Matthew, *General Atlas* (Philadelphia, 1796). The following editions were used: 1796, 1800, 1811, 1814.

Jeffreys, Thomas, *American Atlas* (London, 1778).

Morse, Jedediah, *American Gazetteer* (London, 1798), *Ibid.* (1804).

Morse, Jedediah, *American Geography* (London, 1792; Elizabethtown, 1789).

Paullin, Charles O., *Atlas of the Historical Geography of the United States* (Washington, 1932).

C. Maps

Dutton, John, *Correct Map of Virginia* (Approximately 1800); Also *The State of South Carolina* (1795-1800).

Howell, Reading, *Map of Pennsylvania* (Philadelphia?, 1792). In
   Pennsylvania Archives, Ser. 3, Appendix 1-10.
Lewis, Samuel A., and Arrowsmith, Aaron, *Pennsylvania*, no. 44 in
   Arrowsmith, Aaron and Lewis, Samuel, *A New and Elegant
   General Atlas* (Philadelphia, 1804).
Carleton, Osgood, *A Map of the District of Maine* (Boston, 1795,
   and 1802).
DeWitt, Simeon, *A Map of the State of New York* (New York, 1804;
   and Albany, 1802).
Fry, Jefferson, Scull and Upton, *Map of Virginia*, in Jefferson,
   Thomas, *Notes on the State of Virginia* (originally Paris, 1784);
   2nd London edition (1787).
Lotter, Matthew Albert and Santhier, C. J., *Map of . . . New York
   . . .* (1777). (Reproduction in Jones, Thomas, *History of New
   York . . .* (New York, 1879). Ed. by Edward Floyd de Lancey,
   Vol. I).
New York, entworfen von D. F. Stozman (Hamburg bey Carl Ernst
   Bohn, 1799).
Map of Massachusetts in 1796, *Massachusetts Historical Society
   Proceedings*, Vol. I, 1791-1835 (Boston, 1879).
Myers, E. W., Map of North Carolina in 1783, in *State Records of
   North Carolina*, XVIII (Goldsborough, N. C., 1900).
Purcell, J., *Maps*, see Morse, Jedediah, *American Geography* (2nd
   ed.).

PART II

BIBLIOGRAPHY FOR NARRATIVE MATERIAL

A. SOURCES

1. Manuscript material from United States Government Records, National Archives, Washington, D. C.

House of Representatives, *Bills* (1798).
Senate, *Bills* (1798).
Manuscript Journals, House of Representatives, 1795-1803.
State Department, *Instructions to Ministers and Consuls*, 1797-1801.
State Department, *Domestic Letters*, 1797-1801.

2. Manuscript material

Henry Adams, *Transcriptions* from British Foreign Office, Correspondence, American, 1794-1801. (Library of Congress).
Gerry, E., *Manuscripts* (Boston, Mass.).

Hamilton, A., *Papers* (Library of Congress).
Jefferson, Thomas, *Manuscripts* (Library of Congress).
Lowell *Papers* (Massachusetts Historical Society).
McHenry, J., *Papers* (Library of Congress).
Otis, H. G., *Papers* (Massachusetts Historical Society).
Pickering, T., *Papers* (Massachusetts Historical Society).
Washburn *Papers* (Massachusetts Historical Society).
Washington, George, *Papers* (Library of Congress).

3. Government Publications of Great Britain and Canada

Brymner, Douglas, *Report on the Canadian Archives, 1890* (Ottawa, 1890).
Grenville, W. W., *The Manuscripts of J. B. Fortescue, Esq., Dropmore Papers*, ed. by Walter Fitzpatrick, Historical Manuscripts Commission, 7 vols. (London, 1892-1927).
First Report from the Committee of Secrecy, House of Commons (fifth edition, London, 1794).
Second Report from the Committee of Secrecy of the House of Commons (fourth edition, London, 1794).
The History of the Two Acts (London, 1796).
First Report from the Committee of Secrecy appointed by the House of Lords (fourth edition, London, 1794).
Second Report from the Committee of Secrecy appointed by the House of Lords (London, 1794).
Hailsham, Viscount, ed., *Halsbury's Laws of England*, 37 vols., 2nd ed. (London, 1931-42).
Statutes at large from Magna Carta to . . . 1761 . . ., by D. Pickering . . . continued to . . . 1806. 46 vols. (Cambridge, Eng., 1762-1807).

4. Government Publications in the United States

American State Papers. 38 vols. (Washington, 1832-1861).
Annals of Congress. 42 vols. (Washington, 1834-1856).
Bureau of the Census, *A Century of Population Growth* (Washington, 1909).
Bureau of the Census, *Historical Statistics of the United States, 1789-1945* (Washington, 1949).
Calendar of Virginia State Papers (Richmond, 1852-1869).
Federal Cases. 30 vols. (St. Paul, 1894-97).
Monthly Summary of Commerce and Finance of the United States for . . . 1899, New Series, Vol. 6 (House Document No. 573, Pt. 1, 55th Congress, 2nd Session, Washington, 1899).

Journals of the Continental Congress, 1774-1789. 34 vols. (Washington, 1904-1937).

Journal of House of Representatives of the United States. (1789-1815). 9 vols. (Washington, 1826).

Journal of the Senate of the United States of America . . . 2nd Session, Fifth Congress (Philadelphia, 1798).

Statutes at Large of the United States. 61 vols. (Washington, 1845-1947).

United States Supreme Court Reports. (90 vols. to 1874. Philadelphia and Washington, 1790—date).

United States Senate Documents, 50th Congress, 2nd Session, No. 58 (Washington, 1889).

Wharton, Francis, ed., *The Revolutionary Diplomatic Correspondence of the United States.* 6 vols. (Washington, 1889).

5. Works

Adams, Charles Francis, ed., *Works of John Adams with a Life of the Author.* 10 vols. (Boston, 1850-56).

Adams, John, *Letters from the Hon. John Adams, to the Hon. Wm. Tudor, and Others, on the Events of American Revolution.* (Boston, 1819).

Correspondence between the Honorable John Adams . . . and . . . William Cunningham, Esq. (Pub. by E. M. Cunningham, Boston, 1823).

Rush, Benjamin, *Old Family Letters: copied from the originals for Alexander Biddle*, Series A. (Philadelphia, 1892).

Austin, William, Compiler, *A Selection of the Patriotic Addresses to the President of the United States. Together with the President's Answers. Presented in the year one thousand Seven Hundred and Ninety-Eight . . .* (Boston, 1798).

Koch, Adrienne, *Selected Writings of John and John Quincy Adams* (New York, 1946).

Letters by Washington, Adams, Jefferson and Others . . . to John Langdon, New Hampshire (Philadelphia, 1880).

Adams, Charles Francis, *Letters of John Adams Addressed to his Wife.* 2 vols. (Boston, 1841).

Warren–Adams Letters, Massachusetts Historical Society Collections, Vol. 73 (Boston, 1925).

Ford, Worthington C., ed., *Statesman and Friend, Letters of John Adams to Benjamin Waterhouse* (Boston, 1927).

Wilstach, Paul, ed., *Correspondence of John Adams and Thomas Jefferson, 1812-1826* (Indianapolis, 1925).

Adams, Charles Francis, ed., *Letters of Mrs. Adams* (Boston, 1840).

Mitchell, Stewart, ed., *New Letters of Abigail Adams, 1789-1804*, American Antiquarian Society Proceedings, LV, 95-232; 299-444.

DeWindt, Caroline A., ed., *A Journal and Correspondence of Miss Adams, Daughter of John Adams* . . . (New York & London, 1841-2). 2 vols. (2nd in two parts).

Ford, Worthington C., ed., *Writings of John Quincy Adams*. 7 vols. (New York, 1913-17).

Ames, Seth, ed., *Works of Fisher Ames*. 2 vols. (Boston, 1854).

Donnan, Elizabeth, ed., *James A. Bayard Papers from 1796 to 1815*, American Historical Association Reports, *1913*, Vol. II (Washington, 1915).

Bentley, Wm., *Diary*. 4 vols. (Salem, Massachusetts, 1905-14).

Lodge, Henry Cabot, *Life and Letters of George Cabot* (Boston, 1877).

Rowland, Kate M., *Life and Correspondence of Charles Carroll of Carrollton*. 2 vols. (New York, 1898).

Cobbett, William, *Letters from William Cobbett to Edward Thornton*, edited by G. D. H. Cole (Oxford, 1937).

Cobbett, William, *Porcupines Works*. 12 vols. (London, 1801).

Cobbett, William, *Life and Adventures of Peter Porcupine; with other Records of his Early Career in England and America*, edited by G. D. H. Cole (London, 1937).

Adams, Henry, ed., *Writings of Albert Gallatin*. 3 vols. (Philadelphia, 1879).

Hamilton, John C., ed., *Works of Alexander Hamilton*. 8 vols. (New York, 1851).

Lodge, Henry Cabot, ed., *Works of Alexander Hamilton*. 9 vols. (New York, 1885-6).

Hamilton, Alexander; Madison, James; and Jay, John, *The Federalist* (Lodge ed.). (New York, 1895).

Select Works of Robert Goodloe Harper . . . , Vol. I. (Baltimore, 1814). (no more published).

Henry, William Wirt, ed., *Life, Correspondence, and Speeches of Patrick Henry*. 3 vols. (New York, 1891).

McRee, Griffith J., *James Iredell, Life and Correspondence*. 2 vols. (New York, 1857-8).

Johnston, Henry P., ed., *Correspondence and Public Papers of John Jay*. 4 vols. (New York, 1890-93).

Bassett, John S., ed., *Correspondence of Andrew Jackson*. 6 vols. (Washington, 1926).

Sawvel, Franklin B., ed., *The Complete Anas of Thomas Jefferson* (New York, 1903).

Lipscomb, Andrew A. and Bergh, Albert Ellery, eds., *The Writings of Thomas Jefferson.* 20 vols. (Washington, 1903).

Ford, Paul Leicester, ed., *Works of Thomas Jefferson.* 10 vols. (New York, 1904).

Ford, Worthington C., ed., *Thomas Jefferson Correspondence, Printed from the Originals in the Collections of William K. Bixby* (Boston, 1916).

King, Charles R., ed., *Life and Correspondence of Rufus King.* 6 vols. (New York, 1894-1900).

Steiner, Bernard C., *Life and Correspondence of James McHenry* (Cleveland, 1907).

Beard, Charles A., ed., *Journal of William Maclay* (New York, 1927).

Hunt, Gaillard, ed., *Writings of James Madison.* 9 vols. (New York, 1910).

Letters and Other Writings of James Madison. 4 vols. (Congress edition, Philadelphia, 1865).

Salley, Harriett M., ed., *Correspondence of Governor John Milledge* (Columbia, South Carolina, 1949).

Hamilton, Stanislaus Murrey, ed., *Writings of James Monroe.* 7 vols. (New York, 1898-1903).

Sparks, Jared, *Life of Gouverneur Morris.* 3 vols. (Boston, 1832).

Morris, Anne Carey, ed., *The Diary and Letters of Gouverneur Morris.* 2 vols. (New York, 1888).

Morison, Samuel E., *Life and Letters of Harrison Gray Otis.* 2 vols. (Boston, 1913).

Conway, Moncure D., *Omitted Chapters of History from the Papers of Edmund Randolph* (New York, 1888).

Butterfield, L. H., ed., *Letters of Benjamin Rush.* 2 vols. (Princeton, 1951).

Amory, Thomas Coffin, *Life of James Sullivan, Selections from his Writings.* 2 vols. (Boston, 1859).

Dexter, Franklin B., *The Literary Diary of Ezra Stiles (Massachusetts Historical Society Proceedings,* 2nd ser., vol. 7 (New York, 1901).

Ford, Worthington C., ed., *Writings of George Washington.* 14 vols. (New York, 1889).

Fitzpatrick, John C., ed., *Writings of George Washington.* 39 vols. (Washington, 1933-44).

Ford, Worthington C., ed., *Correspondence and Journals of Samuel Blachley Webb.* Vol. III, 1783-1806. (New York, 1893-1914).

Ford, Emily Ellsworth (Fowler), compiler, *Notes on the Life of Noah Webster.* 2 vols. (New York, 1912).

6. Memoirs

Carey, Matthew, *Autobiography* (Brooklyn, 1942).

Goodrich, S. G., *Recollections of a Lifetime.* 2 vols. (New York, 1856).

Graydon, Alexander, *Memoirs of His Own Times.* Ed. by J. S. Littell (Philadelphia, 1846).

Quincy, Josiah, *Figures of the Past from the Leaves of Old Journals* (Boston, 1926).

Sullivan, William, *Familiar Letters on Public Characters & Public Events, 1783-1815* (Boston, 1834).

Trumbull, John, *Autobiography* (New York, 1841).

Tudor, William, *Letters on the Eastern States* (New York, 1820).

Gibbs, George, *Memoirs of the Administrations of Washington and Adams from the Papers of Oliver Wolcott.* 2 vols. (New York, 1846).

7. Miscellaneous Sources

Adams, John, *Deeds and other documents relating to the several pieces of land, and to the Library presented to the town of Quincy by President Adams, together with a catalogue of his books* (Cambridge, 1823).

Ames, Herman V., *State Documents on Federal Relations* (New York, 1907).

Blodget, Samuel, *Economica* (Washington, 1810).

Destutt de Tracy, or Tracy, Destutt de, Compte Antoine Louis Claude de, *A Treatise on Political Economy* (Georgetown, D. C., 1817, 1819?).

Dwight, Timothy, *Travels in New England and New York.* 4 vols. (New Haven, 1821-22).

Godwin, Wm., *An Enquiry Concerning Political Justice* (Philadelphia, 1796).

Knox, Dudley W., *Naval Documents Related to the Quasi-War between the United States and France.* 4 vols. (Washington, 1935-39).

Mayo, Bernard, ed., *Instructions to the British Ministers to the United States, American Historical Association Report* (Washington, 1941), Vol. III.

Pinto, Issac de, *Essai Sur La luxe* (Amsterdam, 1762).

Pinto, Issac de, *Traité de la circulation et du crédit* (Amsterdam, 1771).

Pitkin, Timothy, *A Statistical View of the Commerce of the United States* (Hartford, 1817).

Quesnay, François, *Tableau Économique* (Paris, 1758).

Raymond, Daniel, *The Elements of Political Economy* (Baltimore, 1820).

Raymond, Daniel, *Political Economy* (Baltimore, 1840).

Seybert, Adam, *Statistical Annals* (Philadelphia, 1818).

Smith, Adam, *The Wealth of Nations* (Cannan, ed.). 2 vols. (London, 1904).

Steuart, James, *An Inquiry into the Principles of Political Economy.* 2 vols. (London, 1767).

Taylor, John, *Arator*, 3rd ed. (Georgetown, 1817).

Webster, Noah, *Miscellaneous Papers* (New York, 1802).

Wharton, Francis, *State Trials of the United States during the Administrations of Washington and Adams* (Philadelphia, 1849).

8. Newspapers

Aurora and Philadelphia General Advertiser (1790-1800).

Boston Patriot (1809-13).

Columbian Centinel, cited as *Centinel* (Boston, 1792, 1796-1801).

City Gazette (Charleston, 1796-1800).

Commercial Advertiser (New York, 1797-1801).

Connecticut Courant (Hartford, 1796-1801).

Gazette of the United States 1789-1801. New York to 1790, Philadelphia after that date.

Independent Chronicle (Boston, 1798-1801).

Porcupine's Gazette (Philadelphia, 1795-1799).

Richmond Examiner (1796-1800).

J. Russell's Gazette, Commercial and Political, Boston, pub. by J. Cutler, *Boston Gazette* after 1798 (1797-1801).

Virginia Argus, Pleasants (Richmond, 1796).

Virginia Gazette and Petersburg Intelligencer, Wm. Prentis (1796).

Virginia Gazette and Weekly Advertiser, Thomas Nicolson (Richmond, 1796).

Virginia Herald and Fredericksburg and Falmouth Advertiser (Fredericksburg, T. Green, 1796).

Washington Federalist (1800-1801).

9. Sources Published as Articles

Adams, Charles Francis, ed., " Correspondence between John Adams and Mercy Warren in Relation to Her ' History of the American Revolution,' July, August, 1807." 5 MHSC, IV, Part III, pp. 315-511. Appendix pp. 493-511 covers 1807-12 (1878).

Adams, Charles Francis, ed., "Correspondence between John Adams and Professor John Winthrop," 5 MHSC, IV, Part II, 286-313 (1878).

Adams, John, "Letters," *New York Public Library Bulletin*, VIII, 240; X, 227-50 (1906).

Adams, John, "Unpublished Letter," *Quarterly Magazine of the Sons of the Revolution of the State of Virginia*, II, No. 2, 35 (1925).

Battle, Kemp P., "Letters of William R. Davie." *James Sprunt Historical Monographs*, No. 7 (Chapel Hill, 1907).

Battle, Kemp P., ed., "Letters of Nathaniel Mason, John Steele and William Barry Grove." *James Sprunt Historical Monographs* No. 3 (Chapel Hill, 1902).

Carey, Mathew, "Letters," *New England Magazine*, VI, 100 ff. (Feb., 1834).

Dauer, Manning J., "The Two John Nicholases: Their Relationship to Washington and Jefferson," *American Historical Review*, XLV, 338-353 (1940).

Dexter, Franklin B., "Selections from Letters Received by David Daggett, 1786-1802." *American Antiquarian Society Proceedings, 1887*, 367 ff.

Dodd, Wm. E., ed., "Letters of John Taylor," *Branch Historical Papers*, II (Richmond, 1903).

Ford, Worthington C., "Letters of Elbridge Gerry," *New England Historical and Genealogical Register*, XLIX, 430-440 (1895).

Ford, Worthington C., ed., *Letters of William Vans Murray, American Historical Association Report, 1912*.

"Letters of Stephen Higginson," *American Historical Association Report, 1890*, I, 711-765.

"Letters on Virginia Politics," *William and Mary College Quarterly*, XIII, 102 ff. and *Virginia Magazine of History*, XII, 257 ff.; 407 ff. (1904-5).

Macon, Nathaniel, "Letters," *American Historical Review*, VII, 100-111 (1902).

Macon, Nathaniel, "Letters," *Branch Historical Papers*, I, No. 2; III, No. 1 (1902, 1909).

Powell, Leven, "Correspondence (1787-1829)." *Branch Historical Papers*, I, No. 3, 217-56. (1903).

"William Heath Papers," *Collections of the Massachusetts Historical Society*, Seventh Series, Vol. V (Boston, 1905).

Steiner, Bernard C., "Letters from the McHenry Papers," *Virginia Magazine of History*, XII, 257-268, 406-414. (1904-05).

Steiner, Bernard C., "Correspondence of William Smith," *Sewanee Review*, XIV, 76-104. (1906).

Turner, Frederick J., ed., "Documents on the Blount Conspiracy, 1795-1797," *American Historical Review*, X, 574-606 (1905).

Taylor, John, "Letters," *American Farmer*, II, 93 (1820).

Wagstaff, Henry M., "Letters of William Barry Grove," *Sprunt Historical Publications*, IX, No. 2 (Chapel Hill, 1910).

Wettereau, James O., "Letters from Two Business Men to Alexander Hamilton on Fiscal Policy, November, 1789," *Journal of Economic and Business History*, III, 667 (1931).

Windham, Wm., *Windham Papers* (London, 1913), vol. I, 121-37, "Letter on American Political Parties."

10. Pamphlets

Anti-Jacobin, or *Weekly Examiner*, Nov. 20, 1797–July 9, 1798.

Anti-Jacobin Review and Magazine (London, July 1798-1800, as far as examined, periodical continued until 1821).

Austin, Benjamin, *Constitutional Republicanism in Opposition to Fallacious Federalism*. By old South (Boston, 1803).

An Answer to Alexander Hamilton's Letter, etc., by a Citizen of New York (New York, 1800).

Bache, Benjamin F., Truth Will Out! — *The Foul Charges of the Tories against the Editors of the Aurora Repelled by Positive Proof and Plain Truth* . . . n. p., n. d. (Philadelphia, 1798).

"A Friend to Regular Government," *British Honour and Humanity, or the Wonders of American Patience* (refers to Wm. Cobbett) (Philadelphia, 1796, preface dated Oct. 8, 1796). Probably by J. T. Callender (Cf. *Prospect Before Us*, II, 129).

"Cato," *A Few Remarks on Mr. Hamilton's Late Letter, concerning the Public Conduct and Character, of the President* (Baltimore, Warner S. Hann, 1800).

"Cobbett, William" [forged] *An Address to the People of England*, (Preface to the address shows this to be an American pamphlet issued during the war of 1812, probably 1813. The address itself purports to have been written by Cobbett upon his return).

Callender, James Thomson, *Political Progress of Britain* (Philadelphia, 1795).

Callender, J. T., *The Political Progress of Britain*. . . . Part Second. (Philadelphia, 1795).

Callender, J. T., *The Political Progress of Britain*, Third ed. (London, 1795).

Callender, J. T., *History of the United States for 1796* . . . (Philadelphia, 1797). Snowden & McCorkle.

Callender, J. T., *American Annual Register, Historical Memoirs of the United States for the year 1796* (Philadelphia, 1797).

Callender, J. T., *Sedgwick & Co. or A Key to the Six Per Cent Cabinet* (Philadelphia, 1798). Preface dated May 22, 1798.

Callender, J. T., *Sketches of the History of America* (Philadelphia, 1798). Preface, iv, dated Feb. 12, 1798.

Callender, J. T., *The Prospect Before Us* (Richmond, 1800). Preface to Vol. I. Dated Jan. 10, 1800.

Callender, J. T., *The Prospect Before Us.* Vol. II, Part I. (Richmond, 1800). Preface dated Richmond, Nov. 3, 1800.

Carey, Matthew, *Miscellaneous Essays* (Philadelphia, Nov. 13, 1830).

Carey, Matthew, *The Olive Branch*, 3rd ed. (Boston, 1815).

Cobbett, William, *Detection of a Conspiracy formed by the United Irishmen, with the Evident intention of Aiding the Tyrants of France in Subverting the Government of the United States of America.* (In *Works*, VIII, 197-230 under date of May, 1798).

Cooper, Thomas, *Political Essays* (Philadelphia, 1800).

Cooper, T., *Political Essays*, 2nd ed. (Philadelphia, 1800).

Dwight, Theodore, *An Oration, Delivered at New Haven* . . . , July 7, 1801 . . . Before the Society of the Cincinnati for the State of Connecticut (Hartford, 1801).

Dwight, Timothy, *The Duty of Americans, at the Present Crisis* (New Haven, July 4, 1798).

Fenno, John Ward, *Desultory Reflections on the New Political Aspects of Public Affairs* . . . (New York), printed for the Author by G. and R. Waite and Published by J. W. Fenno, No. 141 (Hanover Square, 1800). Preface dated June 30, 1800.

Fenno, J. W. and [anonymous], *Desultory Reflections on the New Political Aspects of Public Affairs in the United States of America, since the Commencement of the year 1799.* New York, printed; Philadelphia, reprinted; for R. T. Rawle (1800) (Adv. is dated June 30, 1800).

Hamilton, Alexander, *Letter* . . . *Concerning the Public Conduct and Character of John Adams, Esq., President of the United States.* Third edition, New York. Printed for John Lang, by S. Furman (London, 1800).

Harper, Robert Goodloe, *Speech on the Foreign Intercourse Bill*, March 2, 1798. (Place of and publisher not given.)

Harper, R. G., *Address to his Constituents Containing His Reasons for Approving of the Treaty* . . . *with Great Britain* . . . *to which is annexed A Letter From Governor Jay* (Philadelphia, 1796).

Armstrong, John [filled in ink], *Letters of Verus, addressed to the Native American.* Published by B. F. Bache (Philadelphia, 1797).

A Letter, addressed to Alexander Hamilton, Esq. in Answer to his Letter concerning the Public Conduct and Character of John Adams . . . By a friend to the President (Nov. 6, 1800).

"A Citizen of the States," *A Letter to Maj. Gen. Alexander Hamilton; containing observations on his letter concerning the Public Conduct and Character of John Adams, Esq., President of the United States.* Joshua Cushing (Salem, 1800). Signed "A Citizen, United States," November 10, 1800.

Lowell, John, *An oration, pronounced July 4, 1799* . . . (Boston, 1799).

Pendleton, Edmund, *An Address* . . . *to the American Citizens on the Present State of our Country* (Boston, 1799).

The Political Reformer, or a Proposed Plan of Reformations in the Laws and Governments of the United States of America . . . *to which are added Strictures on John Adams's Defense of the Constitutions of Government of the United States of America* (Philadelphia, W. W. Woodward, 1797). Dedication dated October, 1796.

Price, Richard, *On the Nature of Civil Liberty* (London, 1776).

Smith, William Loughton, *The Pretensions of Thomas Jefferson to the Presidency Examined; and the Charges Against John Adams Refuted* (United States, Oct., 1796).

Smith, Wm. Loughton, "Phocion," in *Gazette of the United States and pamphlet, The pretensions of Thomas Jefferson to the Presidency examined; and the charges against John Adams refuted* . . . (October, 1796).

Taylor, John, *An Inquiry into the Principles and Tendency of Certain Public Measures* (Philadelphia, 1794).

Taylor, John, *An Examination of the Late Proceedings in Congress, respecting the Official Conduct of the Secretary of the Treasury* (Richmond, 1793).

Taylor, John, *A Definition of Parties or the Political Effects of the Paper System Considered* (Philadelphia, April 5, 1794).

A Touchstone for the Leading Partymen in the United States, dedicated to Mr. Sedgwick (1800, Massachusetts).

A Vindication of the Conduct and Character of John Adams, Esq., in reply to the Letter of General Hamilton. Addressed to the Federal Citizens of the Union (New York, 1800). John C. Totten. Signed, "An American."

"Aristides" [Noah Webster], *Letter to General Hamilton* . . . By a Federalist. n. p., n. d. Second Ed., New York, 1800 (Philadelphia, 1800; Boston, 1809).

B. SECONDARY WORKS

11. United States Histories

Bassett, J. S., *The Federalist System* (vol. 2 in *The American Nation Series*; New York, 1906).

Channing, Edward, *A History of the United States.* 6 vols. (New York, 1905-1925).

Hildreth, Richard, *History of the United States of America.* 6 vols. (New York, 1856-60).

Krout, John A., and Fox, Dixon Ryan, *The Completion of Independence* (Vol. V of *A History of American Life*, ed. by A. M. Schlesinger; New York, 1944).

Irelan John Robert, *The Republic*, Vol. II, *History of the Life, Administration, and Times of John Adams* . . . (Chicago, 1886-1913).

McMaster, James B., *History of the People of the United States, from the Revolution to the Civil War.* 8 vols. (New York, 1883-1913).

Schouler, James, *History of the United States.* 6 vols. (New York, 1894-1899).

Turner, Frederick J., *The United States, 1830-1850* (New York, 1935).

Winsor, Justin (editor), *Narrative and Critical History of America.* 8 vols. (Boston, 1884-89).

12. Biographies

Adams, Henry, *Life of Albert Gallatin* (Philadelphia, 1879).

Adams, James Truslow, *The Adams Family* (New York, 1932).

Allan, Herbert S., *John Hancock, Patriot in Purple* (New York, 1948).

Austin, J. T., *Life of Elbridge Gerry.* 2 vols. (Boston, 1828-29).

Barry, Richard, *Mr. Rutledge of South Carolina* (New York, 1942).

Bemis, Samuel Flagg, *John Quincy Adams and the Foundations of American Foreign Policy* (New York, 1949).

Beveridge, Albert, *John Marshall.* 4 vols. (Boston, 1916).

Bowen, Catherine D., *John Adams and the American Revolution* (Boston, 1950).

Brant, Irving, *James Madison, Father of the Constitution, 1787-1800* (Indianapolis, 1950).

Brooks, Noah, *Henry Knox* (New York, 1900).

Brown, William G., *Life of Oliver Ellsworth* (New York, 1905).

Chamberlain, Mellen, *John Adams, The Statesman of the American Revolution* (Boston, 1898).

Chinard, Gilbert, *Honest John Adams* (Boston, 1933).

Clark, Mary E., *Peter Porcupine in America: The Career of William Cobbett, 1792-1800* (Philadelphia, 1939).

Dodd, Wm. E., *Life of Nathaniel Macon* (Raleigh, 1903).

Drake, Francis S., *Life and Correspondence of Henry Knox* (Boston, 1873).

Dwight, Benjamin W., *History of the Descendants of John Dwight of Dedham.* 2 vols. (New York, 1874).

Higginson, Thomas Wentworth, *Life and Times of Stephen Higginson* (Boston, 1907).

Hunt, Charles Havens, *Life of Edward Livingston* (New York, 1864).

Hutcheson, Harold, *Tench Coxe* (Baltimore, 1938).

Iacuzzi, Alfred, *John Adams, Scholar* (New York, 1952).

Jay, William, *Life of John Jay.* 2 vols. (New York, 1833).

Koch, Adrienne, *Jefferson and Madison* (New York, 1950).

Konkle, Burton A., *Thomas Willing* (Philadelphia, 1937).

Malone, Dumas, *Jefferson and the Rights of Man* (Boston, 1951).

Malone, Dumas, *Public Life of Thomas Cooper* (New Haven, 1926).

McCormac, Eugene I., *James K. Polk* (Berkeley, California, 1922).

McLaughlin, J. Fairfax, *Matthew Lyon* (New York, 1900).

Melville, Lewis [Benjamin, Lewis Saul], *Life and Letters of William Cobbett in England and America* (London, 1913).

Morse, John T., *John Adams* (Boston, 1884).

Pellew, George, *John Jay* (New York, 1890).

Pickering, Octavius and Upham, C. W., *The Life of Timothy Pickering.* 4 vols. (Boston, 1867-1873).

Quincy, Edmund, *Life of Josiah Quincy* (Boston, 1867).

Randall, James G., *Lincoln the President.* 2 vols. (New York, 1945).

Randall, H. S., *Life of Jefferson.* 3 vols. (New York, 1858).

Rives, William C., *History of the Life and Times of James Madison.* 3 vols. (Boston, 1859-1868).

Robertson, Wm. Spence, *The Life of Miranda.* 2 vols. (Chapel Hill, 1929).

Schachner, Nathan, *Alexander Hamilton* (New York, 1946).

Scudder, H. E., *Noah Webster* (Boston, 1882).

Simms, H. H., *Life of John Taylor* (Richmond, 1932).

Story, Joseph, *Sketch of the Life of Samuel Dexter* (Boston, 1816).

Wallace, Paul A. W., *The Muhlenbergs of Pennsylvania* (Philadelphia, 1950).

Warfel, Harry R., *Noah Webster, Schoolmaster to America* (New York, 1936).

Wilber, James B., *Ira Allen.* 2 vols. (Boston, 1928).

13. Local and State Histories

Adams, James T., *New England in the Republic, 1776-1850* (Boston, 1926).

Ambler, Charles H., *Sectionalism in Virginia from 1776 to 1861* (Chicago, 1910).

Barry, John Stetson, *History of Massachusetts.* 3 vols. (Boston, 1857).

Belknap, Jeremy, *History of New Hampshire.* 3 vols. (Boston, 1792).

Bidwell, Percy W., " Rural Economy in New England at the beginning of the 19th century." *Transactions of the Connecticut Academy of Arts and Sciences.* Vol. XX (New Haven, 1916).

Fee, Walter R., *The Transition from Aristocracy to Democracy in New Jersey* (Somerville, New Jersey, 1933).

Field, Edward, *The State of Rhode Island and Providence Plantations . . . A History.* 3 vols. (Boston, 1902).

Gilpatrick, Delbert Harold, *Jeffersonian Democracy in North Carolina* (New York, 1931).

Hammond, Jabez D., *History of Political Parties in the State of New York*, Fourth Edition, 2 vols. (Buffalo, 1850).

Howe, Henry, *Historical Collections of Virginia* (Charleston, 1852).

Ludlum, David McW., *Social Ferment in Vermont, 1791-1850* (New York, 1939).

McSherry, James, *History of Maryland* (Baltimore, 1850).

Morse, Anson E., *Federalist Party in Massachusetts to the Year 1800* (Princeton, 1913).

Morgan, Forrest, ed., *Connecticut as a Colony and as a State . . .* 4 vols. (Hartford, 1904).

Pomerantz, Sidney I., *New York; An American City* (New York, 1938).

Purcell, Richard J., *Connecticut in Transition, 1775-1818* (Washington, D. C., 1918).

Robinson, William A., *Jeffersonian Democracy in New England* (New Haven, 1916).

Sharpless, Isaac, *Two Centuries of Pennsylvania History* (Philadelphia, 1900).

Sharpless, Isaac, *A Quaker Experiment in Government* (Philadelphia, 1902).

Stackpole, Everett S., *History of New Hampshire* (New York, 1916).

Tinkcom, Harry M., *The Republicans and Federalists in Pennsylvania, 1790-1801* (Harrisburg, Pa., 1950).

Winsor, Justin, *Memorial History of Boston.* 4 vols. (Boston, 1881).

Wolfe, John Harold, *Jeffersonian Democracy in South Carolina, James Sprunt Studies in History and Political Science*, Vol. 24, No. 1 (Chapel Hill, 1940).

14. Specialized Secondary Works

Allen, G. G. and Fagley, F. L., *History of American Congregationalism* (Boston, 1942).

Ammon, Harry, *The Republican Party in Virginia, 1789-1824* (Unpublished doctoral dissertation, University of Virginia, 1948).

Beard, Charles A., *An Economic Interpretation of the Constitution of the United States* (New York, 1913).

Beard, Charles A., *Economic Origins of Jeffersonian Democracy* (New York, 1915).

Bemis, Samuel F., *A Diplomatic History of the United States* (New York, 1936).

Bemis, Samuel F., *Jay's Treaty* (New York, 1923).

Bidwell, Percy W., and Falconer, John I., *History of Agriculture in the Northern United States, 1620-1860* (New York, 1941).

Buckley, J. M., *A History of Methodists in the United States* (New York, 1907).

Chalmers, George, *An Estimate of the Comparative Strength of Great Britain* (new edition, London, 1810).

Chinard, Gilbert, *Jefferson et les Idéologues* (Baltimore, 1925).

Clark, Victor S., *History of Manufacturers in the United States* (New York, 1929 edition).

Clauder, Anna C., *American Commerce as Affected by the Wars of the French Revolution and Napoleon* (Philadelphia, 1932).

Cole, Arthur H., *Industrial and Commercial Correspondence of Alexander Hamilton* (New York, 1928).

Craven, Avery O., *Soil Exhaustion as a Factor in the Agricultural History of Virginia and Maryland, University of Illinois Studies in the Social Sciences* (Urbana, Illinois, 1926), XIII, No. 1.

Cunz, Dieter, *Maryland Germans* (Princeton, 1948).

Dewey, Davis Rich, *Financial History of the United States*. 9th ed. (New York, 1924).

Dewey, Davis Rich, *State Banking before the Civil War* (Washington, 1910).

Dorfman, Joseph, *The Economic Mind in American Civilization*. 2 vols. (New York, 1946).

East, Robert A., *Business Enterprise in the American Revolutionary Era* (New York, 1938).

Easton, David, *The Political System* (New York, 1953).

Faulkner, Harold U., *American Economic History* (New York, 1929).

Fletcher, Stevenson W., *Pennsylvania Agriculture and County Life* (Harrisburg, Pennsylvania, 1950).

Gray, Lewis Cecil, *History of Agriculture in the Southern United States.* 2 vols. (Washington, 1933).

Greene, M. L., *The Development of Religious Liberty in Connecticut* (Boston, 1905).

Haines, Charles G., *The American Doctrine of Judicial Supremacy* (Berkeley, 1932).

Hall, Walter P., *British Radicalism, 1791-1797* (New York, 1912).

Haraszti, Zoltan, *John Adams and the Prophets of Progress* (Cambridge, Mass., 1952).

Harlow, A. F., *Old Townpaths* (New York, 1926).

Heitman, Francis B., *Historical Register of Officers of the Continental Army* (Washington, 1914).

Hepburn, Barton, *History of Currency in the United States* (New York, 1924).

Hockett, Homer C., *Constitutional History of the United States, 1776-1826* (New York, 1939).

Holdsworth, John T., *The First Bank of the United States* (Washington, 1910).

Hulbert, Archer B. and Moody, John, *The Highways of Commerce* (New York, 1920).

Hunter, Henry C., *How England Got Its Merchant Marine* (New York, 1935).

Hutchins, John G. B., *The American Maritime Industries and Public Policy* (Cambridge, Massachusetts, 1941).

Jacobs, James R., *The Beginning of the U. S. Army, 1783-1812* (Princeton, 1947).

Jensen, Merrill, *The New Nation* (New York, 1950).

Johnson, Emory R., et al., *History of Domestic and Foreign Commerce of the United States* (Washington, 1915).

Jones, Rufus M., *The Quakers in the American Colonies* (London, 1911).

Koch, G. Adolf, *Republican Religion: The American Revolution and the Cult of Reason* (New York, 1933).

Kohn, Hans, *The Idea of Nationalism* (New York, 1944).

Libby, Orin G., *Geographical Distribution of the Vote of the Thirteen States on the Federal Constitution* (Madison, Wisconsin, 1894).

Link, Eugene P., *Democratic-Republican Societies, 1790-1800* (New York, 1942).

Luetscher, George D., *Early Political Machinery in the United States* (Philadelphia, 1903).

McArthur, John, *Financial and Political Facts of the Eighteenth Century* (London, 1801).

McLaughlin, Andrew C., *Constitutional History of the United States* (New York, 1935).

Mahan, Alfred T., *The Influence of Sea Power on the French Revolution and Empire.* 2 vols. (Boston, 1892).

Manross, W. W., *A History of the American Episcopal Church* (New York, 1935).

Marshall, John, *A Digest of all the Accounts . . . Relating to Great Britain* (London, 1834).

Maynard, Theodore, *The Story of American Catholicism* (New York, 1941).

Merriam, Charles E., *Political Power* (New York, 1934).

Meyer, Balthasar H., *History of Transportation in the United States Before 1860* (Washington, 1917).

Miller, Harry E., *Banking Theories in the United States before 1860* (Cambridge, Massachusetts, 1927).

Miller, John C., *Crisis in Freedom: The Alien and Sedition Acts* (Boston, 1951).

Millis, Walter, *The Martial Spirit* (New York, 1931).

Monroe, Arthur E., *Monetary Theory before Adam Smith* (Cambridge, Mass., 1923).

Morais, Herbert M., *Deism in Eighteenth Century America* (New York, 1934).

Morison, Samuel E., *Maritime History of Massachusetts* (Boston, 1921).

Morris, Richard B., *Government and Labor in Early America* (New York, 1946).

Mosca, Gaetano, *The Ruling Class* (New York, 1939).

Mowat, R. B., *Diplomatic Relations of Great Britain and the United States* (London, 1925).

Mudge, E. T., *The Social Philosophy of John Taylor of Caroline* (New York, 1939).

Neill, Charles P., *Daniel Raymond* (Baltimore, 1897).

Paine, Ralph D., *Ships and Sailors of Old Salem* (Boston, 1923).

Parrington, Vernon L., *Main Currents in American Thought.* 3 vols. (New York, 1927).

Paxson, Frederic L., *America at War, 1917-1918* (Boston, 1939).

Paxson, Frederic L., *Post War Years: Return to Normalcy, 1918-23* (Berkeley, Cal., 1948).

Philippi, Gertrude, *Imperialistische und pazifizistische strömungen in der politik der Vereinigten Staaten von Amerika wahrend der ersten Jahrzehnte ihres Bestehens (1776-1815)* (Heidelberg, 1914).

Phillips, James D., *Salem and the Indies* (Boston, 1947).

Pratt, Julius W., *Expansionists of 1898* (Baltimore, 1936).

Pratt, Julius W., *Expansionists of 1812* (New York, 1925).

Rice, Stuart A., ed., *Methods in the Social Sciences* (Chicago, 1931).

Rice, Stuart A., *Quantitative Methods in Politics* (New York, 1928).

Roberts, Christopher, *The Middlesex Canal* (Cambridge, Mass., 1938).

Russell, W. O., *A Treatise of Crimes and Misdemeanors*, 1st American edition by Daniel Davis (Boston, 1824).

Schlesinger, Arthur M., *Colonial Merchants and the American Revolution* (New York, 1918).

Shea, John G., *Life and Times of Archbishop Carroll* (New York, 1888).

Shultz, William J., and Caine, M. R., *The Financial Development of the United States* (New York, 1937).

Simons, A. M., *Social Forces in American History* (New York, 1911).

Smith, Justin H., *The War With Mexico*. 2 vols. (New York, 1919).

Smith, Walter B. and Cole, A. H., *Fluctuations in American Business, 1790-1860* (Cambridge, Massachusetts, 1935).

Sprout, Harold and Margaret, *Rise of American Naval Power* (Princeton, 1939).

Stanwood, Edward, *A History of the Presidency*. 2 vols. (New York, 1898).

Stephen, James F., *History of the Criminal Law of England*. 3 vols. (London, 1883).

Stephen, Henry J., *Summary of the Criminal Law* (London, 1834).

Stevens, Abel, *History of the Methodist Episcopal Church in the United States of America*. 4 vols. (New York, 1864?).

Strayer, J. R., ed., *The Interpretation of History* (Princeton, 1943).

Sweet, W. W., *Religions on the American Frontier, 1783-1850*, Vol. 3, *The Congregationalists* (Chicago, 1939).

Sweet, W. W., *Religion on the American Frontier*, Vol. 2, *The Presbyterians, 1783-1840* (New York, 1936).

Sweet, W. W., *The Story of Religion in America* (New York, 1930).

Swisher, Carl B., *American Constitutional Development* (Boston, 1943).

Trescott, William Henry, *The Diplomatic History of the Administrations of Washington and Adams, 1789-1801* (Boston, 1857).

Tryon, Rolla M., *Household Manufactures in the United States, 1640-1860* (Chicago, 1917).

Walsh, Correa M., *Political Science of John Adams* (New York, 1915).

Warren, Charles, *Supreme Court in United States History*. 2 vols. (Boston, 1926).

Warren, Charles, *Jacobin and Junto* (Cambridge, Massachusetts, 1931).

Whitaker, Arthur P., *The Mississippi Question, 1795-1803* (New York. 1934).

Whitaker, Arthur P., *The Spanish-American Frontier, 1783-1795* (Boston, 1927).

White, Leonard D., *The Federalists; A Study in Administrative History* (New York, 1948).

Wiltse, Charles M., *The Jeffersonian Tradition in American Democracy* (Chapel Hill, 1935).

Weyl, Nathaniel, *Treason: The Story of Disloyalty and Betrayal in American History* (Washington, 1950).

Wood, John, *History of the Administration of John Adams, Esq.* (New York, 1802).

15. Specialized Secondary Articles

Adams, Brooks, "The Convention of 1800 with France," *Massachusetts Historical Society Proceedings*, XLIV, 377-428 (1911).

Anderson, Frank Maloy, "Enforcement of the Alien and Sedition Laws," *American Historical Association Report, 1912*, 115-126.

Bemis, Samuel F., "Relations between the Vermont Separatists and Great Britain, 1789-91," *American Historical Review*, XXI, 547-560 (1916).

Brant, Irving, "Edmund Randolph, Not Guilty," *William and Mary Quarterly*, 3rd Series, VII, 179-198 (1950).

Carleton, William G., "Macaulay and the Trimmers," *The American Scholar*, XIX, 73-82 (1949).

Carroll, Thomas F., "Freedom of Speech and of the Press in the Federalist Period: The Sedition Act," *Michigan Law Review*, XVIII, 615-51 (1920).

Channing, Edward, "Virginia and Kentucky Resolutions," *American Historical Review*, XX, 333-36 (1915).

Cometti, Elizabeth, "John Rutledge, Jr., Federalist," *Journal of Southern History*, XIII, 196– ff. (1947).

Cox, Issac J., "James Wilkinson," *DAB*, XX, 222-26.

Dauer, Manning J., "The Political Economy of John Adams," *Political Science Quarterly*, LVI, 545-572 (1941).

Dauer, Manning J. and Hammond, Hans, "John Taylor, Democrat or Aristocrat?", *Journal of Politics*, VI, 381-403 (1944).

Dorland, W. A. N., "The Second Troop, Philadelphia City Cavalry," *Pennsylvania Magazine of History*, L, 79-87 (1926).

Ford, H. J., " Timothy Pickering," in S. F. Bemis, ed., *American Secretaries of State and Their Diplomacy* (New York, 1928), II, 161-244.

Ford, Worthington C., " John Adams," *DAB*, I, 72-82.

Ford, Worthington C., " Thomas Jefferson and James Callender," *New England Historical and Genealogical Register*, L, 321-333; 445-458; LI, 19-25; 153-158; 323-328 (1896-97).

Hamilton, J. G. de R., " William Richard Davie: A Memoir," *James Sprunt Historical Monograph No. 7* (Chapel Hill, 1907).

Harrison, Samuel A., " Memoir of William Hindman," *Maryland Fund Publications, No. 4* (Baltimore, 1880).

Hockett, Homer C., " Western Influences on Political Parties to 1825," *Ohio State University Student Contributions in History and Political Science, No. 4, Ohio State University Bulletin*, XXII, No. 3 (1917).

Hunt, Gaillard, " Office Seeking during the Administration of John Adams," *American Historical Review*, II, 241-261 (1897).

James, J. A., " George Rogers Clark," *DAB*, IV, 127-30.

Koch, Adrienne and Ammon, Harry, " The Virginia and Kentucky Resolutions," *William and Mary Quarterly*, 3rd ser. V, 145-176 (1948).

Kyte, George W., " A Spy on the Western Waters: The Military Intelligence Mission of General Collot in 1796," *Mississippi Valley Historical Review*, XXXIV, 427-442 (1947).

Lerche, Charles O., Jr., " Jefferson and the Election of 1800," *William and Mary Quarterly*, 3rd ser., V, 467-491 (1948).

Libby, Orin G., " Political Factions in the Washington Administration," *University of North Dakota Quarterly Journal*, III, 293-318 (1913).

Lycan, Gilbert L., " Alexander Hamilton and the North Carolina Federalists," *North Carolina Historical Review*, XXV, 442-65 (1948).

Lyon, E. Wilson, " The Directory and the United States," *American Historical Review*, XLIII, 514-32 (1938).

Lyon, E. Wilson, " The Franco-American Convention of 1800," *Journal of Modern History*, XII, 305-33 (1940).

MacIver, R. M., " History and Social Causation," in *The Tasks of Economic History* (New York, 1943).

Mead, Edwin D., " John Adams, National Statesman (1735-1826)," Ch. VIII in Vol. III of Hart, Albert Bushnell, ed., *Commonwealth History of Massachusetts* (New York, 1929).

Miller, William, " The Democratic Societies and the Whiskey Insurrection," *Pennsylvania Magazine of History*, LXII, 324-349 (1938).

Miller, William, " First Fruits of Republican Organization: Political Aspects of the Congressional Election of 1794," *Pennsylvania Magazine of History*, LXIII, 118-143 (1939).

Morison, Samuel E., " DuPont, Talleyrand, and the French Spoilations," *Massachusetts Historical Society Proceedings*, XLIX, 63-78 (1915-1916).

Morison, Samuel E., " Squire Ames and Dr. Ames," *New England Quarterly*, I, 5-31 (1928).

Morison, Samuel E., " Elbridge Gerry, Gentlemen Democrat," *New England Quarterly*, II, 6-33 (1929).

Morse, Anson D., " Causes and Consequences of the Party Revolution of 1800," *American Historical Association Report, 1894*, 531-40.

Morse, Anson D., " The Politics of John Adams," *American Historical Review*, IV, 292-312 (1899).

Philipps, Ulrich B., " The South Carolina Federalists," *American Historical Review*, XIV, 292-312 (1899).

Purcell, R. J., " James McHenry," *DAB*, XII, 62-63.

Rezneck, Samuel, " The Rise and Early Development of Industrial Consciousness in the United States, 1760-1830," *Journal of Economic and Business History*, IV, 784-811 (1932).

Robertson, Dice R., " Edmund Randolph," in Bemis, Samuel F., ed., *American Secretaries of State and their Diplomacy*," II, 149-159.

Robertson, Wm. S., " Francisco de Miranda and the Revolutionizing of Spanish America," *American Historical Association Report, 1907*, I, 189-550.

Robinson, W. A., " Timothy Pickering," *DAB*, XIV, 565-568.

Schaper, William A., " Sectionalism in South Carolina," *American Historical Association Report, 1900*, I, 237-463.

Seidensticker, Oswald, " F. A. C. Muhlenberg, etc.," *Pennsylvania Magazine of History*, XIII, 184-206 (1889).

Smith, James Morton, " The *Aurora* and the Alien and Sedition Laws," Part I, *Pennsylvania Magazine of History*, LXXII, 3-23 (1938).

Smith, James Morton, " The Sedition Law, Free Speech, and The American Political Process," *William and Mary Quarterly*, 3rd ser., IX, 497-511 (1952).

Spaulding, E. Wilder, " The Connecticut Courant," *New England Quarterly*, III, 443-63 (1930).

Spengler, Joseph J., " Political Economy of Jefferson, Madison, and Adams." In David Kelly Jackson (ed.)—*American Studies in Honor of William K. Boyd* (Durham, 1940), 3-59.

Thorpe, Francis N., " Political Ideas of John Adams," *Pennsylvania Magazine of History*, XLIV, 1-46 (1920).

Turner, Frederick J., " The Policy of France toward the Mississippi Valley in the Period of Washington and Adams," *American Historical Review*, X, 249-279 (1905).

Van der Borght, Richard, " History of Banking in the Netherlands " in Sumner, William G., ed., *History of Banking in All Nations*. 4 vols. (New York, 1896). IV, 188-371.

Wagstaff, Henry M., " Federalism in North Carolina," *Sprunt Historical Publication*, Vol. IX, No. 2 (Chapel Hill, 1910).

Warren, Charles, " John Adams and American Constitutions," *Kentucky State Bar Association Proceedings, 1927*.

Welling, J. C., " Connecticut Federalism," in *Addresses, Lectures, and Other Papers* (Cambridge, Massachusetts, 1904).

Wettereau, J. O., " New Light on the First Bank of the United States," *Pennsylvania Magazine of History*, LXI, 263-285 (1937).

Index[1]

Adams, Abigail, wife of John Adams: 36 ff.

Adams, Brooks: 195 n.

Adams, Charles Francis, on John Adams: 195

Adams, Henry, on Federalist aims: 210, 222

Adams, John: early career, 56, 84; early foreign policy, 61, 78, 79; political ideas, 35–54, 83–84, 86, 262, 263; on monarchism, 45–47, 84; economic ideas, 55–77, 79; election of 1788, 79–82, 83; of 1792, 85; of 1796, 92–111; of 1800, 246–59; on Hamilton, 111, 114, 115, 246–59; as President, 120–259; addresses, 120, 137, 143–45, 159–61, 243; his cabinet, 121–28, 172–97, 241, 251; foreign policy as President, 128, 149, 183, 186, 213, 225, 226, 231, 239, 243, 265; domestic policy, 144, 206, 207, 212–45; splits with Hamiltonians, 225–37, 242, 251, 254; closes administration, 259; retirement, 260, 261; appraisal, 264–65

Adams, John Quincy: 54, 140, 223, 231, 260, 261

Adams, Peter B.: 76

Adams, Samuel, Governor of Massachusetts: 30, 33, 78, 88, 89, 90, 110, 254

Adams, Thomas B.: 231

Adet, Pierre A.: French Minister: 142

Agrarians: 7, 24, 147–49

Agriculture: exports, 18; political influence, 18–25; and banks, 68

Alien and Sedition Laws: 33, 152–71; enforcement, 206, 242–55; opposition to, 227–29; text of sedition act, and amendments, 343–48

Allen, Ira: 173

Allen, John: 142, 167, 225

American Revolution: 3, 29

Ames, Fisher: 33, 62, 91, 98, 101, 118, 195, 199, 210, 244, 256, 276

Anderson, Frank Maloy, on sedition act: 206

Anti-Federalists: 3, 33, 99

Anti-Jacobin Review: 164, 181

" Aristides," *see* Noah Webster: 219

Army: 210, 214, 215, 243

Aurora (Philadelphia): 116, 155, 242

Austin, Benjamin: 76

Bache, Benjamin Franklin: 116, 155, 242

Baer, G., Maryland Congressman: 142

Banking: 14, 15, 66–67, 247, 282

Bank of Amsterdam: 70

Bank of the United States: 14, 53, 67, 71

Bankruptcy Act: 228, 244, 259

Baptists: 26–28

Bartlett, B., Massachusetts Congressman: 142

Battle of Moore's Creek Bridge, North Carolina: 29

Bayard, Jonathan, Delaware Congressman: 139, 142

Beard, Charles A.: 6–7, 16–17

Beckwith, Sir George, British Agent: 62

Bemis, Samuel Flagg: 231

Bentley, Rev. William: 153, 221

" Betweenites ": 276; *see* moderates

Bingham, William, Senator: 98, 169

Bismarck, Prince: 196

[1] Names of Members of the House of Representatives of the United States listed by states on the eight Vote Charts, pp. 288–331, *infra*, are not included in this index, unless also mentioned in the text. For alphabetical listing of those on the Vote Charts, see the biographical section of Poore, Benj. P., *Political Register and Congressional Directory . . . 1776-1878* (Boston, 1878), which contains some errors as to spelling and biographical data, for the congresses studied. The reader may also use the *Biographical Directory of the American Congress, 1774-1927* (Washington, 1928), or the current printing (Washington, 1950). As in Poore, some inconsistencies have been noted in these later editions.